Happy & Homeless

A Handbook of Tips, Tricks, Advice,
Stories and Wisdom for a Life Well Lived.

S.C. Sanborn

Dedication

This book is dedicated to all the assholes, manipulators, narcissists, fair-weather friends, backstabbers, liars, cheaters, abusers, family members, tyrants, neglecters, clock-punching therapists, and the people who tried to murder me.

It is also dedicated to the kind, righteous, fun-loving, good-hearted, forgiving, caring, nurturing, accepting, generous, and otherwise completely wonderful human beings who have shared the path with me.

You all taught me invaluable lessons. How to survive seemingly unsurvivable events. How to get back up, over and over again. How to laugh when punched in the face, when I was crying, and when I was spitting mad. You taught me how to look into the mirror, take accountability, and realize who I am as a person. And then how to love that person unconditionally. You taught me how to smile when things were great and when the darkness was too deep to see out of. You taught me how to take the high road and the low road. Most importantly, you allowed me to transcend my own experience. This is what I hope to pass on to the next person.

Contents

The Handbook

Preface

I began writing this book a long time before I actually wrote it. When I started, I was twenty-two years old and I had graduated college a year before. The high-paying job had not materialized. The self-satisfaction and self-confidence that stems from material success in a competitive world hadn't materialized either. What *had* materialized was a bunch of entry-level jobs, an intense pattern of self-loathing, and a general malaise surrounding the 'real world.' I remember thinking that if I could just write a book then all of my dreams would come true. I would be respected. I would be admired. I would be a success.

Then I started writing for a living and quickly realized just how wrong I was. At first, I was an intern for a music magazine. I got to go to a lot of shows, interview musicians, and hang out with other writers. The good ol' dog days. But it was highly evident any way you sliced it: that world was hard, and nobody respects writers. I had to work impossibly hard just to get an article into print that I wouldn't even be paid for. And when the time came that I might gain a paid position, it still wouldn't pay the bills. I would still have to mop floors and chop tomatoes. I would still have to punch a clock. The future did not seem bright. Rather, it seemed pretty bleak.

So, I looked at my options. There weren't many. It was 2009 and the economy was squeezing everyone like an aluminum can in a shop vise. I saw what I would have to do to achieve my illusory goals. I would have to sell my soul. And I wouldn't do that then just as much as I won't do that now. I can't count how many people have read this book and told me to swear less or to cut out this section or that. To take out some of the stories telling you how much I have fucked up. Fuck 'em. I love them, but fuck 'em. It is what it is. And back then, it was what it was. There were no options, so I took the only option available to me. I left.

I started out working in a gift shop. It was boring, menial, and repetitive. But it was Paradise. Literally. That was the name of the town. Nestled about 6,000 feet up on Mt. Rainier, with wildflowers blooming by the million outside. On the short walk back to the mouse-infested bunkhouse, I would regularly walk through a scene most people wouldn't dare to dream of, lest they 'start to hate their life.' It was the very first time in my life that I realized that nothing mattered but my attitude. That the paycheck, the 'girl,' the shoes, the uniform, the title, the accolades, none of it mattered. What *did* matter was how I perceived it. And I perceived it as heaven. I had finally achieved peace, happiness, and joy. I had finally found my place in this world.

Of course, this all came crashing down two months later. I let myself drink recklessly, didn't deal with my problems, became entangled with a loathsome woman, neglected my physical health and mental well-being, and otherwise put myself in a bad situation. But the fact remained, I had figured out the key to happiness. I had taken the leap and was rewarded with a glimpse of paradise. I had escaped the rigamarole and the path laid out for me by miserable people who thought they knew best. And this vision of peace and contentment is what I have chased ever since.

The key was simple: taking the leap. I had coldly analyzed the situation I was in and had adamantly refused to accept it as my future. I searched and searched for a solution. When I saw the job posting I was scared. Terrified. And when I told my friends and family what I had chosen I was met with disapproval and angry stares. No matter. I wasn't happy. I wasn't satisfied. I wasn't progressing toward transcendence or enlightenment. It had to happen.

Now, that isn't to say that I have found any of those things since. I have had some epically great times. My marriage was an ecstatically happy one at times. I have found locations where I was respected, admired, and appreciated. I have stood on the top of mountains and giggled for hours. My list of achievements and accolades is long. But the path to transcendence and enlightenment is a long one. Life is hard. And when you think it's hard, it gets even harder. No matter who you are, you are going to have to face extremely dark and painful parts of yourself. You are going to have to triumph over mountainous obstacles that others might simply step over. There will be soul-shattering events as often as there are brilliant, beautiful moments. But this is what we signed up for. The search. The struggle. We signed a contract before we were born. We came onto this plane to 'figure it all out.' To grow. To progress. Our birth was simply the first leap we took.

You are probably reading this because you feel stuck in some way. Because you feel the need to change yourself and your situation. And that is exactly what this book is for. Long ago I gave up on my foolish notions of success and went through the world trying everything. The number of jobs I have had is staggering. The number of things I know how to do oftentimes makes people uncomfortable. But that is their problem. Because I had to go through immeasurable amounts of discomfort to learn the things I have shared with you here. I have constantly been the student, always with this book in the back of my mind. This was how I was going to make a difference. And hopefully, it has. Because you are, most likely, going to take the same leap I did. You are going to break out from your patterns in the pursuit of happiness. And it might be fleeting. But the pursuit is all there is. You were born for this. You can do anything you want. Anything you need. You can make a difference and make yourself happy along the way. And hopefully, this book will help you do it the easy way, the safe(r) way, the right way. Or not. Who cares. The point is that you do it. The point is that you leap.

So, tell your loved ones that you love them, close your eyes, pinch your nose…

… and jump.

Prologue

Aside from general survival tips, you will immediately notice that the first part of this book details a whole lot of wellness advice on how to treat your body and mind. And you might wonder to yourself: "But I thought this was a book about traveling for cheap?" And you'd be right. Partially. There are tiers of needs. Mental wellness may be at the very top of the pyramid, but everyone has to eat. We all need a place to sleep, water, toilet paper, gas, heat, shoes, etc. And while we are on the road, these basic human needs become much harder to provide for. With this in mind, these needs are adequately and thoroughly addressed throughout this entire book. So, why all the wellness advice? Because as someone who has been to hell and back, slept on sidewalks and illegally in backyards, climbed mountains, and lounged at million-dollar pools, there is an oft-forgotten concept in today's 'influencer' driven travel: being healthy and happy.

I was at a beach in Greece with a girlfriend. We were sitting there drinking piña coladas and generally loving every second of the day. It was paradise. The weather was perfect, and it was the end of the season so there were barely any people there. There was even a light breeze that cooled all the sweat off of my very pale skin. About halfway through the afternoon, we noticed a couple walking past us. Both of them had makeup plastered on, with bales of clothes under one arm and heavy-looking camera equipment under the other. I remember seeing them sweating and lightly grunting and thinking: "Why on Earth would you ruin such a perfect day with all that crap?"

The couple continued a short way down the beach until they found a good spot near the water. A few young kids were playing in the surf behind them, in their shot evidently, that they quickly shooed away. I saw the man walk over to the beach bar and come back with two very elaborate-looking pineapples. They then proceeded to take each other's pictures, over and over, in different outfits, with different angles. At one point, the woman pointed to the breakwater that separated the swimming area from the open ocean. The man then proceeded to carry the young woman (yes, carry) through the shallow water to the breakwater, where he gently laid her down on the stone. He then trudged back through the water and returned with his camera and spent another full hour taking her picture, pausing only to show her the results from time to time. When she was satisfied, he then picked her back up and carried her back to the beach, where they started to take sunset photos.

The entire thing took around four hours. By this time my girlfriend and I had gone swimming four times, made friends, and were thoroughly hammered. It was positively awesome. I felt like Jimmy frickin' Buffett. As the light diminished past the 'golden hour' the couple left, with their trash and pineapples still sitting in the sand. I hate beach trash, so I strode right over and picked it up for them. Curious, I pulled the top off of the pineapples. Completely untouched. I couldn't help it. Grabbing my new treasure, I walked to the bar and turned around. My girlfriend was already walking toward me with two straws in her hand and a big smile on her face.

I have no idea how social media works, but we were somehow able to look up the beach by the hashtag, and bam! There were our models, greased up, decked out, and smiling. The caption read: "What a great day of swimming and fun in the sun!" Sure was! The pictures weren't nearly as good as those pina coladas though.

The irony of ironies was, after a few more weeks of traveling, we ended up on the same flight as our favorite models. We were heading from Athens to Singapore, then on to the Gold Coast, and then, finally, Auckland. That's a long, long haul. I passed them by and gave them a wave and a smile. The woman snarled at me. As I continued down the aisle, I heard them sharply bickering. Countless hours, delays, altered gates, and changed terminals later, we finally landed in Gold Coast, Australia, where our favorite 'influencers' evidently called home. We were standing in line going through customs to get to the next terminal when I saw them heading toward the baggage claim. They were pointedly not looking at each other, or anyone else for that matter. I couldn't help shaking my head. I truly hope their next vacation was a little more fun.

Overall health, wellness, and meditation are emphasized in this book because they are the most important. Yes, we have to take care of our bodily needs. But after you become adept at that your life quickly evolves into a search for meaning. Every single human who has ever lived has hit this wall, where they realize that they have been missing 'something more.' Examples of this are prevalent in all aspects of our culture. Burnout. Mid-life crises. Obsessive use of social media. Rebellion. Self-destructive behavior. A relentless search for a partner. Or a *need*, not just an instinctual desire, to have children. All these to some degree constitute our attempt to get to the next rung on the ladder; the next stage on the pyramid hierarchy of needs. We strive to find meaning and happiness. Or, in other words, wellness, wholeness, and understanding. I'll tell you right now, matter-of-factly: you are probably not going to find this sitting in your hometown, or on social media. Definitely not on social media.

You will only find this with hard work. You will only find this by seeking the truth of yourself, finding out what makes you tick and why. Does something irritate you? Good! Why? The answer to that question teaches you a lesson about yourself. As Albert Einstein once so famously said: "There are only two ways to live your life: One is as though nothing is a miracle. The other is as though everything is a miracle." By traveling we *force* ourselves into uncomfortable and potentially dangerous situations. We put ourselves through the rigors and trials necessary to achieve knowledge. We are positively forced to work hard, pay attention, strive to be better, and learn about the world, and ourselves, in the process. We are forced to get to the next rung on the ladder.

One of the primary purposes of this book is to help you realize your goals, dreams, passions, and ideals. Maybe even have some frickin' fun. It is designed to help you along your journey of finding out who you are and how you can be the happiest you can be. No one can do that for you. Your wellness is your happiness. Your body is the lens through which we see the world. If you travel and treat your body like crap, your experience is going to suffer. Traveling is already hard. Living a life that is outside the norm is equally so. It is taxing. Stressful. If you don't maintain yourself, you are going to break down. And when you break down, it is going to be a miserable experience. Now, if you have prepared for it, if you have paid attention to your body's needs, your mind's wants, and your soul's desires, you are inherently in a much better place to deal with troubles and trials as they arise. We are all here to venture forth into the world to find success and meaning in our own way. The knowledge contained in these pages can give you an advantage in doing just that.

Breathe

Just breathe.

If you hear or listen to nothing else written on these pages, listen to this. Breathe. Take big, huge mouthfuls as often as you can. Watch your belly go in and out, in and out. Breathing is the essence of our lives. Oftentimes, it is the only thing we can control about our situation. For some, it is the only thing they *want* to control about their situation. Life comes in and out of your lungs one expansion and contraction at a time. Controlling this, or just paying attention to it allows you to be present in the moment. Control what you can control. And it puts you into a frame of mind that is susceptible to all the goodness and positivity the world can provide. It is the crucial first step for every single moment of your life.

There are clickbait listicles with miles of print telling you what to eat and what not to eat, what's causing cancer this week, and how to best organize your room to live, on average, 18 hours longer. From infancy, we are bombarded by information about our health and disease. Every single Hollywood celebrity that has ever graced the screen now has a line of organic, holistic, poorly made, and excellently labeled products that are full of crap. And they want you to believe. Believe in THIS, and you will be healthy, happy, and well off. That is all well and good and I am sure some of these things can help some people. But in the end, spending tons of money isn't what is going to help you the most. And if you're reading this, you probably can't afford the lifestyle this system is trying to sell you anyway. So, what can you do? What can you control?

Your breath.

Just breathe. Count them or don't count them. Focus on the air hitting the tip of your nose, or the point right between the inhale and the exhale. Watch your diaphragm rise and fall. It's free and it is the single best thing you can do for yourself at any moment.

Rules to Live By

Be kind.

Aside from breathing, this is the best thing to know about living. It is up for debate whether most people in this world are 'good' or 'bad.' What we can all agree on is that there are a lot of really bad people and plain ol' assholes in this world. We can also all agree that assholes make this world much harder to live in than it needs to be. The hard part to realize is that we can become assholes without knowing it. I know I did. Suddenly, I was living a life surrounded by negativity and, well, assholes. Everything was someone else's fault and when it *was* my fault, I always somehow had a very good reason for being an asshole to them.

We are all the heroes of our own story. We are not all the protagonists of *the* story. And that is the only thing to try to be in this world. I cannot count how many times I have run into 'highly successful' people, who had nice clothes, more money than they knew what to do with, accolades, fame, you name it… and they were complete assholes. They were miserable! And it's because they failed. They paid attention to everything but the most important goal/tenet/rule. Be a good person. Because, simply put, if you are not kind then you are not a good person. You failed. You lost at life. It is the only certifiable achievement and it is the building block for any kind of success in this world.

Always start a conversation with: "How are you today?"

All too often in this rapidly expanding and online world we forget to be human. It is hard to remember that no matter how much we might *hate* the credit card company we are calling for double charging us for shitty Chinese food, there is still a real-life, honest-to-God *human being* on the other end of the line. They are paid pennies to deal with jerks all day long and do not deserve all our frustration. Also, in a not-so-altruistic fashion, everyone in the world has the power to help our day go smoother and better. By engaging them and acknowledging that they are human and that we care enough to check in, they are much more likely to help us out with whatever might be troubling us. You might just find that your phone bill is $5 cheaper per month (Thanks Evan!), or that they magically found a coupon for $20 off of your oil change. Just like that. Everybody just wants to be treated with respect and compassion. Asking them how their day is going is the best way to start. It really is that simple.

Do not lie, cheat or steal.

Everything in this world has a price. Whether you believe it will come in this world or the next, doesn't matter. What you put out into the world you will get back. If you lie, you will be lied to. If you cheat, you will be cheated. And if you steal, you will be stolen from. Some call this Karma. Some attribute it to the Law of Attraction. Perhaps we are all just part of a simulation wherein people are playing our bodies and consciousness as if we are a video game, complete with 'good points' and 'bad points' that lead to different cinematic endings. Regardless of your opinion, it is a universal truth. Ignore this and you will only have to learn it the hard way.

It is also crucial to follow this rule if you have any intention of following Rule #1. There is no world in which you can lie, cheat, and steal your way to being a good person. So many of us idolize the bank robbers we see in movies. The protagonists always have a *really* good reason for stealing from that particular bank or bad guy. What we don't see is the rest of their lives after they have finished the heist. We don't see the price that they have to pay. Everything costs something. Whether it is the revenge of the 'bad' guy or the ravages of taxes and time, the protagonist is never going to waltz off carefree. It just doesn't happen. You cannot be committed to following the path of sin/crime/negativity and expect to reach true happiness and/or enlightenment. The cost of your actions will always be equal to or out-weigh your efforts.

For what it's worth, it's also just the right thing to do. We have become so accustomed to living with bad people who treat us like crap. It is under-stood and accepted that most of the people you interact with are trying to take advantage of you in some way or another. This does not mean that you have to be this way. The world would be a much better place if we were not accustomed to this. Why not be different? Why not be the better person? Why not change the world?

Save as much of your first paycheck as you can.

I have lived a wild life that resulted in me having more jobs and job titles and locations and everything that goes with it than I can count. Most people do not believe me when I tell them how many jobs I've had, so I stopped doing so. In my experience, which is considerable, I would always follow a familiar pattern:

1. Get kicked out somewhere.

2. Take off and wind up in a situation with very little or no money.

3. Desperately start looking for a job. Usually, this started 10 minutes *after* number 1, but it really kicks into gear when you're running out of booze and you're cold.

4. Take whatever job comes your way, wherever it is.

5. Show up broke.

6. Work hard, bending over backward to make it work. Stress myself emotionally, physically, and mentally, usually to the breaking point.

7. Get paid and blow it all with my 'new friends' and on crap I didn't need.

8. Do something stupid and expensive.

Where I messed up, every single time, is by not saving the first paycheck. If you're in a situation where you are taking the first or 'best' job available, most often you are taking a job that multiple other people have left, meaning that it is bad for you in one way or another. Anyone who has ever waited tables is adamantly nodding their head right now. There is a section on this later if you're interested. The point is the same. You're broke and hungry for so long that as soon as you see that first bit of cash you want to pay off all of your bills and debt and go out to eat with all these friendly new people. Let the good times roll, baby! But hold up. These jobs are like life. They come and go with a flicker. Here one day, gone the next. We are so caught up in the 'here and now' that we want to believe that we will be 'here' forever and that 'now' will last forever. But for me, I was only in that situation because I was running from something else. Or because I had messed up somewhere else. Almost as if I was supposed to learn a lesson, right? Right.

The point is to always take care of yourself first. Always have an escape plan. Because these companies out there don't see you as a person, at least not right away. They see you as a warm body, an 'asset to their company.' It sounds cold but it's true. That doesn't mean they are bad people. It's business. And people want to make money so they can feed their families and fuel their ludicrously large pickup trucks that have never been even slightly touched by a load of construction debris, hay bales, or any other kind of cargo you'll see in a truck commercial. They want their business to operate at peak efficiency and that means getting people 'trained' to do their jobs *exactly* the way that the employee video wants them to and blah, blah, blah.

Are you a robot? Are you programmable? I didn't think so.

Spending eight to ten hours a day in a human-soul meat grinder is going to take a toll on every part of your being. And when it does you are going to react in ways that surprise you. Even if you aren't quite as reactive or sensitive as me, you always need to take care of yourself first. Fight your impulsive nature and your impatience and pay yourself first. Save that first paycheck.

Mental health comes first.

For a long, long, long, long, long, long time I pushed hard against the wall. I refused to directly deal with an intense series of traumas and issues. This held me back from having normal relationships, any kind of meaningful purpose, a job that lasted longer than six months, or fulfilling relationships of any kind.

It blows me away that we have no problem working on our homes, spending thousands of dollars to send our cars into the shop, buying a new cellphone, or blowing hundreds of dollars at the bar getting wasted. No judgment, I have done all these things too. The reason this is so shocking to me is that we have no problem with these expenditures, yet this nation *hates* even the *vague notion* of therapy. Way too many times I have seen revulsion on people's faces when I recommend going to talk to someone. Mindboggling. We live in a flesh-and-bone meat sack, controlled by an infinitely complex organic computer that is self-aware, self-controlling, and utterly independent of anything and everything that has ever existed before it. Our brains, and our existences, are miracles of mathematics, transcendence, spirituality, you name it. We are *miracles*. And we think we don't have to *maintain* our *minds*??? These miracle processing machines made of living matter? Wild. Absolutely wild.

Take care of your brain. It is the only thing that you are 100% certain actually exists. If you need a day off, take it. If you are too anxious to go to that party, *don't go*. If someone makes *me* uncomfortable, I leave. Usually politely but still, I'm gone. When my in-laws get in my face with their unresolved Daddy Issues, I laugh in their faces and walk away. No questions asked. The generations before us had the incentive to work themselves to the bone. *We do not.* I am not saying don't work hard! Working hard is the key to getting what you want out of life! But there is no excuse for working two people's jobs for one person's salary and having zero time for a personal life or to raise your children, all for an income that doesn't give you enough to save for any of those things. If your dog is at home alone for more than 40 hours per week, you are fucking up your life. If you don't see your children till 7 pm, six days a week? Sorry. I know you are working your ass off. *You're still fucking up.* You *will* regret it. Make your mental health, and that of those around you, come first. Even if it means moving to Nebraska (it's cheaper there, damn people) and working at a gas station, do what you need to do to make space for your mental health.

Never trust anyone with clean shoes.

As someone who has worked incredibly hard for everything I have ever gotten, this rule became apparent early on. Look around you as you are working toward one of your goals, traveling through your world, or when you come face to face with an adversary. Take note of their shoes.

I can't even imagine getting to the car with shoes that are still clean. Even when I used to work in an office, I would still carry a rag with me everywhere I went because I couldn't go ten minutes without sloshing mud on them. I couldn't stay away if I tried.

If someone is obsessed with perfectly clean shoes it tells you a lot about what they value and who they are. It's not always bad. There are exceptions to every rule, for sure. But most of the time that means that the person you are looking at values appearance above all else. Let me just straight up tell you that substance is way more valuable than appearance, every single time. If you weren't already aware. That person thinks that to progress through the world effectively, and to achieve their goals, they have to do so *while keeping their shoes clean.* This inherently means scrapping the ideas of 'rolling up your sleeves' and 'getting dirty' and 'working hard.' How do you think one gets ahead by not doing these things? If you said 'taking advantage of others,' you are correct. As a side note, if you think that every company that doesn't pay you (most likely) double what they are paying you *isn't* doing the same thing... well, you are lying to yourself. These people aren't to be trusted, as they are most likely sizing you up for what they can take you for.

Notice the details.

Life will pass you by if you aren't paying attention. Things that are special, sacred, and wonderful happen every second of every day to every person. Make note of this. Be grateful for the miracles surrounding you. When you do, your life will take on a much higher meaning than you ever thought possible.

You may have heard the term 'mindfulness.' It is ambivalent, omnipresent, and ubiquitous. Simply put, it's everywhere these days. Everyone wants to make a buck off of telling people to breathe in and out, myself included. Mindfulness is just paying attention to the details around you. Everything is a miracle, from how the leaves hang from the branches to your very own existence in this particular moment. You are surrounded by miracles, absolute miracles, at every moment. Taking the time to notice these miracles helps you identify the things you can be grateful for, the positives you have in your life currently, even if it might not feel like very many, and the blessings that the world has to offer. This is the easiest way to 'enlightenment,' which by itself means to 'lighten up' your world. Your life will be happier if *you are happier*. And the way to start doing this is to notice the things around you and actively seek gratitude within yourself for the things around you that you like. Do this enough and it becomes automatic. Once it's automatic you will see your outlook, and your life, start to attract a lot more positivity which, in turn, will greatly improve everything around you.

Find a very good reason(s) for living.

The most common attribute shared by happy people and those who have survived traumatic experiences is a well-cultivated reason to continue existing. This could mean anything. Some people call it 'resilience.' Some people call it 'positivity.' Some people call it 'love.' Doesn't matter what it is. Mounting scientific evidence, common sense, and easy rationale all come together for this one: figure out what makes you happy and do it. All the time. And enjoy it as much as you can.

Right now, I love my dog almost more than anything in the world. The only thing I love more? Myself and my experience, sitting here with a cup of coffee at my desk, writing this awesome book while the rain pours down onto the trees across the street. I am warm here, my dog is snoring on the couch, and I can just barely feel the gentle rocking of the washing machine beneath my feet. These are the mundane moments that I live for, and I am excited for as many of them as I can remember every single day. Find out what you live for. Then live for it.

Never watch the ads.

A good mentor of mine once referred to the array of billboards, storefronts, colors, lights, buildings, etc., that compose the landscape of America as the 'cultural matrix' that we are all plugged into and forced to sift through to survive. It is an apt metaphor because it succinctly describes the constant assault on our senses that we are subjected to daily. Just driving down the road for five minutes you are confronted by the urgent needs of hundreds of people, all clamoring: "Buy this!" "No, buy THIS!" Or, "Buy THIS for LESS," Or even, "Hey, how about you buy THIS and pay us MONTHLY with money you don't have!!" And on. And on. And on.

But this is not a treatise on the excesses of capitalism, even though there are many, and how anyone who says so is creepily shushed by people who typically don't have a firm grasp of how the system is screwing them over. I digress. This is NOT, (slaps wrist) NOT a treatise on the excesses of capitalism. This is just a simple reminder to constantly assert critical thinking skills and have your wants, desires, and best interests in mind at all times, rather than those that this 'cultural matrix' wants you to have. I get the fact that everybody has got to eat. I also understand that advertising *is* effective. All I am saying is that every person is better off if advertising doesn't affect *them*, or to the least degree possible.

As an example, my girlfriend loves game shows, and I am a huge fan of American Football. It is amazing the difference in your experience when you keep the remote close at hand and mute the box when the ads start playing. You immediately notice the silence. The calm. The cessation of the onslaught; the overbearing message to consume and insure. Consume. Insure. Consume!! Insure!!!!!

Try it sometime. You might like it.

Take long showers.

One of the first things you will notice if you spend a considerable amount of time in the wilderness or in a country less affluent than the one you are from is that it becomes much harder to bathe when you are there. I have had some glorious experiences in the middle of the wilderness in ice-cold, glacially-fed pools of water. And I have certainly found some great showers in hotels and hostels around the globe. But I have had way more experiences of weeks at a time without safe running water or any running water at all. I have seen my fair share of bathrooms that barely function, sometimes with just a hole in the ground. Pit toilets in faraway campgrounds become a luxury after weeks out in the bush, and even the pump water in the dish cleaning section can be a merciful reprieve when you've gone long enough.

The point is that here in America, so inappropriately titled the 'First World,' we accept and expect a standard of living that most others do not have. We are so used to having the infrastructure, and average median income, that allows for life's 'basic necessities,' that we forget that they are not necessities at all. They are luxuries. And I am certainly not saying to feel guilty about these things. Why would you? Anyone in their right mind is perfectly sane to take full advantage of the situation in which they are born or work their way into. The point is to focus on gratitude. Be grateful for the clean, hot water running out of this pipe in your home, cleansing your body and relaxing you at the same time. Showers are awesome. Just a built-in mini-massage where you barely have to do anything and you become healthier and more relaxed. Not to mention a shower is, bar none, the best place in the world to sing loudly. It is the paramount of daily luxuries in the average American life. If you pay attention to this, and to other luxuries we typically enjoy just like it, imagine what else you'll discover about your life.

Deal with your problems immediately.

Looking back, I am still stunned at how much time I 'wasted' being bitter, angry, jealous, resentful, spiteful, etc., for things that I could have dealt with much more efficiently. The same thing goes for how many times I repeated the same painful mistakes, believing that I was destined to break through for no other reason than that I was a good person and deserved to succeed at what I thought I deserved. Ever been in a relationship with a narcissist? Yeah.

What I learned from my previous behaviors is to simply accept the present and your role in it. If you mess up, just look it in the eye and admit to it. You don't necessarily have to change it. You don't even have to be sorry. Walking around apologizing for everything will make you hate yourself and the people you care about will subconsciously look down on you for it. The important part is to recognize what you did and why you did it. Don't make excuses, don't reimagine the story, don't try to sugarcoat it and make yourself look better. Be real, be honest, and be forthcoming. You will demand respect and you will inherently love yourself more. Consider this the fast track to self-love.

This does not mean to purposefully act poorly. If you have any questions about that, refer to rule #1. Here's a personal example. For a long time, my ex-wife was my 'soul mate,' my best friend, and my accomplice. If she had come home laughing, covered in blood, and saying she had killed someone, I would have just grabbed a shovel and bought a sailboat. I would have burned down an entire city to save her. We fought all the time though and our fights used to get pretty heated. I used to sleep on the couch quite a bit. We both had a bunch of issues from our past that we had never really dealt with. I had tried as she had tried, but not to the degree that either of us needed. When we got divorced, I kept working at addressing my issues. All sorts of things poured out. I realized that I hadn't been arguing with her. I had been arguing with ghosts. Figures long gone from my past had dictated my present, including the image that I held of her, which was no longer an accurate representation of who she was. All this drove me away from any semblance of happiness and ultimately away from myself and where I wanted to go in my life. What was needed was a basic reckoning. My marriage had needed a long set of open, respectful discourses on how we were going to deal with the things we had done and said to one another. How we were going to repair the damage and move forward together. Instead, she turned to other guys and I turned to the bottle.

To progress in this world, we have to tackle our problems as they arise, immediately and with courage. This doesn't mean doing it perfectly the first time. This simply means addressing the fact that some situations can make you afraid or uncomfortable. Or that you know that you are dealing with something in an unhappy way. The problem with doing this is that it is hard to look at ourselves with an unfiltered lens. Whether we want to admit it or not, we are all the heroes in our own story. How can we be *wrong?* Impossible! But we are. Often. And it is this awareness and openness to being wrong that allows us to grow. If you are seeing the same problems come up again and again, you are not learning the lesson. And believe me, there *is* a lesson. If you cannot see it, or find it hard to let your guard down with yourself, don't worry. This just means you're human. That's what good friends, therapists, support groups, sports, coffee shops, meetup groups, and any number of different avenues of meeting with other like-minded humans are for. If you seek the truth about yourself, you will find the answers. And most of the time the answer is to deal with your issues and problems right away.

Find a way to keep laughing, no matter what it is.

You'll hear this a million different times in a million different ways until you finally internalize it. Life is what you make of it. This is a cliché saying for a reason. It might be the oldest truth we collectively know about the human experience. Yet, enacting this supposedly 'simple truth' remains one of the hardest things to do. It takes patience and effort to learn. Sometimes more than you can bear. But once you learn how to laugh when you are in pain, instead of becoming bitter and lashing out, that laughter invites love and kindness. And love and kindness are the only way to heal that pain. Any kind of laughter will do the trick. It is subjective and personal. Find what that is for you right at the beginning. It will save you a great deal of time and missed opportunities to grow.

Fuck 'em.

Always try to be humble, forgiving, and kind. Hold the door open for the next person. Be giving of love and affection. But hey, this world is just as full of love and light as it is with evil and assholes. It is almost always better to take the high road, and it is certainly always better to *try* to take the High Road at *first*. But you are human. You are a walking, talking, mathematical miracle. You do not deserve to be trampled over and ridiculed at a whim. There is a line, and if someone steps over it, *multiple times*, fuck 'em. Let it rip. Tear them a new one, leave them on the side of the road, ghost 'em, or just flat out break their fucking nose. Every grown adult knows where the line is. If they step over it, and you've tried everything you know how to do to be an exceptionally kind and loving person, then they step over the line *again*, fuck 'em.

Never hesitate.

··

The world often tells you: "It's my way or the highway." Choose the highway.

··

Basic Survival

I could list all the places I've been, all the jobs I've had, and all the times I've had to build up something from nothing. I could go on and on about coming up from sleeping on the street, a backpack holding everything I owned, $0 to my name, and no one to call. I know everything there is to know about coming from nothing. And that's because I spent my entire life pushing myself into the most uncomfortable places I could possibly go. Grinding my body and soul into life's great cheese grater as if I was going to come out of it whole. I always thought it would write a good story. I was wrong. It did give me enough material for a book though.

The hard road I took, and that so many are forced upon, does not build character. That's a misnomer crafted by the coddled and wasteful generation before us. The Hard Road shatters your mind, body, and spirit. It is a misconception that it takes strife and heartache to create success. Usually, it is just the opposite. It creates evil just as easily as excess does, along with trauma, stress, cancer, and regret. The fact that so many people have had to travel the Hard Road is one of the reasons that we see the degradation of the world around us. It might just be the *very reason* that we live in the world we do.

There are only three things that help this world thrive: kindness, wisdom, and understanding. That's it. And we rarely see any of it in our daily lives.

I didn't always know that. I barely know that now. When I was younger, I had no heroes or role models. No one showed me the way or taught me what was right and wrong. I was angry, and filled with hate, self-loathing, bitterness, and spite. I was also sensitive. I knew, deep down, that love was the only real way forward. I knew that I craved belonging and connection more than anything, despite my best attempts to be a 'lone wolf.' Man, did I think *that* concept was cool. I was adrift in a world that I didn't know whether to emulate or cast aside.

It doesn't excuse some of the ways I acted and some of the things I did. There are no excuses. But I'm not lugging around Herculean guilt like some of the guys in the movies and I am certainly not even close to 'past saving.' I made just as many mistakes as I had wild successes. Sometimes I put myself into situations, emulating rap stars and men I thought that I was supposed to be, that were not healthy for me or the other people involved. I regularly humiliated myself trying to be somebody I wasn't. I went on long journeys I didn't want to be on from the *beginning*. I took jobs in far-away places that I knew were bad for my health. And I found myself back in my hometown over and over again, in countless failed relationships, and one horrific marriage. I was putting myself in situations where I was destined to fail. And I did fail. In epic fashion. Side of the road, head in my hands, too drunk to stand, too sad to cry, fashion. But I never wavered in my determination to throw myself back at the giant cheese grater of life.

If I had a problem talking to people, I talked my way into a bartending job. If I had to get out of 'there,' I put out my thumb and got *out* of there. If I needed an outlet, I volunteered, interned, or wrote on a pad of paper till my fingers bled. I hurt some people and they hurt me. I routinely made it happen, however, regardless of the odds or the cost. Some call this divine providence, that God has a plan for all of us. I call this determination and grit. Others have called me an absolute moron. Doesn't matter now. Because what happened, happened. Some of it was horrific and some of it was transcendent. One time I was driving along a dirt road in the boonies somewhere near West Yellowstone. I had recently had one of the worst days of my life. So there I was, beer in hand, bathing in self-pity, wondering if I should just drive off the side of the cliff, when I spotted a kid walking along, half-dead. I convinced him to get in the truck and, after an hour-long ride back to town, got him back to his mother. I'll never forget her face. Other times were awesome too. I bailed some people out of jail, changed some tires, and helped some people get out of some prickly situations. Sometimes I intentionally was a friend to those that needed it, if only because I know exactly how that feels. I was given unlimited chances to walk a road of light, love, and respect. Sometimes I took it. Sometimes I didn't.

The point is that I was granted the opportunity to live a life *worth living* and I was oftentimes up to the task. There is no greater pride or satisfaction than giving a starving person half of your sandwich when *you* are starving. I will tell you right now that I am a spiritual man. The things I have seen… I don't know how not to be. And when God, or the universe, or simple happenstance, whatever it is that you believe, gives you the chance to be a good person the only answer is yes. The world forgot that at some point. That is the first thing I learned. Half of what I know.

The other half is how to survive.

I am never going to have children. I am never going to have a family. I am never going to live a 'normal' life. It just won't happen. They got to me too early, too deep. My bloodline, and the cycle, dies with me. I am what some call a 'wounded healer.' A teacher. A mentor. I think. Maybe I'm just a very hot fart on some equally hot wind. Who knows. But I do know that my main legacy will be this book. And that will be enough. Because these pages are a manual, of sorts, for how to break out from the rubric of what everyone around you is doing; what everything around you seemingly wants *you* to *be*. For how to live a life independent of the absolute bullshit that our society is constructed from, how to be a good person, and how to create your own cycle.

I can lambast you with advice and tricks that I have learned along the way. I can tell you story after story that will (hopefully) make you laugh and then learn from my dumbass mistakes. I can tell you how important it is to find out what makes you tick, what makes you happy, and even whether or not to simply ponder your existence once a week. None of it will mean jack if you're hungry, thirsty, and homeless.

This section is a basic blueprint of how to survive until you get it all figured out. You're going to need a job, a place to live, some things to do. You're going to have to get a bank account, then a savings account, even a credit card. You're going to have to pay taxes and bills, sign up for phones, get jobs, and go grocery shopping. All the mundane details of life that we call 'adulting.' And on top of all that, you're probably going to have to get a car.

The details will not be 100% correct for everyone. Certain things will be different in your area. For example, buying a truck in Oregon is much, *much* less expensive than it is in North Carolina. Is that because everyone listens to country music down there and feels like they aren't man enough without an F-150? Who knows? It costs double to buy a truck in the South so someone should figure it out. Either way, there are differences like this in every single aspect of life throughout the country. If this is the case in your area, just take the advice with a grain of salt and apply the basic idea to your efforts.

You don't necessarily have to be a 'nomad.' It's a silly term. You don't have to learn how to code, move to Lisbon and work out of an overpriced commune. You can live in any city you want. Or the desert. Or even Antarctica. They do need cooks down there. I don't know if anyone has ever told you this, but *you can do whatever you want.* Anything. It's all possible. Believe me, I didn't think I could break out either. But here I am. I have left hundreds, *hundreds*, of living situations, jobs, and relationships with nothing but the clothes on my back. I made it. By the skin of my teeth. And I learned a few things doing it. I learned how to make the hard road a lot easier. I learned how to be a successful, decent, philanthropic, outwardly focused person. It's all I know.

I'm assuming you're reading this because you want to know too.

01 | Finding A Place to Live

Getting an Apartment

This can be the most complicated part of survival in the modern-day world, which is frustrating because something so absolutely necessary *should* be really easy. It's not. And yet, every urban area has some kind of vagrancy law that prohibits people from sleeping there, meaning the very act of falling asleep requires that you pay for it if you are to not break some kind of law. For most people, this means that they are going to have to find an apartment to rent.

This is an option if you are planning on being somewhere for a considerable amount of time. It runs opposite to everything that I advocate for in this book, but I have included tips from my experience nonetheless. Breaking out of the mold that 'they' want to pigeonhole us into typically necessitates traveling around, but that is not mandatory. You can still be yourself, live a completely healthy life, and generally avoid the pitfalls of modern society, all while staying in the same geographical area.

Just be aware, every single person who has ever rented out a space is doing so to make as much money as possible off of said space. They don't call them land*lords* without reason. This means that, simply because you are staying in the space, they will blame you for any depreciation of the property (i.e., anything that goes wrong naturally), will hesitate to complete or facilitate necessary improvements/repairs, and will raise their rates at least once a year to maximize their investment. An irritating yet necessary evil. Elsewise, you are on the street. Just heed this: do whatever it takes to get out of the cycle of renting. You are pissing away your money. Money that could easily, and almost for the same amount, be used to purchase your own space.

With that said, here are some tips I discovered along the way:

- **Make your application stand out.** I always hand delivered my applications, showed up in slacks and a button-up shirt, and generally was friendly to the staff. They are bombarded with requests and stacks of applications so anyone who thought to just show up and put a face on their application immediately sticks out to them. The few times I did need to sign a lease and get an apartment (I never made it through the entire lease), I never had too much trouble getting one. This is not the norm.

- **Research the company or the private owners.** When possible, go through a private owner. Be wary though. Feel them out for what they are all about. If they are renting the property out as a means to make some money right before they renovate, or if they are house flippers, then they are expecting you to cause damage and they will charge you for things you did not do. This is not everyone. A lot of people keep their first home as a rental as a means of paying the mortgage on their second home. These are good people to go with, as they want to keep their property well-maintained and will manage any problems that arise.

- **Private owners are just like relationships.** You learn their flaws and quirks as you go along. It is up to you to put in the work, effort, and attention necessary to figure out if it is a good situation for you to be in long-term. Make sure not to enter into any kind of rental situation if you are desperate. It will lead you to not follow your intuition. When you are meeting with prospective landlords, you should be asking a bunch of questions designed to get them to reveal what they are truly like. If they are dismissive and irritated that is a good indicator that they are not good to rent from. If they make excuses for the way that the unit looks, chances are they are lazy. And if they are late, hurried, rude, and there are several things wrong with the property? Definitely walk.

- **If it is a company, make sure to look into the reviews.** They incentivize current and former tenants to write them good reviews with discounts at the end of their leases, or when they move out, so pay little attention to rave reviews. Very, very few property management companies are anything better than slumlords, so pay close attention to the negative reviews. If they mention serious problems that aren't dealt with, like mold or water leaks, move on and find a new company/ new location. With this in mind, check the Better Business Bureau, or whatever functions in a similar way wherever you are located. This is an independent agency that functions as a regulatory body without any real powers. People can still report businesses to the BBB, however, which can be used as a guide for people who come after them. In a way, the BBB functions as the highest form of ratings, as their process to get a 'review' published is extensive, so whatever problems the person had were significant if they went through all that trouble. If the BBB says the company is rotten then they most certainly are and you should avoid them, no matter how much you want to live in that townhouse next to that one coffee shop.

- **Read the lease.** Sometimes people are wholesome and honest. There really are people out there that want the best for everyone and who will look out for your best interests. And these types of people are disproportionately represented in the recreation, travel, and hospitality industries. Unfortunately, these are not the majority of people. Equally unfortunately, if you are looking into an available space, there is a higher likelihood that the person offering this space is *not* one of these people, as the odds that the person before you did not think highly of their landlord are much higher simply because *they left*. So read the lease, twice. Highlight it. Take your time, get some coffee down the street, make notes, and *read* the damn thing. Why? Because most leases have at least one thing in it that will cost you down the line and all of them are negotiable. No lease has ever been written that cannot be changed. It is why the 'cost fields' are usually left blank. Because landlords and rental companies pull a background check and a credit report on you, then *decide* what to charge you and when. So read the thing, ask questions, look them in the eye, and if you think they are trying to pull one over on you, *leave*. It is never worth sinking the boat just to make it over the next wave. You'll thank me later.

- **Always have renter's insurance.** Most people think that when they are renting they are only truly responsible for their belongings. While it is true that the rental company or owners are not liable for your property, you *can* be responsible for a lot of things that can cause damage to the property. If you have a dog that chews up the walls or if you leave a stove on and it causes a fire, you could be held liable, not the property owner. And if you don't have insurance you will end up paying for any damages on your own. In addition, the renter's insurance usually covers your personal property when you aren't even at home, meaning any stuff you leave in your car, at a storage unit, or even your parent's house, is protected (to a degree).

As I said, renting is a necessary evil. Whether you are saving up enough to buy all the gear or transportation you need/want to hit the road or if you're just more comfortable in the place you're at, you need a place to rest your head. Just be aware that it is not the only way. Most, if not all, leases go for twelve months or more. Some are six months, but these are much rarer. During these twelve months, you are paying at least a third of your income just for this space. That is income that goes straight into someone else's pocket and doesn't get you ahead at all. You are also contractually obligated to pay it until the end of your lease. It is a racket, it is criminal, and it is the way things are. Just think about this: the average cost of a mortgage is barely more than the average cost of rent for a decent size space. So why is it so hard to qualify for a mortgage, when you are paying, and have most likely been paying for a long time, the equivalent amount in rent? Just a thought.

Roommates

The easiest way to work around the typically monstrous cost of rent is to find other people to live with. The idea of roommates is definitely not mine. People have lived together since the dawn of time. But I have ritually used a roommate situation as a means of temporarily being in an area and not having to pay the same amount that an Airbnb, a weekly hotel, or any kind of month-to-month stay would cost. These are easy to find, as people are constantly moving in and out of places. Whether roommates don't get along, they find their own place, don't play nice with others, whatever it is, the turnover is high.

A simple web search will find you multiple sites that provide a board for people to post and look for roommates. I have had great luck and success in the past with Craigslist, but this can be a bit sketchy. Regardless of what avenue you take to find new roommates, make sure to follow some basic guidelines. The first is to set up a meet-and-greet before you move in. Always be wary of someone that is totally cool with you just moving into their place sight unseen. Not only is there a high percentage chance that it's a scam, but if it's not, they will have the same openness about the place if you were to move in. Do you want random people from the internet in your house all the time? Probably not.

Next, make sure to always let someone know where you're at the first time you meet up with a potential roommate(s). You just never know. Usually, they are on their best behavior the same as you are. They need someone to fill that room in their house so that they can continue making rent. Never hurts to have backup waiting in case the whole thing goes south. If the meet-and-greet goes well and you think that you'd all play nice together, make sure you can iron out the details right off the bat. How long do you plan on being there, what is the cost, how much are utilities, who has their name on the utilities, and how are they divvied up? If someone insists on having expensive cable/satellite TV and you never watch TV, that can be an issue, especially if they want you to pay half of it.

After that, you'll need to check out the place in person. You want someone to prove that they actually live there as well. People rent Airbnbs for a month or so, get a bunch of renters/roommates, collect the dough, then bounce to another state or country. It's a common and effective scam. So just ask them for a copy of the lease. If they can't immediately provide you this you should be skeptical, *especially* if they are asking you to cover part of the deposit or any cleaning fee. They should have a copy of their lease ready, which clearly shows their name, multiple IDs, and should have no problem contacting the landlord or company if you ask them. I usually pushed that a little, just to see how they were with their landlords. If they got twitchy about it, I assumed that they were trying to rent to me illegally, against the wishes of their landlord, or that it was a scam.

If all this checks out, then all you have to do is agree on a move-in date and have your money ready to move. It helps to have a checkbook, or some kind of online payment software because this leaves a paper trail. Beware of anyone who insists on cash-only. They usually have a good (really, it's bad) reason for not wanting to have a paper trail. Also, take personal pictures of anything that is damaged or needs repair *as* you're moving in. Don't make a big deal of it, 'cause nobody likes a finicky diva and the object is to make friends and have a good time. But you don't want the person who holds the security deposit to get mad at you later for damage you aren't at fault for. And if it's a party house? Take pictures of everything. When the bill comes due, and it eventually will, people will look for anyone to blame. Don't be in their crosshairs.

Also, watch the neighborhood you're in. I always look for kids playing on the street, or kids' toys out in the yard. If kids are playing, then some parents are OK with their kids playing outside. This doesn't happen in neighborhoods where there are frequent shootings or kidnappings, which you obviously want to avoid. Also, on a lighter note, look for coffee shops, restaurants, and bookstores. This is just from my personal experience, but any of these things typically mean that people like to come here to relax and hang out. On the other side, living next to bars, music venues, and thrift stores usually attract a louder crowd than you might want to live right next to. But who knows? Maybe you do. Look for things that would attract the noise level and type of people you will vibe with.

Always take a stroll around the area in which you want to rent. You might not have the wherewithal to go out and do this and that's OK. Sometimes you just have to take what you can get. But if you have the time, take a stroll in the morning and the evening. You can get a good feel of the place you might be moving into just by walking around and being observant. Pay special attention to the traffic and street noise, especially if you're in the city. One of the blocks I once lived on had a resident crazy person, who *loved* to scream obscenities at the top of his lungs, always at 11:11, morning and night. Every day. Not to mention scowl and curse at everyone that walked by. I always handed him cigarettes. He didn't yell quite as loud at me, but it was still super annoying. Make sure to scope out your area if you have the time and energy. Sometimes you'll catch something you wish you had.

Weekly Hotels

Weekly and monthly rentals are a huge part of the nomadic/alternative lifestyle, and you will see them referenced in several other places in this book. There is even a definitive section for how to go about picking one, vetting it, and identifying any potential issues with one of these rentals before it comes up. I've added it here because I wanted to sow the seed that these are available everywhere right when you are starting to immerse yourself in the possibilities and procedures behind living this kind of lifestyle.

Hostels

Just like with the weekly hotels, these are always a cheap option when initially trying to find somewhere to go. There is a section on these later. The important thing to note here is that these are available and popular options that may very well be in your area. They typically do not allow locals to stay there, however, so these will only be a type of solution if you have already left your 'home.'

Camping

This can be a difficult way of starting out if you are still working in a fixed location or are trying to work and save up funds. I have frequently returned to and left Portland, Oregon, in a seemingly endless cycle. This means that I have burned a lot of bridges at times and have had to get creative when finding temporary places to stay. Oftentimes I would camp, inevitably resulting in me getting up way earlier than I had to in order to get to my job or work site on time, working all day, then traveling the extra hour and a half necessary to get back to the campsite. And this does not even take into account the time it takes to cook meals, do laundry, shower, and finish basic chores and upkeep. It *can* be fun if you find the right spot, just pay attention to the gas costs and travel time if you are still commuting to and from work.

Sleeping In Your Car

I have had to pull this move way more times than I would like while I was traveling. It can be very effective if you do it the right way. Keep in mind, there is a distinct possibility of getting a ticket or getting arrested. You are also guaranteed to wake up feeling filthy and with a kinked neck. But this section is about survival and surviving means doing whatever is necessary. No one said it was going to be easy.

There are three main concerns when sleeping in your car. The first is homeowners and people who live around where you want to park. Nobody is going to like people sleeping in their car anywhere near where they live. They automatically assume that you are going to steal from them. The trick is to have a sunscreen that blocks off the windshield. This helps to keep people from seeing that you're in the car. Also, try to pull in at night when no one is outside, pick areas that are less densely populated but not easily identified as dead-ends and corners, and keep the lights low. This means pulling in and immediately trying to sleep, not sitting on your phone for hours.

The second concern you are going to have are the police. Vagrancy laws typically dictate that people cannot sleep in their cars and you will never know that some dickwad called you in until a cop is knocking on your window to wake you up in the middle of the night. This is why it is important not to drink or smoke. It will be tempting. Very tempting. But there is always the chance that a cop is going to wake you up and you are going to have to shoot out of a dead sleep and then immediately take a sobriety test. All cops are going to immediately assume that you're drunk and fell asleep at the wheel. If you fail the test for whatever reason or blow almost anything into the breathalyzer, they are going to cite you for *something*, and it is going to set you back considerably.

Last, you have to remember the street sweepers, loading vehicles, delivery people, contractors, and other early-morning workers that might come near your vehicle. These are hard-working people who will typically have a very low patience for people sleeping while they are working. This, along with the early morning dog walkers, is going to be your biggest threat to getting 'called in.' This usually doesn't matter as much because you'll most likely be getting up early and not sleeping well, but if you are a champion of sleeping, just know that waking up to being towed is not a great way to start your day.

Couch Surfing

It took a great deal of thought, time, and effort to figure out how to write this paragraph. That's because couch surfing is a significant grey area for traveling and existing in general. On one hand, it is good to ask for help from your loved ones when you legitimately need it. On the other hand, this entire book is dedicated to inspiring and instructing you on how to be fiercely independent at all times. Can you see the dilemma? But as you will see often in this book, when faced with a choice of whether to add something or not, I have typically added it in the hopes that it might help even one person. If it ends up harming you, as it harmed me at times, then it will hopefully be a good learning experience.

Couch surfing has an expanded section later on. Peruse that if you are going to take this route. For the time being, simply know that this is an option for only a short time. Whenever you are on someone's couch, you are directly impinging upon their life and their hospitality. Many people will offer you space in their homes with gracious and loving intentions. It is on you to utilize that space to get yourself fully independent as quickly as possible. If you do not do exactly that, you risk ruining relationships, setting yourself back mentally, and otherwise establishing a reputation for taking advantage of people.

When you are staying on someone's couch it is imperative to do three things: keep your stuff together, help out around the house, and fit into the lifestyle of the person you are staying with. Keeping your stuff together is obvious. Never enter someone's home and then create a giant mess. Helping out around the house is the way that you 'pay' for your stay. Nothing in life is free and if you are providing a service to the person offering you free accommodation then you are creating value for yourself in their mind. This buys you more time to either save up money or find your next spot. Lastly, fitting into their lifestyle is key. If they are late-night folks who like to stay up and play video games on their couch it is going to quickly chafe them that you are asleep and taking up their living room at 8 pm. The same goes if they go to bed and rise early. No one is going to want you around for long if you are making loud phone calls and watching TV late into the night when they need to be up early in the morning to get to work. While couch surfing is a cheap option, never forget that it can only work out for a short amount of time and still requires a great deal of work to pull off.

Homeless Shelters

This is an absolute last resort. Just like begging and Food Stamps, you need to approach this type of help tentatively and only in great need. I have legitimately been homeless and have chosen to sleep in the park rather than head to one of these shelters, solely out of guilt. I did use one once. There is a process for getting in and there is a lot of demand for obvious reasons. The one I stayed in was dangerous, not-patrolled, and there were a lot of drugs being done. I couldn't get out of there fast enough. But they do exist for a reason. If you are on your last leg, have already slept outside for a night, have no money, and are starting to slip mentally a little, this can be the place you need to recharge enough to figure something out. Plus, everyone needs a hot meal when they are starving.

02| Food

Grocery Shopping

It is amazing how privileged we are to have a place where we can just walk into and pick our food off of carefully arranged shelves. Not having to spend all of our time creating food has opened the doors for humanity to explore the planet, the cosmos, and the depths of the human soul to an extent not imaginable a mere two hundred years ago. All you have to do is hand someone a bunch of plastic/cloth paper and then they willingly let you leave with a basket of perfectly edible food arrangements.

With that said, grocery shopping is an absolute nightmare of irritated people, garish white lighting, and cheap marketing tactics designed to get us to eat as poorly as possible to improve some company's bottom line. You also need to have some of that 'cloth paper' that they want you to give them. There is no business in the world that is so carefully concocted to subliminally coerce you into buying certain things over others. And as much as possible. But do we want to become farmers? Nope. Yeah, we're going to head to the grocery store! Just pay attention to some of these things:

- **Total up your items as you go.** Always keep either a loose mental tally or a running calculator on your phone as you shop. This rams home the precise notion of how much you are spending, typically in stark contrast to what you were intending to spend.

- **Grocery stores (really all retail companies) utilize lighting of different kinds to draw your attention to different things.** And if they are drawing your attention to something, odds are that it either isn't good for you or has an inflated price. Typically, this lighting is bright white as a means of making it easier to identify products, make products more appealing, and generally get you to look in the direction they want you to look in. All this is carefully designed to distract your attention from what you are trying to do: shop for food as cheaply as possible.

- **All major stores and brands effectively utilize music as a means of slightly manipulating your shopping habits.** Grocery stores thrive off of pushing you to lose track of your budget and exactly how much food you are there to buy. Ever ended up with way too much food? Or a shit-ton of vegetables that will inevitably wilt and go bad before you have a chance to eat them? Yeah. These stores use up-tempo music to get you to move slightly faster. The volume isn't too loud, they still want you to be able to hold a conversation and think, but it is loud enough to influence you. And they mostly utilize popular music, the kind that you'd hear on the radio. These songs are already engineered to have a certain number of beats per minute, utilize certain frequencies, and are formulaic concoctions of 'catchy' hooks and lyrics. All these combine to get your body moving faster, which leads to faster decision-making processes. This, in turn, leads you to spend more. Want to spend less money at the grocery store? Wear headphones.

- **Watch for the 'image of abundance.'** Ever notice how most grocery stores *really* try to get you to walk through the produce section as soon as you walk in the door? And notice how they rarely let their produce sections *not* appear overflowing and stuffed with products? This is to convince your brain that you are surrounded by abundance. That you are, simply by being there, rich. Produce is also relatively cheap so if you start there you subconsciously get the idea that you can get a ton of food for really cheap. Vegetables are also the best thing for your body that you can buy at the store. We all know this. Yet we don't eat enough of them. Instead, we buy a ton of them, leave them in our fridge till they go bad, then throw them away. Grocery stores know that we want to have the health benefits of vegetables, but we don't necessarily want to cook or go through any of the trouble of creating a healthy meal. This is another reason that they put them up front. If you buy a ton of vegetables, you might think that you also deserve some ice cream. It's natural, don't worry. Maybe even some (gluten-free) corndogs that you can cook in the microwave. No shame. It all starts with the vegetable section though. The goal here is to only buy vegetables for that day and the next. That way when you inevitably head home and order pizza instead of cooking, you didn't break the bank on vegetables you didn't eat. And hopefully, you didn't go crazy in the freezer food section.

- **Buy your fruits and vegetables 'in season.'** It is a miracle of the modern world that we can get pretty much everything at any time we want. All we have to do is look hard enough and BAM! Kiwis. This does not, however, mean that these fruits and vegetables are going to be even reasonably priced. Scarcity breeds higher pricing. If you are trying to buy fresh peaches in the wintertime it is going to cost you an arm and two toes.

- **Boxes.** Always be wary of anything in a lot of packaging. This harkens back to the idea of creating the image of abundance and prosperity. If it looks like a lot of food then it is worth the extra cost, right? Not necessarily. Nothing is more irritating about grocery shopping than paying a great deal of money for a product, then opening the box and seeing that it wouldn't feed a small child during snack time. And everything about that box smacks of extra costs and profit margins. Cardboard costs money, designs cost money, logos cost money, the 'nutritional ingredients' section costs money, and on and on and on. Every single thing about that box cost a ton of money to engineer, design, and produce. And this doesn't even factor in any of the actual costs of the food. Remember, everything on those shelves is designed to make someone a lot of money. You are trying to minimize that while picking the products that are best for you, the consumer. Overpackaged, overproduced, and overmarketed products in gaudy boxes are some of the worst examples of this. These boxes also go hand in hand with frozen foods. Not all frozen foods are horrible for you. Some frozen fruits and vegetables can supplement a healthy diet. Are they as good as the fresh varieties? Absolutely not. But they can help. Most frozen food, however, is intensely processed, manipulated, and generally terrible for you in every single way. Again, no judgment. But just know what you're putting into your body and why. Also, pay attention to the box.

- **Marketing will assault and assail your senses.** I haven't found any cohesive or comprehensive evidence that details 'marketing overload' but I have personally experienced it in almost every single facet of American Lyfe. Billboards on the highway. Shopping centers and retail plazas. Anywhere that people are trying to make a buck there is an absolute assault of colors and advertisements, all of them trying to pull your attention. They are just like flowers in the forest trying to attract as many bees as they can. Keep in mind when you go shopping for food that it is no different indoors. Take a minute and *be curious* about the product you are thinking of buying. Why? Oftentimes, just this pause will stop you from buying something you don't need and don't truly want.

- **With this in mind, keep track of whatever you notice first.** A common trick of grocery stores is to put whatever is getting close to expiring or whatever has the highest profit margin at the end of an aisle, the side facing the entrance or back of the store. This gets the highest traffic and, therefore, sells that product much faster. Does that benefit you at all? No. Another trick that they use is to put the products with the highest profit margin (remember: worse for you) at the eye level of the average person. Your brain has already been tricked into thinking that you have more money than you do, you are being goaded on by the up-tempo music, you are overwhelmed, and your perception is intensified by the gaudy marketing and bright lights, and now you are seeing products that are designed to be right in front of you. Make sure to slow down your pace and shop each section. Typically, the products with the best ingredients and most benefit to you, the consumer, will be around your knees or lower.

- **Grocery store deals are never 'deals.'** Most often, these products aren't even 'marked down' at all. They actually have their prices *increased,* but because they have a 'sale' tag on it then everyone believes that they are getting a deal. On the flip side, grocery stores commonly run into the problem of having too much supply with rapidly upcoming expiration dates (at which point they can no longer legally sell the product). To avoid having to throw these products away they will put 'sale pricing' on it. If you are buying this product, then you are paying a relatively similar cost to the original cost of the product but getting a severely diminished product in return. Altogether, you are rarely actually getting any kind of 'deal.'

- **Buy online.** Whenever you are in a store you are paying for the products there, the people that work there, the security, the parking, the lease, the taxes, etc., etc. The beauty of online businesses is that they do not have to pay the same overhead costs as brick-and-mortar establishments. Or it's like Amazon where they move so much product in warehouses that they can substantially undercut the price of grocery stores (although I will loathe them until they are unionized). This method is great for vitamins, dried foods, meal bars, and other products that don't go bad as fast. This is also way, way better for any cleaning, pharmacy, household, or other general products.

- **Don't pay for cut-up meat.** Really you should be heading to the butcher. In doing so you are going to get higher quality meat, support a local business, and generally pay a lower price. Regardless, you should be buying whole 'cuts' of meat and then cutting them up at home.

- **If you can, do the same for your vegetables and naturally pre-pared foods.** Chances are that no matter where you are you can find a roadside store that sells only vegetables and products made in the area. Farmer's markets are the absolute best places to make this happen. This means that your honey, jam, soups, pickles, canned vegetables, etc., are all available without the markup of the grocery store, any of the overpackaging, and none of the GMO or processing concerns that you get with mass-produced/mass-marketed foods.

Food Stamps and Food Banks

I remember when I was twenty-four years old and I moved back to my hometown for the third time. I had just gone through my second intense breakup in the past two years, had gotten unceremoniously let go from both of my jobs, and had alienated my remaining friends with my negativity and jaded behavior. I was swirling the drain and I knew it. I was riding the bus, oh yeah, I had also managed to get my license suspended, and overheard some kids my age talking about Food Stamps. They were lamenting how you couldn't buy energy drinks or cigarettes with them. All I heard was my stomach. Growling. I couldn't remember the last time I had eaten. I was on my way to drop off my resume at a bunch of different restaurants to work a job I didn't want to do in a town I didn't want to be in. It happens, right? So, I didn't have a particularly tough time quitting that potential job and rerouting myself directly to the office where Food Stamps were ostensibly doled out.

That was it for me. Rock. Fucking. Bottom.

It's not that I am or have ever been 'better' or 'above' anyone who has ever needed support with their everyday living. Far from it. I took unemployment during the pandemic just like everyone else. I firmly believe that my taxes (that I pay) should be good for *something*. The reason this was as low as it goes for me is that I built my entire personality, my entire *being*, on being able to survive. On being self-sufficient. A scrabbling, scrapping, hard-nosed yet charming, apocalypse thriver. I could get anywhere, do anything, and overcome any odds. Yet now… I needed help buying food. It didn't compute. I just couldn't reimagine myself, recreate myself from all the shattered pieces, again. I walked into that office and ground to a halt. Just thinking about it, putting myself back in that place, grinds out tears in the corner of my eyes.

I walked up, took a ticket, and sat my ass down.

The rest was a blur of paper paperwork and standing in line. This was way before COVID so I could see everybody's face. They all looked like regular people. One guy was clearly on his lunch break. He still had his reflective gear on. There were a couple of folks who were clearly homeless, but they had people working exclusively with them, most likely 'cause they had a screw loose or didn't have any kind of ID. Understandable. But the rest of the people looked just like me. I should have taken heart in that but instead, I took more shame.

When I finally got to the interview process, it was quick. I sat down and the woman looked me dead in the eye for a half second then immediately got up, beckoned me to do the same, then put her arm around me, and gently led me to a side office. I guess I wasn't the first one to ever break down in their office. We didn't say a word for what must have been fifteen minutes. When I was done crying, she gently took her arm off of my shoulder and led me back to the desk.

"When's the last time you ate?" she asked, reaching out for my hand. I didn't even notice so she just put it over mine. I couldn't remember. I also couldn't remember whose yard I'd slept in the night before or whose garage I'd arranged to sleep in for the next week. It was all just a blur of Craigslist ads, six-hour moving jobs I picked up, multiple-hour bus rides, and sad music on my MP3 player. She handed me half a sandwich and I silently broke down again. I will always remember that woman, even though I can't remember her name or face. I just see her hands reaching over the table to assertively grab mine. Her cracked brown skin was calloused but smooth. That feeling of seeing a small, bright light after sitting in a massive pitch-black room. And that damn good sandwich.

I walked out of there with a card that I could swipe to get some food. Didn't take long to try it out. I was at Trader Joe's, and I had a small basket of stuff to make more sandwiches. I was so nervous to use my new card. What if it didn't work? I didn't even have a credit card, so if it didn't work I'd have to put all this stuff back in front of a huge crowd of super judge-y people… But it worked just fine. And the old lady threw in a chocolate bar I hadn't paid for and gave me a big wink.

Everything is going to be OK, you know?

The reason I tell this story is because this isn't just a book about how to do things, where to put your hands, and what ingredients to use. Just put your feet at shoulder width apart and squeeze those buttocks! Nope, that's already been said and done. I want to (hopefully) show you how to do things the *right way*. See, I didn't have any role models or anyone who gave a shit while I was growing up. And nothing changed all that much as I got older either. But I knew, deep down, that the goal was to end up a good person. So, what happened? I did things the *hard way*. The whole point of this book, which you'll hear over and over, is so you won't have to.

One of the most common things that you hear in places where people congregate after they've fucked up to some degree (AA, jail, the Food Stamps office, rehab, etc.) is that they never thought that those things would ever happen to *them*. We all share the characteristic of being optimistic when we are young. We all think: "Nah, that won't happen to me." Until it does. And when it *does* happen, and believe me, something like this will, then you need to be ready for it. Both physically and mentally. Because the alternative is washing down the drain.

So yeah. This is my section about Food Stamps and Food Banks. They exist everywhere, they are easy to find for good reason, and they can help you out in a pinch. The only advice I give is this:

1. **Only use them when you absolutely need to.**

2. **Respect the fact that these resources are there for you and the people who need the same support that you do.**

3. **Give back to the same places when you can.**

That's it. Just remember that to some people these places are miracles. And places that deal in miracles need to be treated with respect.

Dollar, Discount, and Salvage Foods

I really would add a bunch of details to this but frankly, I have never gotten food at any of these places that didn't make me violently sick. Either the next day or weeks later, doesn't matter. If you play with fire you are going to get burned. A lot of times you don't have a choice and I understand that. If you are starving the Dollar Store will sell you a can of spaghetti rings for a dollar. The problem is, that the can was probably manufactured in the

1980s. It is definitely past anyone's definition of 'still good' and as a result, can have severe long-term health effects. I have zero trust in the FDA, the Department of Agriculture, or any American governmental authority that is supposed to regulate the processes that bring food to storefront shelves. These are the same people that allowed Purdue Pharma to operate without regulation for *decades*. They don't give a fuck about your health, your family's health, or anything at all, besides the millions of dollars they receive from various lobbying agencies. If you think that anywhere along this process your health was taken into consideration when deciding whether to make it legal to sell food past the time that anyone has studied its effects on humans then you are, flatly, wrong. Use these stores in a pinch but never make it a habit.

Cheapest Ingredients

Here's a list of the things I would buy to maximize my nutritional value and the actual amount of food I could afford when I had nothing. I've gotten by on these ingredients for years. I'd add some basic recipes as well but really, you can find those anywhere.

- **Bananas**
- **Apples**
- **Flour (+baking soda and baking powder)**
- **Rice**
- **Tortillas**
- **Lettuce**
- **Peanut Butter**
- **Jelly**
- **Oats**
- **Dried beans and lentils**
- **Potatoes**
- **Tomatoes**
- **Green peppers**
- **Onions**
- **Cucumbers**
- **Watermelon (in season)**

- **Broccoli**
- **Bread. Especially 'day old'.**
- **Pasta (if you can't afford the sauce just get lemon, olive oil, salt, and pepper)**
- **Then take your pick of whatever is cheapest: chicken, ground beef, ground turkey, or canned tuna/salmon.**

Keep in mind when you are shopping that the key is to get the cheapest, high-quality ingredients that your can. Then think of how to put them together into a meal. By thinking this way you detach yourself from the type of thinking that will get you drawn into expensive ingredients and add-ons that you can't afford. And don't forget to get yourself a chocolate bar.

03 | How to Ask For Help

You ask for help by proving that you are worthy of it. Did your car break down, leaving you stranded and hungry? Well, somewhere in your car is a piece of paper or cardboard. Somewhere in there is a pen. You can write a joke on that piece of cardboard. You can write a Bible verse. Trust me, as long as you don't explicitly ask for money, someone will help you. People are good if you give them a chance to be! I learned how to play guitar (See: How To Play Guitar) just to make some money on the road. I only ever had to use it one time, but it was worth every penny of the thirteen dollars I made at that rest stop. Why? Because it turns out that was exactly how much gas I needed to get to where I was going. All you ever need to do is put it forth to The Universe and the good people that live in it that you need help, that you are worthy, and that it is for a good cause. People don't need a sob story. They don't need a victim with a victimization routine. What they need is a reason to believe in you. And the best way to do that is to show them that you can and will use whatever help they give you to help yourself.

This is a separate section because it is bound to happen to every single person and it is so critical to our way of life that we all do this correctly. Yes, there are con artists out there. Yes, there are predators. And yes, some people are lazy assholes who expect a handout from the world. It is these people who have put a stigma on helping out those that need it, i.e., those people by the side of the road who *really do* need a couple of bucks and a bottle of water. These people are passed by countless times by people who could help, who *want* to help, but don't because of the people who take advantage of them.

So, the goal is to teach you how to ask for help so that you don't perpetuate the suffering of others. There is such a deep wellspring of emotion that boils out of me every time I think of someone who begs just to travel when so many people are starving to death or living horrible lives in squalor. Anyway, as I mentioned, the goal is to do it correctly.

If you set out on the road with nothing but a backpack and a dream you are going to run into some hurdles. It is not always going to be easy. It is oftentimes going to be wet, cold, hard, and oppressive. It is also going to push you to the absolute maximum of your capabilities. And occasionally you are going to 'fail,' leaving you in a situation that you don't know how to get out of. This has happened to all of us, whether we knew it at the time or not. Believe me, when you get off a plane in a foreign country and immediately lose access to all of your funds and don't speak the language, with everyone yelling at you and adamantly trying to take advantage of you, *you are going to know.* When you get booted from a job for dating one of the customers, or get mugged, or your car breaks down, whatever, whenever, wherever, *you are going to know.* And when you do, you're going to need someone to bail you out.

The absolute first thing to remember is to never, ever simply ask for something. Traveling is a luxury a lot of people just don't have. They are constrained either physically or in their minds. Approaching someone who is in this state and asking them to help you is just going to reinforce whatever notions or ideas they already had about travelers. They no doubt have them and you just triggered them. People are also highly wary of being taken advantage of. It takes a serious effort for most people to break through most of their mental constructs and personal experiences for them to open either their phone case, wallet, or car door.

The answer to this is to always offer something in return. Anyone who has ever smoked cigarettes (never do this) knows that there is a culture surrounding these horrible death sticks. Everyone is mutually addicted and congregates in the same areas to push the inevitable reality of COPD, cancer, and breathing tubes, further toward reality. Have I clearly depicted that I am adamantly advocating for you to not smoke cigarettes? Great, glad we wrapped that up. Still, there is a culture that surrounds them. That naturally leads to a bunch of people asking each other for cigarettes. If you do this, just walking up to someone and asking for one, some people will offer you one. Most people will not, coming up with some excuse, always thinking of how expensive they are and a million reasons not to give one to you. But if you walk up with a dollar bill and ask if you can buy one? They will give you one every single time. And nine times out of ten they will adamantly refuse your dollar. Why is this? Because people are good and they want to help you out. They are hardworking people who want to achieve their dreams. And they fucking hate bums.

A long time ago I was walking through downtown Seattle. I had just sold almost everything I owned, put the rest in a small backpack, and taken off to go work at Mt. Rainier. I stopped for a couple of nights to celebrate getting out of Portland. I had $100 in my pocket, my hostel was paid for, and I was going to go out and get wasted. I walked past that iconic, original Starbucks and immediately picked up a tail. He was a street urchin with a tattered leather jacket and rags swaddled around his feet instead of shoes. His short dreads looked like they hadn't been washed in months. He was short, real short. Barely came up to my elbows. He was also the best poet I have ever met.

He wasn't really a good poet. Bukowski, Frost, and Feuerstein are good poets. What this man did well was provide a service that you didn't know that you desperately needed. I've been around a bunch of bums my entire life. I know exactly how to get them to leave you alone. This guy refused. He just started rattling off poetry custom-tailored to my pale skin and hiking clothes, right down to the ink stains on my hands. I wrote poetry at the time too. I've got a whole book of it, self-published, living on my shelf. Somehow, he figured that out too. Still rattling off lines, he followed me to the door of the bar I was headed to. I was laughing by now. I grabbed the door handle and the bouncer looked at me, looked at the poet, then started to put up his hand to him. I shrugged him off and, still chuckling, gave him twenty bucks. Best money I ever spent. I will never forget that poem.

The theme here is this: always offer something in return. It is only when life seems the bleakest that we are capable of our greatest inspirations. Our minds, when confronted with directionless terror, immediately orient toward the worst-case scenarios for our behavior. Ours and humanity's greatest failures. Selling your body, dealing drugs, robbing others, and hurting other humans. We are fallible, we are hungry, and we are oftentimes cold. It is understandable to be desperate at times. But those are not real options. Those are the physical manifestations of weakness and unimaginative thinking. That's why you won't be doing them. What you will be doing is innovating. Creating. Plugging into the correct energy sources; refusing to cater to the darkness that nibbles at the periphery. Because when we ask for help, we give people a chance to help themselves; we invite the other person along with us into the collective good of mankind. We become human together. That's how to ask for help.

04 | Essential Gear

I wrote this whole book without one single thought about what gear you would need. I had lived for so long with just a backpack, so long without any of the other trappings of life that most people collect, that it became second nature. For the first nine months of living in a house full-time, I kept my backpack fully packed with all of my essential gear and my passport. Unpacking it and putting all those things in their 'correct' places was a big moment. It was only when I started to accumulate all the stuff that owning a little house leads you to collect that it dawned on me that most people probably have no idea how to trim all that stuff down to just one bag. And that's OK. Believe me, you learn quickly exactly what you do and don't need when all that weight is strapped to your back most of the day.

The first mistake most people make is either to bring too little or too much (mostly this), which can sink your boat almost immediately. You need to be warm when it is cold, reasonably dry when it is pouring, and cozy when you find a place to hang out for a bit. You'll probably need to be able to cook in the woods, have a tent, and need some form of entertainment as well. All these things add weight. And you are probably used to only holding one or two of them at the same time. When all that weight is put into one bag and that bag is constantly on your back, well, fifty pounds becomes way more than it might sound initially. If you don't believe this then lay out all the stuff that you are thinking of bringing and put it in your pack. If it is hard to just get into your pack then you already have a problem. Are you stubborn? That's OK. Get all that stuff in your pack, put it on your back, and pick somewhere a mile away. Then walk there and back. If you are struggling with this, you are going to need to be less stubborn and get rid of some of that stuff. I have walked multiple miles in just airports and getting to and from hotels. This doesn't even factor in the fact that you will most likely be walking *dozens* of miles if you are doing anything more than that. Err on the side of lightness.

Here's a basic list to get you started, in order of importance:

- **Your Passport.** The golden ticket. This is the most important piece of property you own aside from your driver's license. You can get anywhere with this, you can prove who you are, and you can go wherever you want. Always, always, always keep this close at hand or know *exactly* where it is *at all times.*

- **Tent.** Even if you are planning on sleeping in your car, couch surfing, or otherwise finding rooms to stay in along the way, you will invariably hit a point where you wish that you had a tent. It is the single easiest way to create a place to stay wherever you are. And for a lot of reasons, this is the one piece of gear that you do not want to be cheap about. Do not, under any circumstances, buy a cheap tent. Cheap tents are poorly made which means that they will break easily and oftentimes come with holes already in them. Spend one night in a bug-infested area and you will greatly appreciate how essential it is to have zero holes in your tent. The other major factor is weight. Cheap tents are heavy and bulky. You want them to be light, flexible, and small. This means that you are going to have to spend a significant part of your budget on this piece of gear. Spend the money. You will not regret it.

- **Rucksack.** Become accustomed to what the term 'internal frame' backpack means and what your budget is. Basically, internal frame backpacks have the frame built into them. These are essential if you are ever going to get on a plane or if you want to enjoy any part of your life spent with your backpack on. Expect to spend the most money on this piece of gear. I would tell you to search for a used bag, but every single one that I have bought that way has let me down at a key time. If the stitching busts 20 miles from the nearest road or, somehow worse, in an international airport, you are straight-up *fucked*. Spend the money to make sure you have a good one that you can count on. No matter what anyone else says, a 60-lb bag is way too heavy. Every single pound of that will weigh you down exponentially more than the one before. Try to keep it at 45-lbs or under. Also, these bags are measured in liters which can easily be confusing. Be ready to convert. Starting out you are going to try to fit too many things into your bag. You are most likely not going to know what you can live without. You will find out quickly (mailing things back to your home base is key). As such, you will want to start with a 50–75-liter bag, depending on how bulky your tent, cook set, and sleeping bag are.

- **Sleeping Bag.** You are never going to be 100% certain that you are going to have a bed to sleep in. And you most likely aren't always going to want one anyway. Especially if you are living primarily off-grid. A good sleeping bag, with a hood and rated to 0 degrees, is essential to being able to go anywhere you want to go. These are commonly called 'mummy bags' because they pin heat in from every inch of your body and can be contracted to cover everything but your mouth too. You never know how cold it is going to be until you're lying on the ground and you start seeing your breath frost the air around you. If you listen to nothing else I say, get a good sleeping bag that is going to keep you warm, and make sure it comes up around your head and face.

- **Sleeping Pad.** As much fun as sleeping directly on the ground can be, and it can be extremely liberating at times, you want a pad to cushion your back for nights when there isn't soft dirt or loam to be found. It isn't the first night that's going to get you. It's the third. By then you'll be achy and twisted, wishing you had packed a little cushion for your back and had rolled up your sweatshirt for a pillow.

- **Lighter.** I always bring four or five. You can get by with matches but it's way more stressful. You're hoping that they don't go out in time, you're rapidly watching the number of them diminish, they don't give out consistent heat, plus they are just not as good as lighters at providing the constant heat necessary to turn wood from potential into kinetic energy (See: How to start a fire). These are crucial for lighting your propane stove and for starting wood fires. If it's wet at all you are going to want more than one as it will take much longer for the wood to catch flame.

- **Butterfly stove.** These glorious inventions are one of those things that should have gotten someone a medal or an award but didn't because not enough people use them daily. If you are going to be in the woods, you *will* use this daily. And you will adore it. The stoves are small, foldable pieces of metal that hook to small propane tanks (pro tip: don't forget the propane tank) and then give out enough heat to boil water and cook food.

- **Mini-pot.** These pots are designed to maximize efficiency and provide a ton of different uses. In one day you might want to boil water for coffee, then cook eggs in it, then heat up some pasta for lunch and dinner, then boil water for tea. I love the systems that have two pots, one for coffee and one for cooking. That way your coffee always comes out perfect. But I'm picky and you can easily get away with just one. Make sure it is light, has good rubber potholders, and easily fits (space-wise) with your propane tank.

- **Earplugs.** Lightweight and essential. From crying babies in the train station to loud snorers in the hostel, you'll want the ability to be able to mute the masses of humanity when you need to. Don't go anywhere without them.

- **Headphones.** Same concept as ear plugs, but these have the added benefit of being distracting and potentially relaxing. Wherever you go you are going to want these.

- **Headlamp.** You never know how much you need the light until it gets dark. And trying to hold a flashlight while you are working with your hands can be difficult and frustrating, if not impossible. Enter in the headlamp. It takes a while to get used to them but when you do, you'll never want to use anything else. It is an absolute necessity, especially if you need to wash dishes, take a leak, or have to deal with anything in the dark.

- **Flashlight.** Oftentimes you are going to need two lights, usually when setting up camp. I like to have one to provide a basic level of lighting in my tent and campsite to supplement the direct beam of my headlamp. The real tip here is to always have a semi-clear water bottle. I prefer red-tinted because it doesn't mess with my night vision. You take your flashlight and leave it resting against the water bottle. This creates a kind of lamp you can put anywhere in your tent.

- **Sandals (or camp shoes).** I always go with sandals because I always end up in either a hostel or a hotel once every week or so and you need them just to take a shower and not get a bunch of funk growing on your feet. It is also always healthy to air your feet out if you get a chance and it's not too cold. 'Camp shoes', or shoes that are thin, light, and comfortable, will work just fine to get you out of your regular shoes, they just weigh more and don't get as much use.

- **Jackets.** No matter how warm, hot, or humid it might be, always have at least one jacket. I cannot count how many trips I've been on that the weather started one way and took a dramatic turn. You ideally want multiple jackets. This point is doubled if you go anywhere near a mountain, river, or stream. They are cold and you are going to want layers. I have always gotten by with a thin 'thermal,' which I put under my shirt, a basic hoodie or sweatshirt, and an overcoat. Anything that has mild resistance to water, like a fleece. In an ideal world, all these layers are the nice, expensive, lightweight kind. But if you have to get the cheap, clunky ones, prioritize these over all other kinds of clothes. Your second pair of jeans is below your jackets on the priority list.

- **Pants.** Speaking of jeans, you aren't going to need as many pairs of pants as you think you are. You are most likely going to get all of your gear messy or dirty on the first day. Get used to it now. We do not always need to be spotless. You can, despite what you are telling yourself, get by with one pair of pants, one pair of shorts, and either a swimsuit or a pair of athletic shorts. I prefer athletic shorts because while they might be harder to swim in and take longer to dry, I like to sleep in them. Keeps my crotch from getting too sweaty and gross.

- **Three pairs of underwear and five pairs of socks.** This is how I've always ended up overloaded. I would load up on boxers and socks. I figured that it would be a long time before I was able to do laundry so I had to bring along as many pairs of these as possible. Remember though that every single pound, or fraction of a pound, adds up. Even socks and underwear. You'll learn quickly that you can wash a pair of socks every night in whatever stream is nearby and do the same with the undies you wore the day before in the morning. I would always just hang or bunch them somewhere on the outside of my pack or tent to dry. Eventually, I got down to three pairs of both (you never know when you're going to need at least one extra).

- **Phone charger, batteries, sporks and forks, toilet paper, two plastic bags, two small hand towels, and a small thing of dish soap.** These are all the little essentials that you are going to need. You are going to need to power your headlamp, eat, do your business, hold your laundry, wash your face and pits, and clean your dishes. There are more little things listed later but these are the essentials. Everything else is window dressing.

And that's it.

You can probably fit more into your bag and this is when things start to get tricky. You start thinking, "Hey, maybe I *can* get away with bringing some of my favorite things!" And the answer you should tell yourself, resoundingly and over and over, is no. Pick a handful. For me, a book is 1000% necessary, as is a pad of paper and a pen. For some people, it's an iPad to play their movies. Just make sure that you remember that everything weighs something! Here's a list of things to consider adding:

- **Inflatable pillow.** These sound like a great idea but they are always underwhelming to me. I've always just taken a T-shirt and stuffed all the clothes I wasn't wearing that night into it and used that as a pillow. But some people swear by them so here we are.

- **Iodine tablets or a water filter.** You may or may not be planning to take off into the woods for considerable stretches. If you are just traveling then you don't need to consider potable water, because it will already be everywhere. But I always carry iodine tablets just in case. They are light and can bail you out in a pinch if you don't trust the water somewhere. If you *are* heading out into the wild, you will need one of these, preferably both. Some people don't like the taste of iodine, so a water filter that you can just pop into a stream and pump till it gives you clean water is a game changer.

- **Camera.** I always use my phone but there are a lot of photographers out there, both amateur and professional. If you're going to bring a big camera, however, this is probably going to be it for you, because it is going to add a significant amount of weight.

- **Gloves.** I like to have a thin pair of these handy just because I've broken my knuckles so many times that they get intensely painful in the cold. These are especially helpful in the morning before it warms up when you are handling water from the stream, using your stove, and possibly packing up a very cold camp.

- **Books.** Really, a book. Maybe two. I started out loathing the very mention of 'tablets' but eventually switched over wholeheartedly when I realized I could download a movie or two and have my whole collection of books on one lightweight device.

- **Bar of soap, a small thing of shampoo, and deodorant.** I used to forget these and it always really pissed me off when I was in the middle of nowhere and didn't have them. Or worse, really wanted them and didn't want to pay exorbitant prices to get them in heavily populated, touristy areas. Always wear deodorant around people. It's just the right thing to do and you can't smell yourself. Usually. If you can, put more on. Lastly, shampoo can double as a way to wash your clothes in a pinch.

- **Pepper spray.** People are mostly good and awesome and all that. But they aren't always. I carry bear spray whenever I am in the wilderness, but those cans are clunky and over-the-top for most confrontations you might find yourself in. Pepper sprays mostly come in compact, easily pocketable containers that you can slip from your pocket to your hand when the hair on the back of your neck is rising. If the Boy Scouts got one thing right in the midst of all the abuse and boy-diddling it's this: Always Be Prepared.

- **Sleeping pills.** No Romeo, no Juliet, you aren't going to have anything in your bag that is illegal or habit-forming. I always carry some perfectly legal, over-the-counter sleeping aids. You are often going to find yourself cold, so tired that you can't sleep, surrounded by inconsiderate, noisy people, or all the above. These can help get you some shut-eye.

- **Extra pair of headphones.** If you're like me, you will definitely break your headphones. Often and spectacularly. It is always worth it to have an extra pair. You just never know when you're going to be at your wit's end and then there are crying babies.

The deadliest snakes don't have rattles.

05 | Detecting and Avoiding Danger

This is a dangerous world. Human trafficking, abduction, murder, drug-related crime, all these things happen way more than you think they do. We don't hear about it all the time because if we did there would be panic. Is it any wonder that the average U.S. homicide 'clear rate' (how many of the cases get solved) in 2020 was barely under 50%[1]? Add in a healthy margin of error for false imprisonment and outright lies of police officers and this rate drops to a horrifyingly low number. The truth is that there are a ton of people out there committing atrocities and other unspeakable crimes and there is *nothing we can do about it*. But that doesn't mean we can't stay prepared.

There are things that I have done and places that I have been that I am amazed that I have survived. For a long time, I had a death wish. I wanted to die in some exotic place where no one would ever find my body because 'nobody cared anyway.' Yeah, that was me. Somehow, I survived all these foolish situations that I put myself in. I chalk a lot of this up to having

---

1   Li, Weihua, and Jamiles Lartey. "As Murders Spiked, Police Solved About Half in 2020." The Marshall Project, 12 Jan. 2012, www.themarshallproject. org/2022/01/12/as-murders-spiked-police-solved-about-half-in-2020. Accessed 21 May 2023.
"Federal Bureau of Investigation - Crime Data Explorer." Https://Cde.Ucr.Cjis. Gov/, 2 Jul. 2023, cde.ucr.cjis.gov/LATEST/webapp/#/pages/explorer/crime/ crime-trend. Accessed 28 Apr. 2023.

always had a really good ability to detect danger coming my way. As a child I learned how to feel danger, to use all of my senses to guess when it was coming, where it was coming from, and how to best avoid it. As I got older, I only got better at it. Too much 'better' as it turns out, but that is another story entirely. The takeaway from this is that I figured out how to stay safe, even in situations that could have, and should have, been avoided in the first place.

When you're traveling you become a target. You will hear this often in this book. People naturally try to prey on people they do not know and do not understand. It is extremely easy for people around the world to be xenophobic, racist, and 'tribal.' Think you're any different? You're not. Disagree with me? Think of your political ideologies. Then think of people with *opposite* ideologies. How do you feel about these people? Yup, we are all xenophobic. Not your fault though. We are hardwired this way. The absolute only way to remove these base tendencies from your brain would be to remove all of your base instincts. When you figure that out, please let me know. Until then, you just have to be aware that this is a reality in the people that you meet. The inference you can immediately draw from this is that, as a traveler, you are going to encounter this everywhere you go. This can and will become dangerous at times depending on how far and wide you travel.

One of the more despicable tactics used by human traffickers is to wait outside of airports or popular tourist destinations for a pretty girl to come along. When they see said girl waiting for an Uber or hailing a taxi, they forcibly interject and try to convince this unwitting girl to 'share their Uber' with them. What they are trying to do is abduct that person and I don't need to tell you what happens next. Think traveling with another person is going to help? Nope. This actually makes it easier to achieve, as you have another person who you think can defend you. But these kidnappers are known to be advanced and methodical, using tactics from needles in the neck to simply gassing the whole car with sleeping gas. These are real-life situations that happen to real-life people all the time. And this is just one example.

I am not trying to scare you off of travel, particularly foreign travel, at all. I just want to make you aware of the dangers that exist, especially in places where you don't speak the language or look like anyone you're around. These dangers can also be just as prevalent in your hometown. Think I might be a bit pessimistic? Do a quick web search for the sex offenders in your area. You'll be stunned by how many there are, and how *close*. And this is only for *sex* offenders. Add in all the other types of crimes that don't require people to be added to a database and you paint a pretty bleak picture of humanity. Again, this is not everyone. Most people are good people. You have to keep believing that. But it's close. Real close. And the bad ones need to be watched. Here's how I go about it:

Practice feeling the hair on the back of your neck.

Ever had a gut feeling? Or just had the feeling that something was off? Well, chances are you were right to think so. Now, this strays well off the path of practiced science, or anything that I, or anyone else for that matter, can really prove. It is derived solely from my own experience and nothing more. But I'm right so here goes:

The scientific term for the hair on the back of your neck raising is 'piloerection.' There is a great deal of consensus that this reaction is emotional and physiological[2], with little input from your thoughts, and can quickly lead to the 'fight or flight' response, wherein the body dumps a bunch of adrenaline into your system and gets ready to either flee at top speed or fight for your life. It's an ancient response system that developed when we had to regularly fight off large land predators that wanted to eat us. Nowadays, you see it mostly when you watch a scary movie and then spend the rest of the night with a flashlight thinking there's somebody with a mask and silly superpowers sneaking into your house. The point is that piloerection happens without you thinking about it. Keep that in mind.

There is also a great deal of agreement that the body has at least a weak energy field[3]. This gives spiritual people, such as me, a lot of leeway. The heart has an electromagnetic field and so does the body, so then we start talking about things such as people having a 'certain kind of energy.' Or an 'aura,' if you're so inclined. We also intensely look at what is called Heart Math, which is the study and intense appreciation of what is called Heart Rate Variability (HRV). Essentially, a bunch of super smart dudes figured

2   McPhetres, Jonathon, and Janis H. Zickfield. "The Physiological Study of Emotional Piloerection: A Systematic Review and Guide for Future Research." Science Direct, 1 Sept. 2022, www.sciencedirect.com/science/article/pii/S0167876022001556. Accessed 2 Mar. 2023

3   Shields, Deborah, et al. "Human Energy Field: A Concept Analysis." National Library of Medicine, 23 Nov. 2016, pubmed.ncbi.nlm.nih.gov/27881613/. Accessed 12 Apr. 2023.

"Human Laboratory and Clinical Evidence of Effects of Electromagnetic Fields." National Library of Medicine, 1 Jan. 1993, www.ncbi.nlm.nih.gov/books/NBK208981/. Accessed 6 May 2023.

out that people are happiest and healthiest when they are 'in tune' with their hearts. In other words, minimizing their heart variability is the best way to maintain overall health. These are broad strokes but stay with me. These same scientists then came up with an amazing discovery. They constantly measured people's HRV and showed them a bunch of images that were either clearly happy, like puppies, or clearly very, very unhappy, like internment camps. They immediately found that the HRV of the people being monitored changed five to ten seconds *before the people were shown the photos*[4]. This study has been replicated hundreds of times. What does all this mean? To me, it's pretty simple. Your heart can *tell the future*. This simple fact should change your life. If it doesn't, I don't know what to tell you. Anyway, that's where the scientific analysis and fact-based approach ends. I will bravely carry on.

Taking your heart's ability to sense the short-term future as a given, alongside your brain's inherent ability to drop your body into the fight-or-flight response, then we have a clear and present explanation for why your hair raises on the back of your neck when something in your field or frame of reference senses danger. Now this is pure conjecture but somehow, *we all know this is true*. Crazy right?

The takeaway from all this is to learn to pay attention to your body. There are clues given off by every human and whether they are audio, visual, scent, or energy-based, your body and your electronic field are picking these up faster than your brain can process them into coherent thoughts. Your body is going to straight up tell you when to pay attention. And this isn't always via the hair on the back of your neck! If you are paying attention, you are going to be able to avoid most of these types of people/situations.

Now, I know a lot of you aren't going to believe me when I am telling you these things and that's OK. It is still a great practice. My friends occasionally tell me that I am over the top with some of my opinions of other people, especially when I am in traffic. They might be right. But one day I was walking down the street with a friend and we passed a man in his mid-40s with a Hawaiian shirt tucked into khaki cargo shorts. The epitome of the average middle-aged guy in our small community. He was the only one on our side of the street. Before I even looked up the hair on the back of my neck was straight up, my pulse had quickened, and I subconsciously put

4   Bulut, Necati S., et al. "Heart Rate Variability Response to Affective Pictures Processed in and outside of Conscious Awareness: Three Consecutive Studies on Emotional Regulation." National Library of Medicine, 1 Jul. 2018, pubmed. ncbi.nlm.nih.gov/29787784/. Accessed 17 Apr. 2023.

my arm around my friend's back. She was off in her happy little world, so when I tightened my hand around her waist, she came back to attention a little bit. I smiled at the man as he passed and quickened a little bit. After we turned the corner, she turned to me and said:

"I know what you're going to say and yes, that guy gave me the creeps."

I was so proud. It was such a validation to know that we had both correctly identified the predator walking free on our small-town street… Yeah. I can't count how many times this has happened to me, particularly on elevators. I think it has something to do with being in a small metal box together with someone who most likely has someone chained up in their garage. Think that's over the top? It's not. This is America and it is fucked up here. You just haven't been paying enough attention.

Use your phone.

We oftentimes look at this ubiquitous brick as solely a means to an end. It makes calls, it takes pictures, it plays music. It shows us videos of adorable pitbull puppies that we want to adopt. But in any kind of dangerous situation, it is also your best tool to avoid a confrontation.

The easiest way to do this is simply to call the police. If you are uncomfortable enough to think that you are actually in danger, then simply making that call is enough to scare a lot of people away. The easiest way to break up a bar fight is to yell into the throng of bodies: "The cops are on their way!" Works like a charm. But there is also something primal about having someone else that you are talking to that makes people think twice. Predators are hardwired to identify people who are alone and vulnerable. It's just how it works. So, if you have someone on the phone with you, they will immediately hesitate to act, especially if you are actively and loudly telling someone exactly where you are or talking to the police. And if you are in a foreign country, and you never got that sim card, you can still use that brick to make an imaginary phone call as well.

Walk with purpose.

Remember, predators look for vulnerable and alone. If you are drunk, tottering, and meandering from street to street, you are going to quickly attract the wrong kind of attention. The main trick, if you are ever in a shady situation, is to stand up straight, square your shoulders, look straight ahead, and walk *purposefully*. This means having intent and attention to get to where you are going. Not quickening your pace out of fear, but rather intensifying your gait and powering through the area. You need to be on a mission to get to where you're going. I always pretend that 'lives depend on it,' that I have to get back to my hotel to defuse a bomb or something like that. It takes my mind off of the people staring at me and makes me walk like I'm in the White House.

Smother your fear.

This is mandatory. Fear is a lot of things. It is complicated, necessary, and difficult. It is the 'mind killer.' It is also conquerable. And there are certain situations where you just don't have the option to be afraid if you are going to get out of there alive. Whether you are aware of it or not, you have been in at least one of these situations in your life. You simply have to remain calm and push down the terror. In my life, I have either straddled the line between caring and not caring about my death or held something so important to me in my mind that this wasn't difficult. If you can't adopt one of those methodologies, there are a million different ways that you can learn to smother your fear. It is highly personal and oppressively tough to do. Yet it must be done. You are going to have to discover your own way to do this. I will tell you this though: never scream unless you absolutely have to, keep your head down if you hear gunshots, and take off your coat if you have to run for it.

Trust your gut, your heart, and your senses.

We have all heard it from time immemorial. Trust your instincts. Go with your gut. Listen to your 'hunches.' And these things are actually based on a couple of slices of science. Did you know that there are neurons, those nerve cells that communicate between parts of your brain, located in your gut and your heart? There are elements of the brain's reasoning and communication apparatus located in various parts of your body. These are relatively independent of your brain's actual structure[5].

---

5   Underwood, Emily. "Your Gut Is Directly Connected to Your Brain, by a Newly Discovered Neuron Circuit." Science, 20 Sept. 2018, www.science.org/content/article/your-gut-directly-connected-your-brain-newly-discovered-neuron-circuit#:~:text=The%20human%20gut%20is%20lined,have%20eaten%20an%20entire%20pizza. Accessed 9 Mar. 2023.
Carabotti, Marilia, et al. "The Gut-brain Axis: Interactions between Enteric Microbiota, Central and Enteric Nervous Systems." National Library of Medicine, 1 Apr. 2015, www.ncbi.nlm.nih.gov/pmc/articles/PMC4367209/. Accessed 22 Apr. 2023.

I didn't design or adapt our bodies and I know very little about how we function anatomically. But when I learned that the age-old wisdom regarding our intuition actually had a shred of scientific data behind it, that did it for me. Trust your gut. If you don't like a place, bounce. Sometimes you just spend the money and don't get it back. In my life, I have done this countless times. Weird Airbnbs. Swamp motels. One time I even accidentally booked a room at an 'hourly hotel.' It was like walking into a porn set. Nope! If you are uncomfortable or get a weird feeling that something is *off* then there is most likely some kind of information or sensory trigger that your body has recognized before you can process the data mentally. Go with your gut, every time.

Watch for the Bait Man.

Most criminals work in teams. It is easier to abduct or rob someone if you don't have to physically subdue them first. Pickpockets often work this way. One will run into you or adamantly start a conversation with you while the other one nudges you from behind and grabs your wallet. Abduction teams will get somebody who's beautiful or handsome and have them start to flirt with you. Your attention is distracted by their figure, or whatever. Next thing you know, they are either inviting you somewhere private or someone has already snagged one of your bags. Now, it's important to note here that these aren't all people. A lot of people are out there to strike up a good conversation or take you home for very fun reasons. The point of this is for you to identify when it's *not* for good reasons. You have to make sure that that is the case before you extend yourself into a situation that you can't get yourself out of.

Watch what you drink.

One of the closest times I have ever come to death was in Mancora, Peru. I was traveling through South America at a reckless pace, drinking and smoking anything I could get my hands on. I was out of control and had stopped caring for my safety weeks ago. That is why, against any sense of judgment I have ever possessed, I decided to stay at a party hostel near the beach.

I do not belong in a party hostel. I have never gotten along with partying fraternity/sorority kids. I am just different. And that's perfectly OK. What wasn't OK was that I was desperately trying to be something I wasn't. This led to a ton of embarrassment at that hostel. I was lonely, depressed, recently abandoned, and generally just swirling the drain. I was intently reaching for any branch I could get a hold of. In short, I was wounded and was an opportune target for predators.

At some point, I made a big mistake. I won't get into it, but let's just say that I stupidly ran around waving some cash and buying some things I shouldn't have bought. I was already drunk, floundering, and now I had pissed off the very people that you don't want to piss off in this world. For some reason, they let me walk away. At which point I went straight back to the bar. I was in such a bad place that people were giving me a wide berth, despite there being a *ton* of people around. I just kept drinking and completely checked out. At some point, the people who you really don't want to piss off came into the bar and started mingling with people. One of them even sat next to me for long enough to get a drink. I wasn't paying attention and I certainly wasn't following the steps above. It comes as no surprise now, in hindsight, that I suddenly became very tired. So, I gave up and went to bed.

The next few days come back in flashes of memory. Waking up in a pool of vomit three inches tall. Being stuck in the bathroom, calling for help, and looking down to see a bunch of blood in the toilet bowl. Getting carried to the moto taxi. A woman I couldn't recognize soothing me, settling my hair (turns out she was the hostel manager). Then I was lying down on some kind of hospital bed. Now this was a small, small town. The streets were mostly sand. How I had gotten to this clinic baffled me. I remember fighting off the nurses trying to inject me with IVs, thinking they were trying to inject drugs into me. I shit my pants twice that night, both completely blood. I truly don't know how long I was unconscious after that. Whenever I did wake up, I had to tear out the IVs and sprint to the bathroom to fill up the toilet bowl with blood. This happened three or four times a day. I would immediately lose consciousness after that and wake up with another IV in my arm. I remember waking up in the middle of the night to an urgent grip on my arm. It was one of the nurses. She was looking at me with a mixture of motherly concern and irritation (*maldito turista*). I tried to ask her what was happening, what was going on, but the words died before they hit my lips. I simply couldn't speak. She spoon-fed me an entire jug of soup. It was the single nicest thing a human has ever done for me.

All told I was there for six days. If you think that isn't a lot, try waking up periodically in a shitty little clinic with dead cockroaches on the ground and everyone speaking a different language. A few times during this period one of the 'doctors' tried to explain what was going on inside of me. They barely spoke English and I barely spoke Spanish. All I could understand was 'muerte,' which means death, and them holding up their fingers with a little distance between them. Aha! Now we were getting somewhere! This meant I was close! To death! To death? Shit.

After five days of constant IVs, I figured that I probably had the strength to stand for longer than two minutes. I had a gown on somehow, don't remember how I got out of my clothes, and an IV still in my arm. But fuck it if I was going to die without figuring out what was killing me. Despite the loud yelling and protestations from the entire clinic staff, I made it to the sandy streets, clutching my IV in one hand and my cell phone in the other. My ass was prominently displayed, a bright white beacon in the middle of the (mercifully) dead street. I powered on my phone and, miracles abound, it had a little juice. I could feel someone running after me so I walked as fast as I could to the first Wi-Fi signal I could get to. All told I managed to connect to some angel's hotspot and send out a quick message on social media. At this point, I was rudely escorted back to my bed.

The next day the biggest male doctor they had woke me up and rudely gestured for me to get up. This took a while. My body still felt close to death. I could feel the tears in my intestine, and my kidneys and liver felt as if they were filled with small stones. Still, I got up with this guy and walked over to the taxi he had arranged. Turns out they were worried I would leave without paying and he just needed to take me to the ATM (*maldito turistas*). No problem, I paid them and had them stop where I could get some Wi-Fi. My post had blown up. Which meant I could get some answers! An Argentinian friend I had was adamantly asking where I was. Obviously, he spoke Spanish and could figure this out for me. I have no idea how much he must have spent making those international calls, but that man saved my sanity that day. God bless you Rolo, wherever you may be. When I got back to the hospital they had connected to my adamant translator. Thus, after six days, I was finally told what had happened.

I had been fucking poisoned. Somewhere in that first night they had taken blood samples and rushed them to another town. I was also damn near alcohol poisoning. Oh yeah, and I had food poisoning on top of it. The assholes that had come into the bar had slipped something into my drink that was intended to be lethal. I can't remember the name, but I have been told by one of my friends who knows these things that it was a highly lethal poison used in that part of the world. The absolute only thing that saved my life was my decision to abandon the beer that had been in my hands, mostly full, and go to bed under my own power. Even then the things they were pumping into my system weren't designed to counteract that particular poison. I survived solely off of my innate abilities. Since then, I have had serious and intense gastrointestinal issues, absolutely cannot digest certain foods, and dairy is akin to poison to my body. I had ignored all the steps above. I had put myself in a bad position, had let myself become oblivious to any of the danger signs, and had adamantly ignored my heart and gut.

Watch what you drink.

Set the terms.

Life isn't about playing it safe all the time and living afraid. You are going to make mistakes and you are going to eventually find yourself in situations where you are going to have to think your way out. That's OK. It just means you are living your life and trying to discover the world. But if you are going to take big leaps of faith or risks, make sure that you understand what those risks are. You can always take charge and dictate terms. Here's an example. A lot of people like to go to Europe and get laid. It's super common. Frankly, hooking up with strangers has never been my cup of tea. I firmly believe that you share part of your soul during a sexual interaction, a part of your soul that you don't get back. So, to hook up with a ton of different partners… yeah. But that's just my opinion. If you *do* like to do that kind of stuff, no judgment here. You just have to know that there are risks involved.

Imagine you're in a bar with someone and you're hitting it off. Things are moving towards heading somewhere private. You should be sober enough to at least acknowledge that this could turn out very badly. If you aren't that sober, then you need to grab their number and head home. There's always tomorrow. But let's say you get no warning signs and you're both consenting and ready to go. Let's say your partner throws out the idea of going back to their place. If I were you, I wouldn't. You have most likely never met this person before and you very easily could be walking into a trap. It happens all the time. The smart thing to do here is to find a neutral location. Maybe go halfsies on a hotel across the street. Maybe just bribe a taxi driver. Fire escapes are really fun too. Whatever you want to go with, just make sure you don't follow the easily followable path toward getting robbed or kidnapped. Dictate the terms, come up with creative solutions, and adapt quickly and readily to the foreign situation. And if you do suggest a nice hotel instead of 'their place' and they adamantly refuse, they are probably trying to rob you.

06 | Basic Improvisation

We all watch movies. We know the age-old plot: the hero is in a tight spot, death is imminent, and the noose has tightened so much that there is seemingly no way out. Then the hero sees a loose thread poking out from the rug, somehow covered in the faintest whisp of kerosene, just barely leaking from the sconce that has no business being that close to the floor. The laughing villain, gun pointed upward, of course, is standing right next to it. The hero then barely breathes on the loose thread, thereby starting a massive fire/explosion, killing the villain and all of his uninsured henchmen, while somehow sparing the protagonist and sex-symbol accomplice, who escape with zero difficulty. World saved.

Believe it or not, this is not a critique of Hollywood. I dislike movies where the hero doesn't pull some stunt like that and win. Otherwise, it seems way too much like real life. The point is that the qualities of innovation and improvisation are heralded in our society to an unhealthy degree. People think that it is a talent; that it is directly related to an innate intelligence. If you haven't heard this already, let me be the first to tell you that improvisation and innovation are born through scarcity. Hunger. Need. There are of course exceptions to the rule but who gives a damn. We live in an economy *more divided*, and somehow *more* disadvantaged than the one our parents grew up in. We live in a world where 90% of us share the remaining 31% of the wealth[6], a world where we have been divided along ethnic lines,

6   "Wealth Distribution in the United States in the Fourth Quarter of 2022." Statista, 25 Apr. 2023, www.statista.com/statistics/203961/wealth-distribution-for-the-us/#:~:text=In%20the%20third%20quarter%20of,percent%20of%20the%20total%20wealth. Accessed 26 Apr. 2023.

'party lines,' 'state lines,' '*county*' lines… We have been divided and con-quered. We have been defeated by the same business-oriented strategy that we have championed. You live in a time where you will be remembered, in 100 or 200 years, as peasants. Where giant internet-baron assholes built rocket ships and sailed the troposphere as you lived in a rotting apartment with the sounds of gunshots permeating your neighborhood like pollen on a summer breeze.

Believe it or not, this is not a critique of American culture and politics either. OK, maybe it is. To hell with patriotism though. America was con-quered by propaganda in the '80s[7][8]. If you don't know this then you haven't been paying attention. Anyway, the point is that you live in a time where innovation and improvisation are at their highest point in 'recent' history. I can hear you saying: "Well, that's great Sam! All I have to do is be hungry, unhealthy, and *needy* and I'll be an improvisational *genius*!" And you, my hy-pothetical, sarcastic cynic are not *wrong*… but that's not the point. We think of these concepts in terms of who can come up with the first functional fusion reactor, who can develop the best app, or who can master virtual reality fastest. In terms of affecting your life, however, the most revolu-tionary ideas are going to come from crafters, amateur mechanics, and tradespeople. Is a multinational race to the moon or is a trick for reattach-ing the railing up your stairs going to affect you more? Are you going to make more money building jetpack prototypes in your garage or new(ish) camp-stove recipes? The point is that you are perfectly capable of innovat-ing and improvising. It has nothing to do with 'genius level' intelligence. The geniuses of our species are still infinitely closer to apes than they are to transcendence. It has to do with how much you want it, whatever it is, to succeed in any given moment. It is a skill, an *easily honed* skill, and not only can you easily do it, you can easily *master* it. You live at the right time. You are in the right place. You have the right tools and the right demeanor. You can do it.

Here are some tips to make it easier:

Cook without a recipe.

---

7   Shultz, Richard H., and Roy Godson. Dezinformatsia: Active Measures in Soviet Strategy. University Fo Nebraska Press, 1984.
8   "KGB Defector Yuri Bezmenov's Warning to America." YouTube, up-loaded by Persian Atheist, 13 Feb. 2013, www.youtube.com/watch?v=bX3EZCV-j2XA.

This is what got me to start thinking about the environment around me as malleable and changeable. When I was learning to cook, I would get the hankering for some pancakes, or some Pad Thai, so I would look at a recipe, make a shopping list, and head to the store. It was an expensive and inefficient way to make food. At some point, you realize that you just don't want to spend that much money on your groceries. And when you start getting ingredients that are in season, or cheaper than some of the others, then you start wanting to make food that has those ingredients. And when you start getting tired of the same old recipes that contain those ingredients you start to get creative.

You don't have to be a cook all your life to know how to cook. It is simply one of those things that people make a big deal of because they want to increase their sense of self-importance. How do I know this? First of all, I was a professional cook for years. And second, it is exactly the way I feel about writing! It's natural. So don't beat yourself up if you burn the eggs. Everybody does it. This exercise is oriented toward getting you to start cooking with *what you have*, not what you want. Everyone wants pizza all the time. But if all you have is a can of beans, some rigatoni pasta, a can of tomato paste, half of an onion, and half of a pepper, then you can't make a pizza. You can, however, make a very basic form of chili. It isn't perfect but it's what you've got. Starting to cook this way will introduce you to a lot of different foods and recipes that you may have not heard of or tried, and it will start to flesh out the creative neurons and pathways that will lead to more creative thinking elsewhere.

Go camping by yourself.

Ideally in the middle of nowhere. A campsite will work if you're too afraid. And bring an axe. For me, this was the second-most important arena for learning how to make something out of nothing. I would hike into a location, set up camp, and then immediately be inundated with a distinct knowledge of exactly what I did and didn't have. If it was cold, then I would need a fire. Which meant digging a fire pit, finding enough rocks to make a ring, and then collecting firewood and other fuel. If I was by the fire, I would most likely want a chair, which meant taking my axe, cutting down some logs, fitting them in an A-shape, tying them together with rope or twine, and whittling down more branches for a seat… and on, and on. I would spend days in the woods entertaining myself by coming up with cool ways to make my camp better. It is an incredibly efficient means of increasing your ability to think creatively. It is also satisfying in a way that you may not experience often in 'normal' life.

Get ready to fail.

Everything you try isn't going to work out. Like making pancakes with sesame oil (raises hand). It's just not going to taste good. One time I spent hours making a camp chair only to have it violently snap apart when I put my weight on it. It was an entire half-day of effort, seemingly wasted. But after I had thrown its constituent parts halfway across the woods, I started laughing. It was a damn good idea. I just didn't have any rope. The vines I had used hadn't been strong enough. I went back, picked up the pieces I could find, and tried it again.

You aren't going to be successful in everything you do. It is your ability to stay positive and supportive of yourself that is going to maximize your ability to improvise. Live, laugh, and carry on. And never give up trying to come up with a creative solution. In doing so you are developing and honing this skill, effectively teaching yourself to come up with creative solutions to complex problems. It is not our successes that are our greatest teachers, it is our failures.

Remove mental barriers.

We are conditioned and indoctrinated into a system of rote memory and patterns of behavior. Why do you do things the way you do? Well, Dad did it that way… or, Mom did it this way… or even, well, I've just always done it my way. None of these things has any bearing on the present. You can be whoever you want to be and do whatever you want to do at any given moment. You can change and adapt at a moment's notice in every moment that you exist. Nothing is set in stone. You are fully capable of progressing from any one place to another. Oftentimes the best thing you can do for yourself is to unlearn what you've learned, then learn it again in a different way.

07 | What You Do Affects Everyone Else

One of the greatest added benefits of traveling in any manner is that it gives you a greater perspective. You immediately see that your culture is not the only one in the world, that there are a lot of things to be grateful for, and that we are all part of the human race. No one is any better than anyone else. We are all stuck in a huge blender together, getting chopped up and older every second. If you think that you are truly independent and aren't part of the mix, then you are lying to yourself. Do you live in the country and hate the city? Guess what, it's that city's money that is paying for your roads. Live in the city and hate the country? Guess where your food comes from. None of us are going to make it out alive. While we are here we are all infinitely better off if everyone is just a little more considerate of the people around them.

Right now, as I am writing this, I am sitting in my favorite coffee shop in Asheville, NC. I like this place because everyone is either shitty to one another or over-the-top nice. It is a perfect microcosm of this country, all wrapped into one neat little coffee-scented package. I am sitting at one of those long tables designed for multiple people to sit at. And as I type a young man is huffing, puffing, moving the table, kicking the legs, and otherwise irritating the hell out of everyone else sitting at the table. I could say something to this guy, maybe embarrassing him in the process, but I prefer to just people-watch and take notes. This guy has no idea how he affects the people around him. He is oblivious. And because of this, everyone here is already irritated with him and can't wait till he leaves. Right as I typed those words, he slammed the table around getting up and doing just that. Everyone around him relaxed and slumped a little, clearly enjoying themselves more without his presence.

The point of this is that this young man, with his backpack and general demeanor, could be any one of us. This is the world and the world is us. As travelers, adventurers, and maybe just as humans, we want to be *part* of it. We all want and need to be accepted. At least by one or two people. This will become ever more important and present in your mind as you age and will be critical if you spend a ton of time out on the road. The disconnect between travelers and the places they go is real. Let me put this bluntly: if you behave like this young man you aren't going to connect with anyone. You are going to immediately and effectively ostracize yourself from any potential groups or individuals that you might want to connect with. It is therefore not just a general nicety that you can occasionally deign to be nice and thoughtful of the people you are around. It is a requirement for your continued health and survival.

I am not saying to bend over backward, give the first person who needs it all of your money, be a spineless people pleaser, or any of that garbage. I am just saying that if you are one of those people who never consider any of the people around you then you are going to have trouble maintaining basic relationships and making friends. And that is just not a fun way to live. Here are a few things to remember when you're traveling that will help you do this better:

Be conscious of your body.

Don't run into people. Watch the space that your backpack takes up. Generally have some idea of your physical presence. Just because you are standing somewhere does not mean that you have exclusive rights to that portion of the world. My favorite is when people are walking, side-by-side and slowly, down the middle of a sidewalk. Most of us want to get somewhere. But these people have no consciousness of their physical presence and how they block those around them from going about their day. Especially those who are tired and carrying a heavy backpack.

Pro tip: Don't just stop in the middle of a thoroughfare. Move over to the side, out of the way.

Always hold the door open for the next person.

It blows my mind how many people just walk through doors and let them slam behind them. That's not how anyone gets anywhere. We forget that we didn't always have things. Whatever stage of life you are at, you no doubt have experienced highs and lows of 'having' vs. 'not having.' Yet we constantly forget to help out the next person in line. Holding the door is the easiest and most common physical embodiment of this concept. All you have to do is wait an extra five seconds, push it open, and you have done your job to foster an open, helpful community of good humans.

Keep your shit together.

No, this has nothing to do with mental health. You won't believe how many people sit down and immediately spread everything they own widely over an entire public area. Sometimes this is unavoidable. Sometimes your passport slips to the bottom of your bag, and you frantically yank everything out to make sure you didn't leave it behind. But most of the time it simply means keeping your junk in your bag, your bag out of the way, and your trash where it belongs.

Watch for opportunities to help people.

Regardless of how you feel about life at this particular moment, the truth is that we are all blessed to be here. Some situations *are* horrific and terrible, but chances are that you aren't in one of them if you are reading this section at this moment. And at the very least, you can be grateful that you *aren't* currently in one of those situations. You can most likely be grateful that you can see, hear, and flex your fingers, along with any number of a million small experiences that inherently come along with the human experience. We are also inherently blessed by our ancestors, who came up with toilets, automobiles, coffee, and pizza. No matter what country or situation you live in, we are blessed with a standard of living that no generation before us has ever experienced. Yes, I understand that some people live without running water, access to doctors, etc. But the vast majority of us have an infinite number of things to be grateful for. The world has done a lot for us. It is for this reason that we should focus on giving back when we can. Always have half an eye out for that parent who doesn't see their kid darting toward the busy street. Go grab the door for that person on crutches. Toss a few coins in that troubadour's guitar case. There are a million things to be grateful for in every moment. And there are a million ways to say 'Thank You.' Pay attention to them!

You make way more noise than you think.

When you live in group settings like hostels, hotels, and group living situations, you quickly start to realize that people are *loud*. They drag their feet unnecessarily, they bang their dishes around, and they talk and yell way into the night. They have loud conversations in the middle of a 40-bunk dormitory at 6 am, while dozens of people around them are sleeping. I can't imagine being that person but really, no one can. Start to notice how much noise you make. Just be present and try the best you can to be conscientious. You don't have to ruin your life or bend over backward. A little goes a long way. And in the end, you'll set an example for the rest of 'em, so everyone is a little easier to be around.

08 | Act Like You've Been There Before

Growing up I constantly heard about confidence. I was a shaky kid with all kinds of issues, one of which was intense social anxiety. I remember walking home from middle school every day, where I had invariably done the same thing. There was a girl I was obsessed with. But rather than walk up and talk to her I would come up with varying schemes to be near her, to talk to her in passing, to send her notes through her friends. Looking back, it was adorable. She knew exactly how I felt. The entire school did. A couple of times I even drew up the guts to hold her hand or ask her to be my girlfriend. I think one time she even kissed me on the cheek. All I remember about that is keeping it together long enough to watch her walk away, throwing up in the bushes, then walking home while making up new schemes.

It was on these walks that I would always think about what I would do better the next day. I would parent myself through pep talks, telling myself, endlessly, that confidence was the key. It became some kind of a mantra that perpetuated the fabric of my development into an adolescent, and then into a young man. Eventually, it became an obsession. As long as I could be confident, or merely *appear* confident, then I would be successful and achieve my goals. Maybe my dreams too…? Well, let's not get ahead of ourselves. In middle school, my goal was simply to walk right up to this pretty girl and talk to her in coherent sentences. You know, just like the 'cool kids' did.

As I got older my obsession with confidence only became stronger. High school was a nightmare for various reasons, particularly the amount of bullying a skinny, socially awkward kid is bound to attract. And instead of hitting the gym, joining clubs, and truly committing to the sports I was a part of, I started smoking pot and listening to the wrong people. Where I could have been improving my self-confidence and self-image, I was adopting the traits and messages of rappers, sports stars, and comedians. Confidence, confidence, confidence. Show no weakness. Dominate the room. Make it happen. No one mattered except myself. The entire world was a single-use container for my ambitions. I was untouchable yet still had the same intense issues that I had started with. My face was constantly held in an increasingly ineffective poker face. It was an unsustainable mentality, and I was destined to break down.

And break down I did! Multiple times. I kept trying to rebuild the sprawling mansion of my mind on a crumbling foundation that hinged on one single concept: confidence. It wasn't until I finally realized that there was another way to approach and address the world that I was able to achieve the same goals that I had always had healthily and sustainably. And it was so damn simple. You don't even need to pretend that you're more confident than you appear. You don't need to 'dominate' a room in any way. And you certainly don't need to wear fancy clothes or cologne, have a fancy hairdo, drive a sports car, get your toes waxed, or any of these things that people seemingly spend so much time on. All you ever need to do is act like you've been there before.

This is a simple concept that has far-reaching implications. It can mean whatever you want it to. For me, it meant that I could embody the quiet confidence I had always had, voice the soft-spoken wisdom I had acquired through years of intense suffering, and walk into rooms like I knew what I was doing. Because I usually do. When I finally learned this skill, I was amazed at how many times I walked into a new job or social situation and somebody would tell me: "Man, you walk around like you own the place." Now, that certainly threatened or offended a lot of people. It's important to remember, though, that you are going to run into constant opposition over the course of your journey. Not everyone in the world is OK with who they are and what is going on in their minds. Some people are just unhappy and want to take that out on the rest of the world. Some people aren't going to take the time to analyze their response to someone new coming into their arena. Their fears, insecurities, and prejudices are going to rear their ugly heads. You are going to encounter backbiting, judgment, scorn, and even outright hatred. But you can't do anything about that. All you can do is the best you can and that's what this attitude is all about.

The sections in this part of the book are in a carefully selected order. This is because it is through innovation, adaptation, improvisation, and the determination to survive this meat-grinder we are all in, that we can earn the necessary toolset to be able to succeed in any given situation. When in doubt though, just act like you've been there before. If you are the 'underdog' in any situation, up against the perennial contender or the dominating force, the only way that you are going to triumph is to not be intimidated by the moment. To have a concrete sense of what you are and what you bring to the table. To reach down in your soul and grab the very essence of what makes you, you. So, when you walk in the door for that interview, that first day, or that new place that you've always wanted to go to, you believe in yourself and who you are. Then you put one foot in front of the other, assertively and with great belief, as if this isn't your first time. As if you've walked this path a dozen times and can't wait to do it again.

As if you've been there before.

09 | Essential Qualities to Develop

Determination

Determination is the key component to (eventually) living a comfortable life and achieving whatever dreams you hope to achieve. This is not to say that you should go forever 100%, sacrifice your health and well-being, and ultimately throw your morals out the window to achieve your goals. Life is always meant to be lived and lived well. But the matrix of life is going to throw you challenge after challenge. Have you ever noticed that as soon as you are breezing along, everything going smoothly and according to plan, a monkey wrench comes out of nowhere and jams your gears? Or, even more annoyingly, everything is *not* going smoothly and *another* monkey wrench comes out of nowhere and jams the gears *even more*? This is because we are on this planet to learn. And if we do not learn the first time, the world will give us the same challenge over and over again until we do. This is why the most important aspect that we can develop is our determination. Enduring uncomfortable situations. Getting up time and time again off the mat. Effectively handling rejection. Remaining positive in the face of defeat. All these qualities of determination combine to make this quality one of the cornerstones of how to survive.

Compassion

Compassion is important for three reasons. First, the ability to empathize with other people who are struggling is essential to learning how to connect with your heart. A lot of conventional thinking leads us away from anything concerned with emotion or the heart in general. This is exactly why we struggle as a society. You know, intuitively, that your heart knows what is right and wrong. Your heart also knows what is best for you. And there is considerable evidence that your heart also knows what is going to happen *before it happens*. One does not need a shaman to know that it is important to be in touch with the only one of your organs that is tapped into energy like that.

Second, compassion can make us feel better about ourselves. Now I am not advocating to become a social worker or international humanitarian relief worker. Well, maybe I am. I am one of those people and I love my job. Regardless of that, we are all in it for ourselves, at least to begin with. We are selfish beasts and we need to eat. The grand idea is to cultivate compassion over time, eventually reaching the lofty goal of altruism. With that in mind, The Dalai Lama once said:

> *"It is important that when pursuing our own self-interest, we should be 'wise-selfish' and not 'foolish-selfish.' Being foolish-selfish means pursuing our own interests in a narrow, shortsighted way. Being wise-selfish means taking a broader view and recognizing that our own long-term individual interest lies in the welfare of everyone. Being wise-selfish means being compassionate."*

This form of compassion is a very good place to start. Fake it till you make it. Reap the benefits and accolades of helping others even if your heart isn't truly in it. Eventually, the true peace and joy of helping others just for the sake of it will come. Until then, it's still good for you.

Last, this quality can straight up look good on a resume. I can't count how many employees I've hired with little to no job experience simply because they had something listed about volunteering. I remember working as the General Manager at a hostel in New Zealand. I had a revolving crew of cleaners, most of whom had never held a job before in their lives. They all stayed for quite some time and would almost always run out of money, so they needed an extra job. I would create resumes for them, and I used to make up B.S. job titles from work on the property to beef up their qualifications like 'Gardener' or 'Social Media Consultant.' Anything to make their resumes look like they had something in it. Then it dawned on me to set up some volunteer opportunities for them in the local community.

Bingo! Trust me, having multiple references from the local churches and hospitals looks way better than listing your high school and helping out in your parent's yard all summer.

Patience

When I was a lot younger than I am now I did not believe patience was a virtue. I worked hard, recklessly hard, partied even harder, sprinted head-first into whatever I thought I wanted/needed, and generally was careless about how I treated myself and others. I would even go so far as to expound upon how patience was *not* a virtue, but rather that it was the opposite. As if patience was akin to a sin.

What I didn't know was that patience is not just reserved for waiting for seeds to grow into plants or for investments to pay dividends. Patience is the key quality for interactions with others and, far more importantly, with yourself. It is a key spoke in the wheel of love and kindness. Without any patience we are doomed to a series of lightning-quick reactions; sentenced to a life of living with the consequences of not thinking before we speak, learning from our mistakes, and failing to love ourselves.

Patience is incredibly complex, a thought that never occurred to my beer-addled mind back in my 20s. It's a mixture of almost every positive human attribute including tolerance, humility, generosity, self-discipline, and kindness. You can even dive much further than that if you wish but the point remains the same. Patience is an intricate web of all of our best qualities and to enact it is to assume the best version of yourself.

Patience also has the distinction of being one of the only qualities that is easier to learn for use on others than it is for use on oneself. Eventually, to achieve the ultimate goal of peace and serenity, everyone must learn to be patient with themselves. We are human, we learn and grow, and it takes time. It's obvious and we all know it, yet it is almost impossible for most of us to simply be patient and kind with ourselves. Thus, to achieve our long-term happiness goals, we need to practice patience with those around us. Frankly, I struggle with people. I used to be spectacular, a social butterfly who could navigate any social situation. I also hated myself and everything I stood for. When I began to identify with myself, with everything I believed in, cared for, and appreciated, truly defining myself against the backdrop of the world, I began to struggle with interpersonal relationships. I am sure that you are most likely similar if not the same. An underlying urge to be unique and 'separate' is one of the defining characteristics of wanderers/travelers. So, I have to practice patience *even more* than I used to. Most often I simply practice it with my dog but when I *do* practice with humans, I try especially hard to give them the time of day, the frame of mind, and the *time of mind*, to try and understand their position and give them the most patient and comprehensive response or reflection that I can. In doing so I put myself out into the world as the best person that I can be. You will rarely see a transformative reaction or approach from those you use it on. But you will see a distinct transformation within yourself.

Empathy

Empathy goes hand in hand with patience and compassion. It is the distinct characteristic of being able to put yourself in someone else's shoes. One of the critical flaws of America is a fixation on 'Cowboy Culture.' We are proudly individualistic, prizing above all else the qualities of being unique, boldly different from the norm, and antagonistic. There are no qualities in this world that are not necessary to the human race and these are certainly no different. But your greatest strengths are always your greatest weaknesses. By focusing so intently on being individuals we can often lose our sense of community. And by losing our sense of community we directly support a culture that indirectly threatens and endangers us. Don't believe me? Ask yourself this: how many mass shootings have occurred in my state this year? This month? This *week*? Do you feel safe in public? Yeah, I don't either. The answer to this isn't gun-control laws and bullet-proof vests.

It's empathy.

As a nation, we are individualistic, selfish, and self-centered. Look at our prevalence for owning and driving massive trucks. Hey, I am no different here. I have owned several large trucks and currently own a 4Runner. Still, it is essentially an arms race of metal and plastic on our neighborhood streets. To feel safe, we want a large automobile, with multiple airbags and a huge grill in the front. So, we buy an SUV. We are higher up than most cars and feel like we can survive all these people darting in and out of traffic like insane little lemmings. But suddenly all these lemmings are driving bigger cars. So, we upgrade to a pickup truck. Until we see an *even bigger* pickup truck than our own. So, of course, we wait till the next year's massive behemoth rolls off the line and we sign away our income for the next twenty years to pay off the biggest truck ever made, complete with the highest torque, the most pulling power, the best navigation system... always forgetting that these vehicles were designed to haul heavy loads of miscellaneous materials and supplies. Not just one person who has anxiety about the way people drive around them. We forget that the massive amount of gasoline that these behemoths utilize is actively affecting the air that we breathe. We have no cognizance of the effect of these vehicles on our community. And this is just the vehicle that we drive around. I haven't even mentioned the type of jobs we have, the goods and materials we consume, the trash and pollution we create, the ways that our actions affect the mental well-being of the people around us, and on, and on, and on. We are a country intrinsically linked at the hip, yet we are locked in competition for every single good and resource. And no one seems to care.

No aspect of your existence does not directly influence and affect the people around you. The same goes for them. We are all in this together. In this country, however, we are resolutely told the opposite. We are definitively told from an early age that if we work hard enough and succeed well enough we will be above the fray and safe from the middling masses. Except that we aren't, and we never will be. You will always have neighbors. You will always have fellow drivers on the road. There will always be some kind of HOA, coworkers, fellow shoppers, or even fellow coffee drinkers in line. You are directly responsible for the well-being and the happiness of everyone around you, if only in small minuscule amounts. And it's time that you not only took this responsibility seriously but that you embody it so much that people start to emulate you. Because that is the only real way that we are going to change this world. By developing your ability to be empathetic to the people around you, you are going to make the world a better place wherever you go. You will attract the same energy, teach those around you a better way to be, and in a more visceral benefit, make yourself and your community less hostile and violent.

10 | Almost Everything We 'Know' Is Bullshit

The hardest thing in life to realize is that you've been fooled. Happens to me almost every day. It forces you to come to terms with your inadequacies, your faults, your limitations, and your general outlook on the world. It can happen anytime. Your ex-wife cheated on you in your bed. You caught your best friend talking shit about you. Your parents didn't tell you that you were adopted. These are all examples of how the principles/tenets/people in our lives can deeply and irrevocably reduce us to shambles. It happens and it is part of life. The real problem is that it is also happening all the time with virtually everything we see.

We are constantly being hoodwinked. There is a reason that some commercials are oddly oriented toward children, even though children are not the ones buying anything. And I'm not talking about soda and cereal. I'm referring to laundry detergent, coffee, bedsheets, and home repair. Corporations run by a strict bottom line, with zero care for their responsibility to society, advertise to children to build their image so that in twenty years, when these children have income, they will see these companies as wholesome and reputable. *Without ever really considering it.* It is called 'brand recognition' and it is one of the driving forces behind virtually everything that you see on TV. Think about one giant brand that you think highly of. Why do you feel this way? Have you ever been to one of their offices? Have you seen their product on the manufacturing line? Have you met a single one of their employees? The answer is most likely no. So why do you associate that brand with a positive emotion? The answer is effective advertising.

And if anything in the world has millions of dollars of reasons to try to convince you that they are good and wholesome, there are millions of reasons for them to be lying. You've been fooled.

Why does this matter? Well, it ties directly into Critical Thinking (See: Education). It's important to note that I am no longer a pessimist. It may occasionally seem that way as I try to steer you away from the many mistakes I have repeatedly made, but I'm not. I'm not even a realist. I am a devout optimist/positivist and this world is full of beautiful things. But to only see the 'bright side' in this world is to invite a whole world of pain and suffering into your life that, in the nomadic lifestyle, is simply too present and realistic to ignore. Nothing in this world is entirely good and nothing is *entirely* evil. Some things and people come fairly close to the latter, but they are never completely gone. Nothing is black and white. We live in a world that is a myriad of different colors and shades of grey and it is your ability to think critically that allows you to navigate it. From the food you put into your body to the people you choose to interact with, we are all faced with thousands upon thousands of critical thinking challenges per day, all of which have direct ramifications on our lives and well-being.

With critical thinking in mind, why in particular does someone living a *nomadic* lifestyle need to focus on the fact that they're being fooled? Because convenience is expensive. A lot of our modern economy revolves around convenience. Grocery stores are more convenient than having your own farm. Vehicles are more convenient than horses and buggies, or walking. Hotels are more convenient than camping. And so on. And all this convenience makes everything you buy more expensive. Everybody's got to get paid, everybody's got to eat. The problem is, so do you, and on a limited budget, with an eye for maintaining the highest standard of health that you can. A great example is convenience stores. There are no truly healthy options inside these shops. They continue to prosper because they sell two things: cigarettes and gasoline. The rest are all just products that they can buy for as cheap as possible and then sell for the highest margin they can get away with. Simple economics. Do they give a single shit whether you get diabetes down the line? Absolutely not. You could live for quite a long time off the crap in a convenience store. Stuff like beef jerky (salt and preservatives), potato chips (salt and trans fats), sodas and candy (high fructose corn syrup), and microwave dinners (cardboard and whatever else was left on the floor). You'll immediately notice lower energy, weight gain, most likely break out a little bit with acne, pick up some hypoglycemia, who knows. I've been there too. The point is that there is a cost to pay for this convenience of having food right off of the highway. It may be easier than driving the extra mile or two to find a grocery store. But it will cost you more, both in the short term and the long term. These stores advertise 'clean' gasoline, healthy 'alternatives,' winnable lottery tickets, and 'good' coffee. We all know that none of these options are true; that they are trying to fool us into spending our money there. It is up to you to decide whether or not their pitch is worth it.

Everyone in the entire world is going to try to take advantage of a traveler. Kids will try to slash your pockets open. Taxis will try to overcharge by 500%. Rich people will lie to you, liars will beg from you, and poor people will steal from you. Rich people will *also* steal from you. Hell, everyone will steal from you. This notion of taking advantage of you is particularly relevant to businesses. They are intrinsically established with one concept in mind: to make as much money as possible. Is it no wonder that so many companies go through extraordinary efforts to make sure that their employees don't unionize? Is it any wonder that large corporations have marketing budgets in the 100s of millions of dollars? Do you believe that anyone with a base goal of trying to sell as many things as possible to as many people as possible is going to make sure that every product they send out is completely safe, well put together, and effective? Absolutely not. It's why we still have lawyers and advocacy groups. Everything you see is most likely trying to get you to buy something for more than it should cost. People that you don't know are blindly trying to get you to give them money so they can feed and house their families. It is not inherently evil, yet it is detrimental to you. As such, you just have to be aware of what is happening and why. Just take the moment to think about what you are spending your money on. Why do you want to? And what might be influencing you to do so? Ask yourself: who is fooling me? Everything we know is bullshit and that's OK... as long as you are *trying* to figure it out.

11 | Basic Vehicle Maintenance

In most cities and towns, it is illegal to sleep in the park or camp on the side of the road. This means that, if you want to legally stay around one of these places, you have to get a job and spend a lot of that money on rent. For most, the ideal situation is to save up enough to buy their own house, which they technically don't own. Rather, the bank owns it, and they are contractually obligated to pay the bank a massive amount of interest over the next 30 years, and BAM. There goes their youth. The advantage of such a sedentary lifestyle is a high degree of security. Employers love people who will show up for years at a time. Your friends and family are all in the same place. You know where you like to eat, where to shop, where the fun places to go are. But some of us find that when we are in the same place for long enough there is something that tickles at the back of our brains. The desire to see the rest of it. If you're like me, it is way more than a tickle. It's a need. And if you are like me, and you have no interest in a long-term job, paying rent, or otherwise becoming part of the scenery, chances are you'll end up on the road for considerable periods. And for that, you'll want a vehicle.

A nomadic lifestyle is hard. It requires a daily assessment of where to get the basics typically maintained in a standard apartment. Where am I going to get my water? Where am I going to get my food? How am I going to cook and store this food? Shelter? Warmth? Activities? Where the hell am I even? And that's not even mentioning the question of how to pay for it all. Luckily, we address those very issues at different points in this book. For now, the easiest way to start, and maintain, this lifestyle is to acquire a vehicle. Anyone who has lived on the road long enough knows that large vehicles that you can sleep in are the best long-term. But anything will do. I regularly slept in Honda Civics for a few cross-country trips in my early 20s. I will hopefully never have to do it again, but it worked at the time.

Now, you don't have to have a car to live or travel. You can live out of a backpack and hoof it everywhere. I have done it for years at a time. But during that time, I learned that it is infinitely easier to get anywhere on a set of wheels and that simply having a mobile place to store your belongings reduces your stress exponentially. While it does take a significant amount of work and resources to maintain a vehicle, the perks greatly outweigh the downsides.

Once you have a vehicle it is necessary to maintain it. A mobile house is just a house if the engine doesn't run. I am an intermediate mechanic at best, but you certainly don't need to be one at all. Here are the basic tips for how to be efficient and cost-effective in keeping your mobile base running and on the road:

Oil Changes

I cannot count how many miles I have put down on America's highways with cars that were older than me. And those things went through oil. You may think that your car 'eats' gasoline, but what it really 'eats' is oil. The older the car, the truer it becomes. Oil sustains your vehicle and keeping that oil as 'fresh and clean' as possible will greatly improve your chances of keeping it operable.

A simple web search with the make a model of your vehicle can provide you with dozens of videos of how to change your own oil. On older cars changing the oil is very easy. You have to find the drain plug, put a container underneath it to catch the oil, take off the drain plug, let the oil drain out, reattach the drain plug, and fill it back up with oil. You can also swap out the oil filter at this time. It's easy, quick, and one of the easiest maintenance tasks to complete on your vehicle. If you have the pan and the ratchet set, definitely do this yourself. If this is the route you are planning to take there is a How-To section about this with further instructions later on. Just make sure to catch the used oil in a pan, pour it back into the container that the new oil came in, then take it somewhere to be recycled. Most auto parts and all oil change stores will take it. Don't be an ass and contaminate the local water table just because you're lazy.

For this exact reason, I don't recommend this for people living on the road, unless you have a pickup or some way to store the necessary components outside of your vehicle. Most people are lazy and will just pour the oil on the ground. As you will hear many times in these pages, you need to be spiritually and fundamentally opposed to ruining the environment in which you live. Dropping gallons of oil onto the sand is the exact opposite of this mandate. The beauty of paying someone else to change your oil is that you don't have to buy the equipment and the facility safely disposes of the oil. Therefore, for the majority of those reading this, get your oil professionally changed every 6,000 miles.

One simple tip for saving a few bucks is to hop online and look at the locations surrounding you. If you find a major chain, or even one big enough to have a website, chances are they have coupons listed on their site. Either print them off or have them ready on your phone when you show up.

Another simple tip, and arguably the most important, is to regularly check your oil. If it is low, add more. If you add more and soon after it is low again, you have identified that you most likely have an oil leak and need a mechanic. If it is super dirty, you probably need an oil change. Getting either of these fixed greatly improves the efficiency of your vehicle and is the easiest way to proactively prevent your vehicle from breaking down.

Be aware, these oil change places make a great deal of money taking advantage of people who don't know anything about their cars. The most glaring example of this is when they try to sell you air filters (both cabin and engine). Changing these filters is ridiculously easy. Typically, it involves lifting the hood, lifting three or four latches, then removing a lightweight filter and simply sliding the new one in. The cabin air filter, which is most likely in your glove box, is probably even easier. I have had places try to charge me a few hours of labor for this when it takes about 15 seconds. The same thing goes for windshield wipers, headlights, license plates, etc. Make sure to enter into the building with a clear plan of what you want and stick to it. You can always return, or find another shop, if they 'find something' that needs doing.

Last, they will ask you whether you want conventional oil, synthetic oil, or a blend. There are a lot of gearheads with a lot of different opinions about this, not to mention environmentalists, but in a nutshell, synthetic is the way to go if you value your car. If you have an aging clunker that you truly don't care about, or if you're skating by on a razor-thin budget, go with conventional. It is cheap and will work for 3,000 miles. If you love your car and want it to last another ten years, pay more for synthetic. It works better in a wider variety of temperatures, protects your engine better when running it all day on the highway, and usually lasts longer.

Vehicle Inspections

Maybe this is a bit pessimistic, but I don't trust mechanics. At all. I have had a handful of good ones but even those make me wonder. It truly is one of the only professions where most of us have to completely take someone else's word for what needs to be done, how long it will take, and how to go about doing it. One trick that I have learned over time is to canvas mechanics (and auto parts stores) to truly identify what is wrong with my vehicle and what can wait till later. This can cost some money. Some mechanics will give you free inspections. These are worth pursuing if the problem is mostly cosmetic, i.e., readily evident from a brief look at the car. But for an intensive look into some of the most common causes of vehicle breakdowns, it's going to take them a lot of time and thus, cost you money. But it's money well-spent. Frequently mechanics will create issues with your car that don't exist so that they can 'fix' them and charge you for them. I can't count how many times I have brought an old truck or car in for an inspection and left with a long list of things that needed 'urgent attention,' only to be told by the more reputable shop down the street that only one or two of those things actually needed to be replaced. Even then, there was little urgency to do so. In these cases, spending the extra 100-200 bucks for inspections not only bought me the time to save up for these repairs but also saved me money by identifying who the right person/place was to fix my car and what to actually have done.

Bright Headlights

I feel guilty just writing this. I can't count how many times I have been annoyed by people with ultra-bright lights blinding me at night. Yet, there is a reason that they sell them and there is a very good reason that you need them. If you are not reading this then chances are you do not own a brand-new vehicle with brand-new headlights. Double those chances for the likelihood that anyone reading this is going to end up camping, driving in areas where there are no streetlights, and/or exploring areas that are virtually in the middle of nowhere. Elsewhere amongst these pages are detailed instructions for how to locate camping spots, but suffice it to say you will most likely find yourself navigating around these spots in the dark. Camping anywhere can be nerve-wracking at times. Finding a camping spot in undefined areas devoid of any kind of law enforcement, man-made lighting, or any infrastructure whatsoever without being able to see anything can be downright panic inducing. And that's if it's *not* raining! Add to this the fact that most roads in the middle of nowhere are poorly maintained, if at all, and you can immediately see the benefits of upgrading your ability to see further. This is a cheap fix that can drastically improve your chances of avoiding potential road hazards and locating decent spots to stay for the night. Well worth the fifty bucks.

Windshield Wipers

You never notice them or need them until you notice them or need them. I've put considerable miles down on almost every type of vehicle you can own and one thing that sticks in your mind is how they handle being in severe weather. Flash floods, hail, and tornados happen. Occasionally you will end up near them. Every single time this has happened to me I have been one of two things:

1. Extremely grateful that I upgraded my windshield wipers when I had the chance.

Or

2. Begging my Creator to get me through this long enough and fast enough to get to the nearest auto parts store in time to upgrade my windshield wipers.

They are that important. Traveling sixty miles an hour has become standardized and normal in our modern world. That doesn't mean that it is not traveling at an extreme speed. Add a torrential downpour to that and you have the recipe for a life-altering event, one that everyone should want to avoid. Arguably the easiest way to do that is to spend the extra twenty bucks on the wipers.

Battery

Anyone who has lived out of their car or spent a considerable amount of the year camping out of their car knows that they use their car battery very frequently *after* they have stopped the car for the night. Whether charging their phone, using the headlights as illumination to get camp set up, or pumping up the air mattress, the car battery probably gets used more than it should. The problem with this is that it drains the only means of starting the vehicle that is most likely your only means of getting out of the middle of nowhere.

The first way to avoid this is to simply take your battery into an auto parts store to see how much charge it has left. The bonus is that in doing so they add some charge to the battery itself. This is always free and will immediately tell you if you are going to run into problems down the line. If your battery is dead, spend the money on a good one. It'll add a year to the time till you need to buy another one and you will thank yourself when it continues to start when you *really* need it to.

Another thing to consider is what to do if you accidentally drain your battery without meaning to. We have all left the key turned one slot too many and left the radio playing and the phones charging as we danced around the fire and then promptly passed out. I cannot count how many times I have had to jog down miles of country logging roads just to get back to an intersection where I *might* run into someone out joyriding who *might* give me a jump. Fortunately for you, recent technology has improved to the point where, as of this writing, for forty bucks online you can get an extremely portable and handheld jump starter. These jump boxes can hold a charge for three months, can charge your devices if you want to, and can pull you out of a serious bind without having to rely on the compassion of strangers. Highly recommended.

Brakes

Just think of your town, city, countryside, or wherever it is that you live. Picture it in your head. Got it? Great, now picture the other drivers in that area. I can guarantee you that 99% of the people who just read those sentences thought about how bad the drivers were in their area. It is a uniform concept throughout the U.S. that the worst drivers are wherever it is that, well, you are. That may be somewhat true but that's a subject for either a philosophy class or a sociology class. Either way, who cares, the answer is to get better brakes.

We all know what brakes do, right? They stop the giant hunk of metal and plastic that you are controlling with a circle and two rectangles. And this giant hunk has to stop, a lot. Now remember the drivers in your area. Think of them. Think of how good they are at what they do, how often they drive like sane and caring human beings, and how much they care about your life more than their TikTok feed. Aside from the little circle in front of you that you have some degree of control of, your only real way of avoiding these crack, ace drivers is via that little pedal at your feet that makes the car stop. That's why you want good brakes.

Don't go cheap on these if you can help it. All brake shops will want to replace your rotors for you. This is how they make a considerable markup. It's like the air filters. They know most people don't know what they are talking about. You don't *have* to swap your rotors. If they get warped it can make things a bit wonky but the important factor is your brake *pads*. Make sure that these are tip-top at all times and go with ceramic pads. Never let the percentage left, i.e. the amount of the pad that hasn't been worn away, go below 25%. If you have the money, get rotors and brake pads done at the same time. Ideally all four wheels at once but you can also do one axle at a time if you need to.

Tires

Your vehicle has four contact points that connect you to the Earth that you are traveling over at great speeds. This becomes especially relevant when that Earth is not flat and paved, and even more so if only two of your tires are providing the push forwards (i.e., you do not have four-wheel drive). Old and 'bald' tires do not provide the grip necessary to keep you safe in wet or otherwise hazardous conditions. As such, it is crucial to make sure you've got tires on your car that are newish and have decent tread on them.

The problem with this, of course, is that they are really expensive. The solution to this is to start budgeting ahead of time. Everyone in the entire world has trouble saving for the future when they are busy spending their money and having a great time in the present. So, the way that I have always looked at it is to consider each of my tires as one ticket to a faraway place. My rear right tire is the Grand Canyon. My front left tire is Key West. You get the point. We have no problem spending money on plane tickets and cheap hotels to go to crappy gambling towns in the desert or STD-filled beaches on the coast. Why do we balk at the same amount for tickets that take us much further and to infinitely more places? Save up for the tires and get the best ones you can afford before you take off.

"If you are not your own doctor, you are a fool."
-Hippocrates

12 | Body Maintenance

To understand your own body you first have to wonder why Americans are so unhealthy. And we are absolutely unhealthy. More than four out of 10 Americans are obese as I write this[9][10]. The nutritional value of our fruits and vegetables has been on a steady decline for over 70 years[11]. We have a shorter life span, a higher infant mortality rate, more chronic lung and heart disease, more drug-related deaths, and *way* more homicide and injury-related deaths than other similar high-income countries[12]. And this doesn't even account for the prevalence of highly processed and 'fast' food!

Our mental health is no better. In 2023, just over 20% of all Americans identify as having some form of mental illness[13]. Suicide rates, after a brief

---

9   "Overweight & Obesity." Centers for Disease Control and Prevention, 27 Sept. 2022, www.cdc.gov/obesity/. Accessed 15 Feb. 2023.

10   "State of Obesity 2022: Better Policies for a Healthier America." Trust for America's Health, 27 Sept. 2022, www.tfah.org/report-details/state-of-obesity-2022/#:~:text=Nationally%2C%2041.9%20percent%20of%20adults,obesity%20rate%20of%2041.4%20percent. Accessed 15 Feb. 2023.

11   Davis, Donald R., et al. "Changes in USDA Food Composition Data for 43 Garden Crops, 1950 to 1999." PubMed, 23 Dec. 2004, pubmed.ncbi.nlm.nih.gov/15637215/. Accessed 19 Feb. 2023.

12   Woolf, S H., and L Aron. "U.S. Health in International Perspective: Shorter Lives, Poorer Health." National Library of Medicine, 1 Jan. 2023, www.ncbi.nlm.nih.gov/books/NBK154469/. Accessed 1 Apr. 2023.

13   Reinert, M, et al. "The State of Mental Health in America." MHA National, 1 Oct. 2022, mhanational.org/sites/default/files/2023-State-of-Mental-Health-in-America-Report.pdf. Accessed 12 Feb. 2023.

decline in 2019 and 2020, have returned to all-time highs[14]. And to make matters even worse, almost 28% of all adults who identify as having a mental illness are not able to receive treatment[15]. My current job is in mental health services. Won't be for long, because the grant wasn't renewed, but for now that's what I do. And the amount of people in abject denial about their condition is staggering. It's for this reason that I consider the mental health situation in this country an absolute crisis. When you add the number of people with mental illness, drug addiction, records of violence, suicidal ideation, and who are overweight with the number of people who simply refuse to see that there is a problem in their lives you might very well be talking about the majority of this country. It is an understatement to call this a crisis.

Why are all these things true? If most people are good, which we really should assume that they are, shouldn't the same be said for the organizations that provide for our well-being? The answer lies in an age-old economics problem that occurs when a group of individuals all have equal access to a shared resource. In this case, the 'group of individuals' is a nation, and the problem is called the 'tragedy of the commons.' When an individual with said access to this resource, i.e., 'the commons,' has more to gain by taking more of the resource, then they will inevitably do so. The issue lies in the fact that society as a whole is affected negatively by the individual doing so. Take a river, for example. Imagine that there are a million people who rely on the river for their water consumption. No one owns the river and therefore, everyone has an equal opportunity to utilize the water. Everything goes smoothly until a water bottling plant opens up at the source of the river. The water bottling plant takes the water from the river, bottles it, and then sells it to the rest of the world. This makes a considerable amount of money but in the process takes a considerable amount of water out of the river. Thus, there is not enough water downstream for the million people who rely on it. In this example, one actor benefits more from the water than the other people, diminishing the resource for everybody.

14   Stone, Deborah M. Scd, et al. "Notes from the Field: Recent Changes in Suicide Rates, by Race and Ethnicity and Age Group — United States, 2021." Centers for Disease Control and Prevention, 10 Feb. 2023, www.cdc.gov/mmwr/volumes/72/wr/mm7206a4.htm. Accessed 12 Feb. 2023.

15   Reinert, M, et al. "The State of Mental Health in America." MHA National, 1 Oct. 2022, mhanational.org/sites/default/files/2023-State-of-Mental-Health-in-America-Report.pdf. Accessed 12 Feb. 2023.

This tragedy occurs in a variety of ways that directly affect the health of every single person on this planet. Our environment becomes polluted. The air we breathe becomes toxified. The weather becomes dangerously hot. Billions of dollars become intensely concentrated in the hands of just a few people. Our health care system becomes completely ineffective. That last example has more to do with frivolous lawsuits, which muddles the picture considerably, but by now you can easily see where I am going with this. The actions of a few lead to consequences for many.

So how does this affect you in particular? The answer is: you don't know. Every day scientists finish years-long studies detailing the cancer-causing agents of everyday household items[16][17]. From BPA to asbestos, we have no idea how much we are killing ourselves with the items we consume.

Combine all this with our increasingly sedentary lifestyle and the increasingly stressful, anxiety-inducing urban areas that the vast majority of people now live in, and you have the components of a full-blown health crisis. As a society, we have reached the precipice of what is survivable here in 'the commons,' and the mechanisms that have been established to pull people back from the edge are broken. Do you honestly believe a for-profit hospital that won't even (and isn't legally obligated to) give prices in advance is going to give you accurate health advice? Especially when the government agencies that are supposed to regulate them are actually in the pocket of whoever has the most money to buy the high-priced lobbyists that, in their turn, control Washington, D.C.[18]? Me neither.

These hospitals don't care about your well-being. So, it is on you to do so for yourself. Assume everything coming at you is a lie. If you see an ad for a hospital, best to assume that that hospital has its bottom line in mind, rather than your best interest. It is important to remember that no silly

16   Gao, Hui MD, et al. "Bisphenol A and Hormone-Associated Cancers: Current Progress and Perspectives." National Library of Medicine, 9 Jan. 2015, www.ncbi.nlm.nih.gov/pmc/articles/PMC4602822/#:~:text=Overall%2C%20 several%20conclusions%20can%20be,AR%20to%20promote%20prolifera-tion%20of. Accessed 2 Apr. 2023.

17   Campanale, Claudia, et al. "A Detailed Review Study on Potential Effects of Microplastics and Additives of Concern on Human Health." National Library of Medicine, 13 Feb. 2020, www.ncbi.nlm.nih.gov/pmc/articles/PMC7068600/. Accessed 12 Feb. 2023.

18   Light, Donald W., et al. "Institutional Corruption of Pharmaceuticals and the Myth of Safe and Effective Drugs." Social Science Research Network, 20 Jun. 2013, papers.ssrn.com/sol3/papers.cfm?abstract_id=2282014. Accessed 1 Apr. 2023.

conspiracies are ruling the world. There *are* cold, hard, business-oriented truths though. And the truth is that sick people make the system money at the expense of 'the commons.' This entire section is devoted to making sure it affects you as little as possible.

Stretching

You are going to hear me talk a lot about preventative care and this is the easiest step you can take. There is nothing better for the body (that is free) than gentle stretching and loose, flowing activity. It decreases your risk of injury, increases your performance at work and play, helps your joints, boosts the functionality of your muscles, increases blood flow throughout your body, and generally just feels good. Stretch every single day, particularly *after* exercise. For a long time, the general thinking was to stretch before exercise, but recently this has been discredited[19][20]. Ideally, you want to warm up before strenuous exercise and stretch after you use your muscles to alleviate the contraction of said muscles and to speed up their recovery and repair.

Stretching will help you in the short term, in the intermediate future, and when you are much, much older. Take a few minutes every single day to invest in yourself. It is your most precious resource, why wouldn't you lavish it with attention?

Yearly Doctor Visits

When I could finally afford health insurance, I began to aggressively seek out answers to some of the health problems I had been dealing with for years. IBS. Anxiety. Depression. Is this a cancerous mole? Why does my back hurt? Why am I always tired? And on, and on. What I found is that most complaints and ailments end up being nothing and that the internet can be your worst enemy. Turns out that what I was paying for is a much-appreciated and much-desired peace of mind after the tortures I had put my body through in my 20s. I also found a great deal of useful

19   Shrier, I. "Stretching Before Exercise Does Not Reduce the Risk of Local Muscle Injury: A Critical Review of the Clinical and Basic Science Literature." National Library of Medicine, 9 Oct. 1999, pubmed.ncbi.nlm.nih.gov/10593217/. Accessed 21 Apr. 2023.

20   Witvrouw, Erik, et al. "Stretching and Injury Prevention: An Obscure Relationship." National Library of Medicine, 1 Jan. 2004, pubmed.ncbi.nlm.nih.gov/15233597/. Accessed 28 Mar. 2023.

information and general health tips that can keep you healthy and out of the doctor's office later in life.

The problem is that, with the way that our health insurance and health care system is typically set up, most doctors do not treat you for the actual ailments you are seeing them for. For anything even remotely detailed they refer you to a specialist. And a lot of times, health insurance will refuse to pay a claim if you are *not* referred to that specialist by your doctor. This ultimately means that it is very much in your favor to have a doctor that you see once a year. Not only is it a serious pain in the ass to have records sent from six or seven clinics when you finally find a decent doctor, but it also helps to have a continuing relationship with a doctor over time in case your health changes for the worse. Just having a yearly physical can detect a myriad of different things that can be altered by slight changes in diet or activity. These changes can improve or possibly even save your life.

Yearly Blood Draws

I know. No one in the world dislikes that sentence more than me. I can't stand even looking at it. My blood draws are an event. It takes me a full day to prepare my mind and the rest of the day after I am typically rendered incapable of anything aside from walking the dog. But the most useful information about your health and well-being comes from a yearly or bi-yearly panel of tests to measure the levels of vitamins, enzymes, lipids, etc. in your blood. This can tell you how to effectively supplement your diet, instead of just popping a useless Flintstones multivitamin or, conversely, taking fifty vitamins a day.

These blood draws may even save your life. I found out that I have hemo-chromatosis, a genetic blood disorder that eventually leads to an overload of iron. I suddenly knew to stop eating so much red meat and other high-iron foods and BAM! Suddenly I wasn't so tired. I also have a plan of action for how to handle this disorder in my early 30s, rather than finding out much later in life, when it might have been too late. Do yourself a favor and give yourself the same clarity with your overall health.

Genetic Testing

This step can come before or after a doctor visit/blood draw but is another extremely important thing to do for yourself. Through a cheap and simple test (as of this writing a major company is offering a spit test for $50) I discovered that I was at high risk for the common iron disorder I just mentioned. Catching this early has been key to avoiding potentially life-threatening symptoms, not to mention improving my sleep quality and overall energy levels. The technology and accuracy of this testing is only going to increase as time goes on and, combined with the information provided by a comprehensive blood draw, can tell you everything from what food you should be eating/avoiding to maintain peak health.

The Western health care system is backward, taking a wholesale approach to the nation's health that, if you deviate from the norm even a little bit, is not going to treat you effectively. The advent of genetic testing and genetic counselors is the antidote to being treated like cattle. Always remember: in January 2020, the FDA approved a nasal spray that contains cocaine[21][22]. They also approved Oxycontin and Fentanyl. Do you trust anyone to provide you with adequate guidelines for your long-term health? I don't.

Supplements

The typical diet that we eat is not healthy[23]. It's not your fault. Everything available to buy has too much salt, too much sugar, too many refined ingredients, you name it[24][25]. The bottom line is that the food the average person puts into their body may not contain the components necessary to maintain an effective level of health. Even those of us that make a conscious, daily effort to eat healthy, nutritious food most likely *still* are lacking critical components that our body desperately needs. Even supposedly 'organic'

21   Yerby, Nathan. "FDA Approves Cocaine Nasal Spray As Study Casts Doubt On FDA Standards." Addiction Center, 31 Jan. 2020, www.addictioncenter.com/news/2020/01/fda-approves-cocaine-nasal-spray/. Accessed 18 Jan. 2023.

22   "Highlights of Prescribing Information." Federal Drug Administration, www.accessdata.fda.gov/drugsatfda_docs/label/2020/209575s000lbl.pdf.   Accessed 12 Mar. 2023.

23   Clapp, Jenifer E. MPA, et al. "Changes in Serving Size, Calories, and Sodium Content in Processed Foods From 2009 to 2015." Centers for Disease Control and Prevention, 15 Mar. 2018, www.cdc.gov/pcd/issues/2018/17_0265.htm. Accessed 1 Apr. 2023.

24   "PAHO Defines Excess Levels of Sugar, Salt and Fat in Processed Food and Drink Products." Pan American Health Organization, 19 Feb. 2016, www3.paho.org/hq/index.php?option=com_content&view=article&id=11685:2016-paho-defines-excess-levels-of-sugar-salt-and-fat-in-processed-food-drink&Itemid=0&lang=en. Accessed 9 Jan. 2023.

25   "Limit Fat, Salt, and Sugar Intake." *World Health Organization*, 1 Jan. 2023, www.emro.who.int/nutrition/reduce-fat-salt-and-sugar-intake/index.html. Accessed 27 Feb. 2023.

foods often aren't 'organic' at all, raised with virtually the same methods, pesticides, unsustainable farming practices, and general environmental fuckery that plagues most of our mass-produced food[26]. Luckily, we live in a world where nearly every component known to man has been isolated and put in a bottle for our consumption. Take a hard look at your diet and figure out what you are most commonly omitting. Then check out the Supplement section later on in this book and add whatever you are missing into your body. It may take a week or two, but adding anything your body is deficient in will cause a cascade of positive things to fall into place in your body. You *will* notice the difference.

Exercise

One of my favorite sayings that rattles around my brain every day is: "You've got to pay for the day." I first heard it when I was listening to a radio show talking about Willie Nelson, so take that with a grain of salt. I take it with *two* grains of salt because anyone who can put themselves through the rigors of being a traveling musician for decades on end, enduring multiple marriages, and doing it all *high as balls* while still making it to old age deserves a good listen. So go for a walk, do some sit-ups, and chase your dog. Whatever it is, pay for the day. It's good for your body, your mind, and your soul.

Exercise isn't just touted by pot-addled hippies either. It might just be one of the universal truths that both conventional wisdom and science universally agree on. Exercise is going to make you healthier and happier, plain and simple. You'll live longer and better. And most likely be more attractive doing it. Find a way to push yourself. Doesn't matter what it is. If it is simply going up and down the stairs an extra time each day, do that. And then when that stops being hard, do it another time each day. Or hell, get feisty and go for a run. If you are getting your heart rate up at least once a day, then you are doing it right. You will immediately notice the difference in both your overall mood and how you feel about yourself.

Holistic and Active Medicine

When you get older, you're going to be in pain. It is a fact of life. Just like a car that sits out in the elements for years on end, eventually, your body

26   Smith-Spangler, Crystal MD, MS, et al. "Are Organic Foods Safer or Healthier Than Conventional Alternatives?" Annals of Internal Medicine, 4 Sept. 2012,   www.acpjournals.org/doi/10.7326/0003-4819-157-5-201209040-00007. Accessed 7 Apr. 2023.

is going to 'rust' and parts of you are going to wear. In American society, this usually means that you are going to be prescribed a great deal of painkillers[27]. As we have seen with the demise of Purdue Pharma and others, this is because the American legislative body, health care system, the pharmaceutical industry, and the FDA, have all come together over the years, tacitly and directly, to create an environment that pumps out new pills at an alarming rate[28]. The result is that our first, second, and third options for dealing with health problems are all to 'take a pill.' Every pill has a side effect, so what do we do? Take another pill.

Fact: Companies make more money if they sell you more of something.

When I started my health improvement journey, I had a wide array of health problems that I have previously detailed. I spent countless dollars following the advice of doctors practicing Western medicine and enduring dozens of tests and procedures. These were useful only to rule out the worst-case scenarios such as Crohn's disease, cancers, and tumors. Honestly, I would spend the money all over again just for that info. But aside from that knowledge, none of their advice helped me at all. I was still in considerable amounts of pain and discomfort, not to mention being stressed to the absolute limit. Then they started to prescribe me things and the side effects were terrible.

What did help was holistic medicine and physical therapy (i.e., active medicine). Now I am not saying that it was putting quartz and amethyst on my nightstand that helped my back pain. Rather, it was engaging my body in ways using methods that aren't as widely recognized as traditional methods. I stretch in the morning, using yoga movements and breathing techniques. I meditate, focusing my mental energy on the source of the problem and asking my body to focus on that as well. I pursue acupuncture, massage, breathwork, and naturopathic medicine in a controlled, responsible way. And guess what? No side effects. And over time I have felt much, much

27   Muacevic, Alexander, and John R. Adler. "Managing Chronic Pain in the Elderly: An Overview of the Recent Therapeutic Advancements." National Library of Medicine, 10 Sept. 2018, www.ncbi.nlm.nih.gov/pmc/articles/PMC6235641/. Accessed 23 Mar. 2023.

28   Light, Donald W., et al. "Institutional Corruption of Pharmaceuticals and the Myth of Safe and Effective Drugs." Social Science Research Network, 20 Jun. 2013, papers.ssrn.com/sol3/papers.cfm?abstract_id=2282014. Accessed 1 Apr. 2023.

better. I spend way less on my supplements, herbs, organic food, and massages (that feel amazing) than I did on my previous regular trips to every specialist imaginable.

Unfortunately, this isn't an exact science. There isn't nearly as much empirical data and scientific research to back up the claims of a naturopathic doctor. Which means that you have to do a lot more work. You can't rely on just taking a pill here and a pill there. You have to keep a journal, make some regular visits to your naturopath or wellness clinic, and otherwise commit to your health. Some of the herbs you take aren't going to work. Some of them aren't even *supposed* to work for long periods. And some are going to just flat-out taste like crap. Some yoga classes you go to are going to be chock full of stuck-up douchebags. It is what it is. But striving to achieve balance and your own answers is the ultimate reward. And this doesn't mean you'd have to completely shun Western medicine. When you break your ankle, you are going to want an ER and an X-ray machine. When you get a nasty infection, you are going to want antibiotics. But focusing on the conventional wisdom and embracing the healing power that the world offers you, free of hyper-processed pills and overbearing legal constraints, will ultimately maintain your health better than you ever thought possible.

Acupuncture

I was initially terrified of acupuncture. I sat before my first appointment with my best friend and his mom begging them to keep me there so that I wouldn't have to go. I went to my first appointment late, sat there tense as a board while I discussed my array of symptoms, overreacted to each little tingle, kept my eyes tightly squeezed shut for the entire time, and…. walked out of there more relaxed than I had ever been in my life.

I have battled anxiety and PTSD my entire life. I have taken every anti-anxiety medication on the market. I think. I have taken anti-psychotics, sleepy-time pills, St. John's Wort, you name it. And I have never experienced a lasting calm like the one I get from acupuncture. Try it before you knock it. There is a reason that it has been around so long.

Here in America, it is not widely accepted, meaning that practitioners often try to make it like a regular doctor's appointment. This works just fine but if you don't have insurance, or if your insurance doesn't cover it, this can get expensive very quickly. There are tons of clinics, however, that practice in the traditional style, where there are multiple clients in the same room. This makes the cost of acupuncture less than half what others are charging. The reason for this is that one is supposed to go frequently to alleviate their symptoms. It is not supposed to be a once-a-month treatment. It is supposed to be a go-until-the-imbalance-in-your-your-body-has-been-balanced treatment. Find one of the People's Acupunctures near you and go until you see the difference. It'll save you tens of thousands of dollars later on in life, and it might just get rid of the anxiety you thought would be around forever.

Mindfulness

Have you ever wondered why happy people are so happy? The answer is always that these people can find joy in whatever it is that they are currently doing. And the way that they do this is by being fully *in the moment*. This is mindfulness. Feeling what you are feeling. Seeing what you are seeing. Smelling what you are smelling. We are so often stuck in our heads. We live by our words and our thoughts, floating by as our meat-sack bodies trudge through this world. So often we become creatures of habit and routine, simply going through the motions in an attempt to minimize the amount of pain that we feel at any given moment. This is not living. And this is where mindfulness comes in. When we can be *present* in our bodies and live *in that actual moment* then we can find the sources of our joy. It is through this process that we teach our souls and train our minds to be happy. And it all starts with simply paying attention to what is going on, right now.

Why is this important? Because it can directly improve your physical health. Mindfulness has been directly correlated with improved sleep quality, steep declines in depression, anxiety, stress, and blood pressure, and can make a huge difference in pain levels of all kinds[29]. It is why this book starts by imploring you to breathe, as our breath is the easiest and most concrete way of centering ourselves in any given moment. By engaging in even the most minute mindfulness practices every day we can dramatically improve our overall mindset and, thereby, our physical health.

29   "Meditation and Mindfulness: What You Need To Know." National Center for Complementary and Integrative Health, 1 Jun. 2022, www.nccih.nih.gov/health/meditation-and-mindfulness-what-you-need-to-know. Accessed 17 Feb. 2023.

"They say your dream job won't pay your bills, They said change your dream but I just changed my bills. I'm hustlin' baby."
-John Craigie

13 | Making Money On The Road

None of the things in this book are possible without at least a basic income. It is highly advisable to follow the steps outlined in the beginning in regard to saving up as big a chunk as you can, minimizing your bills, having the right gear and supplies, and doing your best to maximize your money. But at the end of the day, any funds you have will run out eventually. The key becomes making dough as you go.

Before I begin, there is one topic that rustles up a primal pseudo-hatred in my gut. I don't hate anything, but this concept makes my skin crawl. I can't stand it, I cannot abide by it, and I certainly will never do it. And that is begging. Just don't. Why is this a problem? You might be saying to yourself, there are plenty of people in the world with nothing, who have been given the shit end of the stick and *need* a handout. They need *help*, Sam! And you are 100% correct.

That is exactly why a *true* wanderer, outlaw, nomad, alternative-lifestyler, a *real* traveler of this world, would never, *ever* beg for money. I can't even write that sentence without feeling gross. Our lifestyle is one of struggle, toil, sacrifice, and ultimately, the greatest payoffs known to man. Tainting this sacred journey and rite of passage with a simple handout is not only taking food and money out of the hands of the neediest people, but it is also a disgusting shortcut to the penultimate destination.

Have you ever driven by someone standing on the median at a stop light with a sign that reads: "Anything helps," wearing $200 jeans, fancy sunglasses, and who can barely be bothered to take their eyes off of their cell phone long enough to approach your car? I have. I have also run hostels where those same people have asked me the best places to go and stand with the 'highest traffic.' I have seen those same people drunk and high later that evening, smoking cigars and laughing at the 'idiots' that live in 'this country.'

I have also spent a considerable amount of my life in Portland, OR, which during my time there repeatedly had one of the worst homeless population crises in the country. I have seen entire families crowded into minivans for weeks at a time, dogs in tow, trying to find work and get back on their feet. I have seen men and women spend years on the street, batshit crazy and in dire need of an institution to take them in, right next to high-school kids begging for loose change because they thought it was funny not to have to spend their parents' money on pizza.

There are systemic and endemic problems in this country regarding our homeless population. We have an ineffective and costly War on Drugs while we do relatively nothing to help those people who need it. It is precisely where our system fails, and perhaps most importantly, *who* it fails. The prevailing myth surrounding people begging for money is that they are going to spend it on cigarettes, booze, and drugs. Or that they are living better than we are, with jobs and bills and dependents. These myths come from somewhere. And they certainly aren't helped by people who have chosen to live a certain lifestyle and who choose to subvert those people who actually need the help.

This isn't to say that you shouldn't look or ask for help when you need it. That's why there is a dedicated section for doing just that. There is just a giant difference between a can-do, solution-based attitude, and an entitled, 'gimme-gimme' attitude. And that difference not only hurts those that need it. That attitude becomes you in every possible way, reverberating down to your core and into your soul. Trust me, you will pay for it. It's best to just leave it to the people who truly can't fend for themselves.

With that said, here are a bunch of awesome ways to make money while traveling around:

Seasonal Hospitality Work

For years I followed the trail of seasonal hospitality work. This is the gold standard for a nomadic life because it is amazing living and working in places that most people only get to vacation to once in their lives. Naturally, these large resorts and hospitality establishments are usually tucked away in beautiful, remote locations. The local employee talent pool is very small in these places, yet the number of visitors is very high. As such, these resorts desperately need a large number of employees who will do difficult jobs. From dishwashing to waiting tables, there are thousands of little things that need to get done to adequately take care of these guests and visitors. So, the companies who run these resorts know that they are going to have to import their employees from outside of the area, which results in workers coming from all over the world. And all these employees are going to need a place to live, basic supplies, and typically help to get in and out of the nearest town. It's a dream set-up if you need a place to stay, play, and save money.

The problem is that the work sucks. Washing dishes, bussing tables, cleaning rooms, and checking people in and out isn't what we typically dreamed of doing when we were kids. Hell, I legitimately thought I was going to be an astronaut. Surprise! Anyway, it is no secret that the hospitality industry is highly demanding of its employees. Simply put, it will drain your soul. That doesn't mean that it isn't worthwhile and incredibly fun. It just means that it can also be toxic and harmful at the same time. Every job I ever rolled into was a total crap shoot. Suddenly, I was living and working with hundreds of people, very few who had ever met each other before, most often with several people living in the same room. Add these factors to a job that can be highly stressful at times with vast amounts of alcohol, and you had the potential for combustion. And some damn good stories. It's no wonder that a lot of the best and worst times in my life came during my time doing this type of work.

With all that said, getting one of these jobs can either be super easy or highly competitive, depending on which of the jobs you are willing to do. Anyone, anywhere can get a dishwashing job at virtually any location. It is hot, wet, backbreaking work that will bore you to tears. But it pays, and you still get to live in a beautiful place. Is it worth it? That's for you to decide. If, however, you want to be a bartender, you better have years of experience, a pretty-looking resume, and good references (more on those later), not to mention some experience. The first thing they will ask you is to make them a drink. Better know how to make that drink, and how to appear physically competent doing it in front of them.

Seasonal work like this is what I recommend to everyone, regardless of age, station, or life plans. It is a quintessential experience that everyone should do. You will gain an in-depth knowledge of humanity while developing an appreciable knowledge of what you are made of and what you want from this world. If you are just starting your journey I highly recommend starting here. You will make friends quickly and discover what your passions are. If you are far along the path of your journey outward, these places are ideal for reflecting and saving up for the next step. There are a ton of very good reasons why a lot of people that start working at one of these places return year after year, or simply never leave at all.

'One-Off' Gig Work

I want to make it very clear that this type of work is inherently dangerous and exploitative. The listings for this type of work are online and for people you have never met. The work is hard, offers no insurance if you get hurt, and typically results in someone else making a *ton* of money using your labor. Still, it's cash, you don't have to sign up for anything, and at the end of the day, you are on your merry way with zero commitment. These types of jobs have turned into some of my best, and worst, job opportunities. Just be very, very wary of what you are walking into, and do not hesitate to walk away immediately if you get a bad feeling. No amount of money is worth your health and safety.

I have listed some of the most common types of gig work in no apparent order. I have done all of these around the country and the world but that doesn't mean that all these will exist where you are. Or there might be completely different opportunities there. And some of these jobs are riskier than others!

● **Moving Jobs**

The most common and popular gigs posted are for moving people's stuff. It is physically demanding, time intensive, and easy to con people into overpaying. These jobs usually require responding to a Craigslist post, then being on time, ready to work, and with the proper gear. I have shown up to these jobs five minutes late and promptly been told to scram, as they had over-staffed and didn't need me anymore. Always bring gloves too, because after a few hours of lifting heavy boxes and furniture, your hands can get pretty torn up.

Typically, these jobs involve showing up at a location and then driving to either a storage unit or another house, where you will unload what you've loaded. Sometimes this even involves multiple trips. The scam here is that someone will pretend to operate a 'moving company,' wherein they locate and contract someone who needs a company to move their stuff, then gets on Craigslist and 'hires' a bunch of workers. These workers drive out to the location, follow all the instructions laid out by the homeowner/client, and finish the job. At that point, the person who 'owns' the moving company shows up and collects the money.

When this happened to me, I was working as a mover, and I had just busted my ass for 10 hours for $15 an hour. I was exhausted and had been speaking to the homeowners the entire time. Because I was the only one of this random group of workers who had any actual moving experience, I had been in charge all day. Then a seventeen-year-old kid rolled up in a brand-new Mercedes and proceeded to take a huge wad of cash from the homeowner. The homeowner never took their eyes off of me the whole time. I walked outside and I am not proud of what happened next. Let's just say that kid didn't exactly make a profit. Just something to keep an eye on if you take these kinds of jobs.

I despise these gigs because they are the most exploitative of all the gig work you can find. The people running whatever moving 'company' you are working for are making at least a thousand dollars for the move and they are most likely paying you in the $10-20 dollar per hour range. This means that you are risking long-term injuries (always possible moving furniture) and making jack while helping someone who might not be a very good person make a boatload of cash. I have never been stiffed on a job like this, but I have heard stories of people who have. After a full day of busting ass, they get to the final location, unload the furniture and boxes, and the 'owner' of the 'moving company' is nowhere to be found. But hey, if you need to make some cash, don't mind working up a sweat, and can be friendly to the homeowner, you can usually make up for the crappy wages with tips. Just be wary of who you're working with.

● **Landscaping**

These jobs are pretty much the same as moving gigs, with the added bonus of being even more repetitive. The main plus is that if you get along with your coworkers and can tolerate the working conditions, these gigs can span a week or two. That kind of quick, under-the-table cash is usually enough to get to the next town if you budget well. However, if you don't know how to use power tools you will most likely spend your day in the hot sun digging holes and smoothing patches of rocks, neither of which are even close to as easy as they sound. Bring a wide hat, a ton of ice water in a thermos, a pair of gloves, sunglasses, sunscreen, and an MP3 player if you've got one. Also, don't lie. If you don't know how to operate a mower or a trimmer they will know immediately, which might get you fired on the spot. This can be problematic if they are working somewhere far away from your vehicle, as you might get hit with the cost of an Uber or be stuck waiting on a bus for a while.

● **Yardwork/Gardening**

Not to be confused with landscaping, where you are typically working with a group of people on several different jobs around a neighborhood. These gigs usually involve a homeowner who needs help getting their property in order. A lot of these are listed in the Fall when the leaves drop and people are getting ready for the winter, but look for them all year as well. I have done everything from mowing lawns to cleaning chicken coops, and everything in between. This is hard work, but it is usually a little easier than landscaping due to the single location. Make sure to gauge your employer. If they look like they are about to scam you, chances are that you're right.

The trick to succeeding in these gigs is just to work hard, relentlessly. People hiring for these gigs are accustomed to slackers and people who just need a little cash to keep their habits going. If you bust your ass and break a sweat, odds are that they will find a reason to need you for a few extra days and typically buy you lunch or throw on an extra $20-50 bucks at the end of the deal.

● **Trash Removal/Furniture Moving**

These are lumped together because they both require either a pickup truck or a large SUV and are a separate class of gig work. It's an old adage that 'everyone needs a friend with a truck.' As a frequent and current owner of a pickup truck, I can say that owning one immediately conscripts you to haul and move things for your friends *all the time*. Still, it is a great way to make money if you do it right. Trash removal is a bit trickier, and occasionally disgusting, as you have to factor in dump fees and potential spills/leakage. If you have a good handle on how much a full load of trash costs at the dump and charge accordingly, this gig becomes simply charging for your time to and from the dump. Be wary of taking people's old trash, however, as the bags rip easily, and you can be stuck moving some vile, repulsive garbage.

Furniture moving is way more straightforward but comes with its own set of challenges. Usually, these are couches, mattresses, grills, etc. Anything that doesn't fit inside a regular-sized vehicle. These gigs typically consist of going into someone's house and hauling whatever it is they need to be hauled out to your truck, driving over to a separate location, and lugging the item to wherever the client wants it to go. The challenge here is that you become responsible for the condition of the item from the time you pick it up to the time you put it down. And you are most likely not insured as a real moving company should be. This means that if you drop the couch you have been paid to move or if the couch falls out of your truck while you are driving, you can then be held liable for the cost of the couch. Make sure to negotiate this accordingly. I always tell people that I am not a moving company and that, while I will do my best to maintain their property, if anything out of my control happens, I am not liable. Most people don't care as they are happy to pay way less for you to do it as opposed to a 'real' moving company. Regardless, use straps to tie the object down inside your vehicle and use a tarp if there is even a remote chance of rain. Blankets between the bed and the object are always a good idea as well.

● **Catering**

These types of gigs can be either one-off jobs or a more long-term type of employment. The important thing is to not work for a staffing agency, as they take a high percentage of your wages and tips. These jobs are all about working hard and efficiently. Typically, it is a dining room style event, where either multiple courses are served directly to the tables or buffet style. Either way, you are shuttling food quickly to the tables, removing plates just as fast, and filling drinks at a frenzied pace, all without looking frenzied. Some people love these jobs because they can anonymously work in large crowds and the pay is pretty good if you find the right gig. I could never stand it because all the old farts attending the events treat you like garbage. It is what it is. If you need a quick cash influx and own a pair of slacks, you could do worse with your time. The best of these gigs are smaller weddings where they are not using a major company to cater. These are typically family-run, which means that they are highly disorganized and less efficient. It also means that if you are willing to bust your ass, they will definitely notice and typically reward you handsomely.

● **Cleaning**

This is my least favorite gig. I can't stand cleaning up other people's messes, but some people have no problem with this at all. The other reason that I don't like these jobs is that they typically require a large number of chemicals and small tools to do the job correctly. Even at the dollar store, you are looking at $20-30 to have a cleaning bucket, rags, and cleaning supplies for what could be a one-day, one-off job. It depends on how much money you are making off of the job and whether it's worth it to you.

Just like with yard work, landscaping, and moving, the key is simply to work hard and fast. Break a sweat and make sure to let them see you doing it.

These are jobs that people are hiring you to do because they just don't *want* to do them, meaning that they are going to have a little bit of guilt swimming around if they are watching you work your ass off. Take advantage of it. These are underpaid positions already and chances are your client can afford it. I have done a handful of these in my life, typically after the client has hosted an event. I always worked up a sweat and got the place into shape. Almost every single time I was either tipped at least 25% of what I was making, was invited back for more work, offered a free meal, or some combination of the three.

Make no bones about it, you'll have to clean a few bathrooms. This is where I usually draw the line. But if you can handle it these gigs are everywhere, and you can easily 'get by' doing them. Some apps can help you with this, but they are evil. You are always, *always* better off finding 'clients' on your own.

- **Festivals/Fairs**

These are easily my favorite of all the short-term jobs I have ever done. It's almost hard to write because a flood of memories hit me that make me laugh, cringe, and smirk to myself. These are the types of gigs I recommend to everyone, regardless of what life they are trying to live, simply because they are such an experience.

The key to finding these is to find out where the events are held. Craigslist is the king of these types of gigs, mostly because it is free. I'd add a list of sites to look at, but they are constantly changing, adapting, and adding paywalls. Spend a few hours looking up seasonal work and gig jobs and you'll come across a handful of good sources. Again, the key is always to find out where the events are held. For example, I spent a good amount of my 20s near Portland, OR. The town itself held tons of events, so there was always a lively Craigslist gigs page. In this town alone I picked up food cart gigs like rolling vegan sushi at the convention center, bartending at the PBR Festival, serving ribs at the Waterfront Blues Festival, and helping out farmers downtown at the weekly Saturday Market. These were all great and nearby.

There were also several large venues in the vicinity that I would often keep an eye on. The trick was to find out exactly where they were and to *seek out* the Craigslist page specific to that venue. For instance, The Gorge is a famous venue located in Washington State, well within driving distance of Portland. I just typed in 'Washington Craigslist' and found the list of pages, then pulled up the map and looked at which of the towns with Craigslist pages were closest to The Gorge. Then I pulled up three or four of them, plus the Seattle and Portland pages, found the section for Gigs, and scanned them all a week or two before any of the shows I wanted to see were playing. It was never a guaranteed thing that anyone would need the help but more often than not there was some kind of ad. I worked at beer stands, corndog stands, lemonade stands, you get the picture. I made good money and I always got to see a little bit of the show for free.

This type of search is easy to do when sitting in the passenger seat of a car heading down the highway. I regularly found gigs just like that, which would pretty much determine where the car was headed and when. I can't say we always actually showed up when we were supposed to, but it was always an adventure finding the next place to make some money. If you keep aggressively searching for cool things going on and fun things to do, there is most likely some work to be had in that area.

● **Paid Studies**

I used to love these and would aggressively seek them out wherever I could find them. One thousand dollars to go in and brush my teeth, spit in a cup, and flirt with a beautiful receptionist once a month? Sign me up. Then I walked into a lab in one of the halls of Montana State University on a tepid, -8-degree January evening and had a bit of a change of heart.

The study involved maintaining memory with a series of electronic stimuli going on at the same time. I had wanted to closely emulate the local collegiate population, so I had stopped by the bar on the way there. Just fitting in, you know. Let's just say I was feeling pretty good when I walked through the doors. The hallways were dark, which should have been a warning sign, so I didn't see the lab tech until he opened a side door on me. At least I had thought he was a lab tech. After five minutes of awkward conversation, I found out he was just a student of a 200-level class in the department. He was 18, reeked of marijuana, and sat leaned back in his chair as if he couldn't get far enough away from the images he was seeing on his laptop. "This seems highly professional!" I thought to myself as I followed the child to a nearby desk.

He proceeded to hook me up to a, I can't emphasize this enough, *slight* electric current. I've been juiced by a car battery, a faulty smoke detector, and a full-blown 120-volt raging river of electricity before. This current was relatively mild in comparison to all those. OK, I said to myself. Shortly after that, images started to pop onto the screen. It didn't take long before I realized that I was failing pretty miserably at the experiment. I have no short-term memory to *begin* with, not to mention rampant ADHD and an intense series of triggers that take me out of normal situations on a minute-by-minute basis. So yeah, this series of short-term memory quizzes was probably not the best use of anybody's time. Still, your handsome protagonist needed to eat, so on I went.

Remember how I told you that I've been juiced by varying degrees of electricity in my time? Yeah, well that means that I have a pretty good idea of when an electrical current is *increasing*. Especially when it's attached to my ears and temples. Which it was. When I pointed this out to the child at the controls he attempted to simply shrug and ignore me. My indignation was fierce. I started answering the questions as fast as I could with zero regard for the context or the images on the screen. It was no surprise then that the current continued to increase. Soon enough I could take no more. I ripped off the connectors and threw them against the screen. I could feel a trickle down the back of my neck, which my then-girlfriend later reported to be emanating from the newly and electrically formed holes in my skin. The child got up quickly and, instead of checking on me, immediately started fretting over his cheap equipment. In no uncertain terms, I demanded to be paid, stormed over to his computer and snapped a picture with my phone, and walked out of there. It was all I could do not to put an extra hole in the kid's face.

I made it a few blocks from campus before the rage and shame started to kick in. And being the responsible and well-adapted person I was back then, this meant that I immediately went back to the bar. I ordered a vodka and called my main squeeze. Soon enough, she was there, fretting over the long streaks of blood streaking down my neck and the large, angry, red holes beneath the back of my ears. And, being the responsible and well-adapted people we were back then, we proceeded to get rip-roaring drunk. It was Tuesday. Around midnight we were teetotaling, swinging back and forth amongst the press of bodies, when I heard a familiar voice. Somehow the child from earlier had a fake ID and had used that, and some money he had connived from some other victim, to buy a bunch of drinks. Because this child was drunk. And he was talking, loudly. The subject? Me. And how he had intentionally put a ton of extra volts into his 'last subject.' Because he was bored.

This did not go over well with either me or my then-girlfriend. Nor did my next actions go over well with the bouncer, who was a friend of mine. But I will tell you, with absolute certainty, that our favorite lab technician was probably not keen to juice another unsuspecting subject for a long, long time.

Paid studies are what they are. You can head to an office, do something that a lot of people probably wouldn't bother to do, and get rewarded fairly handsomely. What you have to be wary of is what, exactly, they are planning to study and whether or not that type of study is healthy for you *long-term*. You have to make sure that the study is reputable, that you are not the first person they are trying this on, and that there is a plan in place in case something goes wrong. A reputable lab will have all this. A disreputable lab? Yeah, well, best to avoid those.

● Surveys

One of the most popular types of gig advertisement you will see is for surveys. Straight up, they are a gigantic waste of time. Any time you ever see surveys as the primary element of a service or supposed benefit to yourself, immediately disconnect and try something else.

The real issue here is one of opportunity cost. How much you are giving up to participate or engage in whatever it is you are doing. The most common way that we look at this is through an hourly wage. Say you perform a job for $15 an hour. You are directly stating to yourself and the universe that your time is worth $15 an hour. If that pays your bills and provides you with everything you need, and you are happy, then great. That is an effective worth for your time. Surveys do not pay even close to $15 an hour. They pay south of $3 an hour. This is where opportunity cost comes in. Yes, you can perform surveys for countless hours laying back on the couch with only carpel-tunnel syndrome to worry about. You could maybe make enough for a sack of cheap groceries without ever craning your neck. But in those four hours or so you could have gone somewhere else and made 5-10x that amount of money. You could then be doing something else with your time that is much more fun or beneficial. Simply put, surveys are just not worth your time.

Aside from my personal beliefs about them, there are also a bunch of risk factors associated with surveys you should be aware of. First, they are typically taking personal information from you, and you most likely do not know who is ending up with that information. Second, even if they aren't just a front for pirating your personal information, the owners of the survey are only 'paying out' for this information so that they can sell it to someone else for a considerable profit, thereby creating a situation in which multiple entities have your personal information and you *still* don't know exactly what they are doing with it. Lastly, if you found that link to paid surveys on Craigslist or a similar site, beware. Those are usually just scams to get your email, phone number, and/or address. All of which can be quickly sold on the dark web to spammers and hackers who send you a bunch of crap.

Avoid it all!

● **Carnivals**

I've been writing this book in my head for fifteen years. That is why I ended up doing some of the things I've done and taking on some of the jobs I have taken on. It was always for the grand purpose of experience and a story to tell. Working as an actual carnival worker was one of the only things I did that I know, deep down, that I will never do again. You can try it if you want, and I won't judge for one second. But here is my experience.

I had worked at a bunch of Fairs and Faires (you just have to be there to know the difference) but I had never actually been a 'Carnie' before. So, when I was presented with a few weeks of downtime I jumped at the opportunity. I was still reeling from my last job, and I needed to get out of town for a bit, which might explain why I ignored all the warning signs. My rat trap car, a different one than the other stories I assure you, actually *died* as I was pulling into the parking spot. It never started again, and I made only $50 selling it for scrap. I was there then. I cracked a beer, took a sip from the flask, and ventured on.

Thirty minutes later I was walking the grounds when a greasy, shady-looking guy with a lisp came up and asked who I was. I introduced myself with a smile and put out my hand to shake. The man simply grunted and turned away. Not a good sign. I decided to follow him despite him giving no indication that I should. The next thing I knew, I was in the middle of twenty people all sitting around and talking to each other. They all went deathly silent as I approached and stared at me, all of them staring laser beams through my skull and into my suddenly *very* sober body. Luckily the 'manager' appeared and heartily introduced himself. The next two hours were a blur interspersed with intense manual labor and me trying to be friendly and have fun as the people I was helping pointedly ignored me. Looking back, they had only agreed to take me on for free labor, which they got. I helped five or six groups of them put up their very heavy tents, then moved on to the next. What I didn't know was that these people aren't paid by the hour. They receive no money for their travel or their labor. The only time they get paid is if they sell tickets or tokens to the games/

rides that they are working at. So, my manual labor was completely *pro bono*. Awesome.

After a day of hard labor, I was informed of the fact that tomorrow I would be making tons of money. Heaps of money. Loads. The 'manager' kept trying to sell me on it. By now I was already on to them. I had sold myself as a salesman through my experience bartending. Real talk though? I am a piss-poor salesman. I couldn't care less about upselling or getting people to buy things that they don't want. And I can tell a racket when I see one. I knew, already, that they just needed someone to take advantage of. But this book you're reading, you know? This had to be told. So, there I was, exhausted, both physically and mentally, in the middle of a dusty Montana parking lot. I set up my small tent as far into the farthest corner as I could find and immediately laid down to try to get some sleep.

Little did I know, the sun going down was just the beginning of the crazy life these people live. Many people might not know this, but carnies live and travel this way all year. They never really stop for long. And they not only pull their rides, games, and stands behind them. They also pull housing units. These are extremely portable tiny little apartment complexes on wheels, complete with tiny little bathrooms and tiny little showers. So, as I was lying on my back in my tiny tent on the dusty, rocky ground, I started getting a little irritated. But rather than get frustrated and mad, I decided to walk over to where everyone was gathering and attempt to work my way into their good graces. It was tough sledding but when they figured out I had a lot of cash on me they couldn't help themselves. Suddenly they were competing to see how much of me they could 'take.' Again, remember, I knew what I was there for, so I let it happen. I wanted liquor, so suddenly someone offered me a tiny little pint bottle. Only $15 there. I needed food and water, well, someone had some somewhere, only $20. Beer? Another $20. Fantastic. I couldn't care less. I had been, at least tacitly and unknowingly, accepted. For the moment.

The next thing I knew, everyone was hammered. It only took an hour. We were gambling and I was holding my own, much to the amazement of the people around me. I kept feeling things tugging at the corner of my pockets throughout the game. It is not wise to accuse people of things, especially carnies, but I knew someone was trying to get at my cash. What they didn't know was that it was rolled up in a leather pouch and strung across my neck. I only opened it when I stepped around the corner to take a leak. I was doing this often because I drank like a fish back then and I was trying to keep up. Conversations bounced between and off people like pinballs and it became clear very quickly that everyone was banging, or had banged, everyone else. Hey, to each their own. No judgment here. But you don't want to get in the middle of a feud. This is why, only two hours after sunset, when the first pushing match began between two rival suitors of some woman, I tottered back to my dingy little tent and laid down. They were just getting started.

The next day I shook off the hangover and headed over to the crack-of-noon meeting. Everyone looked exactly as rough as I felt, and any progress I thought I had made the previous night into the warm graces of this group was gone. Long gone. The 'manager' was nowhere to be seen and today the strategy was clearly to ignore me at all costs. Maybe I hadn't stayed up late enough? Maybe I had spurned a suitor I didn't know I had. Maybe I was *supposed* to lose at poker and dice. Who cares? It was opening day and after an hour of awkward silence, I was put in charge of a game where people are supposed to spray a water gun in the mouth of various colored dinosaurs.

This is where it got interesting. You never really know what it's like to do something before you do it. Which is why you never trust anyone with clean shoes. They just don't have the empathy for you that they should. Working as a carnie might just be one of the extremes of this. See, carnies only make money if they are selling you tickets to the game that they are standing at. If no one is playing, they are making absolutely nothing, and the effort that they have gone through to stand in that exact spot is for nothing. So, they hustle you. It's why they cat-call, it's why they crack jokes, it's why they have all those canned lines. I had grasped this already and was doing my best impersonation. I had a headset on that was attached to a loudspeaker and I was talking to everyone going by. It was the single most awkward and uncomfortable experience of my entire life. It is hard to revisit it even in memory. But I went all out. I cracked awkward jokes. I made awkward remarks about the weather and people passing by. I even managed to get some people to play my game! But it was no surprise when the 'manager' came and pulled me.

Next thing I knew I was off the main strip, the 'drag,' and on a barren 'side street' managing a game where people could dump quarters into a machine in the hopes that they could push more quarters off into a hole. It was called The Dozer. I will never forget standing there for the next five hours. I saw maybe three people. As soon as someone stopped by to pull from the cash box, I asked them to watch for a little bit. I ran to my tent, grabbed the rest of my whiskey, and chugged it on the spot. I then went back and stood in the bright lights of the bedazzled Dozer machine, watching the blinking lights, choking on the dusty air, and generally laughing at myself for getting into this situation. The sunset that night was beautiful.

Afterward, I didn't even bother trying to mingle. I knew I was gone. The 'manager' had told me that I hadn't 'broken even' into 'the black,' his words, and that I'd need to pull in more money the next day to get paid. I laughed and told him I was going to take off in the morning. Oddly, he looked intensely disappointed. I hadn't seen that coming. I never ask for money, but in this case, I pretended I was broke and asked him for ten bucks for bus fare. He begrudgingly obliged. I hate asking anybody for anything, but I wanted something to show for my efforts and labor. I think I had worked a total of 14 hours at this point, which equates to about 74 cents per hour. And I had to ask for it! Still brings a smile to my face.

I whistled as I walked to the gas station, bought a 12-pack and a cigar, then walked back to a picnic bench just within earshot of where all these crazy carnies were just getting started again. A couple of the cars in the employee parking lot were rocking back and forth pretty strongly, so hopefully the two suitors had worked out their differences and everybody was happy again. I watched everything play out till my cigar was long burned out and I was out of beer, then turned in. Soon after daylight returned, I was up and going, pack across my back, also carrying two heavy bags of stuff I had previously stored in my scrap-heaped sedan. I called a cab to meet me at the nearest hotel and started walking. I never looked back.

14 | Side Hustles

Not to be confused with 'one-offs', these gigs are longer term in nature simply because you can do them for as long as you want to. I have supported several people at a time driving for major food delivery and rideshare services. At other times I subsisted completely on furniture assembly gigs. You can build your own business(es) based on these as well, particularly using the lead-based services described later. These types of gigs are referred to as side gigs because you don't punch a clock. You can check in and out or schedule yourself whenever you want. They are great ways to add to your income if you are underemployed, especially if you are being kept at 39 hours per week for a company trying to avoid giving you benefits (quit immediately) or just kept at 19 hours in part-time status purgatory to keep your from accruing paid days off (quit immediately). I used these gigs, and continue to use them, at various times when I am committed to giving up my free time to save up money or when I am not in the mental state to work with or for anyone else. This happens quite a bit these days!

Side hustle jobs are the backbone of the modern nomadic lifestyle, whether people have caught up to this or not. As humans, we need a wide variety of passions, interests, and goals. Traditional 'wisdom' wants us to specialize, maintain a relatively narrow focus, and maximize our productivity at this specialization through nearly infinite repetition. This is why we burn out. We spend our lives doing the same thing day in and day out, missing out on huge swaths of the human experience, for goals that we did not make for ourselves. If the COVID-19 shutdown taught us anything, it is that there is more to life than work. And that the current way our working lives are set up is for us to fail to see the true worth of our time so that someone else can profit.

We have to focus on our own goals to be successful and we have to focus on our own interests to be happy. The problem is that jobs that require a great deal of specialization typically pay considerably more than those that don't. If you do a job that most people cannot do, you get paid more, simple as that. This means that by following your interests and passions you are most likely giving up, to some degree, the safety and security of a larger income.

This is where these side gigs, really side incomes, become a necessity. If your passion is laser engraving custom jewelry, you are going to have to hone your craft, find buyers and local stores to sell in, gather reviews, etc. It is going to take time out of your day and may take a long time to see enough income to live off. If ever. So, you get up in the morning, pour a nice cup of coffee, and make your jewelry for the first few hours of your day. Around noon you go to your car, turn on the food delivery app, and work for 2-4 hours. You come home, do some yoga, tinker with a necklace project that you have, then hop in your car for the dinner rush. You come home having made a living wage while also following your passions, interests, and best overall well-being practice.

That is just one scenario. The point is to get you thinking about how your life is not a rigid, linear set of data points from birth to death. You are not obligated to follow the routine and pattern of those around you. We do not *have* to go to high school (you can get your GED), go straight to college (why not go to a technical school?), get a job your parents approve of, get married right away, have kids before 25, and on and on. I am not knocking this type of life. A great many, perhaps the majority, dream of this life. Live for it. And that's fine! The point is that there are a lot of people who don't want this and most likely feel pigeonholed into pursuing it, despite having other interests, goals, and passions. The previous scenario of driving for food delivery is one example of how you don't *have to*. How you can use the burgeoning gig economy to diversify your life by diversifying your activities, income streams, passions, and hobbies. By having a flexible concept of what it is exactly that you do for income your life becomes more flexible in terms of how you can best find your happiness.

Ridesharing

There is a distinct reason that there is a long and detailed driving section in this book. Ridesharing is a dangerous activity, if only for your car. Large companies that provide these services have a horrible track record of providing for their 'employees' (Yes, Uber, they are *employees*). It seems so easy. Just hop in the car and drive people around. But when you are on the road for considerable periods you dramatically increase your risk of exposing yourself to risk, not to mention the effects of considerable stress on your mental health. The people that get into your car are rarely polite and respectful of your property/space. They can and will treat you like a bicycle. If one of them 'acts up,' either violently or with sexual aggression, they are already *in your car* and the major companies you work for will do little to protect you. You are on your own regardless of what happens.

That said, you can make a good amount of money driving people around. You have to learn how to do your taxes correctly, find the cheapest places to get gas, have an electric or fuel-efficient vehicle, generally know how to get places, have a somewhat decent rapport with strangers, and be comfortable gently pushing traffic rules, but it does pay the bills. Not to mention you can hop on and off whenever you want. I struggled with the people. I'm still trying to figure out whether I am an introvert or extrovert, depends on the day really, but most of my rides were jackasses in some sense or another. From 'young professionals' who stayed glued to their phones and actively demeaned me at every opportunity, to older socialites who spoke at length about their daily activities and demeaned me at every opportunity, I rarely found that the people in my car had a vibration/energy/attitude that I wanted in my life. Or, more specifically, within twenty feet of me. I struggled with this. I found myself taking two or three rides, then having to turn the app off for fifteen minutes to recharge. It's not for everybody and, frankly, I preferred food delivery. All the driving, none of the chatter. But to each their own. Here are some tips and tricks I learned along the way:

- **Pay attention to the bonus times.** I always avoided rush hour, but this is also when you make the most money. My favorite times to drive were in the morning doing airport runs and then right after rush hour ended. There were usually still bonuses during these times and you don't have to deal with as much traffic. The fares that these services offer aren't always worth your time. Sometimes they will pay you $3 to drive across an entire city. You actually *lose* money when you factor in gas and vehicle depreciation. If you are going to turn enough of a profit to make this gig worth it, however, you have to drive when these companies offer boosted rates. And this means at peak hours of demand and traffic.

- **Ride with a few other drivers.** It's just good to see how they do things. What they do right and wrong becomes immediately apparent. As an objective rider, you can get good insight into how you can do well on your own.

- **Always track and record your miles.** And keep your gas receipts. These are key to actually making money because you are allowed to write off the miles that you put on your car when you pay your taxes. Not only does this mean that you pay less taxes but with enough miles you will most likely get a refund. I always download an app that I run in the background on my phone. It automatically tracks every trip I make and adds them up for me, making it easy to crunch the numbers come tax time. Don't forget to write down the odometer readings from when you started to when you ended. You'll have to figure out how to effectively depreciate your car come tax season and it pays to have these numbers later.

- **Don't be *too* chatty.** The recurring theme I see with rideshare drivers is a shared sense of inferiority and a tendency to overshare, maybe to compensate. I have no idea why this is. There is nothing shameful or degenerate about giving people rides for money. Yet the trend exists all the same. Don't be one of those drivers who have to prove to everyone that they are 'above' their job. Or a driver who tells their passengers everything about their lives. It is uncomfortable for everyone.

- **Make your money at the airport.** The best rides are always found at the airport. It helps to have a good idea of when planes land in your town. They are more regular than you might think! It also helps to have a good idea of how your local airport runs, where they let you park, who's going to give you a hard time, etc. Eventually, you can get into a rhythm of doing airport rides, thereby increasing your efficiency.

- **Drive for multiple companies.** Different companies have different perks and bonus times, not to mention it's always better to stay busy. Depending on where you are you'll notice certain days and times that people use certain apps. If you're staying busy and switching between companies, you'll most likely be making more money.

- **Don't listen to people who want you to hurry.** A lot of people in this country want to play dictator. Barking out orders, paying no attention to anyone else, and generally just being an ass. You'll get them eventually. And they always want you to hurry, as if they aren't in *your* car and *your* safety isn't on the line too. Don't listen to them. They will be just fine at whatever speed you drive.

Food Delivery

As I mentioned before, I greatly preferred food delivery to ridesharing. I didn't mind the driving aspect and I was in a relatively rural location where the big major companies were jostling to enter the market. They offered decent bonuses for each delivery that I took full advantage of. Later on, delivering in some of the major cities, I discovered that without those bonuses there were entirely different tactics. And payouts. I didn't last long there but again, to each their own. Regardless of where you're at, this is a great job if you like driving and don't want to constantly interact with people. Here are some tips to get you started.

- **Always be nice to the restaurant workers.** I quickly made friends with the counter people at the restaurants where I accepted orders. I remember watching this guy fly in, hair and pants on fire, and angrily demand that he get his orders. FAST. I was chuckling, standing behind him, when the counter girl handed me my orders around him. I gave her a thumbs-up and a wink and took off. My orders weren't too far away so, I dropped them off and immediately took two more orders from the same restaurant. As I got there the man was angrily pacing in front of the counter, still waiting, ranting quietly under his breath. I walked in, cut the line, threw the three bucks the last order had handed me in the restaurant's tip jar, and again the counter girl reached around the register to hand me my next two orders. I gave her prayer hands, a half bow, winked again, and took off. The angry guy was still pacing and ranting as I left. The point is, always be nice to the people who work at the restaurant. Take care of your people and your people will take care of you.

- **Know which restaurants to decline.** Some restaurants just don't know what the fuck they are doing. They take forever, they get your orders wrong, and they move slowly. A lot of restaurants generally prioritize the people they have sitting down to eat. This isn't exactly a bad thing, but it can seriously affect your bottom line when you're waiting around. Your customers don't know that it's usually the restaurant's fault too, so there goes your perfect rating. There are always at least four or five restaurants in my area that I won't accept orders from.

- **Use a hot bag.** This is a no-brainer. You want your food to stay hot on the way to the customer. You'd be amazed how fast it can cool down. These bags are game changers. They will make a serious difference and make you look professional at the same time.

- **Always be nice to the people you're delivering to.** No matter how pissy or hangry they were when I showed up, I was always nice and polite. These folks are hungry assholes and as soon as they eat some of the food you're handing them then all they will remember is you telling them to have a great day. Trust me, if you stay super friendly, you'll end up with a lot of belated tips.

- **Take the shorter deliveries and stack them up.** You'll be completely forgiven if you think that the longer rides are worth more money. All things considered, they aren't. You may make more money *going there*, but you are most likely going to have to come back the same way as well, without being paid for the return journey. On longer trips, this takes time and gas, not to mention losing out on the opportunity of taking more orders. If you can, take the short orders down the street and do multiple orders at a time.

- **Try to do your own maintenance.** This is a tough one for a lot of people. It's really hard to look at an engine and figure out what's going on. But having a ratchet set, hopping on YouTube, and tinkering for a bit, could save you a few hundred bucks for a half hour of your time. Especially the cosmetic stuff. Keep in mind, brands always try to make their products look more complicated than they are so that you have to rely on them for their lifetime and keep paying them to maintain it. You *can* fix your own car and it's way easier than you think it is.

Dog Walking

To be honest, I didn't last long as a dog walker. I have a furry terrorist at home who already gives me tennis elbow and I'm not a huge fan of cleaning up dog poop. If you don't have a beast of your own and don't mind waste collection though, this is an awesome way to make extra cash. There are loads of dogs who simply want company, need to be given their medications on a schedule, and otherwise just need to be let out of the house in the middle of the day. You can set your hours, choose your pay, and pick your clients. It's a pretty sweet deal all around if you are an animal lover. While there are a lot of gigs like this that are for other animals, this one is primarily catered toward dogs because I only care about dogs. If you want to walk a duck or a ferret with these tips, be my guest.

- **Get to know the owners.**

First of all, you're going to need to get comfortable meeting people off of an app or a website and then immediately going into their homes and meeting their fur babies. It can be pretty strange. You have to trust them just as much as they trust you. The way to alleviate this is to take the time to get to know them. Of course, you'll want the job and feel like you're in an interview. But try and let those thoughts go. Look into the person that you are talking to. Try and learn about their lives and who they are as people. While you are doing this, be open and honest about yourself. Tell them some about your life and what you stand for. This creates a mutual bond. You will be entering their home, most likely with them gone to work, and taking their beloved dog out into the world. As such, having a bond that extends beyond a simple exchange of money for services makes any potential for tension much lower than it would be otherwise. This also helps to build your business. If your clients can trust you around their home, then you better believe they are going to tell all of their friends about you.

● **Be picky.**

I have a difficult dog. He is enthusiastic, to say the least. There is not a mean bone in his body but when I say that he loves me and other people, that is an understatement. He *aggressively* loves everyone. It is a routine occurrence to see him jumping five feet high in the air to try and kiss someone's face. I have received two chipped teeth, a dislocated shoulder, multiple cuts on my nose, and more fat lips than I can count trying to train this wildebeest. Is it any surprise that it has been difficult to find people who are willing to walk him while I am at work? The answer is, resoundingly, no.

There are some difficult dogs out there. A lot of owners simply don't know how to raise a dog to be friendly. Just like humans, dogs can be defensive, possessive, and mean. Dogs can also be exuberant, maniacally energetic, and nippy. It is up to you to decide what you are willing and capable of dealing with.

If you are going to pursue this gig, you're going to want to be picky. My dog and I have been 'fired' several times by various dog walkers and doggie daycares. I took it in stride because I understand. He's a lot to deal with. I did, however, eventually stumble upon people who enjoy the way my dog behaves. He *is* a wonderful beacon of love and joy. You might think so, you might not. It is up to you to decide what you want. Most owners are going to want their dogs taken for an actual walk so make sure they are trained enough to obey commands and not drag you toward every passing squirrel. Some owners have older dogs that simply need to go outside for five minutes and then lay their heads on your lap for an hour or two. Some clients may just need you to let their dogs out in the backyard for an hour.

Find situations that work for you and what you can do, then build your clientele from there.

- **Short leashes.**

Under no circumstances should you ever have someone else's dog on a long leash. This means any leash over ten feet long. The risk of them straying into the street or tying up your legs is just too great. When you are taking care of a dog you are in charge of their wellbeing just as much as your own. By having a short leash, you minimize the chances of having something go drastically wrong.

- **The Rule of Two.**

OK, I am a serious Star Wars nerd. If you are too then you caught the reference. If not, just move on. The point is that you are only going to want two dogs at a time. You have probably seen someone walking four or five dogs at once. While this may be a way to maximize your income when walking dogs, it is certain to cause trouble at some point. There are just too many factors to consider. First, you're going to have to clean up the poop of all of them and when you are doing so there is always the chance that one of them will slip away. Second, you just never know how a dog is going to react to any stimuli. When you are holding six dogs the chances of one of them having a wild reaction to a cat, siren, or even one of the other dogs you are walking becomes unacceptably high. And last, it's just stressful. There is so much going on when you take on that much responsibility. As such, you're going to want to keep your focus on two dogs at once.

- **Avoid dog parks.**

A lot of dog walkers pick up their client's dogs and then take them straight to the dog park. This can create a ton of challenges. Dog parks are sketchy in general because you just never know how two dogs are going to interact. They are also a breeding ground for sickness and disease. While they may be fine if you take your dog there and continuously supervise him, they are certainly not the place that you want to take someone else's pride and joy to.

- **Meet and greets.**

If you are going to walk more than one dog at a time it is your responsibility to make sure that the dogs get along. You may have several clients that trust you with their dogs and that's great. That does not mean that each of your clients, or their dogs, are going to get along. Therefore, you are going to have to arrange a meet and greet to make sure that they do. Just make sure that the dogs are off-leash when you do this and that everyone is on board. Most owners are enthusiastic about their dogs being around other dogs. It makes them happy and tires them out more. Some owners are intensely against this though. Just feel it out. Have the dogs get to know one another before they are both walking with you at the same time and have both owners on the same page and you'll be fine.

- **Have treats.**

This one is obvious, but I included it anyway. Have treats. Make sure that the treats you use are OK with the owner first, but always have them. Most times your clients will have their own that you can use, so fill your pocket with them and head out. Having a treat is the easiest and best way to distract a dog if you need to redirect its focus. And they are all such good boys. They deserve a treat or five.

- **Lights at night.**

Most of your clients will need you to work during business hours when they are at work. There are, however, some clients who will need your services at night. This means walking a dog without a ton of light. You're going to want to leave your black hoodie at home. Instead, you're going to want something bright and visible so that you can be seen easily. The same thing goes for whatever dog you're walking. Because dogs don't usually wear clothes, you're going to need to attach something to their collar. There are several great products for this, ranging from LED lights to disposable glow sticks. Whatever it is, make sure that the dog and you are very visible. You will look professional, caring, and keep yourself safe at the same time.

Furniture Assembly

This was my favorite side job of all time. I still do it occasionally and still have a small business presence related to this because of how much I love putting the pieces together. It is like a beautiful puzzle that everyone else hates and can't figure out that pays a lot of money. This section is particularly oriented toward setting yourself up with your own business as soon as you become comfortable with the practice. One note: Major companies like Handy are evil and best avoided. Handy in particular. I truly do hope they sue me so that I can start a David vs. Goliath class action suit. Really. Plain, unadulterated evil. Anyway!

Furniture assembly is all about having the right tools for the job. I've listed those below. Just having them puts you head and shoulders above your competition and, typically, your clients. Most people see the ads and think

that they need to head to Home Depot and buy themselves a brand new…
Ryobi toolset. Don't do this. Not only are they absolute garbage tools but
they are made to only work for one or two jobs before their power and
effectiveness dramatically decrease. If you don't have the budget for good,
new tools, canvas your nearby thrift stores and resale shops. You're looking
for older versions of top-brand power tools. These won't have the same kick
that they used to, but they are built to last and they are still way better than
the bottom-drawer crap from the Big Box stores. Also, they have the added
benefit of making you appear as if you have been doing this for a long time.
Just make sure to score an extra battery pack and a charger to bring with you
on the job. The worst thing that can happen is running out of battery when
you're in a hurry. Knowing how to use these tools is also a plus, but mostly
you learn through trial and error. If you're nervous just hop on YouTube and
type in exactly what you want to learn. I can't count how many times I've sat
outside a job site and either refreshed my memory of how to do something
or learned it right before I walked in. Regardless of how confident you are,
just remember to start slow. At first, you are just trying to minimize the er-
rors. The most common of these are listed below as well.

Tools You Will Need

1. **Drill (with a full set of drill bits)**
2. **Rubber mallet**
3. **Regular hammer**
4. **Hex key (set of Allen wrenches)**
5. **Long flat head and long Phillips head screwdriver**
6. **Short (stubby) flat head and Phillips head screwdriver**
7. **Glue**
8. **Level**
9. **A decent set of pliers and wrenches**
10. **Box cutter (watch out when opening, you can easily scratch the furniture)**

*People will commonly ask you why there are extra parts. All companies
add extra parts to their part sets because there are so many defective nuts,
bolts, and whatnot. You will always end up with extra! I keep them in a
separate bag. Eventually, you'll have quite the collection, which can bail you
out if something is missing on a later job.*

Common Errors

● **Having the drill set too high.**

Most of this furniture is made of particle board so it isn't that sturdy. You are inserting cams, screws, and pin nails into this flimsy material. If you have your drill on too high, you'll go right through and cause a huge blemish, at which point there's usually not a whole lot you can do about it. Some people adamantly say not to use a drill at all but if you've got multiple pieces to assemble you just don't have the time not to. Just make sure it's not set too powerfully.

● **Leaving parts and pieces in the box.**

I can't count how many times I've had a mini-panic putting a piece together and thinking I lost a piece. It is always in the box, hiding amongst all the cardboard and other packing material. Start every job by pulling out each piece, examining it for major defects, and carefully arranging it around the room. It is a pain in the ass, but it makes the rest of the job go super smooth. Worth the time.

● **Pay attention to the directions.**

My greatest nuisance in this line of work was coming into a situation where the homeowner had started to put the piece together themselves, messed it up, and then called me. A handful of times they had messed it up so bad I couldn't fix it. It is what it is. Just make sure not to do this *yourself*. Even with pieces that I absolutely know how to put together, I still follow the directions as I go. Those tricksy Swedes change things around sometimes! Take your time if you have to. Refer to the picture as many times as you need. Breathe, slow down, and make sure to get it right the first time.

● **Don't hesitate to ask the homeowner for help moving it into place.**

I would always frame this with the question: "Where exactly did you want this to go?" This is directly insinuating that I need an extra hand to nudge the enormous armoire I had just constructed against the wall. These pieces come unassembled for a reason. They are not the best furniture, and they are certainly not designed to be moved around a ton. You can do this step by yourself but if you have any worry that the thing will break then absolutely ask for a quick hand.

● **If it shows up broken, don't put it together.**

Regardless of whether it's your fault or not, the homeowner is going to blame you. When you are pulling out the pieces and you see one that is broken, you need to immediately let them know and see if they want you to continue. You need to make it clear that this happens all the time in transit (it does) and that they have the option to send it back and get a new one. It's a pain in the ass for everyone but it will help you in the long run to just point out flaws immediately.

A Few Tips

- **Glue can save your ass.** Occasionally you might fuck up, put a nail through the corner into the front, or bust out the back of this cheap particle board. This is why you always have glue. I carry superglue, regular wood glue, and clear epoxy as well, depending on the color and material I need to put back together.

- **IKEA hands out free spare parts.** The furniture overlords have a designated section for extra little parts that you might need. If you really can't find one of the little pieces, and you haven't been collecting all the extras as you go from job to job, then you can make a trip to IKEA and get some of these.

- **Furniture companies will always replace broken pieces.** Even if you're the one who broke it, just show the homeowner and tell them you'll order it and come back and finish assembling it then. They are never happy when this happens but fuck 'em if they think you're just going to snap your fingers and magically make particle board appear.

- **When you are pulling out the pieces, have some order to it.** The pieces are usually lettered or numbered. I like to arrange them off to the side in order. This reduces the time it takes to keep sifting through and finding each piece as you go. Also, it's common that there will be a piece or two where the sticker fell off. If you know what all the other pieces are, it's much easier to identify the one that isn't marked.

- **Keep the screws, nuts, and bolts in their respective marked baggies.** It is intensely annoying to lose one or, even worse, get all of them mixed up.

- **Use the rubber mallet, not the regular hammer.** Your regular hammer will leave marks and divots. Your rubber hammer will not.

- **Don't overtighten the cams!** They aren't supposed to hold the atmosphere to the planet, they just need to do their job. If you overtighten them, you can crack the whole board. I always do the cams by hand, rather than by drill, because this is so easy to do.

15 | Driving

This is a separate section because of the particular relevance and importance it has to staying alive on the road. As Americans, we are uniquely
oriented toward the automobile. The infrastructure and landscape of this
nation were designed around the highway system and our cars. We *think* we
invented the automobile, but we did not, although we did invent the mass
production system for cars, and highways, and we absolutely, 100% invented the drive-through. The drive-thru, specifically, because most people still
can't spell 'through.' We are a nation of flag-waving, monster-truck-driv-
ing, gas-guzzling, hot-dog inhaling, gearheads. We rely on automobiles for
virtually our entire existence, from transportation to every single good and
service we buy.

So why is it that most people are terrible drivers?

The answer to that has a lot of factors. More than I could ever point to and
certainly more than I could ever prove. Cell phones immediately spring to
mind. Our individualistic, 'me'-based, self-centered culture is also a huge
culprit. Maybe it's that we have too many drive-throughs and everyone is
eating too many tacos. Or perhaps most important is the lack of effective education centered around driving available today. Simply put, most
people are taught to drive wrong, both by their parents and by the driver's
education programs most young drivers are forced through in high school.
Everyone is taught how to drive, yet very, very few are taught how to drive
well. And it is driving well that will eventually save your life.

Think that is melodramatic? Think about how many times in your life you
have seen a collision, been in a collision, or seen a near collision. Those
events probably happened on the way to work or school, or to get groceries. A short trip that lasted mere minutes most likely followed by a short
trip after you finished whatever you were doing. But what if it isn't a short
trip? Imagine how much exposure to this you will have when you spend

countless hours in the car, at higher speeds, in more isolated environments… maybe you see the picture I am painting here. The idea in life is always to learn the lesson before the epic fuck-up. So, here's a brief tutorial on how to be a good driver:

- **Always expect everyone else to mess up, every single time.**

It's an extremely simple notion that's easy to forget and very hard to apply. And it's not pessimistic! I have (almost) solved my road rage by learning to give people the benefit of the doubt. Now, instead of accusing everyone of being incestuous, knuckle-dragging, failures of humanity, I say things like: "Well, I hope you get where you are going!" and "They are probably having a bad day." But that doesn't mean that any of these super nice, regular people can't make a mistake at any time in their five thousand pound minivan going sixty miles an hour surrounded by hundreds of other vehicles.

Does this mean you have to be ultra-vigilant at all times? No. That's impossible. No one can stay that way without suffering a mental breakdown (raises hand) and those are certainly a no-no in the whole concept of total wellness. The goal is simply to see the possibility of someone messing up and either be ready to react before it happens or anticipate it with enough time to avoid it entirely.

For example, imagine you are driving along and you are coming to an intersection. You have a green light, it has been green as long as you have been driving toward it, and you anticipate that it will stay green long enough for you to drive through it. Imagine you are heading to this intersection, and you see a car to your right, slightly pulled forward over the white line, clearly about to take a right. A selfish instinct is going to come first, which is natural, and that is to speed up. "It's MY right of way and MY green." The problem is, they see it the same way. They are wrong, but that doesn't matter. If they pulled in front of you, they would be liable if you weren't speeding. They would have to pay for the repairs to your vehicle and body, not to mention any collateral damage at the scene. But is it worth it for all that? Absolutely not. Nothing is. Hence, when you are coming to that intersection, slow down slightly, let that dickbag who is tailgating you see your brake lights a little, and get ready to slow down dramatically if someone pulls out in front of you. Worst case scenario in that instance? You have to wait at a single light. Definitely worth your time.

This notion of expecting failure applies to all kinds of situations on the highway as well. We forget that the speeds we drive at are too fast for our minds to adequately process all the information we are seeing. It's why you see a blur if you look horizontally out of the window. Do you really need to tailgate someone else going 90 mph? Nope. Expect them to doze off or swerve to avoid a lizard. Or worse, merge lanes *into* the car next to them in the other lane, putting them in *your* way. Very fast. Give them *tons* of room. You have nothing to lose. You are not going to get there any faster, you are only going to waste money on gas, and your stress level will be much higher. Not to mention, you raise the risk of getting hit at a very high speed.

● **Drive five hundred feet in front of you.**

This goes right along with the first segment as it is another unique half of the same whole. While you are driving along, expecting all these people to constantly do stupid things, you are now *noticing* it as it happens. The next step is to start doing so farther and farther away from your car. Why? Ever heard the adage: 'It takes 5 miles to turn around a battleship?' It's true. With that much weight and momentum, it takes miles for a ship of that size to make a 180-degree turn. The same concept applies to your car. Never, ever forget that you are driving a five to 10-ton hunk of fused metal and plastic with enough force to instantaneously liquify an entire family. Think of the last dinner table you were at. Then think of all those people reduced to their constituent parts, screaming for God and dying in agony, on a crappy Idaho back road in the winter. That is what you and your vehicle are capable of *at all times*. It's morbid but completely true. Now, are you going to mow down people on a daily basis? No. But if you ever did? Game over. Prison, PTSD, or both. For life.

The goal is to always expect other cars to behave erratically and then to expand that awareness and observation further and further away from your car. You should have, at least, a passing awareness of the cars *behind* you, the cars that are 100, 200, 300, 400, then 500 feet in front of you, and the basic knowledge of whether someone is in your blind spot as well. At all times. Forever and ever. And this isn't limited to other cars. Are there people walking on the side of the barren highway? Good chance there's either a broken-down vehicle or a wreck ahead. Time to slow down. Is there a line of yellow signs? Probably means there's a curve up ahead. Time to give the car in front of you some extra room and get ready to slow down. Is that narcissistic lipstick jockey who's swerving in and out of all three lanes going to have *just enough* time to cut me off while passing me in the slow lane before she hits the car in front of her? Who knows? Better slow down and make sure she doesn't cause a pileup. This is the preeminent skill of driving. Being aware enough to identify what is happening way before it happens, then doing something about it and generally keeping everyone around you that much safer. Bonus points for extending your range.

● Don't panic.

Hey, you're human. You're going to mess up. Or you're just going to be unlucky and something is going to go wrong. The trick is to always stay calm and try your best to mitigate the damage. I remember driving an old rat-trap Honda Civic across the country for the first time. I was young and broke and trying to make time. I had woken up in Cleveland. At some point the night before I had pulled over, grabbed five hours of sleep, and there I was in a rest-stop parking lot. One massive jug of coffee later and I was on my way to Vermont. Hours went by. I think I was in Pennsylvania. Or was it New York? Doesn't matter. I was zoning out to a book on tape and didn't see the signs that my lane was closing. Fuck. I was one of those guys who rockets to the front of the line and then cuts in at the last moment. Don't be *that person*.

Turns out my pride and image were the last of my problems. Cones were coming up fast. Really fast. And no one would let me in. I still remember my heart pounding out of my chest, my hands clenched around the steering wheel as if I could force the car to become airborne by sheer force of will. But I didn't panic. I slowed down. Kept watching all of my mirrors. Popped my blinker and waved at the people around me. I think I even pointed to my chest in the universal 'my bad' gesture. I only hit seven or eight of the previously lined-up cones at 70 mph and even managed to miss the huge blinking sign by a few feet.

The message here is not to panic. A lot of people are going to jerk the wheel when they see a squirrel, or they are going to slam on the brakes at the first sign of trouble. Not only is it usually too late for this to help, but most often, this is going to make your situation *worse*. You are either going to flip your vehicle, lose control, or put yourself in the opposing lane. Some things in life are going to hurt. Sometimes you are going to crash. By panicking, you guarantee the worst-case scenario. By staying present, trying to minimize the damage, and otherwise keeping your wits about you, you can make a terrible situation *much less terrible*. And who knows, you might just skate out of there with only a few dented cones as witnesses.

● Get some sleep.

Everyone thinks they can drive for days on end and be just fine. They are wrong. Your performance on the road drastically declines after eight hours, tops. You think you are doing OK, but remember, you are driving a five-ton wrecking ball at high speed in an environment your mind *cannot comprehend*. You, at best, are driving just well enough not to cause a catastrophe. Most likely, the people on the road near you are the ones keeping you safe, giving your car distance and space as you furtively try to keep it between the lines. And no amount of disgusting, metallic, witch-potion energy drinks, or delicious, dirt-flavored, gas station coffee, will make a difference. The only thing that will change that? Taking a break. Getting some ZZZs. Letting someone else drive for a while, no matter how terrifying that might be for you. There are rest stops, Walmarts, and hotel parking lots for a reason. And that is to take a nap. Maybe a long one.

- **React appropriately.**

As I mentioned earlier, stuff happens. Despite your best intentions, or maybe even despite them, people are going to mess up and crazy stuff is going to go down. The surefire, guaranteed way to make those things worse is to overreact. For example, take the age-old dilemma of zipping around a bend and coming face to face with a deer standing in the middle of the road. A large number of people will grab the wheel and yank it in either direction to miss the deer. This is panicking, which we are not going to do, and will invariably cause the car to flip and kill anyone and anything (your dog) that isn't tied down. There is no right answer in this situation. Should you have been going that fast? Probably not. Are you going to regret going that fast as soon as you see the damn deer? Oh yeah, absolutely. But the answer is definitely *not* to yank on the wheel. Depending on the situation you'll have to come to your own conclusion, but if I were there, and I've been there before, I'd slow down as much as I could without locking the brakes, keep my car on the road for sure, and try to either hit as little of the deer as I could or hit it at an angle so it doesn't flip directly over the hood of my car and flatten me and my dog in the front seat. The point is to not panic and *keep thinking*. Time does slow down in these instances and if you try your best to mitigate the damage, you are going to have much better results than simply wrenching the wheel of life and hoping for the best.

- **Never tailgate.**

I don't understand why people do this. It makes the person in front of you nervous, which is going to make them slow down, not speed up. If the tailgating person hits the car in front of them then they are going to end up paying for the whole mess and considering that is much more likely due to how close they are, makes it a bad idea all around. You are not going to get there faster, you are going to aggravate yourself and everyone around you, and you are going to demonstrate to the entire world that you think that you are much more important than everyone around you. Frankly, tailgating is one of the stupidest things you can do behind the wheel.

- **Avoid busy times.**

If you haven't guessed by now, half of being a 'good' driver is just avoiding 'bad' drivers. Collisions always take two people, just like arguments, and who ends up paying is nothing more than the person who is *most* at fault. There are exceptions to this, as anyone who has been t-boned by someone who ran a red light can attest to. But we are talking about the vast majority of collisions. And what's the easiest and best way to avoid the highest amount of bad drivers? Stay off the road when they are there!

This is harder said than done, however, and requires a commitment to avoiding these situations. We all know the classic story. You're tired. You've been driving all day. You want to get to that cheap hotel you found on that app you used and you are blaring along, ten over the speed limit, and you look at the clock and… it's 4:30. Just in time to be surrounded by all those psychopaths gunning it to beat rush-hour. I get it. You want to push through, just deal with it, and get it over with. But if you want to truly avoid the highest possible chance of getting nailed, pull over to the nearest diner, grab a cup of coffee and a burger, and wait it out.

The same goes for winter weather, heavy rain, weekends, and holidays. You couldn't pay me enough to drive into *any* city around Thanksgiving. And I make dedicated plans to avoid the same cities and heavily congested areas around weekends. It may seem obnoxious to always be trying to avoid people but if you think about it, the cheapest way to travel is to only go on 'shoulder seasons,' hit the places where people *aren't* going at that time, and travel/drive when the least people are traveling/driving. It becomes second nature. Sometimes it's unavoidable. You're going to wait in lines. But when you *can* avoid it, do so. It's the best way to stay safe and mentally ready to either continue traveling or enjoy yourself at the place you were heading to.

- **Know what you're driving into.**

Most times when you take off, you're just trying to get out of where you are and you don't care where you are heading to. But nowadays, with the advent of Google Maps and universal weather alerts, it's super easy to pull up the map and check what the weather looks like ahead of you. It can easily ruin your day to drive into a tornado or hurricane warning.

I remember driving an ancient chariot down I-95 on my way to Florida, ironically to *escape* a hurricane, and getting to North Carolina, where I was immediately greeted with a massive flashing street sign that read: Beware Horizontal Flying Debris. Well, fuck *me*. They were serious! Another time that vividly comes to mind was driving a full car of people out of New Orleans a few years later. I have never seen so much rain in my life (see: Windshield Wipers) and every single town had their emergency siren blaring. I turned on the radio only to be blasted in the face by constant warnings about how we shouldn't be on the road. It was all I could do to keep rolling as the rain was coming down in dump trucks. It was as if God was forcibly pissing on that particular part of Louisiana and trying to blast us off of the side of the bowl. The sky above was the darkest gray I think I've ever seen and to my left, I saw that there were downspouts. Multiple downspouts. Good times! Both of these events could have been easily fixed by simply checking my phone or asking someone at the local gas station why everyone was panicking.

This section is most relevant if you're going to be driving through the mountains, particularly a mountain pass, at any point along your route. These places will have snow in the winter, could have snow any other time of the year, and are much more likely to have wind and rain conditions that can stress you out. There are a bunch of apps you can download for this if you don't already have one, or you can just call 511. The information all comes from the same place so they can all save you a ton of time and stress, not to mention giving you time to detour if the highway is closed.

● **What to Do When You See an Ambulance/Firetruck.**

It's easy to see an ambulance or a police officer blaring by and not care. It really is. We can get so wrapped up in our lives, goals, and daily tasks that we forget that, at any time, something horrible can happen. But the fact is that life is short, and it can end any day. Most times you hear that siren? At least one person is scared that it is happening to them. Have you ever been in a life-threatening situation? Have you ever *lived* through a life-threatening situation? Have you ever experienced the gratitude and eternal relief that comes from coming out 'no harm done?' From cheating death and getting to hug your favorite person one more time? Well, I'll tell you, I've been through a lot of those. From ambulances, to back seats (in handcuffs and not), to waking up in hospitals you have no recollection of entering, there is a sacred aspect to the act of trying to save a life. And that is something we have an inherent duty to aid in its process.

While I was writing this book, I went through a PTSD rehabilitation program, multiple separations with my ex-wife, a divorce, and more bullshit than I should conceivably be able to shake a stick at. But after all of it, on the worst day of my life, I was confronted with a message. I had just lost everything, again, and been brutally deceived and betrayed in the process. Suddenly, I had nothing. No hope, no future, no dream, no assets. I was driving a creaky old '95 Ford Ranger I had bought simply as an emergency plan, sweating in the 90-degree heat and wondering what I was going to do with the rest of my life. So, I drove to the park to consider my options.

I was just starting to sweat when I noticed the car behind me take off. It was a back corner of a huge park in Hendersonville, NC. I always watch cars come and go, an old habit, so I thought nothing of it. Until I noticed the woman lying in the grass. Her car door was open, which I thought was weird, but the way she was laying made it look like she was peacefully enjoying the grass, the sun, and the beautiful day. So, I finished a hotel booking, made some other plans, and otherwise started moving on with my life. I started up the old truck, flipped her around, and started heading out of the park. Then I saw the bubbles coming out of her mouth.

I slammed the truck in park, damn near ripping the engine mounts out. I was on the phone with 911 moments later, a foot away from the woman. She had crusty clothes, track marks, and otherwise smelled like she hadn't taken a shower in a long time. Honestly, I was scared to touch her because I was afraid she would wake up and swing a knife. But touch her I did, as the wonderful 911 operator coached me on how to give CPR. I followed her instructions for ten minutes until the police arrived. Then I sat there and chain-smoked as they loaded her up into the ambulance. When an officer finally walked over to me for a statement, she simply patted me on the shoulder as we watched the ambulance roar off. I asked her if she was gone and was told she would let me know later. She did end up calling me and said that she was deemed DOA at the hospital. A nice lady even gave me some hand sanitizer.

Now just think. What if that woman had been a member of your family? What if you *were* that woman? It probably took them ten minutes to get to the hospital from there. And maybe, just maybe, if things had worked out better for her, those ten minutes could have saved her life. That is what I am getting at. You never understand till you understand. And I am telling you, *under-fucking-stand*. These emergency vehicles are trying to save lives. Stories. Families. The most precious of all gifts. Get out of their way and let them do their jobs. Chances are that one day you are going to be in one and when you are you'll be praying for speed.

S.C. SANBORN

16| Van Life

I have only recently gotten back onto social media and plugged back into society after the rigors of the pandemic and all the crazy mental-health shenanigans that followed after that. As such, it would be disingenuous not to say that my idea of common themes and popularized images may be a little tainted. But the overall picture of what the popular image of taking off and hitting the road has become seems to be a customized Sprinter van filled with impossibly attractive people and thousands of dollars of customized equipment, not to mention a carefully designed array of decorations complete with a color palette designed to impress on Instagram. This popularized image of van lifestyle is bullshit and is nothing like what our media outlets and 'influencers' (ugh) make it out to be.

Don't get me wrong, van life is awesome. It is amazing to have everything you need to survive on four wheels and to be able to park and live anywhere you want. This does not mean that it's not hard, occasionally frustrating, and that it doesn't have a ton of drawbacks. For instance, you're going to need a bathroom. You can't just whip it out or squat in the middle of a neighborhood if you want to stay out of jail. And occasionally you want to be in a separate room from your dog or anyone else you are with, without having to go outside to do it. But the overall experience is one of freedom and self-reliance. Combine this with your general ability to simply pack up and drive away on a moment's notice and you have all the ingredients for a very happy alternative lifestyle.

There are a lot of things to remember when it comes to living in a van. Most people that I know are used to having a fairly large amount of space. They can collect obscene amounts of stuff. Want to generally be messy and untidy? No problem, just clean it up in the morning. This is not possible in a van. Unless you are completely comfortable living on top of all of your stuff, you are going to need to have a very limited amount of crap. Even then, you are going to want less than you need because of how complicated it becomes to store everything. It's like a backpack. Every item adds weight and all that weight becomes more of a burden with every mile.

Your social life will also change when you live in a van. You can no longer have everyone over to your house for a party. You can't travel for long periods with more people than you're comfortable sleeping in the same bed with unless some people are willing to sleep outside. And if you're mostly introverted like me, even having people in your personal space in the first place might be a big no-no. That's not to say that a social life isn't possible *outside* the van but you'll quickly realize that even that requires more work and set-up than you're used to. All told you are going to have to adapt to a much smaller space that contains tools for your survival that you haven't had to use before. You are going to have to come up with a routine that is completely different from one of living in a house or an apartment. And that's OK! Just go into the adventure knowing that it is going to be a massive change. Here are the main things to know and remember:

Give it a shot before you spend a ton of money.

When I first took off, I constantly dreamed of having a van. I landed a job at Mt. Rainier where I made a buddy who owned a baby blue Volkswagen bus. It was awesome. We took a bunch of day trips and had a blast packing everyone in there and riding off somewhere fun. Later on, after I inevitably got myself fired, I met up with them on the coast as they meandered down the highway.

Quickly, the wheels fell off. I wasn't stable, mentally or physically, and I was trying to be something I wasn't. I was packed into a van with three other guys and two girls. I started drinking heavily and, long story short, they left me behind. I don't blame them a bit. I was being an asshole. But the weird part was that I realized halfway through the trip that van life wasn't going to work for me, especially not in an old VW. I was way more into grabbing my backpack and taking off into the woods. Soon after that, I was presented with an opportunity to buy my very own van. I politely declined and bought an old AWD Subaru instead.

The trick here is to make sure that you like it before you drop a ton of money into it. We are all susceptible to the image of a beautiful, well-maintained hippie van traveling down the highway, beautiful models in the back seat, and surfboards strapped to the top. It smacks of freedom and the beauty of travel. But it is not until you do it for a week or two that you are going to have any idea whether it is for you. As I got older, I started to love van life. I became relatively more social and didn't like to have to spend so much time and money getting to the middle of nowhere. My tastes evolved. How did I figure that out? Renting a van for three weeks and taking it down the coast of Australia. It was a perfect amount of time to understand what it took to live in one permanently, without the financial commitment.

Figure out what you need.

Your build-out is going to determine how you are going to travel. I won't get too far into what to have and how to do this. I have traveled in fancy vans with all the bells and whistles just as much as I have traveled in vans with nothing but a mattress in the back. The key is to determine what you can't live without (and if that fits into your budget).

I travel. A lot. And while I can still live without a lot of stuff, my tastes and needs have definitively changed. I used to need nothing. And when I say nothing, I mean *nothing*. I would have no problem pulling up in my old F-150 and sleeping in the back of the truck with no pads, no blankets, *nothing*. That is not how I am anymore. I need an air mattress. I need an extra bag for boxers, sweatpants, and dog toys. And an extra bag of… whatever the hell it is that makes me happy. I do not, however, need a sink. Or a mini-keg. Or a portable shower. These are just the things I have found out about myself as I went.

If you're buying a van and doing a build-out, you're also going to figure these things out for yourself. You could very easily just have the van. A lot of us are very happy to simply have the space necessary to roll out a sleeping bag. Small air mattresses fit well inside these spaces as well. The same thing goes for a small mattress. Some of us, however, want to create a nest-like living space. And with the bigger vans, this becomes possible. There is room for a small bed and dishwashing space. Or a fridge and a desk. Or maybe just storage/shelving. All of these things, however, require a build-out. You have to remove the elements of the van that are already there and replace them with the electrical, plumbing, and hardware components necessary to affix these units into place. This takes time and money. This means that you aren't going to want to undertake these projects without knowing exactly what you want. Here are some very good ideas for what you *might* want to add:

- **Deep cycle batteries.** When you have a constant power draw, like a fridge, you need batteries that can provide power for long periods. It is so easy to forget about the van when you're off adventuring. Especially if a side adventure comes up. But you don't want to return days later to a dead battery and a fridge full of expired food. Plus, the smell… Don't skimp on the batteries.

- **Fans.** Vans are stuffy. You're in an enclosed area that is often well-insulated. Even with the windows open it is hard to keep the air moving. These fans, usually put in the ceilings, create airflow that moves the smells to the *outside*, where they belong.

- **Windows.** A lot of these vans start with no windows. It can seem too costly and intimidating of a project to take on but remember: you can do anything. And windows are a necessity. It can get really dark and lonely quickly without windows.

- **Curtains.** For some reason, everyone always wants to look into vans. It's a weird fact. People are weird. Have curtains.

- **Fridge.** This is lower on the list of potential stuff because of how long I have lived with just a cooler. Or just dry food. But jerky and PB&Js get old pretty fast. And even with a nice cooler, you are always spending money on ice. A fridge is an extremely handy piece of equipment. Monetarily it will pay dividends quickly if you have good batteries. It will also allow you to keep leftovers and store better, healthier ingredients to cook with.

- **Cooking area.** A fold-out table can work just as well but these can also be a giant pain in the ass to lug around and fit in the van all the time. Having a designated cooking area in the rear of the vehicle or built into the wall can be a game-changer, if only for your peace of mind.

- **Sink.** The same thing goes for a sink. I have lived for years just pouring water out of big jugs to do dishes. But having a designated area that is connected to fresh and grey water, that you simply drain and switch out as necessary, is a huge time-saver. It can be the difference between enjoying your day and being too tired to do anything fun.

- **Solar panels.** This is all about pure independence. When your power needs are taken care of by the sun you have little need for anything besides gasoline and food. Maybe some other basic supplies too. This is the best upgrade you can have for your van. They are very expensive and can make you a target for thieves, however, so keep that in mind.

- **Organizers.** I'm pretty OCD about organization. I have shelves inside my drawers and leaves inside my shelves. Everything has a place in my 'office.' So, when I travel, I do my best to have bags for certain things, shelves, and basic areas for others. Make sure you have some kind of plan for all of your stuff. And account for stuff you are inevitably going to pick up along the way.

Have the right gear.

Even if you have the perfect van you are going to struggle without the right gear. Ideally, you paid attention to the essential gear section and have all that stuff. Van life is just camping with metal around you. You're still going to need a sleeping bag for extreme cold and headlamps to see. But there are some particular pieces of gear you are going to want and need just for having around the van. The reasons for this are twofold. First, you have more room than you do with just a backpack. Second, it is a more permanent form of existing/traveling, meaning that you are going to need tools in which to facilitate that kind of lifestyle. Here are some of the things that I have found helpful to have in my van:

- **Garbage container.** Plastic bags aren't always going to cut it. Ideally, you are a person who doesn't litter and respects the Earth that we all live on. That means that all of your garbage goes into a place where it is taken care of better than simply being tossed on the ground. And when you keep this garbage, you know that eventually, it is going to smell, especially if it is left in a van all day. These containers are great because they have a bag in them and they *seal*, keeping the smell inside of the container. You know, where it belongs.

- **Food storage container(s).** Not all of your food is going to need to be refrigerated. And if you have ever stayed in actual bear country you have heard the stories. I have lived in Yosemite, where bears will regularly tear the doors off of a car to get to the peanut butter jar left on the front seat. These containers keep you and your van safe and have the added bonus of keeping all of your less-perishable food in one place.

- **Shovel.** I don't believe in port-a-potties or using a bucket for a bathroom. Then again, I am the kind of person who will walk for miles to do my business. I also keep a running list of the best-kept 'public' bathrooms in every city. So, there's that. I always keep a shovel for this reason. *Do not* be one of those assholes that behaves like dogs do. Bury your business, at least a foot below the ground.

- **Bear spray.** This is the $40 you never knew you had to spend until you see or hear your first bear. Because when you see one of these giant trash raccoons you want a sure-fire way to make them leave if they get too cozy. Unfortunately, nothing is going to do that save a high-powered rifle. But the closest thing you can get to a true bear deterrent, without killing the poor thing, is to have bear spray. A word of caution, however. Do not spray this into the wind or with the doors of your van open as it ruins the world when it goes off.

- **Netting.** I love this in vans because it can make placing regularly used items, like your phone, really easy. It can be as easy as a few screws to install and can really declutter your life. Plus, it's usually super cheap.

- **Portable toilets.** You are required in a lot of places to have a bathroom present on your vehicle. I carry a bucket for this reason. I use that bucket to soak my pans, but they don't know this. A lot of people actually use their portable toilets. And that's OK. I am not one of those people. Do your research on this one.

Commit to the work.

Everything in a van is just a little harder than in other places. Nowadays there are lots of these vans with running water, enough electricity for appliances, attachable bathroom units, complex shelving and storage space, and any number of other amenities that you can think of. But nothing will ever be as easy as having a home. You have to constantly replenish your drinking and grey water. Your electricity needs to be charged, either by solar, a hook-up, or the battery. Your food needs to be cooked, cleaned, and then the dishes washed. Usually immediately. Trust me, you are going to go nuts quickly if you aren't always tidying up after yourself. Plus, you are going to forever be taking gear in and out, rearranging bags, packing clothes, etc. It is a lot of work. If you're not ready for it, you can quickly find yourself miserable.

Commit to cleaning.

You never quite realize how important it is to keep something spotless until you use a small space to sleep, cook, hang out, and drive in. We spend a lot of our lives having different areas for all these things. Not to mention, a lot of us spend half of our time in a different place than the one where we sleep. But when you are living in a van any laziness you engage in piles up instantaneously. There is no space for dishes. Your toothbrush will immediately fall on the floor or get wedged into the sheets. Empty cans and used socks will stink up everything you own. And food will attract all manner of pests into the same sheets that you sleep on! You're going to need to keep things clean and that takes constant diligence.

Places to park and camp for free.

Part of van life is living a cheaper, less work-intensive lifestyle, and this most often means finding places to stay that don't cost 30-40 dollars per night. Who knows, this could be every night. Forever! It's up to you. And these places do exist. Some of them are obvious and a lot of them are the 'you pay for what you get' variety. But here is a basic list of places where you can stay for free. It is certainly not comprehensive, and all of these are subject to local laws, regulations, and petty local officers. The main objective is to point you in the right direction so you can start finding and locating these on your own.

- **BLM land.** BLM stands for the Bureau of Land Management. This land is public-owned and used to be (almost) completely unregulated. That has changed significantly in recent years, with some areas closed to public use and some sold off to private ventures. I am still not sure how this is legal but it is what it is. Still, there is a *ton* of this land, and it is perfectly legal to camp on for free because it is ostensibly public. This is called boon-docking and this is where a lot of the regulation involving bathroom waste and trash waste comes into play. Make sure that you are ready for someone to check you on it. It may never happen. But if it does, and you're not ready, it'll be expensive. BLM lands are also facing scrutiny and closure because so many people have treated them like crap. Either by throwing their garbage everywhere, polluting, or otherwise enacting violence on others, people have made these otherwise pristine areas an uninhabitable wasteland, which has led to the aforementioned closures. Don't be one of these people. There are tons of apps, websites, and books specifically devoted to finding this type of land.

- **National Forest land.** These are areas that are also public, and you can legally camp on them. These are *much* stricter, as they are regulated and patrolled. Have all your stuff together and you'll be just fine. And follow whatever the signs say. Waking up to a Ranger or a tow truck is a guarantee for a frustrating day.

- **Trailheads.** Trails are everywhere you want to be. Hiking is the best thing about living in this country. And it is no coincidence that the best hikes are farther away from civilization. These trailheads are often great places to park as well. Make sure to watch the signs. I've been towed from a few trailhead parking lots because I didn't take the time to read the sign. But if there aren't any signs then you can stay there for the night and get a hike in to boot.

- **Free campsites.** These used to be way more common but now everyone wants to make an extra buck or two. But they still exist! Especially out West. They are usually 'unimproved,' meaning that they don't have any running water. But they will often have pit toilets, fire rings, and designated parking spots. There are plenty of apps for this too.

- **Rest stops.** I have used these countless times. They are public, dangerous, and easily accessible. If you are driving long distances and need some rest, then you could do worse. I used to like to stop here when I was hauling ass and putting in some nighttime hours. As soon as the coffee and energy drinks (don't drink those) started to wear off, or if I couldn't think straight anymore, I would just pull off at one of these and sleep until I wasn't comfortable being there anymore. They were built for a reason. The problem is, everyone knows about them. I have woken up to foreign faces looking into my vehicle more than once. Use these often but be aware of your surroundings.

- **Visitor centers.** These are the same as rest stops, except that only half of them are cool with you parking there overnight. Look carefully for signage. And go on in and ask around. They are paid to be friendly, and often they will know good places to go if it turns out you can't stay there.

- **Truck stops.** This is a different beast. Every single truck stop is different. Different spots, different rules, different clientele, different workers, different dangers. You have to be on your toes. They are loud, busy, and potentially dangerous. But they are also chock-full of amenities and can be extremely convenient. Follow your gut on this one.

- **Walmarts.** Think rest stops that are even more dangerous, with glaring bright lights, and even louder and more frequent traffic. I hate staying in these. But no one will ever tell you to leave.

- **Sam's Clubs.** Think less populated Walmarts.

- **Cabela's.** These can be great options, especially if you need gear.

- **Cracker Barrels.** I mean, in a pinch, right? Plus, the gift shops are top-notch.

Safety.

When you have everything you own stowed in an expensive, well-built vehicle, you are going to attract the wrong kind of attention. All the places I just described above come with their fair share of danger. When you live on the road, you lose the security of walls and fences and property. The aluminum of your vehicle or the polyester of your tent are the only things separating you from the general public. And we all know what the general public is capable of. Here are some tips to keep you as safe as possible:

- **Don't put fires near your tires.** This seems simple but it is commonly forgotten, to disastrous results. Make sure that your campfires are a good distance from your van. Otherwise, you might be dealing with a bunch of damage or, God forbid, something blowing up.

- **Locks are essential.** I've owned a lot of old, old vehicles. And one of the first things that break down are the doors and lock mechanisms. You might not care about an old truck or a beater. But you are going to care with your van. If your locks don't work, you have to fix them so they do. The same thing goes for anything stored outside of the vehicle as well.

- **Have your curtains drawn.** As I mentioned, everybody tries to look inside the van, with better or worse intentions. Vans are targets for 'worse' intentions because people are assuming that you've got everything you own in there. And that some of those possessions are valuable. The easiest thing you can do to avoid break-in attempts is to simply keep your curtains closed when you're away or not paying attention.

- **Always have a hidden key.** Getting locked out of your van when you are in the middle of nowhere is terrifying. Especially when it is really cold outside. It can be a huge, life-threatening problem. The easiest way to remedy this is to buy one of those magnetic key holders, make a spare key for the outside doors, and attach it somewhere on the vehicle. I prefer to keep one on the underside of the car and one inside the engine space.

- **Make sure someone knows where you're going.** This is commonly overlooked and can be a game-changer. It's understandable to not want to bug people or to want to go recklessly exploring on whatever whim takes you that day. But if you have a buddy or a family member that you just check in with when you're heading off the grid, this can give you serious peace of mind if something sketchy happens to you while you're out there.

- **Have an extra battery pack.** Who knows, you might actually need your phone. And you might *really* need your phone after you have drained the batteries in your van. This is where a spare battery pack becomes very handy.

- **Have a weapon.** Even if you're never going to use it. It can help just to have the ability to fight back. Cheap bats, knives, and even golf clubs, all of them work. Just having a weapon and showing it off to someone acting sketchy can be enough to ward them off. I live my life by the philosophy that it is better to be a warrior in the garden than a gardener in the war. I learned this the hard way. Now you don't have to! Have something to defend yourself if the worst-case scenario occurs.

- **Keep your hood propped open when parked.** A lot of campsites have a ton of mice in the area. They gravitate towards places where there are a lot of humans because there is so much food. They have been known to crawl into the engine area of vehicles because it is warm and because something in the wires appeals to them. They chew on the wires and there goes your next day-trip plans. The way to ward this off is to pop your hood and keep it slightly raised with a stick or a piece of plastic.

- **Back into parking spots.** This is called an 'exit position' and needs to be drilled into your brain. Always, always, always be ready to take off if you need to. You don't want to ever get caught flat-footed, especially in a less-populated area.

Wisdom is seeing the end in the beginning.

The How-To Section

I remember sitting in a small closet when I was 22 years old. I was smoking pot with my friends in what we called the Green Room. It was just a closet set off to the side of the house but to us, it was a great place to hotbox and talk about life. I am not glorifying marijuana use. I was constantly high back then and it led to me going nowhere fast. I was an emotional and psychological mess, and it was only through divine intervention a few months later that I was saved from a life of mediocrity and self-pity. Anyway. I was sitting in the closet, bong between my legs, when suddenly it hit me. What if there was a manual? It was 2010 and the economy was still in the crapper. It was hard to get a job and even harder to get ahead in life, even with a freshly minted college degree. I knew for sure that I wasn't going to get any advice from my parents. So. what if there was a guidebook? What if there was a way to thrive after simply *surviving*?

What if I wrote it?

Of course, the inspiration quickly faded after another bong rip, as coherent thoughts tend to do under the influence of mind-altering chemicals. My friends shrugged off the subject and I forgot about it for a time. I was an amateur writer then as I am now, so I had a huge stack of half-used notebooks standing on every surface of my room. After taking yet another bong rip one day, I opened one of these notebooks and quickly saw that in my constant stupor, I had been taking notes about this project. Most of them were purely ego-driven, idealistic fantasies of what travel should be, but they were a beginning of sorts. I had, unwittingly, started the process of finding out what I wanted to know.

Soon after that day I gave up the bong rips and hit the road. I kept the notebooks and began to immerse myself into travel as a lifestyle. It was rough at first. As my father once told me: "I have made every mistake I could have possibly made. And you are going to make more." Great stuff from that guy. The real problem was that he was right. I found myself pushing in odd directions and doing things I wasn't comfortable with. That *is* kind of the point, but I could have avoided some of the situations I put myself in and been the better for it. I frequently found myself gambling, and not with money. With opportunities. This led to a lot of time spent with little funds trying to figure out how to not spend them. And voilà! I was forced to figure out how to survive in the woods for three days while I waited for a call back from the hiring manager. Or how to reattach my tailpipe in the middle of a desolate Wyoming highway. You get the picture.

As I went along the notebooks piled up. Due to a mixture of negative be-liefs, thought patterns, and trauma I picked up in my childhood, I always talked myself out of actually writing the sections. But I still collected notes and paid attention whenever I learned something new. Which was *all the time*. It took my horrifically awful marriage to push me over the top. I knew some things alright and now I had the alone time necessary to put them on the page. If you're going to have a quarter or mid-life crisis, might as well just go for it, right? Right. So without further ado, from a closet full of smoke, to some extremely well-traveled steno pads, to your hands, here is a section about how to do all the things. Hopefully, it will save you some trouble down the road.

17 | How To: Be In a Car Wreck

Sometimes you're going to get fucked. Anyone who has ever been in a bicycle or motorcycle wreck knows that there is a full second where you know you are about to crash, you know there is nothing you can do about it, and you know it is going to *hurt*. The same thing goes for a car wreck. You can drive slowly, own the safest car, wear your seat belt, and have zero potential projectiles in your cupholders. And you should do these things if you can. But sometimes that doesn't mean jack. Maybe some dumbass is trying to pick up their donuts from the foot space of the passenger seat while their beat-up minivan is rapidly crossing into your lane. Or a drunk is blowing through the red light and t-boning you. Life happens and it isn't fair. Here are some things you can do to help your chances:

- **Don't overreact.** This is included in the Driving section but bears repeating. I can't count how many collisions I was able to narrowly avoid by not yanking on the wheel or slamming on the brakes. When you start sliding or see something in your path, never yank the wheel. It might save that squirrel but it is going to flip your car or put you in the ditch. The same thing goes for stomping on the brakes. You aren't going to stop immediately. And slamming the brakes is the easiest way to go into an uncontrolled skid. You want to do what you can do, without losing control of the vehicle.

- **Mitigate the damage.** At this point, you're going to be in a wreck. There's nothing you can do about that. What you *can* do is to make the damage and danger as little as possible. That means avoiding a head-on collision or slamming into a tree. Those are the worst-case scenarios. If you can help it, and you usually can, you want to hit the ground or the bushes. No matter what you do, it's going to hurt. You want it to hurt *less*.

- **Loosen up.** This sounds impossible, and it oftentimes can be, but try your best to not tighten up, clench, or hunch forward. Your body is going to get tossed around like a ragdoll. The only thing that is going to make this worse is if you are already tensed up to the absolute max. When that happens, and then you are hit with great force, your body is fighting itself, maximizing the damage.

- **Look straight ahead.** In a major wreck, it is almost a guarantee that you are going to come out of it with some serious neck pain or injury. The whiplash alone is enough to concuss you, not to mention cause intense issues with the muscles and fascia in your neck. The only way that you can make this worse is to be looking sideways or diagonally. This puts even more strain on your poor neck. If you can, look straight.

- **Praying doesn't hurt either.**

18| How To: Buy a Used Car

This section was tough to write because every single piece of advice comes with the caveat of potentially not being true. Luckily for you, I don't give two shits about potentially being wrong. Because if I can help one person who needs it, then this was all worth it. Also, hopefully, I am sitting on a small slice of beach that I own by now, drinking organic ginger ale and watching the world burn. Anyway!

There are a ton of ways to buy a used car. None of them are fun and all of them are going to try to have you pay more than the car is worth. My favorite method is using Craigslist because that is where you are going to find the most people who are selling their car person-to-person. There are other options for finding these as well. I like old, used cars that look like crap but have good engines, so take this opinion with a grain of salt. Here's a rundown of your options:

Craigslist

These listings are super cheap for the car owner and are virtually unregulated, so this is kind of the Wild West of car sales. You can find a ton of 'lemons' (cars that look good but are bound to fail quickly and cost the new owner a ton of money) and you can find a ton of deals. What you are looking for is a motivated buyer who wants to get rid of their car. These people are often moving, selling the car for someone else, or just needing money due to some misfortune. This doesn't mean that you should try hard to haggle and take them for all their worth, this just means that you are most likely to get the correct price for the car that you are buying.

I always go to Kelley Blue Book and punch in the values for the car before I go to look at it. This gives you a basic range for what the car is worth before you even show up. Then, if you discover a bunch of things wrong with the car while you are there and still want to make an offer, you can adjust the numbers accordingly.

I'm assuming that you're looking for older cars as these most likely fit into your budget. What you are looking for with these older cars is an engine that sounds good and looks good and then has purely cosmetic things wrong with it. As cars age things are going to stop working. Sticky door handles, a broken glove box, torn seats, etc. These are easily fixable and, most importantly, the parts are cheap to get. What isn't cheap are crucial parts of the vehicle that have broken, like the fuel gauge, catalytic converter, and transmission. And rust. Always look for rust. This is likely most prevalent on the bottom of a car. If there is a ton of rust, walk. There's no going back from a rusted-out frame.

Always do a basic search of what common problems are with the car. When you show up with a list of said problems, ask the owner if they've ever had them fixed. If you think they are lying about anything you are most likely right. Cosmetic issues can be dealt with. What can't be dealt with easily are problems with the engine. And if you aren't comfortable gauging the quality of an engine by looking at it? Congratulations! You're just like everyone else. Most people will try to pretend they know more about cars than they actually do. So be prepared for people to throw around a lot of technical terms and jargon. They are typically just trying to prove that they have done a lot of work on the vehicle themselves. It's up to you to decide whether they have or not. Most often I walk when this happens. I tend to buy cars from people who don't know that much. They are usually more honest, so if the car breaks down and I get screwed on the deal, then at least my money went to a good person.

Once you have done the visual inspection the engine has to be checked, unless your gut is telling you otherwise and the price is right. This is a great time to take the car to a mechanic. If the seller says this isn't necessary or recommends a mechanic, that's a red flag. If they do offer up 'someone they know' don't take the car to where they want you to. Go to a random mechanic or, ideally, your own mechanic, and have them do a brief inspection. This should either be free or cost less than $150 (don't quote me on this, inflation is a bitch). This won't completely remove any concerns, but they can check a lot of boxes. Have 'em give you a thumbs up or a thumbs down.

As I mentioned before, I like to buy old cars. I look for a lot of cosmetic faults and an engine that works pretty well, with less than 175 thousand miles. Ideally less than 150. If it is an automatic, this is the mile range you might start to see problems with the transmission. For almost all cars a faulty transmission is a deal breaker because of how much it costs to replace. If that isn't an issue, think about what you could fix yourself. I like to buy these cars and then put some sweat into them. Not only does it make me feel good to replace what I can replace on them (you'd be surprised what you can do yourself), but it also dramatically improves the value of the car. So, when I sell them later on, I usually make a good chunk. Regardless, after the deal is done and I am the new owner, I always take the car to a transmission specialist and get their opinion. This should be free or cost very little.

I also 'poll' various mechanics that offer free estimates. This is a little exploitative, so I tip the mechanic that did the work $20 for their time. They will invariably give you an itemized list of all the things they recommend should be replaced. If you do this 2-3 times you get a really good idea of what *actually* needs to be replaced by what pops up multiple times. The added bonus to this is you can see which mechanics are trying to take you for all you're worth. If you have ever done this you are smiling and nodding right now, because mechanics are famous for adding things you don't need. This is also a great way to find a good mechanic if you do want to make some immediate repairs.

This is a good time to mention that with these old cars, you are frequently going to run into issues with the odometer. This isn't as much of an issue with newer cars because the odometers are now electronic and have typically been recorded with the DMV. This wasn't always a requirement. This means that with a lot of newer used cars, you can pay for a service online to take a look at the history of the vehicle and that there is a paper trail of odometer readings. If you are looking at one of these next to the odometer reading that should be on the title and the numbers just don't add up, then the odometer has likely been tampered with and you should walk. If the car is *really* old and they say that it has 'rolled over' (meaning that there wasn't a sixth digit and the numbers only go up to 99,999), automatically assume that the car has 100,000 more miles than they say it does. This isn't automatically a deal-breaker. Some people, yours truly included, take exquisite care of their automobiles. If you stamp out rust, minor faults, leaks, and faulty parts as they arise you can keep a vehicle going indefinitely. But, if you don't know much about cars and you're looking at a very old car with a bunch of new parts that you don't understand (and they keep saying: "Well *this* engine is new, all *new* parts!") then definitely take it in for an opinion or walk. Just make sure to be respectful, because even if you don't understand, they still took the time to meet with you and might know what they are talking about.

Here are some quick additional tips to watch for with odometer fraud:

- **A ton of cars have their odometers manipulated.** Get a report on the car and intensely look at the numbers presented. If there is any discrepancy, politely ask the owner why that is.

- **Check for oil change or maintenance stickers that might have a mileage marker.** These should line up with what the seller is claiming as well.

- **Look at the tires.** If the mileage is as low as they claim it to be there should be plenty of tread. With old cars, this doesn't necessarily mean that they should be original, but if they are heavily worn down this can be a warning sign.

- **Check the pedals.** Another sign of heavy use, maybe higher than they are representing, will be shown on the gas and brake pedals. If they are worn to a nub and the owner is telling you that this was their grandpa's truck that mostly sat in the driveway, they are lying. The same thing goes for the front seats and truck beds.

- **Check the maintenance logs.** Even seasoned 'gearheads' take their vehicles in for certain services. While they may be very capable of swapping an alternator, certain services require the engine or the entire car to be lifted, which they might not have the equipment or time for. This means that they should have maintenance records from this being done. At the time of service, there should also be an odometer reading.

- **Never buy an old truck expecting the perks of a new one or for it to work perfectly.** I will never forget a couple I showed an old truck to in Portland, OR. I drove halfway across the city to accommodate them, then they were snobby, rude, and wouldn't listen to anything I had to say. They treated me like a used-car salesman and seemed to be shocked that the windows and door handles were creaky, all for a really good older truck that I had put a ton of sweat into. Newsflash! Don't expect the car owner to let you test drive the car without them in it! Bless their hearts. I ended up selling the truck to a gearhead a week later. He still messages me occasionally with gratitude and pictures of things he fixed in the truck. Somethings just work out, you know?

- **Pay attention to the details.** With a person-to-person sale you'll also really want to make sure the paperwork is right. The seller should have two types of ID. One will do but most sellers know they should have two. You'll need to print out a Bill of Sale. Every state has a place on its website to print one out that accurately details the information needed later to register the car. Do this! Twice! Then lay out their ID, your ID, the Bill of Sale, the title for the car, and their proof of insurance. The proof of insurance isn't necessary at all but if they are who they say they are they will have a copy. The point of all this is you are confirming that they indeed own the car. This is achieved by comparing their ID to the title and their insurance. Once you prove that you're talking to the real owner go ahead and check the signature on their ID. When they sign the title over to you (there is a place on the back for this), and sign the Bill of Sale, all the signatures should match. Once all these things are completed and you've handed them cash, electronically sent them money, or transferred crypto, then the car is yours and you can drive away. I usually pull over just out of sight of the old owner, get on my phone, and buy a cheap insurance policy. You never know. You can wait to do this till you get home but why risk it?

Auto Trader

There are other sites just like this but as of the writing of this book, this is the most prevalent and widely used. I like these kinds of sites for buying what I call 'mid-range' cars, or cars that aren't really old but that are not new. This is a much more streamlined process than privately listed vehicles. Typically, this will lead you to a dealership. Only go this route if you are buying in cash. Dealerships will buy a car for a discount, invest in a minimum of maintenance and repair, then make a ton of money off of the interest you pay monthly after you take a loan from them for the car. Hence, only buy in cash. Because the actual margin on the sale price is so low, they probably won't haggle. The same thing goes for listings on these sites made by private owners. They have also done their research and homework, investing money to maximize the sale price of the vehicle. There isn't as much wiggle room if the vehicle is in top-notch shape.

These cars usually have a lot less wrong with them. The key then is to look at the car, look at how many similar cars are available, then do a basic web search of what common problems are with that car. Ratings and reviews are typically worthless but, in this case, they can oftentimes help you avoid bad car models and years. Because sites like this will only sell cars without cars having been in 'the system' their entire existence, meaning that you can pull electronic records. Make sure to do this. You're looking for the maintenance records, particularly for those issues commonly associated with the vehicle. If there are common problems that aren't addressed in the vehicle records, this can give you leverage when you're negotiating terms and pricing.

CarMax or Carvana or whatever.

I had always dreamed of this, and I am glad I never pulled the trigger on it. My experience with one of these kinds of dealerships came when I had to sell a used Toyota. I was in the middle of my divorce, and I kept finding myself talking to my ex-wife in the passenger seat… even though she wasn't even in the same state. Yeah, I had to get rid of it. So, I started to go through the motions, listing it in various places and taking it to the local dealerships to see what they would offer me. Luckily, when I went into CarMax, I didn't have high hopes, so I wasn't disappointed.

The salesman took his time looking over my exquisitely maintained truck. Sure, it had some little things wrong with it, but it was in excellent mechanical shape, especially considering it has such high mileage at this point. He even remarked to me about how well it was working! And yet, when he handed me an offer it was low. Way low. As in, three or four thousand less than the scumbag dealership I had just walked out of an hour before. I looked at him and he sheepishly asked me what I thought. I said nothing, aside from thanking him for his time, and walked out. That's all I ever need to know about one of these services.

These companies exist because people hate buying cars. You are paying an absolute premium for not having to do any shopping and not having to deal with annoying salesmen. This premium can be hefty as you end up paying 5-10% more than the 'fair' price for these vehicles. In my case, I was selling a vehicle and they offered me less than half what I ended up selling it for. Phew! I always advocate for people to avoid having a car that they cannot afford because for me it ends up being cheaper to fix the car as I go along than to continue to pay a company for the privilege of driving their car till the day I own it. But I'm opinionated and I completely understand anyone's desire to have a solid, safe vehicle of their own to get them around. If that's your jam and you're cool with being in debt for a while then this is the easiest and most convenient way to get a car.

Dealerships

Unless you are buying a used car at one of these lots with cash, and you can avoid it, don't go this route. It's like credit cards and rent. You are paying someone a ton of money just for the privilege of driving the car you want and paying for its repairs until you actually own it, which can take a long time. Car dealerships exist and survive by buying cars for as cheap as possible, paying an in-house mechanic to do the bare minimum of repairs necessary to pass inspection, selling right at the recommended margin that most people will pay, and then getting you to voluntarily sign up for an exorbitant interest rate on the loan that they applied to a rapidly deteriorating investment. Indeed, an investment that loses a massive percentage of its value the second you drive it off the lot. Wait what? All that sounded normal till the last part? Exactly.

Just like a credit card company, dealerships want you to spend money that you don't have. They couldn't care less what you 'haggle' the price of the vehicle down to. They are trying to get you to take a loan from them that you pay a ridiculous amount of interest for. Dealerships are just credit card companies that only let you spend the money on the car you 'bought.' On top of this, they want you to buy maintenance packages, upgrades, infotainment systems, etc. All in the name of increasing the amount you are borrowing and thus, the amount of interest that comes into their pockets. And if you miss a payment? They can take that car right back from you.

If you need a car and don't have any cash saved up, well, everybody's got to eat. Sometimes we have to do things we'd rather not do to get ahead. I would rather take the bus and struggle for a few months so that I could afford a junk car as opposed to being tied to a loan for a car I couldn't afford, but that's just me. You are you. Just know that buying from a dealership comes with a hefty cost. And there is a reason that they have such a bad reputation. Go into any negotiation at one of these places with a stern wariness and you'll be fine. Always be ready to walk, even if that means that you are literally walking away. And if you are signing up for a loan, make sure it is the smallest possible number, with the lowest number of monthly payments that you can afford. You want to pay off any loan as fast as you can. The alternative is being stuck in a job, lifestyle, and financial servitude that you might not want to be in for longer than you ever wanted to.

19 | How To: Change Your Oil

Alright, I might have said not to do this but some of you are going to do it anyway. It's cheaper, it's more satisfying, and damnit, this is America. I also started getting really into automotive maintenance while I was halfway through this book, so I figured I'd add this section so that if you *are* going to change your oil, you can do it cleanly and efficiently. Now, not all cars are the same. Some are much more complicated than others. These are just the basic practices and methods for changing your oil. Proceed with caution. When in doubt, ask YouTube. With that in mind, here's a list of the gear and tools you'll need:

- **Latex gloves.**
- **Drip pan (at least five quarts, probably more).**
- **Socket wrench set or adjustable wrench.**
- **Jack stands.**
- **Wheel blocks/chocks.**
- **Torque bar.**
- **Oil filter.**
- **New oil (probably five quarts, maybe more).**
- **Paper towels.**

Don't omit any of these tools or materials. Starting to see why I recommended just going to the shop? You're looking at more than the price of an oil change just to get the right tools *and* you then have to haul them around with you to make it worth it. You can make it work with just an adjustable wrench in a pinch but then you risk over-torquing the bolt or, even worse, *under*-torquing the bolt. Then you are leaving yourself with a mess and an un-functioning vehicle, most likely in a far-out location. With that said, here's how to do it:

Park on a flat surface.

You're going to want to raise your vehicle. You can get under a lot of cars without doing so but it isn't recommended. You want to make sure that your car isn't going to fall or roll on top of you, and this means raising the tires above the ground. To do this effectively, you need to be on a flat surface.

Put the car in park, remove the keys, put the parking brake on, then place chocks behind the back wheels.

Pieces of wood can work as chocks, but it is always recommended to have actual angled chocks for this.

Raise the vehicle.

A simple jack will work, it is just a much more laborious process. Ideally, you are in a garage somewhere and you have a floor jack but that isn't always going to happen. If you *do* have a floor jack, just find a sturdy center point of the frame and pump it up high enough to fit the jack stands underneath each side of the frame. If you are using a simple jack, locate the divots in the frame that show you where to place the jack, then raise one side of the vehicle. When it is elevated, place the jack stand underneath that side of the frame. Then repeat for the other side.

Let the car sit for 15-20 minutes.

You want the engine, and the oil inside, to cool off enough to be tolerable. If you don't, you risk scalding yourself with hot oil, and trust me, that is a very painful and expensive lesson to learn.

Push down on the hood and gently wiggle the car around.

You're making sure that the car is stable and isn't going to move and/or fall. If the car is moving a lot, especially back and forth, then either the jack stands aren't level or your wheel blocks aren't effective. Either way, you're going to have to put the car back down, find a flatter spot, and try again.

Put your oil pan beneath the drain plug.

Once your car is stable you can start draining the oil. You should have no problem finding the drain plug. It'll be within a foot or two of the front of your car and sits directly beneath the engine. Your drain pan should be more than five quarts so that it catches all the oil.

Remove the oil cap from the top of the engine.

It will say 'oil' on it, unless the car is so old that it has worn off. In that case, it is a cap that is about two inches wide, and it will be sitting directly on top of the engine. Wipe off the threads then place this face-up on top of a paper towel. Keep the threads clean, as any dirt or debris that finds its way onto the threads is going to end up in your engine.

Put gloves on.

You are at the (potentially) dirty part. And getting oil off of your hands is not always the easiest thing to do, especially if you aren't near a sink.

Un-torque the drain bolt.

Grab some sockets and figure out what size fits the drain bolt. Once you do, take your socket wrench and apply pressure in a counterclockwise manner until the bolt starts coming loose. A crescent wrench or adjustable wrench will also work here, just be careful not to damage the bolt. As soon as the bolt is loose put the wrench down and unscrew the rest of the way with your hand. This is important because as you are unscrewing the bolt, you want to apply pressure *back* toward the oil pan. This is to stop the rush of oil from drenching your arm. Once you think you've got the bolt all the way loose, swiftly move the bolt downward and away, while keeping your hand away from the stream of oil headed toward the pan. Try to get the metal washer in between the bolt and the pan along with it so that it doesn't fall into the pan. If it does, you're going to have to fish it out. If it sticks, just wait till the oil is finished draining and come back for it later.

Wait for it to drain.

I have always heard that it takes three or four minutes for the oil to finish draining, but I have never actually seen it happen this fast. Maybe my cars are older and bigger than the norm. Or maybe it's just because I have OCD. Whatever. I always let it sit for ten minutes.

Reattach the drain plug bolt.

Gently wipe down the drain plug and bolt threads, pat dry the oil pan threads, reattach the metal or plastic washer to the drain plug bolt, and thread it into place. Once it becomes too difficult to thread with your hands, grab your torque wrench. You'll want to find the specifications for your vehicle for how much torque your bolt will need, then (as gently as you can) apply it till the wrench clicks. This is how to get the bolt as tight as it needs to be to stay on but not too tight as to break anything. If you don't have a torque wrench, that's OK. You'll have to feel it out. Keep in mind, this is where the whole thing can get messed up. If you over-torque it, the bolt can snap, or worse, crack the oil pan. It's best to err on the side of caution. Just tighten it a reasonable amount, tight enough that it gives you some resistance, but not so much that you're going to tear a bicep. Also, make sure that you pull over after a few miles and scope out whether the drain plug is still on there. If it's not, you will definitely know!

Swap out the oil filter.

You don't *have* to do this for every oil change. You *should*, but you don't *have* to. It's usually not too tough but if it hasn't been done in a while, or if the last person to do it torqued it on way too tight, you might need a special tool to extract it. Before you start make sure to correctly identify where the filter is for your respective vehicle. There is no standard place. They can be on the back, the front, or either side of the engine. The good part is that, because of this, oil filters are often made in bright colors. Whenever I replace my oil filter I always tend to get bright orange ones, regardless of the actual quality, because they are easier to find on the next swap. Of course, these are only the 'older' versions. A lot of newer cars have custom jobs where you need a special tool to open the filter cartridge, then you have to insert the filter into the opened housing.

When you've located the filter, put your drip tray underneath it. There's not always a ton of oil in it but sometimes there is, and this can cause a serious mess. Once you've got the tray in a good spot, twist the filter or filter housing counterclockwise (to the left). This is when you'll find out if some jackass 'torqued' it on, making it almost impossible to get off. This is where an oil filter wrench becomes essential. They are designed to fit into the 'grips' of the filter. Suddenly, the last twenty minutes, where you were desperately trying to apply enough pressure and torque to get your filter off, seem much more futile as this wrench will pull the filter off easily. As soon as the filter drops, pull it out of the pan and make sure that the gasket is on it. If it's *not*, reach into the now vacated hole and pull it out. If you install the new filter, typically with a new gasket already attached, and the old gasket is still in there, you're going to cause a leak and a host of other problems.

The last step is to install the new filter. It's very, very satisfying. Grab your new filter, with the gasket gently installed onto it, and rub some oil around the gasket ring. This makes it seal better and ensures that you'll be able to get it off on the next go-around. If you're comfortable with it, and if it's possible, you can also add a couple of teaspoons of oil into the filter, which will speed up the process of regaining oil pressure. If you forget to do this (raises hand), just make sure to run the vehicle for a considerable amount of time before you drive it. Screw on the filter, gently at first, making sure that is threaded correctly. If you find intense resistance halfway through screwing it on, then it is cross-threaded and cattywampus. If this is the case, gently back it off and try again. If it continues to smoothly screw in, apply more pressure as you go. You can check the torque specs but usually, the maximum hand strength of the average person is right on the money, so just squeeze and turn as hard as you can.

Add oil.

The amount is different for every vehicle. The same thing goes for the type of oil. You'll have to look this up. The oil cap, however, is much easier to find. It's on the top of the engine and always says "oil" right on top of it. If you've followed all the steps I have listed, then this cap should be sitting face-up on a paper towel in a clean location. I carry around a small funnel at all times because my old trucks are leaky bastards. These funnels are cheap and can work for all of your fluids. If you don't have one of these, grab a piece of paper and roll it up from one of the corners until it's in a funnel shape. Then rip the bottom corner ever so slightly so that the makeshift funnel can sit flat on the oil pan. These makeshift funnels can only hold up for so long, so make sure to get all the oil you need in on the first or second try.

Replace the fill cap.

Did you hear me? Replace the fill cap. Replace it! It sucks when you forget to do this, and it is arguably the easiest thing to do in all of car maintenance.

Start the car.

You'll want to check the dashboard to make sure the oil pressure gauge reads right, and you'll want to leave it on for a while so that the oil pressure can stabilize. This is a good time to go check the dipstick too. Make sure that it reads a healthy amount, not too much, and not bone dry.

Check for leaks.

Don't worry too much if there's a little smoke or a few drops of oil here and there. Being your own mechanic is a messy job. Do worry if there is a ton of oil coming out. That means that you messed something up or forgot one of the steps.

Get rid of the old oil.

Most drip pans these days have a spigot or pour spout built into the actual pan. And most times you do this you'll be buying the big five-quart containers of oil. Put some paper towels underneath the used oil container, then gently pour the drip pan into the jug. A funnel is perfect here as well. When you're done, wipe off the sides and take it to the next auto parts store you find. Almost all of them recycle oil. If they don't, go to the next one down the street. Recycling centers usually take oil now as well.

20 | How To: Chop Wood

To me, there is no better feeling than turning a tree into a pile of highly burnable pieces of wood. The feeling of accomplishment, of providing for myself, and of mastering a basic tenet of survival, gives me a boost of confidence and satisfaction. If you don't know the feeling, go chop some wood. Then make a fire with it. You'll get what I'm talking about really quickly.

Even if you don't particularly like chopping wood it is often a necessity. We have to stay warm and a lot of us do this by burning firewood. You *can* buy your firewood already chopped. But that makes it expensive. To make it worth it, you have to chop your own. And if you do it wrong, and with the wrong tools, it can be exhausting. It might even cause injury. So, with that in mind, here's how to properly chop a bunch of firewood:

Have the right tools.

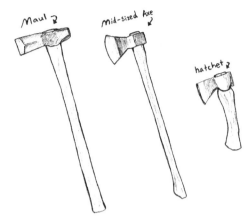

There are a lot of people out there who think that they are going to chop major logs with just a hatchet, or with a $20 mid-sized axe. Because they heard that you're 'supposed' to use an axe. What you need is a maul. It is much more like a sledgehammer than an axe. It is heavier, yet it's easier (more on that later). And yes, you do need a mid-sized axe and a hatchet, but the majority of the work will get done with a maul.

Get the right base.

You're going to need a solid surface to chop on and you don't want this surface to be on the ground. What you want is a raised surface about knee height. This means that the logs you're chopping will most likely come up to your belly button or sternum. If you are swinging your axe/maul and your swing ends up with you reaching downward or bending over, your surface isn't high enough. Ideally, you have a massive stump or log for this purpose. I always take the log that looks the hardest to chop and use it for this first. If it somehow splits, good for me! If it doesn't? Well, screw that log anyway. If you can't find a massive stump or equally massive piece of wood for this purpose, do your best to find the most level piece of ground you can.

Set your log.

Take the log you want to chop and set it so that it stands vertically on your base. You want this to sit dead center of the base because you don't want it to fall off. Also, make sure that any knots or burls on your target log are closer to the base log. If you are chopping straight into the burl or the knot it can prevent the log from splitting and make your work harder.

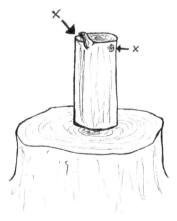

Chop with the grain.

Wood is 'arranged' in a visible pattern. It is called the grain. You can easily see what direction this is 'flowing' by looking at the log. You want to chop so that the direction of the blade goes with the direction of the grain. This will dramatically increase your chances of getting a clean split on the first try.

Let the maul/axe do the work.

A lot of people tire themselves out unnecessarily by trying to drive *through* the log. Not only does this increase the chances of you missing and thereby hitting something besides the log (i.e. your foot), but it is also completely unnecessary. Gravity, acceleration, and the weight of the blade itself should be enough to split the log. If they aren't there is most likely a knot or burl in the way, and you need to flip the log to the other side anyway.

Adopt a wide stance and line up the blade with the target (dead center of the log). Then raise the blade behind you and as you bring it down on the target let the blade 'fall' into the center of your target. Keep a good grip on the maul/axe.

Keep cutting in half.

Don't try to 'shave' a log. Always aim for the middle of whatever you are cutting. And as you continue cutting pieces in half, keep cutting them in half. You should end up with at least four pieces for every log you chop. If you keep missing, switch to either your mid-sized axe or your hatchet. If a piece is just too damn stubborn then just leave it as-is and go to the next one. Don't waste all of your energy on one piece of wood!

Pile as you go.

Stacking the wood is just as important as chopping it. You want it to 'season,' meaning you want it to dry out and weather so it will burn easier when it comes time. I find that if I chop 8-10 logs, I end up with about 40 pieces of wood. Then my work area is intensely cluttered, and I need to stack them to get them out of the way anyway. This is also important for avoiding injury. It's really easy to roll an ankle on a piece of wood laying on the ground. Stack them as you go, and this won't be a problem.

Cut kindling with the hatchet.

I usually take the straightest and most uniform pieces of wood and start to chop them into smaller and smaller halves. You are looking for the thinnest pieces you can get without lopping off part of your hand. Ideally, these are about the width of your thumb and a foot long. This process is physically easier but requires a great deal more attention because narrower or smaller pieces of wood typically don't stand upright on their own. This usually means that you have to hold them in place, at least temporarily, as you chop them. I take my chosen piece and try to have it stand alone on my base. I then take my hatchet and cleanly slice through the middle. Because this requires focus, don't emphasize cleanly separating the piece in one swing. If you can do that, great! But if you can't, just get your hatchet firmly lodged into the target log on the first swing, then pick up the log with the now-attached hatchet and bring the whole thing down on the base. Repeat as necessary.

If you cannot get these smaller logs to stand alone, or if you keep missing, you're going to need to hold them up with one hand as you swing the hatchet with the other. This is dangerous as you can easily cut your hand. As such, I don't recommend it. If you're like me, you're going to do it anyway. So to do this, hold the target log upright on your base and as you (gently) swing down with your hatchet pull your off-hand away. I mention the word 'gently' because you want to focus on hitting your target rather than chopping through the whole piece. Smaller logs require much less force and kindling even less so. Safety first! At least, that's what my lawyer tells me.

21 | How To: Cut Down a Small Tree

Anyone can cut down a tree. The important word to remember here is 'small.' Now, I am not saying that anyone can't cut down a large tree. It might be exactly the same as cutting down a small tree. But I am not saying that. I am saying, explicitly, that this is how to cut down a 'small' tree. Because if you get killed cutting down a big tree it's on you and I am not liable. So definitely don't do that. But if you need firewood, or if you're making a shelter, and need a 'small' tree to do that, this is how you do that. Are we all on the same page? Fantastic. Now, for all these instructions, I am assuming that you're going to be using an axe. If you want to use a chainsaw the directions are basically the same. But not exactly. And using a chainsaw means you need a bunch more safety gear. For this, I am assuming that all you have is a maul (for chopping), a medium-sized axe, and a hatchet for the smaller stuff.

Pick your tree(s).

There are a ton of factors that go along with this. Don't bite off more than you can chew. Remember, you're using an axe, so you are going to have to manually chop this thing down. If I have the choice, I like to pick trees that already have a slight bend to them. I automatically expect the tree to fall in the way that it's bending. And this way, I can visualize how much space I am going to need/have and thereby plan how I am going to get the hell out of the way. It's really important to try and size up anything that might catch it on the way down. Trees are unpredictable when they are falling. It's not out of the question for them to fall a little, then flip the other way as they come down. Try and gauge if there are any other trees, lines of any kind, etc. Anything that could catch on the branches and send it back in your direction.

Start your notch.

You are going to cut two of these but the first one needs to be in the direction that you would like it to fall. Ideally, you've picked a tree that has a slight lean in one direction, the 'pathway' is clear of anything that will catch it on the way down, and the terrain allows you to take clean swings at the trunk. You want to cut your notch at a height that is good for your natural swing. You're trying to get the vast majority of the tree to fall. You can always come back and cut off the rest of it later.

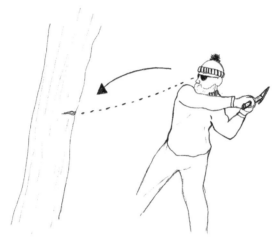

Aim somewhere from waist to knee high and put some force into it. The first swings are going to define where and what your notch is going to look like.

You want to hurt the tree on these cuts. Come in horizontally with as much force as you can reasonably muster and make sure your blade sinks in.

Once you've set the 'bottom' of this notch, then carve out the rest of the notch by cutting *downward* toward the 'bottom' that you created with the first swing. I like to do three horizontal chops and then two chops that are downward at an angle. This keeps me from tiring out and starts to carve the notch. Don't go deeper than a third of the way into the tree. If you do the tree might start to 'pinch' the blade. Once you are satisfied with the notch, give a couple of swings in a slightly upward fashion to carve out a downward slope to the bottom of the notch. If the tree doesn't follow the exact path downward that you are intending, which happens, then you'll have a higher chance of having the trunk still fall in the direction of the notch. After you are done you should have a notch that looks like this:

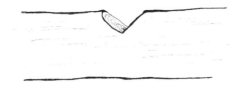

Start your second notch.

Head around the tree and line up a spot about a foot higher than your first notch. This should be directly across from the first notch on the other side of the tree. You are now standing on the opposite side of where the tree is going to fall. Never, ever take your eyes off of the tree at this point. You just never know. Some trees are stubborn, ruthless bastards, and some flop and crack with the flimsiest breeze. Start your notch with a bunch of serious, deep horizontal cuts. Again, you're trying to hurt the tree with these swings. Give it a few more horizontal swings in the same spot to set the horizontal 'bottom' edge. Then give it two or three downward, angled swings. You are aiming for a notch with a horizontal 'bottom' and a 45-degree angle toward the middle of the tree from the top. After I size up where the notch is going to be I like to alternate with one or two horizontals then two or three downward, angled cuts. Don't go deeper than a third of the tree. You aren't fully ready to knock it down yet.

Bring it down.

This is the part that can get hairy. Remember how you are never taking your eyes off the tree? That continues here, except now you add an intense skittishness to your mentality. You are a rabbit in a closed pen with a bunch of wolves. Have absolutely no hesitation to drop everything and bolt at the very tickle of a floating spiderweb strand. Because now you return to your original notch and start to deepen it. You should have a good idea of where the tree is bending and in which direction you want it to fall. Therefore, you need to be standing to the *side*, parallel to the direction you are trying to get the tree to fall along. There are two schools of thought here. One is to give swift, intense, powerful cuts to *make* the tree fall. The other is to give 'half' swings that drop the tree a little slower. This depends on your mentality. Each of these tactics works, but if you are nervous then take your time. Most trees will groan as they go down, giving you a solid half-second to react. Some, however, are evil little shits and come down directly toward you as a last, solitary middle finger. By the time the top of the tree can move five feet, you should already be ten to fifteen feet away. And don't stop till you *know* that you're clear.

Chop it up.

I always head back to the stump that I created when I dropped the tree. I don't believe in wasting something that *was* alive and blessed me with its being. But I'm spiritual. If you don't think that way, then just think about the next person to come along. Leaving jagged stumps behind can be a serious hazard. I always take the time to cut it down to a less hazardous height.

Next, you're going to want to head to the tree itself. Start by hacking off all the branches and breaking those down into their constituent parts, then drag them to their relevant piles. You'll need all these pieces later on so it's easier to deal with them immediately. When you're done with that the real work starts. You have to cut up the tree itself into 'log-sized' pieces. If you're doing this with solely an axe, then you're going to want to cut these into fire-sized pieces right off the bat. When you're done with each log it's going to be difficult, if not impossible, to stand it up and split it. Make it 'fire ready' in the beginning and it will make your life easier later. Even if you chopped this tree down with an axe, this is the point where you will want a chainsaw. If you don't have one of those, well, take breaks and remember to hydrate.

22 | How To: Deal with a Fear of Flying

Flying sucks. I've never understood people that like it. You're crammed into an aluminum cigar box, pressurized, dragged 30,000 feet in the air, inundated with high levels of radiation, virtually forced to make inane small talk with nervous and chatty travelers, and generally herded and abused from airport to airport. And the booze they sell is a filthy lie. No matter what the label says it's always the cheapest, nastiest concoction that they can get away with giving to humans. And for what? To save a few hours or days of travel? Flying sucks.

We're still going to fly though. I'm certainly not going to swim across the Atlantic and you won't be finding me on a cruise ship any time soon. So, we have to get over the fear, that gripping, crushing anxiety that sends earthquakes of stress across our chest with every bump of turbulence. We have to keep it together. Here's how to make the best of it.

Ignore everything everyone has ever told you.

Everyone tries to tell you that flying an airplane is the safest way to travel. That *statistically* it is way safer to fly on an airplane than it is to drive on the highway. It's *only* one in every seven million flights that crash and kill everyone aboard! Yeah. Don't pay any attention to that crap. You are strapped to a fucking rocket, flying through the air at 500 miles per hour, with someone at the controls that you don't know and certainly don't trust. The airplane you are in is mechanically supervised by the completely unreliable Air Traffic Organization and the Federal Aviation Administration. These are the same people who blindly authorized the roll-out of the Boeing 737 MAX. Yes, the only thing between you and the abject degradation of capitalism on the mechanical operations of this aluminum coffin is an organization that has been *proven* to be political and unreliable.

Ready to panic? Don't. These are all the facts that your subconscious already knows. The anxiety of flying comes from trying to tamp down these perfectly reasonable fears and anxieties. We lie to ourselves. We try to pretend like none of it is going to happen to us. The reality is that it might. You can never know. Realistically, you can die at any time. Heart attacks, aneurisms, drive-by shootings, etc. We are fragile and can be wiped out *at any time*. It was when I embraced this, and stopped looking at airplane flights as the height of danger in my experience, that my fear of flying was toned down considerably. We are all going to die. And if you are real with yourself about how lucky you are to exist and how easily it would be in everyday life to have that taken away, then flying is less of an event and more of just a slight uptick in the level of danger that you're in.

Make a deal with yourself.

Face it, we all have the fear deep down in our souls that we are completely alone in this universe. That somehow, we are the only sentient beings and that we have created this entire human experience as a means to entertain ourselves in the oppressive expanse of eternity. Maybe even that Heaven and Hell are both equally present in every moment and whether we are in one or the other is purely a result of how well we can rationalize and manage our solitude. Is that just me? Hello?

Anyway, these thoughts and concepts come intensely to the forefront when faced with the potential of imminent death. And if you're anything like me then that potential is at one of its highest when entering a makeshift aluminum can launcher. So, make a deal with yourself. I do this every time and it is one of only two things that actually calms me down on a flight. I typically make a deal that involves what I am going to do when I land. Either cure cancer or go and hand out food-based gift certificates to the homeless. Or just kiss some dirt. Whatever it is, make a deal with yourself to do something. That way when you are bouncing around in midair you are either looking forward to something or holding yourself accountable for everything you are going to do in the future. You know, after you land.

Make a deal with God.

This is the other thing that helps. I put the section above first because I recognize that not everyone is a spiritual person and that everyone may not have the same belief structure that I do. Tolerance and understanding, there we go. But turbulence will make a believer out of us all. Even the most steadfast atheist or agnostic will be adamantly questioning those ideas when they are being tossed around like a ragdoll as they are flying impossibly high above the Atlantic Ocean. This is why we make these 'foxhole prayers' to make deals with our higher power.

I always bargain from a place of strength. I have always held myself like one of God's favorite lieutenants, one that regularly cusses, barely swears allegiance, and refuses to go to church. That's me and for all I'm concerned it owes me a conversation about some of the things I went through. But every bargain requires a give and take and I always offer things that might make a difference. It's usually to treat my friends even better than I already do. Once, coming into Honolulu with the heaviest turbulence I had ever seen, I promised my girlfriend a dog *and* a parakeet. I also swore that I would write this book, find a way to change the world for the better, and try harder not to swear. It's fucking hard. And I never did buy her that parakeet. But the fact remains the same. Whatever bargain I made must have worked because I am still here, and that plane didn't go down.

Altitude is life.

The number one thing that always leads to a gripping terror is just how *high* I am while I am flying. I am not able to compartmentalize like some people. I just can't do it. I am brutally and viscerally *present* whenever there is a dangerous situation, to any degree. When I am in one of these jittering air torpedoes, I am constantly aware of the 30,000 feet between me and the soft, luscious ground beneath me. This terrified me until I talked to a pilot. You know, one of these crazy bastards who spends the majority of their life flying through the air. He explained to me that 'altitude is life.' The higher they fly the more time these cockpit jockeys have to figure out *how not to die*. I reminded him that is great if you're behind the controls. For the rest of us in the back, we just have to trust that the pilot is sober, experienced, and not going through a rough divorce. First, believe in your fellow man. Then remember that the higher you are the safer you are.

Breathe.

It is way, way too easy to hyperventilate on a plane. We are looking around, bumping up and down, and generally focused on the visual and auditory clues that, in reality, mean nothing to our continued survival. The only thing you can truly control is yourself. And the most important element of self-control is breathing. So, breathe. Deep, slow, intent lungfuls. I do this for as long as it takes. And this has the added benefit of indicating to the people next to you that you are striving to regulate your anxiety. Oftentimes this will lead to them offering to hold your hand, which is an awesome gesture of humanity and always helps me greatly.

Ignore all the other stuff.

There is a staggering amount of crap out there about how to reduce your fear of flying. Meet the crew (*definitely* don't do that), 'educate yourself,' rationalize things to yourself (yeah right), and make sure to sit on the aisle! Absolute, unadulterated horse shit. These are just clickbait articles based on absolutely nothing. If you're afraid of flying that just means you are *paying attention*. It is never going to go away. And for good reason. It is unnatural and intensely dangerous. Ignore all that crap and get yourself accustomed to your fragility, take gratitude for your life up to this point, make a promise to God or yourself, and then regulate your breathing.

23 | How To: Deal with a Tire Blow-Out

This section isn't about how to swap a spare tire once you get to a safe place by the side of the road. This is how to deal with a flat tire if it happens while you are driving. This is called a 'blow-out' and it is one of the greatest dangers you can encounter while on the highway. It can pull you into the other lane, into the path of other vehicles, or just into the ditch, all of which will cause massive damage to your vehicle and everything in it. If you are driving along, minding your own business and otherwise following all the advice in the Driving section, and suddenly you hear a loud noise followed by a dramatic pull to one direction, follow this advice:

Keep two hands and a firm grip on the wheel.

It'll be tempting to 'mom-arm' the person in the front seat or reach out toward the dash to steady a potential impact. But as the driver, your first and foremost responsibility is to keep both hands on the wheel and maintain as much stability as possible if the car is becoming out of control. If you maintain a firm enough grip, and have just a little bit of luck, simply doing this is often enough to keep your vehicle in your lane.

Do NOT stomp on the brakes.

At this point, you are operating with three wheels. If you apply the brakes you have a good chance of causing your vehicle to spin, which could mean death if one of the cars around you isn't paying enough attention. Without the cushion of the tire, you are now riding on the tire rim as well. This is inherently unstable and sudden, intense pressure from the brakes can lead to further damage to your vehicle.

Gently reduce the gas pedal and let the car gradually slow to a stop.

If you are in the left lane you are going to *want* to move to the right, as that is typically where the wider shoulder is. In this case, however, you want to take what you can get. If it is safe to do so, do so. Just remember to be gentle with the wheel. Refrain from yanking and tugging in any specific direction. If you are in heavy traffic, however, you are probably not going to be able to do this, so you're going to have to go to the left shoulder (if there is one). You only need as much space as it takes to get the entirety of the vehicle out of the lane you are currently in. Find the space available to you, maintain a slow, steady deceleration without slamming the brakes, and get your vehicle to the safest spot available.

Put on your flashers.

I have been a delivery driver for a long time, so I use these a ton and can do so reflexively, even in an emergency. This is a great habit to develop. These are useful because everyone behind you, who are still probably moving at a high speed, knows that you are in trouble and are trying to get to safety. If you *don't* know where the flashers are, that's OK. Just get them on as soon as you get to a safe spot. In 'newer' cars these are often placed in the middle of the dash. If it isn't there then scan around the wheel for the button with the red triangle. And if you have a co-pilot, instruct them to hit the button while you maintain control of the now three-wheeled vehicle. You'll want to keep two hands on the wheel as you slowly guide the vehicle to a stop.

24 | How To: Dodge a Punch

Let's first say that there is no winner in a fight. The entire purpose of life is to detach yourself from all the attachments and heal all the trauma that leads to fighting in the first place. Fighting in any form will only lead to misery and jail time. We should be striving for peace, harmony, and balance at all times.

But sometimes life is a bitch, and you have to fight your way through the crowd to stay alive.

The first thing everyone wants to know when they are angry is how to throw a punch. Whoever it is that 'deserves it' is right there and you want to punch them repeatedly in the face. With your fists. Repeatedly. Over and... yeah OK, you get it. But what is commonly forgotten amongst all of our anger and self-righteousness is that there is someone else involved here. And I will guarantee you that that person is not going to be happy about being punched in the face. To the point where they are going to want to punch *you* in the face. Repeatedly. And if you are ever going to achieve *your* dream of landing multiple hits on this (hopefully) very deserving person, then you are going to have to know how to dodge their punches.

There are a few way ways to go about this. All these tactics start with the A-frame position described in 'How To: Throw A Punch.' You want to keep your non-dominant foot in front, with your heel still under your shoulder, and your dominant foot in back, with your toe just under your other shoulder. There should be about a 45-degree angle formed between your feet. Also, always have your hands up. Punches are fast and if your hands are down, you're going to get tagged. By keeping your hands in front of your face you are naturally barring it off and keeping your hands in prime position to strike fast when you want to. With that in mind, here are your basic tactics.

Moving backward.

This is the easiest way to dodge a punch. You are essentially just dodging backward out of reach. It is highly effective but not always desired. Keep in mind, you are trying to neutralize your opponent. By going backward, you are taking yourself out of striking range as well as them. It *is* the most highly effective tactic if your goal is to tire out your opponent. If you are up against a person with a massive advantage in either size, strength, or skill, definitely start with a few of these.

First, you are going to want to rotate slightly to your back (dominant) leg. I like to slightly pick up my back leg as I do this. This activates your hips slightly as well, all of which come together to free up your torso and neck to dodge backward. It is key if you are trying to move forward quickly to take advantage of their overreach, thereby using their momentum to inflict damage. You dodge backward and immediately step into a punch of your own. If you are just trying to dodge, however, you will want to use the momentum of your feet, hips, and knees to carry yourself dramatically backward. And don't forget to still move your head backward as well! People can lunge into a punch at the last moment to close the gap. Even if that takes some of their power away it can still cause damage.

Moving forward.

Sometimes you know you are going to take a hit. It happens. None of us are Jackie Chan. And you are definitely slower and less agile than you think you are. If you're in this situation you are going to want to take the punch with your forehead. This is the most effective way to absorb a punch with the least injury. The alternative is your nose, which is extremely painful, or your chin, where you can easily get knocked out. Trust me, take it with your forehead. It has the bonus of being the place with the highest likelihood of breaking their knuckle as well.

To complete this move, you are essentially going to 'dodge' their punch by moving towards it. Moving forward is a great way to aggressively counterattack as well. To do this you move with your waist. Your feet are still balanced and beneath your shoulders. As soon as you see any movement, or sense that they even *might* be moving, then you immediately lower the shoulder closest to your assailant and bend your knees. You don't have to end up on the ground. You are trying to quickly get your head a foot lower than it was a half-second before. As you duck, lowering your shoulder and bending your knees, you are also pivoting your body to remain facing the attacker. As they finish their punch, ideally you have moved under it, they are now overextended, and you can cause serious damage.

Rolling, Ducking, and Weaving.

If you can help it, you never want to take a punch straight on. This is harder said than done. When punches are flying you don't have a whole lot of time to make decisions. And contrary to what the movies display, most fights only take a few punches. No matter how tough you think you are, it only takes a few well-placed blows to knock you the fuck out. The idea then is to make them *less* well-placed. And this is why you try to roll out of them.

When you are in a fight you are going to want a careful balance between breathing heavily and flexing your abs to keep your organs protected. This is advanced stuff and very hard to do. The easier way to stay protected is to constantly be ready to 'weave' away from punches. If you can, see the punches coming and 'weave' or 'slide' slightly in a direction. Ideally *away* from the strikes but it doesn't matter. You just need to be moving as the strikes land. This slightly diffuses the blow. And if you can be blowing past the strike to reach the undefended position of your attacker after their punch then all the better. Just keep moving, stay twitchy, and try to physically roll and weave away from any potential strikes.

25 | How To: Get a Credit Card

With how aggressive banks and companies are to hand you a credit card you'd think it would be easy to get one of these. The point of this section is to get you thinking about how to get a *'good'* credit card. We all know why we need these. And Grandma's voice comes into the back of all of our heads saying, in a high, screechy tone: "It's just for emergencies and unexpected expenses!" Oh, no one else heard that? Just me? Alright. Anyway, that's how so many of us talk ourselves into having these cards. And for travel, they become extremely important. Either you lose your debit card, your debit card just doesn't work in whatever area you're in, or you bail suddenly from a place you don't want to be and need to take the nearest place to stay. Whatever the reason, sometimes you've got to borrow to make it happen.

It's important to understand how these companies work and just how evil it is. They make money off of you in three ways: interest, yearly fees, and transaction-based charges. All these are different and the parts that affect you are usually buried deep in the user agreement. They want you to get bored and complacent reading it, so they start with their benefits section and whatnot. Side note: the trick to most complex documents is to read them backward. But the fact remains the same. They attempt to lure you in with various incentives as they are charging you every which way that they can.

The interest is simple. They take what you owe, assuming you haven't paid off the full amount, and charge you a very high percentage of it as a fee. Most new borrowers will be inundated with junk mail offering new credit cards and personal lines of credit. The main reason behind this is that most people will, at least once in their lives, get behind their payments. The best thing to always do is pay off your balance as soon as you can. These companies do not post their balances immediately as they are wagering that you will forget about it. If you do, and don't pay it off immediately, you are accruing interest that you will have to pay later. But we sometimes get behind the 8 ball. And when you do, that is when the extremely high interest rates kick in. For those with bad credit and new borrowers, this is somewhere around 25%. Which is insane. Because suddenly they are giving you a 'minimum payment' option that barely covers even the interest they are charging you! This is how a lot of people get buried. They pay the minimum, which isn't enough to actually reduce the amount of their debt, and constantly get oppressed each month by the 25% interest they are now paying.

Annual fees are just as bad. All these cards offer some kind of incentive. Whether it is cash back, airline miles, or even gift cards for other companies, these companies want to make you believe that by using their cards you can 'get ahead' or benefit in the long run. What they don't tell you is that the vast majority of these cards offer these benefits for only the first year. Or they offer these benefits continuously, but you have to start paying a yearly fee after the first year. Or even pay immediately. Depends on the card. Regardless, these fees are pricy and, in my experience, they have never justified any kind of 'benefit' I would have received. You also have to think, if they can afford to provide these kinds of 'benefits' to people, then where are they making their money? How are they taking you? Because they *are* taking you. Food for thought.

Third, credit card companies always charge random fees. Service fees. Finance charges. Transaction fees. Penalty fees. They are going to charge you a fee for whatever they can legally get away with. These dickbags are like carrion. They circle and circle, thinking constantly of new ways to slowly bleed you and then get to your carcass. That sounds dramatic but it is true. Credit card companies only exist to take advantage of you when you are either weak or in a financial bind. Then, when you are dragging weight, that is when the fees appear. Watch them closely.

Here's how to go about getting a credit card:

Never get a card that you don't have to apply for.

If it randomly showed up in the mail, then it is a crappy deal. It is called 'predatory lending' for a reason. Somewhere in that small piece of plastic is something designed to keep you in a life of indentured servitude. OK, maybe that's a little much, but those cards should be treated with the same disdain that the companies sending them have for you. Recycle if you can, or otherwise throw them in the trash. You are going to want to hunt down the credit cards you want. I resolutely demand zero fees and absolutely no transaction fees. That way I can keep my cards in the freezer where they belong, use them sparingly and only for big purchases that I immediately pay off, and not have to pay a single cent in fees. They do exist. Find them, research them, then apply for them.

Get multiple cards but never more than three.

The older you get the more that you realize that you're only ever using a credit card to get a higher credit score. And the only reason that you ever care about your credit score is when you need to take a big loan. And the most common major loan that you'll most likely ever take out is going to be for a house. So, in short, the only reason we use credit cards long-term is to eventually buy a house. Therefore, you are paying attention to your credit score. And one of the major factors of a credit score is how many accounts you have open. They want you to have a bunch and they want you to have them for a long time. But really, you don't need eight credit cards. It's ridiculous. But you also want to insulate yourself from disaster and emergency. And using certain cards at certain times *can* be advantageous. For example, I use a 'miles' card whenever I pay for plane tickets. And I use a 'cash back' card whenever I pay a hospital or doctor bill. But never get more than three. It will only trick you into thinking you have more money than you do. These companies also add fees of all kinds over time. And they link your debit card to them to pay for it. So over time, after you have forgotten that you even have the card, you'll get a charge for $49.99 or something silly like that.

The limit you are looking for is dependent on how much you trust yourself.

I have always been fairly prudent with how I spent my money. I've never racked up too much debt and I certainly didn't do a lot of things financially that I didn't have to. Yet I still got in some binds and owed a filthy company a few grand. Damnit! But if you have ever looked at your credit score then you will immediately see that they want you to have a high limit, but they dramatically reduce your score if you are holding a high balance, i.e., you've spent a lot of your limit and haven't paid it back yet. These companies thrive by giving you the highest limit that they can reasonably give a human. They are counting on you seeing only the short term, not the long term. They want you to go on that IKEA shopping spree, pay only the minimum that you owe, and end up paying the interest for the next 40 years. And if you have a high limit, you are thereby convinced that you have more money than you do. Make sure that you can trust yourself. Think of it this way: credit card companies are expecting that for every dollar of theirs that you spend, you are going to have to spend three to five dollars to pay back. So that couch you just bought for $500? It ends up costing you about $2000. Only have the limit you can handle.

Freeze your credit cards.

When I first heard this idea, I was floored. It might just be the smartest thing I've ever heard. The idea is this: take your credit cards and put them in a Tupperware container, fill it with water, and freeze it. That way if there is ever something that you think you should use your credit card for you will have to wait till it thaws to do it. Genius! Because most of the things that we think that we want we will reconsider the next day. Everything in this country is designed to get you to buy, buy, buy. And buy it now! Oftentimes when we sleep on it, we are way less inclined to buy it the next day. And that's why this trick is so effective. Pro tip: fill the Tupperware halfway and then let it freeze. Then put your card in on top of the block of ice, fill the remaining space with water, make sure that the card stays in the middle, and then let it freeze again. This makes sure that the card stays in the middle of the block for maximum effectiveness.

Secured credit cards.

These are pure genius if you don't trust yourself or if you are prone to impulsive purchases. These cards take a 'security deposit' equal to the amount that they 'lend' out. If your limit is going to be $500 then you have to put $500 down up front. If you miss your payment or don't pay up at all, the amount that you owe just gets taken out of the $500. Now, this is still exploitative. Of the real $500 that you have put down then a lot of that can get absorbed in fees and interest. Therefore, you don't actually get to spend your entire $500. But this is an excellent way to build credit if there is benefit in that for you. These are great as 'starter cards' and for turning around your poor credit decisions in the past.

If you do end up with credit card debt, don't give up on the credit cards.

You are eventually going to want a good credit score. Everyone gets tired of flushing money down the drain with rent and all the costs associated with not owning a home. You may even travel your entire life, but you will still want to own property. It is in our DNA. So, you don't want to just walk away from your credit score. As I mentioned, shit happens, and you may end up with a hefty balance. Most of your brain will tell you to stop using the card because you are paying a hefty interest rate per month, and you are trying to get that balance down. But you want to use your card more in this instance *as long as you can pay off your purchases immediately.* That is a very key point. If you cannot do that then stay away from your card like the plague. Freeze it and leave it. But if you have a high balance, and can afford to pay your stuff off immediately, then use the card, sign onto the credit card, and immediately pay off whatever you just spent, plus $10 or $20. The credit card company will only add this to your bill a few days later in the hopes that you forget about the charge, but altogether you'll end up with a balance that is $10 to $20 less than you would have originally.

Watch for fraud.

This has happened to me a handful of times. People take your card and plug it into a fake card reader that stores the information for later. They then go home, upload your card data, and sell it on the Darkweb. It is incredibly easy and common. Once I made the mistake of eating at a diner in North Plains, Oregon. It is a middling little town with an excellent taco/burrito joint and we had some great clients there. One morning the weather wasn't cooperating so, against my better judgment, we went into this flimsy little shack.

I immediately got wary because the waitress mentioned that she had been up all night working next door. The only thing 'next door' that I saw earlier was a strip club. And if this poor woman was working doubles as a waitress after stripping all night this meant only one thing: she was desperate. The breakfast was great. And maybe it was serendipitous that I accidentally gave her my credit card when it was time to pay. My girlfriend was telling me something, but I was tired, so I was doing what I usually do, staring into her beautiful eyes. I had a feeling that something was off, but I couldn't put my finger on it. I got the receipt, tipped the waitress, and left.

My spider senses were tingling so after an hour or two of working at the job site I paused, took off my respirator, and signed onto my credit card's website. I had two messages already describing strange behavior and several pending charges from somewhere in Southern California. It took the rest of the day to get the company to believe me that I was, in fact, still in Oregon and that my card number had been stolen. And, because I hadn't used the card in a year, I knew exactly who the perpetrator was. They had no interest in solving this issue and reluctantly took the charges off my account. I would put good money that this woman is still ripping people off left and right. I cut that card up as soon as I got home and let it expire. The lesson was simple. Watch for fraud. It is everywhere.

Money transfers.

Don't do them. It's a racket. It's predatory lending. It's completely illegal yet somehow common everywhere. These are essentially credit card transactions that charge you a ton of fees up front, insanely high-interest rates, and then more charges if you pay it off faster than you agreed to. It is evil and the definition of usury. If you have to send money, use Bitcoin! Or PayPal! Or Venmo! There are too many companies that offer these services for pennies on the dollar to waste your money paying for a cash advance or a money transfer.

Pay more than the minimum.

I mentioned this earlier, but it bears repeating. Do not just pay the minimum. The 'minimum' is a misnomer designed to get you to think that you are paying something that is within the terms of your agreement. It's not. You are only paying the interest charges that have been added to your 'balance' with a few dollars of the actual amount that you owe added on top. If you have a significant balance, really anything over $500, then it will take a *decade* to pay off. 10 years! Always pay more than the 'minimum.' If you have ever gotten behind in life and you racked up some debt your sole focus should be paying off that debt and not much else. Don't disregard your health while you're doing it, but make it a focus. Your quality of life, and your finances, will dramatically improve when you aren't paying a tenth or a quarter of your income in interest fees!

Have a savings account.

And put money into it! I've struggled with this in the past as well. It is really hard to look at the state of the world and say to yourself: "Yeah, I'm going to invest in the future of this place." As I write this, Russia is invading Ukraine and threatening the rest of the world with nuclear weapons. I cannot imagine a more selfish, entitled, and petulantly childish endangerment of the entire world than saying: "Hey if y'all try to interfere with us massacring this ethnic group, we're going to make the entire world unlivable." And this isn't limited to Russia. This is how the world hierarchy works. It is all in the interests of money and the 'security' of that money. It's really hard to bet that your money is better spent *later* as opposed to *now*. But, on the other hand, some investments can seriously pay off. And it is investing *in yourself* whenever you put money aside for later. Because despite inflation and the silly crap that goes on in this world, it is going to cost you one of your nuts/ovaries if something goes *wrong* in your life. Therefore, it is beneficial to have a chunk of change for when that happens. It's not just healthcare either, which is easy to disregard when you're young. Plane tickets. Train tickets. Towing. Speeding and parking tickets. Broken bones. All this stuff costs a lot of money and if you're not prepared then you are going to end up using a credit card and thus, spending a lot more than you have to. Invest in yourself and save some of your dough.

26 | How To: Get a Job in a Foreign Country

It is important to note that I have only done this in the hospitality industry. And the hospitality industry is far more accommodating of foreign workers moving somewhere, usually sight unseen, to a new country for a job. But regardless of your current occupation or desired occupation, there are a few steps to take to be able to get into the country and then work there. Once those are completed you can then start hunting for jobs.

Get a basic visa.

These can be different depending on where you are from and where you are going. Seemingly every single country has a different relationship with every other country. Luckily, these are all listed on your country's embassy website, so you can always start there. If you are American or European all of this is dramatically easier, mostly for economic and racist reasons. It is what it is. Look into what kind of visa you'll need. These basic visas typically fall under the 'traveler' category. I recommend these first because you never know what you're going to get. A long time ago I worked for a year in New Zealand, then went on vacation in Australia before I headed back to the States. I got a worker's visa, despite it being more expensive, with the intention of working the entire time. A few months in I regretted it. I became acutely aware that I should have *worked* in Australia and *traveled* in New Zealand. I also became acutely aware that I was paid primarily in cash, meaning it *didn't matter* which visa I had. Pro tip: get a cheaper traveler's visa, see if you like the place, and then get the worker's visa if you want to stay.

Get a worker's visa.

See if you like the place first. Then spend the money on this extra visa if you fall in love. These visas oftentimes require a workplace to sign off on it as a form of sponsorship anyway, so going there and working under the table for them for a bit makes this step dramatically easier. If you already know that you want to be in a place you can always correspond via email and video chat and secure the sponsorship that way. Just keep in mind that many of these agreements are flimsier than they appear, so be careful with what you agree to and why. I have always regretted signing a contract before arriving. For some reason or another, it has never worked in my favor. Be wary of what they want from you and never hesitate to question why that is. *Then* spend the money on the visa.

Hostel jobs.

This is my favorite way to get a foot in the door in a foreign country. There really is no better way to enter a country on a traveler's visa, find people you can communicate with, and then cheaply live while you look for long-term opportunities. Most often, if you are friendly and hang around long enough, the hostel itself has work that needs to be done. Look for the bulletin boards and make sure to ask the front desk, after you've befriended them of course.

Backpacker Boards.

These are the best examples of how to get jobs in any foreign country that you are in. Remember, there are a nearly infinite number of businesses that want to take advantage of you for low wages. But you don't usually care. You're in a foreign country, you just want to make enough to break even and get to the next place, and you generally are willing to put up with sub-par accommodation to do it. And those are exactly the conditions you are going to find on these boards. From service industry jobs to picking fruit, all these companies are very used to the idea of using temporary labor who might not even speak their language. Make sure to work hard, stay friendly, and wear sunscreen.

Government sites.

I have used these a handful of times and generally had bad experiences, but they are a means of getting a working visa immediately and with less headaches than more conventional means. The deal with these is that you agree to work at a certain job for a certain period. Most of these are jobs that a lot of people won't do, like picking fruit. They claim that there were penalties for leaving your designated company and for not working as long as you said you would. I saw zero indication that these threats were enforced. On the contrary, I saw many people use those visas as a way into the country, two or three weeks of work and housing, then they simply took off and traveled till they ran out of money. Food for thought.

27 | How To: Get Your Car Out of the Snow

━━━━━

Before I moved to Alaska, I thought that I knew about snow. I had lived in Montana, on Mt. Rainier in the spring, on Mt. Hood in the winter, and in Vermont during a particularly snowy winter. Truth be told, I had no idea what I was in for. Weekly blizzards and sub-zero temperatures were the norm. I quickly went from wishing for snow to praying that it would just stop snowing long enough to get to work and back. And then, an abject acceptance that it would never, ever stop, and to just get used to the mountains of whiteness everywhere you looked. Until the brief, fleeting, and utterly spectacular summer of course. But the snow... so much snow.

What I am getting at is that there are times when you are going to have to get somewhere and Mother Nature is going to have something to say about it. You might not live in Alaska but as our climate changes you are going to run into snow and you are going to have to be prepared for it. So, here are a bunch of different ways to get your car out of the snow, regularly employed by the good people of Girdwood, Alaska.

Whatever method you choose, dig out your car first.

You need to remove most of the excess snow around your vehicle or you're not going anywhere. Not only is it heavy and will push back on your car, but it's also slippery, so if you do get any traction then it will slip you right back to where you came from. Don't be lazy with this step, especially if you're digging it out in the morning. It'll be tempting to skimp because it'll most likely be cold as balls and it is a lot of work. But you don't want to have to do it twice. Clear out as much under the car as you can and pay special attention to the front and back of your car. You might not get clear in the direction you were hoping for. And even if you do get your car to head in that direction, you might have to rock back and forth a bit to get there. A snow shovel is a plus for this step. In Alaska, everyone had one in their car. It was common to come out of the bar and be snowed in already. If you don't have one of these you might be stuck using your hands, so have gloves handy too.

Don't spin your tires.

If at any time in this process you hear one of your tires dramatically spinning then immediately stop, unless of course your car still has enough momentum to keep going forward. If you truly are stuck, then just spinning your tires is going to make the process of getting out that much harder because you are turning the area directly around your tires into a solid brick of ice. It is extra hard to chop that up and you'll be sliding all over the place doing it.

The 'back and forth' method.

This can be masterfully done just as easily as it can be messed up. Remember, you don't want to spin your tires. If you hear your tires rapidly spinning immediately take your foot off the gas. I find it's much easier to successfully pull this move off with someone next to the car, out of range of a drift, talking you through it.

Start in low gear. If you've got 4-wheel drive all the better, just engage the 4-wheel 'low' setting. Turn off 'traction control' if you have it. Then turn your car on and give it the littlest bit of gas. You aren't trying to get free here, you're only trying to give it a little bit of forward momentum so that the car will roll *backward* on its own. You can either simply let it roll backward after your first push or quickly switch it to reverse and give it a bit of gas. You'll have to feel that out for yourself depending on how much snow you're in and what your car is like. Make sure not to spin the tires! Ideally, this will tamp down the snow behind you, allowing your back tires to get some traction. If you do this successfully, oftentimes you can then use this traction to give the car a little gas and shoot out of there.

Just push it.

Sometimes you can simply muscle the car forward enough that it can get some traction. Two or three people are usually enough. Make sure that there is still someone behind the wheel. I have seen several scenes of the driver getting out to push, only to watch their now directionless vehicle slide down the hill and either hit another car or end up in the ditch. And the driver always, always, *always* slips and falls, only to watch their car slide away from the ground. Pay particular attention not to spin the tires too much here, as it will spit snow into your pushers and potentially make their job a lot harder. You are looking for a good amount of spin but not a ridiculous amount. Rocking back and forth can also help here.

Cardboard and kitty litter.

A favorite method of many Alaskans is to use cardboard and kitty litter to get out of heavy, wet snow. The tactic is easy. Dig out as much as you can, flatten it out, then take your cardboard and wedge it as far underneath the tire as you can get in the direction that you are hoping to go. Next, take the kitty litter and sprinkle it *past* the cardboard in the same direction. If you only have one piece of cardboard, then still dig out the tires and put kitty litter in front of them. Ideally, you are going to catch enough traction with the single wheel and then the rest will catch enough with kitty litter. Keep in mind, most cars are rear-wheel drive, so you'll most likely want to focus on one of the back tires.

Chains.

Frankly, I hate chains. I've always made sure to have good, all-season tires and I usually have bought 4x4 cars as I frequently find myself in cold places. But if you don't have these things, or you weren't expecting winter weather, then chains are the next best thing. They can be a serious pain in the ass to put on but stick with it. These are the last best option if you truly are stuck. Just make sure to have cleared out the snow around your tires as best you can, as you are going to need room to put these on. And make sure to put them on correctly and that they are the correct size. Do not use chains that will not fully connect or are too large. This will *quickly* chew up the underside of your vehicle.

If all else fails...

This can be the most frustrating of events. So far you have diligently followed the instructions of your favorite wanderer and you still can't get your dumb, stupid, no-good car out of that jerk-face, godforsaken hole. You most likely have to be at work fifteen minutes ago and your partner is getting cold and antsy and you are working your *ass off...* Yeah, I have been there too. Try this: let some air out of your tires. Put cardboard down where you most likely have had a tire spinning. Then put a chain on the other tire. Take anything rock-like and small that can create traction and put it on both sides of the back tires. Then have the driver gently rock it forward and let it fall back. Do this twice, or three times, until you see the car gaining momentum forward. Then PUSH and holler at the driver to PUNCH IT! If done correctly this should work, at least to the point where you can hit some better snow and try one of the other methods again. Try not to get frustrated! Easier said than done, but still try and breathe, take your time, and patiently chip away.

Make sure to reverse everything you did once you're unstuck.

Turn on the traction control. Take the vehicle out of low gear. If you let some air out of your tires, go put some more back in. And if you put chains on, or just one chain, take them off if you think you can now get around without them. And don't forget to breathe.

28 | How To: Handle a Break-Up

There is only one real way to deal with your relationship ending: self-love and compassion. That is all we are ever going to truly need in this world. Is it no wonder that the road to serenity is through calm, quiet self-reflection? Because it is in this pursuit of ourselves that we see how we are. We see what it is we are seeking and what we think we are lacking. We see who we are and, hopefully, that we are enough in the exact state that we are in. But enough of that. You are probably hurting and wondering how to make it stop. You are going to have to deal with the fallout of the ending relationship and everything that comes with it. So here are some general tips and tricks. You don't have to agree with or use all of them. Pick and choose as you will but pay attention to all of them. You are most likely highly emotional and volatile and that is only going to hurt you in the end.

Take some space.

I know from hard experience that *all* you want to do at this time is reach out to your former partner and bend over backward to either fight with them or 'get them to love you again.' But what you need right now is *yourself*. If this is how you feel, then it is a clear indication that you based some of your sense of self-worth and self-esteem on your ability to make a relationship with *someone else* work out. You need to block out the noise, take some time away from everyone else, and learn how to apply those same efforts to yourself. Watch some movies. Listen to some TED talks. Take quiet walks by yourself. Meditate and do breathwork. Nurture your mind, body, and soul. In no time you will find yourself appreciating you for *you*. And that is what really counts.

Give yourself time.

We *should* be living every day like our lives like we might end tomorrow and just be grateful for the day but in reality… you probably have a lot more time. And that means that you can give yourself some time to process what is going on in your mind without feeling like you have to be in front of the whole world or talk to whoever it is that you are most likely thinking about. You can take a day off. You can take three days off. You can find a little bit of separation to 'get your mind right', and then come back a more settled and relaxed person. It is still going to hurt like hell, but the first step is to get out of the 'shock' phase where we say and do irrational things, i.e., things that we will regret saying and doing later.

When I was in the process of getting divorced, who knows when it really began, I was acutely aware of the fact that my ex-wife had been having an affair. I had seen their conversations, I had the phone and text records in a pile on my desk, and I had even seen the guy(s) coming out of my con-do. Yup, denial is a bitch. So is shadow work! Anyway. A few weeks later I was in the process of getting sober, rebuilding the barn I was staying in, grieving my marriage, starting a new life from scratch, raising a puppy and, on top of all that, I was unraveling the PTSD and C-PTSD I had endured my entire life thus far. I wanted everything to be alright, *right now*. That was always going to take a lot of time, but it still didn't compute. One of the most traumatic experiences of my entire life was packing up all of my stuff in the house that I own, stuffing it in the car, and tearing out of there, only to see the same guy I had seen before pulling into my parking spot right as I left. How was it fair that I could feel the things I was feeling and this monster that I had loved so deeply was able to move on *so quickly*? How was any of it possible? Was I broken? Was I any of the nasty things she had called me so many times? Was any of it real?

The answers only came with time. That's a bitch because I am a steadfast believer in the notion that there is an alternative path to everything; that I can work hard enough at any given time to *force* my way *through* challenges. Despite this, it took some time. At first, I needed a cabin in the woods. I needed to cry and get in my car so that I could scream as loud as I could without scaring my dog or having the cops called. I needed to hike, watch movies and play with my puppy. I needed to hit some meetings and make new friends, without the constraints of regular life. After a while I needed something more, so I got a job. That was a good distraction, but it wasn't what I wanted so I got another one. Three jobs later I ended up at something semi-stable. One day at a time, and sometimes one *minute* at a time, I took care of my bodily needs and established myself in a small community. This was easier said than done. I was traumatized, rattled to the core, and utterly fed up with people in general. Trusting other people? Not easy. But I knew I couldn't be alone forever, so I had to try.

And try I did. Over and over and over again. Most of the time I was met with mild failures and disappointments. But every so often, maybe once a month, I found something worth keeping. And those 'somethings' started to add up. I began to achieve some semblance of peace of mind, forgiveness for myself and others, healthy relationships, and productive habits. My days became something so much more than just putting out the next fire. I was building myself in ways that I never had before. I was rising above the chaff and seeing through myself and others. It was, and is, the greatest undertaking of my life. Every morning I wake up, hop in the shower, and do my gratitude exercises. The first thing out of my mouth is always a giant thank you for removing me from the situation I was in and giving me this opportunity to grow into something so much more. What!? Crazy. That only came with time and effort. Mostly time. So, give yourself a lot of leeway. Do not compare yourself to others or try to put yourself in anyone else's shoes. You are on your very own journey and only you are going to feel what you feel in the way that you feel it. Take the time that you need. If that means a month off in the Bahamas, well, go for it. If that means going down to two or three days a week at work to give yourself a few extra days to be in the dark on your couch, go for it. There is no wrong answer. Give yourself the time and the answers will come.

Get hammered.

As someone who has had to go through a lot of recovery, I have a distinct outlook on alcohol and substances. For me, they have always been a way for me to mask my deficiencies and the intense pain that has always existed in my head. That being said, a lot of people do not have those issues. And if you have ever heard a country song in your life, then you know what the first, second, and third purposes of whiskey are: heartbreak. I used to love how some people told me that you shouldn't do drugs when you're going through a breakup. I mean, sure, you shouldn't do drugs at all. And you shouldn't get drunk ever, I guess. But if there ever *was* a time to get obliterated with your friends it is when you're going through a breakup. Getting blasted might just be the *only* part of the entire process that is actually any fun. Just remember, turn your phone off, have your friends nearby, and make sure you have somebody you trust chaperoning you home. And I mean all the way home. Bringing home somebody random is just going to make you feel worse. And you don't want to be sending late-night texts to someone you've been fighting with all week. Or who just cheated on you.

Then get sober.

You are never going to get over someone you used to love if you are constantly under the influence of intoxicants. Drugs have a way of making our brain fuzzy and inhibiting the healthy processing of emotions. I would go so far as to say that it is *impossible* to process your emotions with even the faintest hint of chemical influences. I get it. I am currently (still) going through a divorce. For a long time, it constantly felt like being murdered. There were times when I legitimately thought that my heart couldn't survive that amount of pain. But survive I did and that is solely due to my decision to quit drinking. It has allowed me to feel and process the pain, rather than simply numbing it down to a 'manageable' level. Instead, I have focused on as many healthy pursuits as possible and engaged in an intense period of personal growth. I have learned lessons, met people, deeply connected with true friends, and ultimately grown as a person more than at any point in my life. And that is all due to the decision to stop drinking and simply acquiesce to the concept of dealing with my pain.

Do new things.

Whenever I have been put in a situation where I needed to forget someone, someplace, or something, I always tried to be positive and focus on how this seemingly negative trend has allowed me to become a better person in the end. It really does work that way. Sometimes we need to break ourselves down to build ourselves up the way we want to be. Or maybe add a new addition to our mental mansion. Regardless of how you see it, try a bunch of new things. Go to a climbing gym. Try a yoga class. Go see the symphony. You'll be surprised how these new experiences will start to push you forward.

At various times I have found myself in this situation, yet each time is equally significant in what it has taught me about myself. It was through the process of trying new things that I learned that I hate surfing and love board games. Surprisingly, I enjoyed Dungeons and Dragons! Never saw that coming. I love to hike, always knew that, but I absolutely cannot stand the culture around rock climbing. I am good at snowboarding but just don't *enjoy it*. Weird. I would much rather sit in a coffee shop on Saturday doing the crossword and shooting the shit with the people next to me than go to a crowded Farmer's Market and hobnob. I jumped out of a plane once and will be keeping my feet on the lovely, lovely ground as much as possible from here on out, thank you very much. I love to work on cars, read sci-fi novels, go to concerts, take random adventures, and generally find every excuse to get away from people. I hate shopping! And I can't stand movies, dance clubs, crowded stadiums, dog parks, or public gyms. Yoga is OK, sometimes. The point is that it is this knowledge that helped me define *my-self*. I had, for so long, been trying to fit into wherever I was that I frequently found myself in places I didn't want to be, doing things I didn't want to do. When I started trying new things it was equally important to find what I *didn't like* just as much as what I did. Finding those hidden gems made me happy, so I pursued them, and for those brief periods, my troubles eased. I was able to be fully present in the moment and thereby, not in the past. This is the way forward.

Exercise and eat a salad.

The exercise is a given. One of the best ways to get through any kind of sadness is to get a sweat going and tire yourself out. Just keep working out till you feel better. It is that simple. The salad part is an internal joke I've always had with myself. I've gotten in ruts before where I ate very unhealthily and led myself into a slew of unhealthy habits as a result. So, I always tell myself: eat a salad, Sam. And then I do and I feel great! It's hard to always remember that what we eat directly affects how we feel during the day. When we are already down this effect is magnified. We may also be looking to comfort food to assuage any sad feelings we might have. And we may have already eaten six pizzas this week (who's counting though, really). So, eat a salad.

Block 'em.

This is probably the hardest part, but it has always been the part of the process that has helped me the most. It is really hard to do. Going through the social media accounts and your phone and systematically blocking access to all of their information and social history can easily feel like cutting a piece of you away. It can also feel like you are walling off your closest friend. To a degree, you are. You are removing your ability to hurt yourself by actively participating in communication with someone who is no longer in your life. Someone who may have hurt you, really badly. It is the first step along the road to redemption. I set time limits for myself. Because it is really hard to stick with it. Start with a day. A full day, not a half day. Then move up from there. As the weeks pass, you'll notice it helps keep you on your path of self-love, self-acceptance, and moving forward with your life. You know, instead of stalking.

29 | How To: Interview

Just like with cover letters and resumes, it is important to note that the vast majority of interviews I have been to (and succeeded at) were in the hospitality and tourism sector. I have held jobs in offices that required all the pomp and circumstance that the commercial sector can provide. But I found those jobs to be soul-crushing, boring, and ultimately futile. As a result, I am simply going to focus on what I know best: menial yet fun jobs.

The key to interviews is to find out what the person interviewing you is looking for and then respond to them in a way where you 'fit into' exactly that. Every time I have ever hired someone, I have always been looking to get it over with. I had a job that needed to be done and I didn't want to waste my precious time going over countless resumes. To avoid this, I would identify basic traits that I wanted them to have and then I looked for a good personality, especially a funny one. I wanted people who were going to fit into the dynamic of my company but were going to bring a spark and some uniqueness. Now, this isn't to say that you shouldn't be yourself in your interview. Just the opposite. You should be *remarkably* yourself. You're not there to kiss ass and bend over backward to make sure everyone likes you. You're there to make money and kick ass. That's why when you walk in, you have to walk *like you've been there before*. Everyone loves confidence and competence. If you can demonstrate to them that you are a person they can get along with, that you bring something new to the team, check the boxes they want 'checked', and that you can do the job effectively, they won't waste any time and will hire you on the spot.

Competence and uniqueness will get you 80% of the way but that's not all you have to do. The last 20% is to get them to concretely believe that you can do the job and do it well. And this is where the dumbass questions come in. You can easily fake or embellish your work history. Especially in hospitality and customer service. As long as you stay confident any mistakes will quickly get swept underneath the rug. That's the easy part. The hard part is nailing the rote questions that these people want to ask you. They are invariably trying to guess just how juicy of a lemon you are. Don't get it twisted. Unless you're drinking martinis with them and then *definitely* get it twisted. Anyway. Every company is looking to exploit you for as much labor as you will give for as cheaply as possible. Every manager and owner knows that they are pulling one over on you and that they are making way, *way* more money than you. That's what these questions are designed to pull out of you. They want to know if you're willing to subserve your success to get a paycheck. They want to know *how desperate you are*. Because desperation is a stinky cologne that they can take advantage of, whether they are singularly aware of it or not. Here are some basic questions and how to answer them:

What's your biggest weakness?

Answer: *My biggest weakness is my biggest strength.*

For example, I am a naturally gregarious guy. I like to talk to 'my tables.' Sometimes I get a little caught up in the conversation and this can slow down food service.

This question is designed to find out how much confidence you have. They want to know if you are going to bash yourself. Or if you're an egomaniac who thinks that nothing is wrong with them. But most often they want to know if you're pliable and have low self-esteem. Don't be those things. This answer subverts that by immediately responding with what your *strengths* are. Remember, you own the place. And that place is a run-of-the-mill food shack that you are going to grow out of in a few months, tops. Remind yourself that they are trying to impress *you*, not the other way around.

Why do you want to work here?

Answer: *Because I think I can thrive here.*

This flows into the point I should have made earlier about doing three minutes of research before the interview. All you need to look up is the business you're looking for and find what they are trying to brag about. If it's a sports bar then they are advocating a fun, lively environment. If it's a fancy hotel then they are advocating for upward mobility, most likely job opportunities around the world, and a 'professional ecosystem.' If it is a sales job, then they will talk non-stop about company culture and attitude. Whatever it is, find what they are bragging about and then say you can thrive in that environment.

What is the last time you provided good customer service and why?

Answer: *Yesterday. Because I like to do it.*

You can put in any story here. From holding the door for an elderly person to moving your neighbor's Amazon packages from the shared front door inside for them. Doesn't matter. We all *should* be doing these things *all the time*. If you're not, well, make shit up, I guess. Ideally, there are a lot of good examples to pull from. And after you've come up with one and are telling it to the person interviewing you, then tell them why. Again, we should all *like* to help other people. If you don't, you're probably going to need to pretend for jobs like this. If you do, just tell them why! Easy peasy.

Tell me about a time you messed up.

Answer: *Every day. I'm human.*

For example: Even on my best days I can't be perfect. One time I dropped an entire tray of champagne glasses! I was so embarrassed. But I started nervously laughing and everyone else seemed to join in. After only a few long hours/seconds it was cleaned up and over with.

The trick with this question is to be humble and not arrogant. Everyone messes up and everyone knows this. Yet when we are in interviews or the public eye, we like to pretend that we don't. The problem is, we still do. Often. Just be open and honest with yourself and who you are talking to. This is not nuclear science or brain surgery. You can mess up and you and everyone else involved are going to walk out of there alive and unscathed.

Why are you leaving your current job?

Answer: *I wanted to find a better opportunity that better matched my skill set and my personality.*

Chances are you're applying for this job because you wanted to get the hell out of the last place that you were living. Or that the last workplace was toxic and nasty. Or the last manager couldn't keep their damn hands to themselves, so you knocked them out. Whichever it is, you can't just say this. What you have to do is be gracious and understanding, then *move for-*

ward. It is called deflection and it is a diplomatic way of grazing over your last negative experience, then immediately complimenting the person you are talking to and their workspace.

Tell me about a time you overcame an obstacle.

Answer: *Today*.

Example: Walking into this interview! I was thinking about whether you were going to be a pompous narcissist and then when I sat down, I realized, yes, you are! So now I have been trying to keep a straight face and get this job because I'm broke and want to get ghetto-rich ASAP, all while forcibly not telling you to fuck off and die.

OK, so you can see why I don't work in the service industry anymore. It's really hard being this funny around people with absolutely no sense of humor. Anyway! The point of this is to demonstrate how you are supposed to answer. Again, start with humility. Always say 'today.' It demonstrates that we all conquer obstacles every day and that we are constantly striving to be better and more capable. These folks love people who can be 'coached' or 'trained.' By saying 'today' you are automatically fitting into the rubric in their minds of someone who, indeed, can be 'trained.' Maybe don't tell them about the douche part. Maybe talk about how someone cut you off in traffic, or the last time you had to 'comp' someone's meal. They just want to hear how you faced a problem and then how you *solved it*. Everything else is a bonus.

Finally, as you have probably noticed, all these answers share a few characteristics: dictating the conversation and anticipating potential pitfalls. You know that these people are trying to milk your tits/nuts as hard as they can. You know that they want you to be pliable and subservient. But you aren't going to be like that, rather, you are taking the initiative and making yourself an equal. As such, when they ask you these rote questions designed to get you to 'expose yourself,' you are changing the course back to places you are comfortable. Back to where you *shine*.

The second component is anticipating where you might not look as good as you want to. Intermittent job history can be an issue. I just say that I saved up a ton of money and went on vacation. Which is usually true! Crappy behavior and a lack of relevant experience are also potential challenges. Whatever it is, you're not perfect and you will have weaknesses. Again, redirect to your strengths and where you are comfortable. If you do this successfully and act with the confidence of having been there before, you are almost guaranteed the job. If not, head to the next interview and try again. Believe in yourself and breathe.

30 | How To: Jump a Chain-link Fence

This also works for any other type of barrier, especially ones where you can get a toe hold in the middle of the vertical part of the fence. If you are jumping a wooden fence, particularly in a backyard or residential area, make sure to compensate for the fact that it might be rotten or tilted. This can cause the fence to snag or bend, which you might not care about at the time, or some of the boards to snap, which you will care about as you are flying toward the ground.

Place your hands on the top of the fence.

Put your foot on any kind of hold halfway up (or as far up as you can go). Make sure not to over-extend to the point where you can't pull yourself up.

Use your hands and your toe hold to pull yourself up halfway. I find it easier to combine steps three and four into one (semi-) smooth motion.

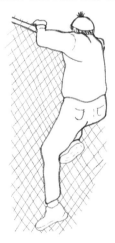

Get your chest up. Continue pulling from the top of the fence with your hands and pushing up with your foot from your toe-hold until you can either get your chest to lie 'flat' on the top of the fence. It also works to get both hands on top of the fence and your foot sideways, also on top of the fence.

If you can only get your chest to the top, don't worry. Your legs are either dangling or still stuck on the original toe-hold. You need to get your leg horizontal, running parallel to how the fence runs. Either grab another toe hold with your non-dominant leg and use the leverage to swing your dominant leg up to this position or push up with your arms so that your chest is elevated off of the top of the fence till you achieve this.

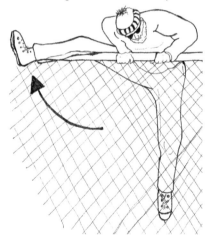

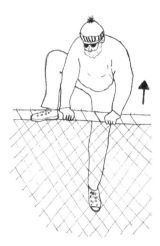

Depending on how high the fence is you'll need to take various courses of action to get back down. When I was in my 20s and un-breakable, I would just pull my dominant leg (the one already parallel to the top) slightly upward, push up with my hands, tuck my non-dominant leg in, and swing over, all in one motion. Pay attention to how to land if you do this. The problem with this method is that if you catch your shoe, you are screwed with a capital F. With shorter fences, this might not matter as much. The smarter method, if you care or have the time, is to take your leg that is parallel to the top and pull it down over the 'far' side as you rotate your body so you're straddling the top. Watch. Your. Crotch. Keep pushing upward and you'll avoid an unpleasant pinch.

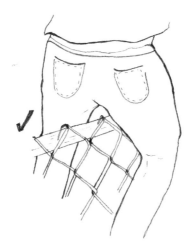

Now that you're straddling the top, you'll want to do this all in reverse. Make sure to lean forward (DO NOT lean back) and as you're doing so lift your non-dominant leg upward and outward (toward the side you came from), bending that leg at the knee. Still, be pushing up with your hands as you hold as much weight as you can. As you're doing this you want to rotate your body so that you are facing the fence again, this time on what was the 'far' side. When you can, try and grab at least a partial toe-hold in the middle of the fence's 'far side'. This should leave you with your arms outstretched or partially bent, holding on to the top of the fence, and your body hanging down what was the 'far side.'

Quickly scan the ground for hazards. There may be holes where a dog tried to dig under, rusted cans, rocks, etc. All these can turn your ankle as you land. Once you've identified a (hopefully soft) place to land, let go. If your desired landing spot isn't right under the fence (recommended) then give a *little* push to separate you from the fence. As you are falling you want to adjust your feet according to the rapidly changing landscape. As soon as you hit the ground, bend your knees to compensate for the momentum. Always, always, always bend your knees as soon as you hit the ground. Some people go so far as to let this bending movement turn into a full-blown barrel roll, which you can do, but if you aren't certain about trash or anything sitting around the fence this can end up messy and uncomfortable.

31 | How To: Jump a Barbed Wire Fence

The only difference between this and the chain-link fence is that these are designed to deter you from going over them. So just know, using this technique is probably going to result in pain, it has a high likelihood of inflicting some kind of injury, and you are most likely entering territory that people *really* don't want you to be on. Your choice. But sometimes there is no choice. It is what it is. Follow these steps and you'll be alright:

- **Read the previous section.**

- **Omit everything about putting your crotch anywhere near those ball and vagina-killing barbs.**

- **Put on heavy, thick gloves.**

- **Pick a spot near a post.**

- **Take the thickest material you have and drape it over the top of the fence.** I have used an old Carhartt jacket, a leather 'blanket,' and a piece of carpet before. If you are trying to go over an exceedingly tall barbed-wire fence, forget it. The chances that it's for illegal purposes are too high and you're on your own figuring that out.

- **Place your hands in between rows of spikes and test, test, test.** Then test it again. The last thing you want is a rusty barb through your hand.

- **Either push down far enough so that you can just jump over or climb just a little bit so you can *gently* sling yourself over.** Take your time with this. If you get poked, you will be nervous about having tetanus for weeks.

32 | How To: Jump-start a Vehicle

When I was staring at an empty page thinking of how to write this section, I tried to go back in my mind to count how many times I needed a jump. I made it about five years back before I lost count. It is one of those things that you never think about. It seems so easy after you do it for the first time. But the first time is the problem! And then if you don't have to do it for a year or two... All that knowledge goes right out the door and you're back to square one. So, here are two ways of doing this very easy thing. Just make sure no one sees you peeking at the pages in case you want to look like you already know.

Using Cables

You should always have jumper cables in your car. We can sometimes ride the tide of humanity's good graces but eventually, you are going to leave the music blasting in your old Subaru, or your glovebox is going to magically open (turning on the glovebox light you didn't know you had) while you are on a six-day backpacking trip. Or maybe some slimeball mechanic is going to charge you for a brand new, top-of-the-line alternator but is actually going to take the old, piece-of-junk alternator from his own car and put it in yours (true story). Whatever the situation is for you, your car is now dead and won't start. And it's usually in a faraway location, there are not many people around, and you need cables. So have them! Here's how to use them.

Put the cars next to each other.

I can never remember what car brands put their batteries on the right or the left. I swear they change randomly, like quantum batteries that consistently exist in two separate yet identical places. Right? Right. Put the cars next to and facing each other so the batteries are close enough for the cables to reach both batteries. This can oftentimes mean parking so that the cars are bumper to bumper.

Start by attaching the positive (red or black) cable to *your* battery.

It will have a (+) sign on the clamps. The same thing goes for the positive terminal on your battery.

Attach the positive (same color) clamp to the working battery.

Make sure to connect the clamp with the (+) sign to the terminal on the working battery with the (+) sign.

<u>Pay attention</u>. Connect the negative cable (-) to the *working battery only*.

You are not going to attach the remaining (so far) unused negative (-) cable to the dead battery. Rather you are going to connect it to a 'ground.' I always use part of the car's frame. Someone once told me to make sure to always use an unpainted part, something about resistance, so I always adhere to that. Make sure that this is your last step and that it has a firm grip somewhere on the frame of your car.

Start the 'working' car.

My knowledge of electricity and batteries is severely limited. I have been told that it should be almost immediately that you should be able to start your car up if you have connected the cables appropriately (sometimes they slip). I have never experienced this. It has always taken 5-10 minutes of having the car with the working battery running, at least, for my car to start up. So have patience.

Start the 'dead' car.

Your car should fire right up. If it doesn't, look for signs that your situation is improving. If the engine is turning, the lights are flashing, and your radio comes on when you turn the ignition, but your car isn't starting, then the process is working and you just need to give it more time. If your car fires up the first time, then head to the next step. Just make sure not to turn your car off for a while. This will let the battery charge up so it doesn't happen again.

Pay attention. Disconnect the cables.

Do this in the exact opposite order than you started. If you have a memory like mine, then I have these steps listed.

- **Disconnect the negative (-) clamp attached to the frame.**
- **Disconnect the negative (-) clamp from the other car.**
- **Disconnect the positive (+) clamp from your car.**
- **Disconnect the positive (+) clamp from the other car.**
- **Store your cables in an easy-to-find place.**

Using A Battery Pack Jumper

Despite how I have written this big 'ol book completely on a laptop and have various sections about internet message boards and cell phones, I can't stand technology and the effects it has on us as a species. It's just not healthy. As a direct consequence of our technology usage, we have lost touch with the very elements of experience that make us human. Maybe we are evolving. Or maybe, just maybe, we haven't successfully bridged the gap between the increasing use of technology and the base aspects of our animal nature. Regardless, I am not a huge proponent of technology. There are, however, a few notable exceptions. And those are percussive electric massage guns, yoga pants, and battery pack jumpers.

Battery pack jumpers are roughly the size of a loaf of bread, or smaller, and can hold a charge for three to six months. I spent $30 on mine a year ago and it has already saved my ass three times. I have charged it twice. I cannot even express how much worry and stress this little thing takes off of my shoulders. I don't have to worry about double-checking my truck before I go on a hike, I don't ever have to rely on anyone else to help me if I get stuck, and I can send my girlfriend off brazenly, despite her penchant for forgetting everything important to her survival at the absolute worst times. No matter how often she might strand herself in the cold, I do not have to worry because that magical little box will be able to turn the car back on and keep her warm long enough for me to get there and ruthlessly make fun of her.

Just buy one. You won't regret it. And follow whatever directions are on it. They are all different. Mine are super simple. Red wire, black wire, turn on. Day saved.

33 | How To: Locate Free Camping Spots

OK, so now you have the vehicle, you've got the gear, you've left everything behind and you are finally, *finally* on the road. Now you have to set out and find places to sleep that don't cost a lot of money. I have pursued this goal in a lot of different ways. From sleeping in my car in Walmart parking lots to laying out my tent and bug screen in the middle of a field, the options were truly endless. The best of these, however, always ended up being free campsites that I found along the way.

The upside to these campsites is obvious. They are free, there are significantly smaller crowds (if any), and the sense of adventure every time you pull into one gives you an intense feeling of being *alive*. The downsides are easy to spot too though. There is no running water, meaning that you are going to have to bring in your own and poop in the woods. Well, I mean, you're supposed to have a waste-disposal method attached to your vehicle but... I've always just dug a hole. To each their own. Just keep in mind that you are going to need to plan for your basic needs much more than you normally would.

We live in a new era. No longer is this country teeming with undiscovered free gems. It is still chock-full of free gems, but the *undiscovered* part is no longer true. Ultimately this is a good thing. You can now download an app or access a website that provides a map of all these locations. You are looking for the terms 'boondocking' and 'dispersed camping.' I prefer any site that is listed as 'dispersed camping,' as this means that it is usually publicly owned land that I found via a government website. Occasionally I still find spots that are unlisted and I hoard these in my memory banks as if they were pieces of gold in a dragon's lair. Hopefully, you'll find some of your own. In the meantime, however, here are a bunch of resources that can point you in the right direction:

Apps

Below is a list of apps that you can use. I have attempted to not promote commercial interests at any point in this book but here I have no choice. These are the apps, in order of my personal preference, that I have used successfully in the past.

- **US Public Lands (paid)**
- **FreeRoam**
- **BLM Public Lands Map USA**
- **Campendium**
- **BoonDocking USA**
- **The Dyrt (paid)**

Now this is certainly not a comprehensive list and I take no responsibility for how well they work and when. These are simply the apps that I currently use. It is a common occurrence for apps such as these to be outdated, give false information, or otherwise cease functioning at any time. I have three or four downloaded onto my phone at all times and regularly make backup plans just in case. I highly recommend you do the same.

BLM Land

This refers to land 'owned' by the Bureau of Land Management. This means that it is public land for public use. There can be different rules in different areas but typically there is very little regulation. There is always the chance that a federal agent of some kind might stop by. They have every right and reason to do so. But as long as you're not up to anything illegal and you have some kind of method for disposing of your trash and human waste then you'll be just fine.

Find a map with BLM land on it first. These come in various shapes and sizes. Some of them come on an app on your phone that registers your location in comparison to your location on the BLM map. Oftentimes, however, you have to look at the map on your phone, which shows your actual location, and compare that to the other map you are looking at, which shows where the campsites are. This can be a little tricky for some. When in doubt, go with your gut. There is a significant overlap between some maps and information is not always accurate. At some point in your journey, you are going to be notified, oftentimes rudely, that you are going to have to pack up and move. Just expect it to happen. Always be respectful of whatever space you are in and leave no trace behind you and you will always be alright.

When you are camping in public lands it's also important to keep your camp as 'mobile' as possible. I have seen a ton of folks set up shop in these places for months at a time. To each their own, I guess. These spots invariably turned into trash-filled, messy heaps. To me, this ruins the entire thing. I don't head into the woods to create a homestead. I want to hang out with a bunch of trees. As such, I have always wanted to remain as flexible as possible. I typically have a good amount of gear to set up, including a few pop-up tables and tents, but I kept most of my stuff organized and in the car. These locations are often too exposed for me. They work extremely well for up to a few weeks as a base of operations and a place to breathe away from the city. But they are also subject to having neighbors move in quickly. There is a human tendency to set up shop near other humans. Which can be irritating if you're looking for some solitude! So I keep it light, breezy, and ready to roll if need be.

There is a caveat to BLM land. Because it is in the public domain and typically in a remote location, then there is little enforcement of any laws. BLM land has a well-deserved reputation for attracting a dangerous subsect of people. When using this land, you have to be very wary of who you are around and when. While on the one hand, it is extremely freeing to be able to so easily find solitude, on the other hand, it can be a serious problem if you run into the wrong people that far out there. This has rarely happened to me. When it did, I simply stared right back, didn't back down an inch, then calmly packed up my camp and moved on.

National and State Forests

The U.S. Park Service does a damn good job as an underfunded and overworked agency tasked with holding back the tragedy of the commons in this country for as long as they possibly can. This means that they aren't willing or able to take any of your shit. There are rules in these forests for a reason. These areas are heavily utilized yet the *modus operandi* is to keep it as clean and pristine as possible. Therein lies the rub.

These forests are open for the public to use. There are, of course, campsites available that you can pay for. But we are looking for dispersed camping sites. The maps you need for these are from the U.S. Forestry Service (USFS). These maps detail the areas of the forest, give a general idea of where the paid campsites are, and most importantly, tell you how to get to the unmarked or undermarked roads scattered throughout the area. This is where you are going to find the prime camping spots. You want to find a road that has a number rather than a name. You then want to follow that road until you find a good pull-off. That's it. Make sure to set up your camp off of the road and keep the road open for anyone else to pass.

There are more rules in these types of parks. National Forest land is pretty standard and well-marked with what they allow. State parks and land can differ greatly, however, so close attention to what the signs say. If there are no signs there are no rules, unless you have unwittingly strayed onto public land somehow. Make sure to follow the rules. These almost always involve having a means of disposing of human waste. I carry a bucket with me for this purpose. When they ask where the waste is going, I point to the closed bucket. They have never offered to open it. In reality, I am hiking ten or twenty minutes away, digging a large hole, taking care of business, and then covering it. But they are typically obligated to make sure that you have an alternative method to that. Mostly because most people like to walk ten or twenty feet away, leave their business on the ground, and then deal with the fallout of the smells and animals it attracts. Don't be one of those people. As I mentioned, the rules are there for a reason. They are not for you, or any human for that matter. The rules are there to protect the forest. And if you think you are better than the forest, or any of nature for that matter, then you are due for a rude awakening.

34 | How To: Make a Tarp Shelter

A long time ago I was a teenager and had a knack for getting into trouble. I also had an explosive relationship with my family, including my mother. We hadn't been getting along and I was actively going through the motions of getting emancipated. I had a lawyer and a job and was couch surfing on my friends' couches until I could find a place that would let a fifteen-year-old sign a lease. I would have made it too if I hadn't made the mistake of walking along the same road that was on the way to my mother's house. Someone called her and told her where I was, at which point she dropped everything and came screaming down the road toward me.

I heartily ignored her for a few minutes as she nicely pleaded with me to get some lunch. I finally relented and hopped in. Despite our differences, and the criminally poor parenting, she was still my mom. We talked. It didn't go well. We were arguing back and forth, spitting venom and hatred when she finally calmed down enough to ask me if I wanted a cell phone. This is how old I am. I was in high school when suddenly *everyone* had one of these things. No one had any idea what the hell a smartphone was. Forget about texting and watching YouTube. So, when she offered me one of these, and to pay for it for six months, I couldn't resist. The only thing running through my head was how much easier it was going to be to get a better job and an apartment with a *cell* phone. We went right then and she bought me one. So of course, I said yes when she offered to 'let me' stay at the house that night. I kept my stuff close, still in my backpack, falling asleep only after everyone else had, and lightly at best. Turns out I was right to be wary.

The next morning, I was awoken early by my bedroom door slamming open and two very large, thug-looking men strolling into my room. "Get up," one of them demanded. "Get the fuck up!" said the other. So, I did. I knew immediately what was happening. And I was *pissed*. I didn't realize that I had my knife in my hand. Or that I was buck naked. I saw them adopt combat stances and I knew that I was faced with a huge decision. I could go to prison for the foreseeable future, either for murder or attempted murder, or I could go to whatever 'treatment program' that they were there to escort me to. I laid down the knife and started to put on my clothes. One of these douchebags had the nerve to try to stop me from putting on my pants. I reminded him of how perverted that was and suggested that he was better suited to working at a summer camp for young boys. That went over well. I was immediately escorted out of the room, past my mother and her boyfriend, both staring as if I was the one who truly needed help, and into an unmarked van out front.

Turns out my mother had deceived me into staying the night so that she could rush me into one of those Wilderness Therapy programs. You know, the ones that all got shut down and sued due to wildly reckless human rights issues. All the people involved in this program deserve to be put through the same program and then put in prison for a few months to think about it. We were forced to hike at least ten miles per day, work for no pay, not allowed to talk outside of mealtimes and 'therapy' appointments, constantly badgered with asinine 'advice' and 'wisdom' (their words) and otherwise ridiculed, abused and belittled by the entire staff. Oh yeah, and we weren't allowed to bathe. For seven weeks. This might sound bitter but it's not. I still hold a degree of irritation toward my mother for enacting her inability to confront her shortcomings on me, but the truth is, I enjoyed my time there. I loved being abused and thrown into the wilderness. I had been constantly alone, afraid, and in survival mode since I was a small child. Now this was the first time I got to put it into practice in the *wild*. Despite how pathetically incompetent and abusive the staff was, they gave me a reason to push *on*. It was the incentive I needed to figure everything out. Or so I thought, at least.

That very first day they put us on a bus and drove us to an unknown location. That's after making us all take turns getting naked, going in a closet-type room, spreading our butt-cheeks and bending our knees, then spinning around in a circle two times. I shit you not. These people belong in prison. Right? Right. When it was time to go, they refused to tell us *where* because so many kids had tried to escape. And they legitimately thought it was because the *kids* were the assholes.

We pulled into a trailhead in the absolute middle of nowhere, pitch black aside from the stars, were handed a 50-pound pack and a headlamp, then 'instructed' to start hiking. We hiked for hours. Finally, they 'instructed' us to stop. No one had a watch, and no one was allowed to talk but I figured it was around 2 am. One of the counselors, a tall woman with blonde dreads with an absolute hatred for anything masculine, came over to me to 'help.' All she did was pull out a piece of paper with instructions on it. On it were diagrams showing eight different types of shelters that could be made with just a tarp. Then she walked away.

It took me an hour after that to finally get something resembling a shelter. Good news too because by this point it was pouring down rain. I had to find a stick that was the appropriate size because we weren't allowed to have metal of any kind, which took time, and I had to improvise stakes for the same reason. Hopefully, you won't have to do this, as stakes are the only thing you can't really improvise very well. Over the next seven weeks, I learned a couple of other methods of making a tarp shelter. There are dozens of different ways to do this but all of them share the same basic requirement: adapting to your surroundings. If you have trees to use, use them. If you have soft brush to lay on, lay on it. Have any kind of natural overhang to use? Use it. It's that easy. You are simply taking a tarp and using it to protect yourself from the rain and wind. The rest is all dependent on your imagination. These are the designs I used, and still use, the most:

Necessary gear:

- **Tarp**
- **'Guy' rope.** These are made specifically for this, so they are narrow enough to fit through the holes on the sides of the tarp and strong enough to hold up to the elements.
- **Stakes**
- **Hiking pole** (or a big stick you find)
- **Knife or axe** (for trimming big sticks you find)

The A-Frame

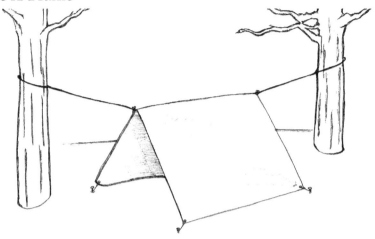

This is first because it's simple, sturdy, and it takes the least amount of time to put together. Funny story, I was on week five or six in the program, time blends in captivity, and I had made an A-Frame tent for the night. I had found a super soft little gully and had put the edge of the tarp right up along the sides. It was a cozy little nest. As such, it was no surprise that I had some company the next day. I had longer hair at the time. I can't tell you why. Just thought it was cool, I guess. But that explains why I didn't wake up right away. When I did, I awoke to loud chewing and tearing noises. I was exhausted so it took me a while to realize that SOMETHING WAS EATING MY HAIR. I started swatting everywhere and yelling, which was a big no-no. I got 'written up' for this later. Worth it. I jumped out of my sleeping bag wearing only my long-johns and tore after the offending squirrel with a huge stick. I was determined to beat some respect into that little bugger. When I cornered it, however, it didn't seem so important. Poor bastard had to eat hair that hadn't been washed in more than a month. Can't get mad at something for being *that* hungry. I watched him tear off through the woods and smiled, then sat and waited for the douchebags to come and yell at me. Anyway, here's how to make an A-Frame:

Find two trees with flat ground between them.

These trees should be about ten to twelve feet apart. This is important if you plan on getting up in the middle of the night to pee. It hurts to shimmy out of your shelter and then walk straight into a tree. Ruins the mood. A lot of times I pick a 'back' side and then have this side be closer to one of the trees than the other, but this does make it more difficult and puts more strain on the rope. Still, it does help with the problem of running into trees. Your call.

Tie the rope to the first tree.

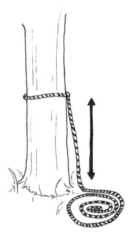

You want the rope to be high enough to allow a little bit of sag. You also want to account for the height of the tarp and any clearance you might want between the bottom of the tarp and the ground. A lot of people just want the rain coverage, so they don't care. I like to feel snug and secure, so I usually make the edges of my tarp come to the ground or close to it. Completely your preference, just make sure you can get in and out easily.

Run the line to the other tree and put the tarp over the rope.

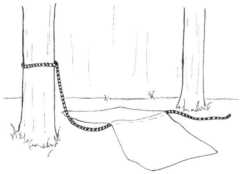

The idea is to get the weight of the tarp on top of the rope before you finish tying it. You're most likely tired at this point and you want to get it right the first time. It is extremely annoying to finish tying your knots and then see that the weight of the tarp is too much for them, causing it to sag, and have to do it all over again.

Tie the rope to the second tree.

Now you have a clear idea of where the tarp is going to line up and whether the sides are going to touch the ground or not. It's also important to note that it is much easier, and requires fewer ropes, to have the stakes go directly through the holes in the tarp into the ground. So, when you are tying the rope to the second tree you are going to want to be sizing all that up and seeing how high you want the rope to go.

Put stakes in the corners.

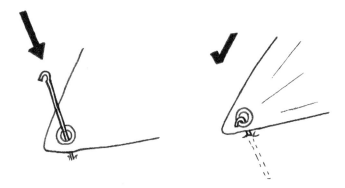

You want these to be as taut as possible without breaking anything. This will maximize the room you have available and make the tarp work best at deflecting rain if the weather turns bad. If you have any extra ropes or stakes it doesn't hurt to put them in where needed to keep the tarp as tight as possible. If your tent is off the ground, you'll need to tie ropes to the corners, then to stakes in the ground or nearby trees.

Put your pack behind where your head is going to go.

I always take my food bag out and hang it from a tree. I have run across my fair share of bears and, frankly, one was enough. But don't do this move if you're planning on keeping your food in your bag. You don't want to wake up to something sniffing your head. This happened to me once, and I almost crapped my pants. The bag is great behind your head because it stops any stray breezes from getting into your shelter. And if it starts pouring it has the added benefit of keeping your head dry as well. Just make sure to put your pack cover on before doing this if it is pouring. It'll make your life drier and more comfortable the next night.

The Holden Tent

This is the tent I had to figure out in the dark on the first night of my wilderness retreat. It is considerably harder to get right than the A-Frame, but it is the most multi-use, all-season type of shelter and should be the first thing you think of. It also has the added benefit of being great for weather that changes quickly. If you are planning on hanging around for a couple of days, or don't know what the weather is going to do, this should be your type of shelter.

Stake in both corners of one of the long sides.

You're going to have to un-do one of the corners shortly to make it taut, but this helps to get the shelter as tight as possible.

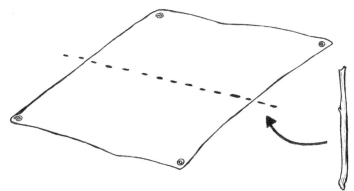

Take the other long side and find the middle, then put your stick or walking staff there.

You are propping up the tent with this pole. Occasionally it will fall backward as you are securing the sides. If this happens repeatedly, do the fourth step before the third.

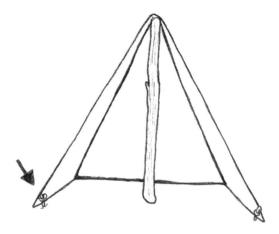

Secure the 'corners.'

You'll want to look at the diagram for this one. You can either put stakes directly into the ground or tie strings and put them through the same holes that you would have used, then attach stakes to the ropes.

By using different size ropes you can make the entrance wider or narrower depending on how the weather is and how much airflow you would like. If you have to cut some ropes for this, make sure to leave some extra room on each one. It's alright if they're too long. If they are too short you might run out of rope before you are finished.

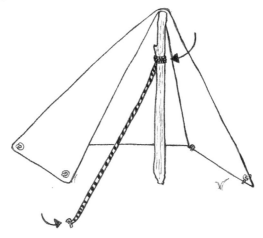

Take a string or rope and wind it around the hiking pole or stick.

I usually carry a hiking staff for this explicit purpose and I have a small keyhole screw attached. What you are trying to do is create tension from the back of the tent through to the front. Not only will this create more headroom, but it will also make sure that the pole doesn't fall in towards you while you are sleeping. Pull the string or rope down to the ground at a 45-degree angle and then use a stake, or two, to secure it.

Go back to the first step and make sure that the back of the tent is as taut in all directions as possible.

35 | How To: Make Friends as an Adult

This is a classic example of the adage: "Those that cannot do, teach." But whatever. As a lifelong outsider and wallflower who has always craved connection and belonging, I have tried seemingly everything there is to try in this world with the sole purpose of finding a connection. Have I been successful? Not always. But that's not for a lack of *trying*. I have been wildly successful at times, which leads to this section of the book.

We all make friends in school. From kindergarten to high school, we are surrounded by other kids and told to learn, participate, and play. At least, that's how it went in public school. Even if you were an alien (raises hand), all the other kids were just looking to have fun so there were plenty of opportunities to be automatically included in almost everything. Sports were mandatory in the schools I attended so you had that to count on. And if you had any social skills at all (puts down hand) then you were almost certain to find at least a few kids that you had a lot in common with.

All that goes out the window after you get out of school. Suddenly all the pretenses and waiting are over. You are free, independent, and can do whatever you want. Suddenly, you realize, you are expected to start a 'life' and 'be successful' in that life. Frankly, I had to start this way before I even got out of high school but some of the people I knew were awkwardly and uncomfortably shoved off that proverbial cliff. They have the scars to prove it and still bitch about it to this day. Everybody typically makes it, maybe with one or two extra stops in their parent's basement. The point is that they *do* make it. This means a job and a place to live, at the minimum. All good, this is to be expected, blah blah blah. What they *don't* tell you about, and what nobody talks about all that much, is how hard it is to meet people and develop relationships outside of work and school as you get older.

Now, anyone who has ever traveled extensively on a shoestring budget probably has worked in the hospitality industry at least once. And everyone who has ever worked in 'the industry' probably knows the awkwardness that typically ensues when the work shift ends and you're hanging out together and *all you talk about is work*. And this isn't limited to the service industry. As adults, we are thrown together willy-nilly into organizations designed to achieve a collective task, whether that's developing software or pedaling tacos. Little to no thought is typically put into how these people are going to get along. Of course, there are exceptions, but the vast majority of places don't give two shits about how their workers interact. They want customers to eat tacos or play on their apps. Bing, bang, boom. This *is* a problem for *you*, however, because a massive number of people spend the majority of their time at their jobs. This means that you might be spending the majority of your time with people you don't care for and don't particularly enjoy. Therefore, the need for meaningful interaction and connection with people you *do* get along with becomes essential.

The question then becomes: "How do I make friends outside of work?" And the answer is complex and difficult. It boils down to how hard you are willing to work and grind. As an adult, you have to go out of your way to make friends. My favorite method was to take jobs that were in the middle of nowhere, where everyone lived and worked together. This either resulted in a bunch of like-minded, connected people that worked well together and formed solid, long-lasting friendships, or a disjointed, emotionally and ethically different group of people who created drama and malice and ultimately all ended up quitting or getting fired at different times. There was rarely any in-between. But hey, it made for some great stories. For those of you who have worked in 'the industry,' you are emphatically nodding your head right now. If you haven't, well, you'll see.

I mention my 'method' because there's actually science behind why some of the worst jobs, hardest encounters, or epic adventures lead to some of the best friends you'll ever have. Turns out adversity breeds companionship. Rebecca G. Adams, a sociologist from UNC-Greensboro, is often (loosely) quoted as stating that the necessary ingredients for friendships are 'constant unplanned interactions' and 'shared vulnerability[30].' And this is exactly what you get when you're either thrown into a public school at an early age with zero life skills and no familiarity with any of the people you're around or tossed into the workforce. Obviously, we don't have countless hours and twelve years of development to burn. Plus, who wants to go through high school again? We need shortcuts.

Good thing there's a study by Jeffrey Hall published in the 'Journal of Social and Personal Relationships,' where he took the time to calculate how long it takes to make varying degrees of friendship. As it happens, it takes around fifty hours to consider someone a casual friend, a modest bump up to ninety hours to consider them 'real' friends, then double that to be 'BFFLs[31].' I don't believe or trust in these numbers at all, but it is still a good framework to work off of. So, it's going to take some work to make friends. It's not going to just arrive, or be handed to you on a platter, like it was in school. You are going to have to make a serious effort to try to identify new chums, swallow that ever-present fear of rejection, create opportunities to hang out, and then keep at it. Relentlessly. Easy right? But we all need connection and human interaction. So, lace up them boots cowpokes, those happy hours aren't going to happy themselves.

Here's a list of all the things to try that might help you meet friends:

Meet-up Groups

Either through Meetup or Facebook, if you search for 'new to the area meet-up groups' you are bound to find a bunch of them. These can be great places to meet like-minded people and they can also easily devolve into shotgun, blind-date groups as well. It's as close to a random assortment as you can get. I've had friends who have had great success with these and even I, the begrudging curmudgeon, found a few good buddies this way. But usually, they are too damned awkward for me. As such, I search for the weirdest and most awesome groups I can find. My all-time favorite was a nighttime, light-up, ultimate frisbee group. The frisbee was OK, but the followup at the pub afterward was the highlight of my week.

---

30   Williams, Alex. "Why Is It Hard To Make Friends Over 30?" The New York Times, 13 Jul. 2012, www.nytimes.com/2012/07/15/fashion/the-challenge-of-making-friends-as-an-adult.html. Accessed 27 Feb. 2023.

31   Hall, Jeffrey A. "How Many Hours Does It Take to Make a Friend?" Sage Journals, 15 Mar. 2018, journals.sagepub.com/doi/full/10.1177/0265407518761225?journalCode=spra. Accessed 30 Jan. 2023.

Gigs

One of the main components of any 'alternative' lifestyle is bringing in income in a variety of different ways. We've all got to eat. I highlighted gig work early on as a great way to do this. This also happens to be a great way to meet other people. It surely falls under the categories of 'unplanned' and 'shared vulnerability' because these gigs usually provide an environment that is something different than what you've experienced before. As an introvert who often tries hard to be an extrovert, I found these gigs a welcome challenge toward staying positive and making friends. Whether it was working at a corn dog stand stuffing processed meat with little sticks, rolling vegan, plant-based sushi at a convention center, or clearing out a massage school of all of their old equipment, it was always something new. You know that the people you are working with are at least a little bit like you and that the experience was just as new to them as it was to you. The key is to always keep an open mind and when in doubt, get your coworker's number and try hanging out at least once.

Sports Groups

Ah, these are easily my favorite. Well, they were my favorite till I snapped my tibia and ruptured my spine. Now physical therapy is my favorite until I get the OK to go back to these activities. In no other place will you find something close to 'playground rules.' All you have to do is show up and ball, and if you suck, *no one cares*. If they *do* care, you just sign up for another group. Wham, bam, thank you, ma'am. And you'd be amazed by just how many types of sporting groups there are. Badminton? Yes, please. As you get older you learn to really appreciate the 'work hard, play hard' mentality. And the adults who play in these leagues do too. Good times all around.

Work

Just not the way you might think! I've worked a ton of different jobs in a dozen different careers. I understand that everybody's job is different. But if you ever have a connection with a client, customer, or colleague, make sure to reach out to them and let them know. If someone from your company has a fit about it? Fuck 'em. This does have the highest chance of failure due to human nature and how people tend to act toward people they are doing business with, but people are brought together for a reason. You pick the reason; the truth remains the same. I used to keep a business card for my business interests and a personal card that read: "We're friends now, get over it." In hindsight, maybe a little overbearing, but it was always worth the laugh. Pay attention to everyone who comes into your life. It is always for a reason. And just because we are at work, which we are a lot, doesn't mean that you can't make a good friend while you're doing it.

Also Work

But this time it's exactly the way that you think. We spend so much time at our jobs that it is completely understandable to think that the people we talk to *all the time* are already our friends. That isn't necessarily the case. As I mentioned, we usually talk about work, work-related things, kids, or any of the other standard conversation topics. Because being vulnerable and talking about real issues at work is usually pretty taboo, we never get to a place where there is any 'shared vulnerability' or experience. In other words, we never really get to know our coworkers. If you can maintain your professionalism at work but also completely disassociate from work when you are hanging out *outside* of work, then you might just be able to pick up some friends this way. Just make certain that you shut down the 'shop talk' as soon as you are out of there.

Fun Ways to Recreate

When I was younger, I thought that the only way I was going to make friends through exercising was to talk to people at the gym or join a soccer team. It wasn't till I got older that I realized that I could join a climbing gym, a kayaking group, or even a curling team, and get the same effect. As a matter of fact, the weirder the activity, *the cooler the people*. It was bizarre and awesome at the same time. Just type in your city or area and then 'fun sports'. You never know if there is a costume-only softball league or an ultimate frisbee team nearby. Give it a shot, you'll be surprised.

Trivia

This is a super easy way to make new friends. First of all, you know they are either going to be a little nerdy, a little competitive, or both. Personally, those people are my jam. I also love trivia, so there's that, but rarely do you have a situation in which everyone is talking about random nonsense, hollering at each other, and you have something to focus on other than awkward introductory talk. I go to as many of these as I possibly can and highly recommend them.

Be Direct

Talk about things that matter to you! I can't count how much time I have wasted talking to people I didn't click with about things that didn't matter to me just so that I could feel less alone. Especially considering how those conversations made me feel *more* alone! It's amazing how far down the rabbit hole of societal conventions and anxiety we can go for a sense of attachment. The answer to this is to just be real. Anyone who doesn't vibe with you, or doesn't like what you have to say, isn't going to be in your life for long anyway. Simply bringing the conversation to a place where you are talking about things you are passionate about or ways that you truly feel about a subject is going to have a profound impact on you, as well as the people around you. By doing this you can quickly sift through what I refer to, in my head of course because I am a positive ray of fucking sunshine, as 'the trash,' and possibly even find some real connections between you and other real human beings.

36 | How To: Meditate

The best thing that I have ever learned to do is to meditate. I find it that important. It is one of the only ways that we can truly get to the core of our existence. I think it is a fundamental responsibility of every human to examine themself and to find what makes them tick. In other words, to find out what has affected us in the past, why, and what makes us happiest *now*. Not to mention, this world is full of anxiety-inducing factors everywhere you look. And it's only going to get more stressful as time goes on. What is the remedy to all this stress? Mindfulness and meditation. In a world of increasingly complex and differentiated truths, meditation is the one thing that remains simple.

The first thing to remember about meditating is that there is no wrong way to meditate.

Anyone who tells you differently is too far up their own ass. You can meditate for five seconds; you can meditate for two hours. You can meditate staring at the ceiling of the bus as some smelly dickwad pushes past you for the second time just the same as you can meditate in a quiet, ambient-lit room with serene pictures of baby deer and multiple types of nature sounds pumping out of fancy, wall-mounted speakers. There are better ways to meditate than others, for sure. But there is no *wrong* way.

Start every meditation with a sense of gratitude.

One of the best sayings I hear is to 'adopt an attitude of gratitude.' I'll let you walk your path and discover what that means for you. Just make sure to try and be grateful for at least one thing as you start your meditation. This can be anything, from the fact that you are wearing shoes (life without shoes sucks), or that you are still breathing, despite it all. Whatever it is for you, just the simple practice of being grateful for five seconds per day will cause a dramatic shift over time. Now, if you can be grateful all day, every day? That might just be nirvana. I'm not sure though. I haven't made it there yet.

Just start.

It can be for as long as you want and it can be in any way that you want. You can get into the ideal posture and form later. The point is that you start to make it a habit. It can start with brief, three-minute-long episodes where you are struggling to maintain focus. That's OK, everyone struggles. It can be by laying down with some headphones on the couch and drifting off into sleep and/or a nap. Whatever it is for you, the important thing is to make it a habit that you do *every day*. Once it becomes routine there is a small shift. With repetition, it becomes something you do automatically when your body 'needs' it. It also becomes something that you look forward to.

As you practice start to identify what *kinds* of meditation you prefer.

There are thousands of different variations. Some have positive affirmations where you talk to yourself about how awesome you are. Some are guided trips through your psyche. Some are just weird music that makes you feel like you're floating through space. A lot of times I like to just listen to my dog breathing as he sleeps. Find out what helps you get to where you want to be when you want to be there.

Posture.

I learned how to meditate with a broken leg and a ruptured spine. At first, before the injuries, I would either sit with my legs underneath my tailbone or crossed in front of me as I sat up straight against a wall. There is something about sitting up 'at attention' that keeps you 'in tune' with what's going in on in your mind and your body. It has always helped me stay focused. Now, it just hurts, so I find either my bed or my couch, both of which are ridiculously, awesomely comfortable, and find a pain-free way to lie down. Either this or the ergonomic chair that I am sitting in as I type. These help me arrange my spine and body in such a way as to maintain my focus and attention to the best of my ability. Not everyone is the same and not every method is going to work for you. This point is that you *try* because in doing so you are physically participating in the efforts of your mind.

That's it! It is that simple. It is in developing a 'practice' that you start to reap the rewards of meditation. Here are some more tips as well:

Meditation groups are great.

Know this though, you don't always have to drink the Kool-Aid. A lot of people can be thrown off by just how far out there some people will go. Frankly, 'crazy' people are the only ones I want to be around, but this isn't necessarily true for a lot of people. Communal meditations have a power to them. Try one and you'll see. That doesn't mean you have to hang around for the hob-nob after they are finished.

Find a free app that provides guided meditations.

Try Insight Timer. It's free and it has yours truly on there. If not that one, there are dozens of apps just like this. They can track your mood, give you reminders at certain times, and even give you statistics on how much you meditate. They are a great tool for fostering a growth mindset and for keeping you engaged in meditation as a process.

Be easy on yourself.

It takes a lifetime to even get 'good' at meditation. You are going to struggle. Either by keeping your mind from shooting off in different directions or your body still. You might straight up forget to meditate for a week. Who knows? Be gentle and patient with yourself. Do the best you can. In the end, your best is all you can do.

If you can, meditate with your dog.

There is no better way that I know to feel grateful than to have my dog next to me. Sleeping or licking my face, doesn't matter. I always feel like the luckiest guy on the planet. Doesn't hurt to rhythmically pet them while you're meditating either.

Make time during the day.

My 'favorite' time to meditate is when I am running errands and, invariably, get stressed out. I always pull over in some sleazy-looking strip mall or next to some intense-looking factory. Wherever I may be when I am feeling stressed, I pull over, put it in park, and *check out* for at least five minutes. You will be amazed at how much easier the rest of your day becomes when you take time to calm down your mind and your emotions.

Use nature.

I routinely take a hike or a walk in the woods with my huge headphones on, blasting all kinds of weird meditation music. Sometimes it works beautifully and sometimes it doesn't. The point is that I am then in nature, observing the day and my relationship to it, breathing intently, and generally surrounding myself with natural beauty. It can help to generate the 'receiving' mindset we are all looking for where we can turn off our brains and simply hear what the universe is trying to tell us. If that doesn't work, thank a tree. Then thank the next one too!

Use yoga, exercise, or EFT tapping to relax your body before meditating.

Some of us are hyperactive all the time and some of us are hyperactive every so often. Regardless, we all understand how it feels to have a bunch of thoughts ping-ponging their way through our brains while our hands are twitching and we seem to be bouncing off of the walls. This state can make it exceptionally hard to meditate. I actually wrote a meditation that helps to deal with this, but suffice it to say that there are a lot of methods to help you calm down enough to get to where you want to be. My favorite is taking a jog. But yoga and EFT work just as well.

37 | How To: Patch a Tent

If you're anything like me then you are going to put your tents and tarps through absolute hell. I have been accused of being abusive toward my equipment on many occasions, which has rewarded me with several opportunities to learn how to *fix* my equipment. And now I get to share what I learned from those opportunities with you. See how positive I am? I am *learning*! Anyway, you'll most likely discover that your tent is ripped when you start hearing mosquitos or it starts to rain, so when this happens, keep in mind: this is why we always check our equipment *before* we are in the middle of nowhere. Oh well! For this fix, you're going to need a kit, which you're going to have to buy in advance, either online or at a sporting goods store. You *can* use random materials in a pinch, like Saran wrap or random pieces of thin plastic, but they won't work for long. So, make sure to carry a patch kit with you. Here's how to fix your tent when it gets a hole:

Clean both sides of the tent around the rip/tear.

If the tear is jagged enough you might want to cut some of the torn pieces to make the shape more uniform. This can be difficult, so if you don't think you need to then don't. Just make sure that you clean the affected area well so that the glue/sealant can seal well. Ideally, your patch kit has an alcohol wipe for this exact purpose, but water and a t-shirt will work just fine in a pinch.

Cut your repair tape.

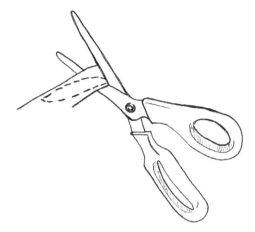

Apply this tape to the outside of the tent. You are also going to want to cut this in a circular shape. The rips and tears will be most likely jagged and your repair tape is only so big. By cutting the patch into an oval, rather than a circle, you can effectively cover all the affected area and seal the tent.

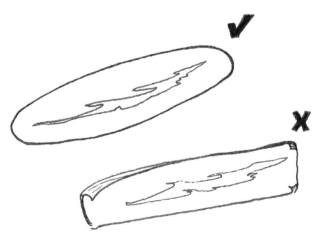

These rounded edges also ensure that the repair tape lasts longer. I have no idea how this works. I'm guessing it's because square patches catch and are ripped off faster. So, make sure that the patch is cut in an oval. If you have an L-shaped tear, or multiple tears, cut the tape in multiple directions as ovals.

Apply the tape.

You'll want someone to help you position and stretch the tent into the shape it will be when it is put together. Find some kind of a flat surface to use. If you can't, use the ground as best you can. The idea is to get the right amount of tension that will be applied by the tent poles and by the occasional swaying back and forth, both by the weather and, ideally, by having a good time. If you are 'in the field' make sure to apply the tape to both sides, just apply the inside tape when it is already set up. It won't do much in the long run, but it will help for that night and the next couple of days.

Check your seams.

Hopefully, you have a seam sealer in your patch kit. And you have set up camp early in the day. And it is beautiful and sunny outside. Because to apply seam sealer you are going to have to let it sit all day and try to stay out of the fumes. It is not going to work well in the rain. If you've got an old tent, then the seams are bound to go eventually, and you are only going to find that out when it's pouring and you least want the tent to be leaking. Also, if you have a patch that you've applied and you have the time on a dry day then you should apply the seam sealer to your patches. It will help to keep them attached and provide a water-resistant layer to your tent as well.

38 | How To: Patch Your Jeans

To be honest, I was going to add a lot more sections for how to patch things. Clothes, walls, packs, tires, etc. It was the section I wrote on how to patch a bike tire that broke me. I hate bicycles. Riding bicycles has messed me up worse than just about anything I have ever done. And some of the things I have done have been insanely dangerous. So, forget bicycles and their stupid tires. Ditto for patching all the things you might need to patch. Except for your jeans. I have had to patch my jeans more times than I can count. This society, unfortunately, makes us wear pants. As such, you are most likely going to have a pair. Maybe two, if you have room in your pack. And you are probably not going to want to spend the money on a new pair anytime soon. The obvious answer is to know how to fix any tears that might happen between long-term stops. I am only going by the hand-sewing method because that's all you're likely to have in you or be able to find. Here's how to apply a basic fix to your jeans:

Before you start sewing you are going to need one of two things:

Fabric mending tape.

Or

Patches.

I have had better luck with fabric mending tape myself, but whatever floats your boat. The difference is that fabric mending tape is better if the cut is small. You flip the jeans inside out, cut the tape to a shape bigger yet similar to the tear, then either iron it into place or use a hair dryer. I always then sew the thing on there, going over the tear and into the fabric mending tape. Be warned, this can be very tricky and frustrating. But I usually buy myself an extra month of use by doing it, so it is worth it to me.

Patches are best if the tear is irregular and/or large. Fabric mending tape just isn't going to be able to keep it all together. You're going to need a patch that is large enough to cover the hole. You can either sew it on top or underneath. It's the dealer's choice. They also make iron-on patches that you can simply cut to size and then apply over the hole. All you have to do is iron it! In my experience these don't hold up for long though, so I like to sew them on. This is a simple process. All you do is undo the film on the back of your patch, once it is cut to size, and apply it to the jeans. Then you whip out your sewing needle and your fabric. You can try to match the color if you want to. I always use black because it's easier to see.

Start by pushing the needle through a corner.

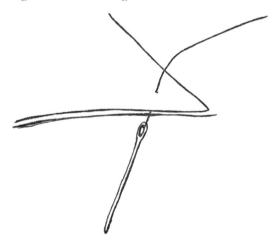

Then pull it out the other side about a quarter to a half inch away.

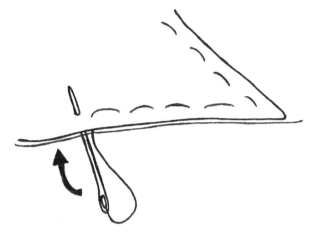

Continue along the outside of the patch, going in on one side and then in from the other. You should be leaving about a quarter inch (if possible) in on the jeans to make sure it doesn't tear out.

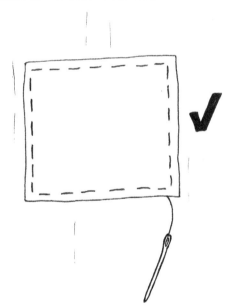

Do this until you go all the way around the patch.

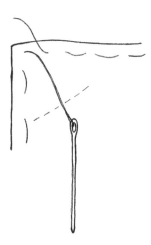

When you are finished sewing you are going to need to tie off the thread. If you have a lot of thread left on the needle this can be easy.

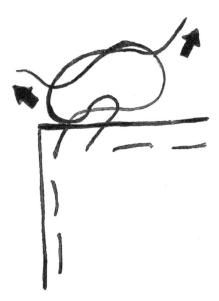

Cut both sides of the thread and then tie them like you would a knot. Then cut the remaining thread from the knot.

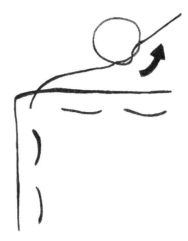

If you only have one thread coming off of the needle or don't have enough to do the last move, just use the thread you have left to create a basic knot.

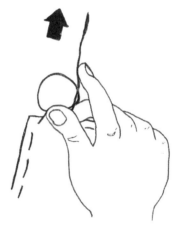

Last, use your finger to hold the knot, then tie it off.

39 | How To: Pay Your Bills on Time

I'll bet you're thinking something along the lines of: "I know how to do this. I just sign up for Autopay." And hey, that can be a great way of doing things. But there are two assumptions that you have to make if you are going to do that. First, you are assuming that you will always have a large enough balance in your bank account to cover any amount of bills that you ostensibly can't remember the due dates of in the first place. And for those of us traveling on a tiny-tiny budget, that's a big if. Second, you are assuming that these companies are always going to charge you the correct amount *and* that they are going to keep charging you the same correct amount the entire time. And therein lies the rub.

Most companies give you a discount for enrolling in Autopay because they are most likely offering a temporarily incentivized rate for their services. Deep down in the fine print that you probably didn't read, 'cause who has time for that crap, it clearly states in size three font that this rate is only good for a short period, say, three months. And in three months that rate is going to jump up significantly. Except that you aren't going to notice because you have everything set on Autopay.

Now, this might be peanuts and raisins to some of you. You might be saying to yourself: "It's not worth my time to care that much." The problem is that you're wrong. These bills always jump up a significant amount for a reason. And no, I am not going to research these statistics because A: I don't care, B: Statistics can all be manipulated (Thanks Matthew Berry!), and C: I am right, and we all know it. Let's move right along. These bills always jump up a significant amount for no reason. Look at it this way: each bill you pay is worth a set number of hours of your time. If you do some basic math, then you have a vague idea of what you're making per hour. Then look at the extra amount that they charge you and turn it into hours of your time. Do you care now? I'm going to guess, yes. And *now*, getting on hold for a half hour to call the company about why your bill mysteriously went up makes a lot of sense, doesn't it? And if you are paying your bills by yourself every month you notice when this is happening. So, when you follow the basic method I've got below, you'll not only notice it happening, but you'll know the precise moment to either switch to a different company or eliminate the service.

Brainstorm a list of all of your bills and put them in some kind of order.

I use a little notebook app on my phone. This should include your phone, internet, streaming, utilities, insurance, etc.

Order them all by how much they cost, with the most expensive one first.

After each bill, detail exactly what they cost, roughly, per month. This helps when you are adding them all up.

Underneath each bill, write the website to visit or the phone number you have to call to pay them on time.

We all do the same thing. We register for our bills online, get everything squared away, then promptly forget our password. Or, even better, we call in our monthly payment and then immediately lose the phone number we waited on hold for twenty minutes. This is one of the things that makes America so interesting too. We are so driven toward buying and consuming that we voraciously acquire credit cards and other kinds of debt. And yet, this country makes it hard to *pay people*. Why this is, who knows? Keep the info handy and make it easy on yourself.

Set up your due dates so they are all roughly at the same time.

This step is the hardest. This means logging into all of your accounts and going through the process of changing your due date, which almost all companies offer as a service. This is key to paying your bills on time because you have that one week of the month where it's Bill Week.

Get a month ahead.

This is the second hardest step. The real key to always paying your bills on time? Being ahead. And getting ahead means doubling up on the first month of your bills. Some companies make you pay for their service before you even use it. Phone companies immediately come to mind. But a lot of companies, like utilities, have you pay after you use their service for a month or so. By setting up your dues dates to be around the same time you link these two things so you're never falling behind. And by double-paying on the services that you have to pay for *beforehand*, you are effectively getting ahead one month. Therefore, if you run into a short-term money crunch, or if you just forget, then you are not going to lose your phone number and the water will keep running.

40 | How To: Pay Your Taxes

I wrote this section because of how many times I have heard people complain (through memes) that they had to learn the quadratic equation in high school but weren't taught basic life skills, like how to pay taxes. I can sense you, right now, trying to remember the quadratic equation. Shhhh, give up, it's not worth it. Just be OK with yourself for having tuned it out. Not all of us were born to care about math. Having a flashback to sobbing while studying for that math final? It's OK. Shhhh… don't cry…. there, there. Anyway, paying your taxes is simple and relatively straightforward as long as you remember two things.

1. **They are designed to be needlessly complicated.**

2. **Anything that is needlessly complicated is just as indecipherable to those reading it as to those writing it.**

Whether we care to admit it or not, there is a part of our mind that thinks that the government is an omniscient and extremely capable array of institutions that actually care about what you do. It is exactly the opposite. The government has no idea what it is doing and is run by career civil servants who neither care about the average person nor have anything close to resembling an intense desire to hunt you down. They are just people who want to be paid like everyone else. The only difference is that they are members of institutions that are subject to politics. And because of these politics, they are criminally underfunded. Thus, their employees are overworked, overstressed, and generally overburdened to the point that they are not going to move mountains to make sure that you are compliant with every single law and line that exists on your tax file.

All you have to do is not raise any red flags. And to do this you simply have to file *most* of your stuff in as honest a way as possible. Do you make tips? Great. You're going to have to report some of them. All of them? Hell no. We are not saints! Plus, you don't get paid anything close to resembling your true worth. Nor is it a 'living wage.' There is also no real way to prove that you really did make any tips. It is no surprise that the law assumes that you are only going to make eight percent, in tips, of the gross sales of food and drink. Eight percent! Anyone who has waited tables or bartended before knows that is a ridiculous number. But that is the line drawn in the sand. Everyone knows that they can't prove it. *But neither can you.* Which means that you have to toe the line. That doesn't mean you have to go above and beyond. Just pony up this paltry number and no one will come calling.

This same concept applies to just about everything tax-related. Most people are going to have W-2s, which are the easiest for paying your taxes during the year and come tax time. Essentially these are an agreement with the government that your employer is going to take money out of every paycheck and pay the government more than you owe. The government is going to hold that money until tax time when you can then prove that you overpaid and thus get a refund. The government gets paid, they get to hold your money and make interest off of it, and you eventually get your money back. Everyone wins.

The way that you can get more of your money back, however, is with deductions. The best tax deduction you can possibly have is to bang out a lot of kids but I doubt that you want to do that. As such, I highly recommend donating to various charities throughout the year. It is not only an awesome thing to do, but it also helps you out when you file them under deductions. Just make sure not to give to big corporations. They have repeatedly proven that they will waste and embezzle money, and otherwise use their means ineffectively. Give to local food banks, toy and coat drives, and even local church events. There are few better feelings than seeing someone walking around in a coat that you once donated, or knowing a kid is opening the Lego X-Wing set that they wanted on Christmas. And you end up getting the money back anyway? Everyone wins.

As far as ease and difficulty are concerned, you might want to consider paying a company for the use of their software. Because I own small businesses and use software tied to a certain company to track my business spending and expenses, I am practically tied to using one company over the others. But you've got your pick of the litter. All of them help you find every deduction that applies to you wherever it is that you live. Some states offer deductions for moving, or starting a company, or paying registration and property taxes on your car. Ponying up the bucks to pay a company to walk you through it can oftentimes be extremely beneficial. But if you don't want to pay there are free options as well. As of this writing the IRS even offers its own free service. It doesn't work very well but it's easy. And if you are only filing with W-2 I highly recommend this because you can start and finish within the hour.

If you are freaking out about your taxes, first just remember to breathe. Maybe crack a seltzer. I can't remember the last time I finished my taxes in one sitting. Take breaks, go for walks, watch a movie or two. Breathe. Here are some tips as well:

- **If you do owe money, and don't have any to give, don't panic.** You can always set up an installment payment plan.

- **Start filing your taxes on Jan. 1st.** Most people delay and this is how they get fucked. I have a small business, so I am constantly collecting receipts and other paperwork. I keep these in a big ass box that is poorly 'organized.' So, on Jan 1st, after a big breakfast, I sit down and start to organize them. I also start to make a list of what I might be waiting on, or what I need to pull from other places. This planning makes it much more manageable.

- **File before April 15th.** This is Tax Day, usually, if you weren't familiar already. You want to have everything go as efficiently as possible and the highest chance of this is before the IRS gets slammed. Get in before the rush, get your refund back before anyone else, and call it a year.

- **Drive for work? Track your miles.** There are apps for that. As of this writing, the standard deduction is 57.5 cents per mile. If you did 1,200 trips for Uber that year, you probably just got a tax write-off in the thousands. If you track your miles, that is.

- **Deduct your medical expenses.** I spend a lot of time at the doctor. And the therapist. It is just the facts of life. I pay them and move on along my merry way. But I *can* deduct these. Yay, Capitalism! Keep track of your receipts, or just scan through your bank statements, tally 'em up, and deduct them.

- **Pay into your IRA.** If you don't have an IRA, get one. It is a tax-free way to save for your later years and when you put money in you can directly deduct that amount (up to a certain amount) on your taxes. It's not only investing in your future; it's investing in your bottom line at the end of the year.

- **Yes, you can deduct your student loan payments.**
- **If you do go and have someone do your taxes, or if you pay a website to file through them, you can deduct those fees as well.**

41 | How To: Play Guitar

I'm not going to lie, I learned how to play guitar because I had a lot of angst, needed an outlet for my depression, and I thought it was a great way to meet girls. I'm still not sure if it was great for any of those things but the point is that I *believed* it. And because I believed it, I enjoyed it. And after years of enjoying it, I became good at it. I still only know 15 chords, definitely can't play anything resembling 'difficult,' and sometimes get very frustrated with various things. But I can hold a rhythm and pluck some strings. It's fun and I enjoy it and that's all that matters.

I think most people are hesitant to start playing music because we are constantly surrounded by music that is so good that we think we can never 'match up.' I've heard so many people say something similar when talking about the fact that they play an instrument, things like: "I'll never be able to do that." Or, "I sound like crap." Or even, "I suck." And most people stop playing! I know I have. For long periods, even. And when I come back, I am always wondering why on Earth I ever let myself stop! So, the first thing to remember is to forget about the Big-Name Bands, the angelic voices, and the supreme talent you may be hearing on your headphones. Just because there are some insanely talented musicians out there doesn't mean it isn't worth your time to play an instrument. If you enjoy it, do it. It's that simple.

Now that you've pushed through the most common mental hurdles surrounding playing guitar you have to learn how to play. I am not going to do an in-depth example of how to do this. There are so many YouTube videos and offerings that you can look up. Plus, music is all about finding your passion and method anyway. Trying to copy someone else's exact way of doing things is only going to detract from your joy of *doing it,* which is the only reason you are playing. I am just going to share the basic means by which I learned guitar, complete with some basic chord diagrams. If you start this way, you might just find that you are writing your own songs and singing along faster and better than you ever thought you could.

Learn these five chords:

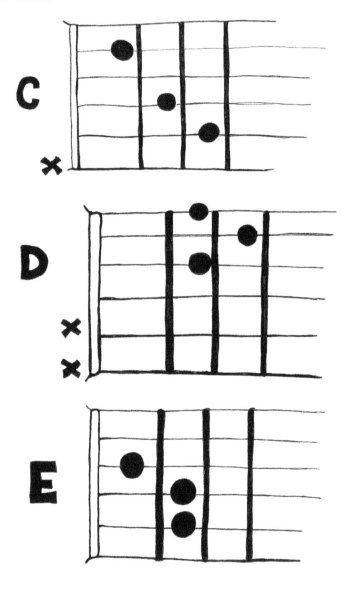

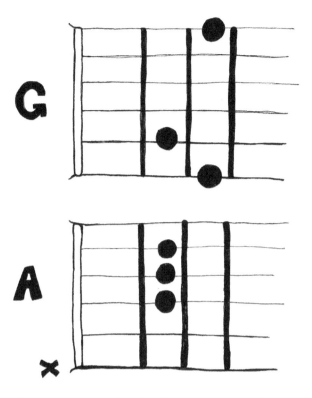

First of all, the way that I teach guitar has always been about empowering others to figure it out for themselves. I want people to learn how to use their fingers, then learn how to strum chords that their fingers know how to play. Once you do that, you can play anything. That being said, you still might be wondering what you are looking at here. These are called 'tabs' and they depict the fretboard of the guitar as if you were looking down on it from above. The dots represent where one of your fingers needs to go to make the desired chord. The 'x' hovering above any string you see simply means to not play that string for that chord.

As a side note, you'll hear all kinds of jokes about people writing songs with these chords and how everyone sounds like everyone else. Don't let it deter you. All music is recycled. There are only so many notes to play and so many ways of playing those notes together. It takes a great composer an hour with a full orchestra to fully separate their piece and distinguish themselves from their peers. You are one person with one voice and one guitar. Fuck 'em.

These chords form the backbone of most songs you are going to want to strum, especially those that are easy enough for beginners. Plus, they're fun! Once you learn these you can easily move on to chords with increasing levels of difficulty and complexity. Start with these though. Repeat them endlessly. Switch between them in random patterns. Learn them back and forth, so that you can play them without even looking at the guitar. These chords will teach your fingers how to push the strings and how to hold their form as you create. It is essential that you also build calluses on your fingers for when you start to play faster. It will sound strange and off-key at first. Do not be deterred. Everyone starts somewhere and you are starting here.

Once you are even remotely confident playing one or two of these chords, you are going to want to learn how to sing. Want to know a secret? Everyone can sing. Everyone. We constantly lie to ourselves that we can't. I used to be that way. I would only sing in private. And I would wince every time I missed a note or didn't sound the way that I wanted to. But I would sing, and sing, and sing some more. I quickly found that just hitting certain frequencies at certain times made me feel better. And then one day I was strumming those five chords above and I decided to sing. And what do you know… it sounded great. Finally, it hit me: I just needed a rubric; a measuring stick. I found that by using the chords that I knew reflexively from strumming them so many times, I could then sing notes! And I was somehow *in tune*. Absolutely wild.

The trick is to strum your chords, over and over, building your calluses and teaching your fingers to make the music. And while you do it, sing the chords you are strumming. That's it. If you're strumming a G-chord, sing a G-note. Strumming a C-chord? Sing a C-note. I guarantee you'll do this for barely five minutes before you start to get it. After this, you'll start improvising. Before you know it, you'll be writing a song, you'll be making music, and you'll be playing guitar.

42 | How To: Play Poker

Poker is the ultimate game for learning how to lie, deceive, and cheat your way to a solid payday. I have been horrible at it just as many times as I have won. So, I figured I would add this section just to throw some ideas and pointers your way. It is handy to know a little about it because this is one of the most popular gambling games you will find and it happens to be fun to play with the right group.

First, keep in mind that there are a ton of different kinds of poker. The one that we will be discussing here is called Texas Hold 'Em. It's the most fun, the most played, and is prominently featured in mainstream media. There are a ton of other versions, so make sure to note that this is just one of those many. That way you won't get confused if you sit down to play and everything is much different than you expect.

Second, if you are looking for a detailed exposition on the mechanics of how to play this game, you are out of luck. I don't care enough to teach you and frankly, I have never learned anything from reading about it. I am a kinetic learner, through and through, and when it comes to games of this complexity, I don't see any other way to be. You can read about it endlessly, but you'll never truly know how to play until you play. So, look up a guide or ask someone to show you. Whatever floats your boat. What I am going to teach you is how to read the table.

See, in poker, you aren't playing your cards as much as you are playing *your hand*. And playing the people around you. At any time you can bluff in a game of poker. You can make it seem like you have a great hand and you can make it seem like you have a terrible hand. You are trying to get the people around you to think one way or another. The main way that you achieve this is through your behavior. Once you realize that it really doesn't matter what cards you have the game takes on a completely different meaning. Obviously, you are going to want some 'good' cards and a 'good' hand. And you are going to want to wait for those 'good hands' to materialize. But you can't wait your whole life. And 'good hands' don't mean donkey dick if the cards on the table aren't in your favor. So, we are going to focus on how to maintain a poker face and what kinds of 'tells' are present, both on your face and theirs.

'Tells' are exactly what they sound like: things that tell you what the other player is intending. 'Tells' can be a nervous heightening of the pitch in their voice, they can be lots of blinking, or maybe they always talk about their dog when they are anxious. Could be anything. It's up to you to find out. Also, keep in mind that you could be showing the same things. The name of the game is to be paying attention to the humans around you and how they are behaving.

Watch their eyes.

There are a ton of ways that the eyes can tell more than we wish they would. This goes both ways. A lot of professional players will wear sunglasses for this very reason. The eyes are the windows to the soul. They show what they show. Watch for other players not making eye contact, making *too much* eye contact, etc. For example, if a player is bluffing hard and just laid down a big bet, their tell might be that they are suddenly not making eye contact with anyone else. This could also be an intentional way of luring you in. This game is fantastic.

Watch their hands.

A lot of players will hide their hands when they are nervous or crack their knuckles when they are confident. These are the easy ones to spot. Make sure to also watch what players *do* with their hands, particularly when it comes to their cards and their chips. Some players will anxiously play with their chips. This can indicate that they are bluffing and that they are worried about how much they are losing. Some players will hide their cards, which I think is technically against the rules, but whatever. This could mean that they have really good cards and they don't want anyone to know. Are you getting the gist of this? You are playing the people at the table, not the cards. This game is about observational skills. Watch everything about your opponents.

Listen to their voice.

A player talking can mean just about anything. Most games you are going to play in aren't going to be high-stakes. Rather, they are going to be friendly games with groups of friends. As such, you don't have to pay as much attention to the table talk. What you *do* want to pay attention to is the tone and pitch of the other players' voices. A lot of people will talk a lot faster when they have a really good hand as well. I always listen for high pitches. They mean that someone is nervous. And that is usually the time to bluff!

Attention.

This is especially relevant in friendly games. There's money on the table, for sure, and you are trying to win, but it's not life-changing money. You're there to have fun. Which makes it all the more valuable to notice who is paying attention and when. It's easy to fold at these games, especially early on, so if a player is giving a certain hand a lot of attention, then they probably think they are going to win. Or they are full of it and trying to bluff you out. A lot of times I will spend the money to get them to show me their cards, even if I know that I am going to lose. This is just to make them, and the table, aware that they like to bluff. This can seriously take the wind out of some especially fervent bullshitters.

If you haven't caught onto this already, this game is played mostly on an observational level. You are using your senses and intelligence to effectively (or ineffectively) guess when people are bluffing, lying, cheating, deceiving, etc. And it is an absolute blast. Your cards do mean something. The best hand is always the best hand. And when you are starting it can help to only play when you have something. But as you go, just remember to watch everyone around you throughout the game. Watch what they look like when they win, watch what they look like when they lose.

You can also start paying attention to what *you* look like as you play. I like to pretend I am Daniel Craig, accent and all. It makes me look stoic, or so I like to think. I also love to create my own tells. I make an exaggerated tell, like getting overly excited about a hand. Then I make sure to get in a situation where everyone sees my cards. The first time, I try to lose on purpose. Then I wait for a really, really good hand. And a really, really big pot. Then I throw down the same exaggerated tell I created earlier, baiting the other player(s). They think they have me, all the way up until I *take their money*! Good times all around.

43 | How To: Regain Your Positivity

Just yesterday I was reconnecting with people on the Big Social Network. I deleted it years ago when I met my ex-wife. I had shunned society as a whole and generally took a deep dive into myself, as opposed to connecting with people and my community. I wouldn't recommend it to anyone. It created a whole new set of problems. But the point is that I was correcting this and reconnecting with people I hadn't talked to in a long time. I immediately reached out to an old buddy I hadn't talked to in years.

It immediately became clear that my old buddy had no interest in the same type of relationship we'd had before. No problem, people change. What also became extremely clear very quickly was that a *ton* of horrible things had happened to my friend. His family had been decimated by drugs, suicide, and crime. His partner and he had fallen apart. He was alone and back in his hometown, where he had never wanted to be, 'stuck' in a situation that he didn't want to be in. He was clearly in a bad spot and in a bad way.

I assumed that I could take up the same mentor-mentee relationship we'd had back then. Yeah, well, I was *wrong*. My friend didn't want any of the old advice or support I had been used to giving. He was caught up in the negative, shielding himself from the horror of his current experience by pushing me away. Probably pushing *everyone* away. Even in our brief conversation, I could feel the pain and malice radiating off of him. He was down in 'the hole,' and when you are down there, it is hard to see the light, it is hard to hear anyone, and it seems impossible to scrabble your way out. You are constantly faced with incomprehensible grief and sadness. Impotence and rage. You are a victim of circumstance and of your limitations. It is a waking nightmare; a hellscape of experience. I have been there, multiple times and know it well. So of course, when my friend cussed me out and told me, in no uncertain terms, to fuck right off, I understood.

We are going to be tested in this life. Some people are luckier than others. Maybe we truly do live multiple lives, accumulate negative and positive karma, and are reapportioned back into the world in various situations depending on how 'good' or 'bad' we were in our past lives. Maybe the universe gives us different situations and lessons to teach us how to transcend our own experiences. Maybe all this suffering is just paying for admission into the Great Beyond. Or maybe none of it means jack and we are all just transitory participants in a random chaos that means absolutely nothing. Regardless of what your opinion is, we are all going to be tested. That is the universal truth. You are going to face untold and unspeakable tragedy. You are going to lose people you love. You are going to lose yourself. And because of this, you are going to come face-to-face with lessons. It is up to you to choose whether or not you learn from them.

In the case of my buddy, he is wrapped up in his tragedy. Can't blame him. All I can do is hope that he faces it, sees the lessons to be learned, and contacts me some time. Because the fact is, we can feel sorry for ourselves, focusing on what happened, how, and why. We can focus all of our attention on making sure that we never get hurt again. That we build walls so impossibly high that no one will ever be able to scale them. We can change our personality and the very core of our being to become different people, 'unhurtable' people, 'dominant' people. We can scrabble around and swim in our victimhood and negativity... or we can learn. Instead of looking at yesterday, we can look at today. We can free our minds. Now, answer me honestly, did you just scoff at that notion? Did you immediately disregard it? Because if you did, why? Why is it so impossible for you that you *could* or *might* be more of a positive person? If you can answer that question honestly, and I highly suggest that you do, then you have already tackled the main issue that might be in your way. The rest is all downhill from there. Because if you can see your tragedies as lessons, and your challenges as opportunities to learn and grow, then these tragedies and challenges *stop being difficult.*

The answer is to look at your life as an opportunity rather than a burden. Everything might be a cascade of crap and horrible things might be occurring to you or around you. But that doesn't mean that you aren't still fortunate to have your eyes, your ears, your fingers. You still woke up this morning. These are just the basics but the point is the same. It is up to you to find a positive spin; *your* way of triumphing over your challenges. Because that is how we regain our positivity. By challenging our negativity. We are only here because of the light. The light of the Sun, the light of God, whatever it is to you. We require light to survive. And by challenging these negative thoughts with optimism and positivity, you are shining light on yourself in your hole. You are actively regaining control of an impossible situation. That is how to regain your sense of self and your direction in life, regardless of what you are facing.

44 | How To: Start a Conversation

The preamble for this is that the vast majority of the conversations I have started in my life have been at bars, airports, bus stations, train stations, and other places where people are trying to get somewhere else. I have no idea why, but it's easier to start conversations in these places. Maybe it is because everyone is waiting and bored. Maybe it's because we feel like we *should* be talkative and friendly. Or maybe it's because we are all sharing a unique experience. Who knows? It's easier. So don't start barking at me if you use these tips and they don't work talking to Karen next to the melon stand in Whole Foods.

Start immediately.

I am an introvert. I have, frequently, been forced to be an extrovert. It is exhausting. But one thing I have learned when being forced to be an extrovert is that the best way to start a conversation is to not overthink it. The longer you wait the more awkward you are going to feel. And the person is going to come up with their assumptions about you. Which you are then going to think about. And then you're going to either overthink your overthinking or you're going to panic. How long have you been thinking about this? How long have I been standing here? Did I just say all that *out loud*? Yeah, you know the spiral. The best way to derail any potential awkwardness is to just jump in and say hello.

Ask for information.

This works well when you're in a new place and genuinely don't know anything about it. Usually, I would look up some things to see and places I wanted to go, then ask people what their favorites were. If any of them lined up with that then I was definitely going there. More often, local people were happy to share some of the cooler spots to go that weren't listed anywhere else. This is occasionally a good way to make friends, as fellow travelers will often invite you along to wherever they are going. Even if you aren't traveling you can still ask people questions about the area too. People love to tell you about where their favorite Chinese restaurant is.

Throw out a compliment.

Make sure to read your audience beforehand. Conversations die quickly if you come off the wrong way, like seeming flirty when you're not trying to. Stick to superficial compliments about what people are wearing or how they hold themselves. Everyone loves a little bit of affirmation, though. So, if you're not hitting it off in conversation, at least you're making a positive difference in the world around you.

Ask about them.

People love to talk about themselves. They love to tell their story and talk about their passions. If you ask them what they are doing in whatever place you are in, chances are they would love to tell you. Starting a conversation can be as simple as asking why they are sitting where they are sitting. If not that, ask about their family. And if that doesn't work, ask them about what they are going to eat for lunch. I love this one because it throws people off just enough that they leave their comfort zone.

Sports.

I was a bartender for a long, long time so I was constantly around sports. I learned them in and out. It is almost another language that you can speak that has absolutely nothing to do with the world that we live in. If you don't know anything about them, or can't be bothered to care, no matter. You don't have to know anything about sports to pull this off. If you see someone watching a game of some kind, just ask: "Who are we rooting for?"

Don't linger on small talk.

Everyone is obsessed with small talk, yet most people hate small talk. It seems that the world is constantly prattling on about the weather, politics, traffic, etc. It's boring. Don't be boring. Say something original. Go out on a limb. If they don't like it? Fuck 'em. Start with the weather, of course. Or their cool ass tattoos. But then move quickly onto another topic that means something. Ask someone what their dreams are, or where they see them-selves in five years. See if you can get them talking about their day. You'll be surprised what tumbles out of people's mouths when they are discussing something they are passionate about, even with a complete stranger.

Ask for an opinion about some drama.

Whenever I am around people it is usually because someone in my life is stressing me out and I need a break from it. As I mentioned, I am an intro-vert. If I am in public there is probably a good reason for it! Anyway, it is no mystery that there are some bad apples in this world, and a lot of times these are people who are so miserable that they just need to take it out on me in any way that they can. I publicly shame them by asking people what they think about the situation. I am certainly not a saint. It is usually funny, always cathartic, and a great way to make some acquaintances.

45 | How To: Survive a Mugging

Traveling and living a low-income existence is naturally going to lead you into less developed and 'rougher' areas than you might normally be in. You will find yourself in situations where you stick out and become a target, more so than you already are as a traveler. In such situations, it is common to run into trouble and the worst version of this is when someone tries to rob you. A lot of times these people are desperate and desperate people do very stupid things. These situations are very, very dangerous. A single wrong move or word can very easily get you killed. As such, make sure to follow the advice below if you ever do find yourself face-to-face with an assailant.

Prevention.

The first thing to do is to lower your chances of getting mugged in the first place. Muggers will most often gravitate toward dark, isolated places. Stay in the light and stay within earshot of a crowd and you will dramatically lower your chances of running into this. Muggers also frequently hang out near ATMs, where they surprise their victims with a knife or a gun and then force you to pull out money and give it to them. Avoiding ATMs at night is key, especially if they are on a side street. Lastly, you want to always be wearing neutral clothing. You want to blend in, if possible. If you can't do this then you need to prepare accordingly. Dressed up for a night on the town? Great. Take a taxi or an Uber straight from the hotel to the restaurant and back. Don't get caught on the street. If you pay a little attention to how you appear and where you are at certain times you can drastically reduce any potential thefts.

Don't fight.

Just give 'em what they want. Remember that you are dealing with someone desperate enough to approach a random person with a weapon and try to rob them. Imagine what must be going through their minds. Or, perhaps more importantly, *not* going through their minds. They might be insanely high. And drugs mixed with desperation are a very toxic mix. Just give them the money and comply with what they tell you. It's just not worth it to get stabbed.

Don't get close.

When you do give them your stuff, don't hand it to them. Judge the situation closely. You aren't trying to piss them off or push them further over the edge. But there is no reason to get within striking distance. You want to calmly and slowly toss your stuff either to them or on the ground. I am fast and was much faster a decade ago. Tossing my cash on the ground was a great way to get their eyes directed downward, which I took as an opportunity to book it in the opposite direction. Not everyone is going to be confident in their ability to outrun someone, so make sure to stay out of range of whatever weapon they've got in their hands.

Get gone.

If you can book it, book it. Usually, the mugger will take your wallet and phone and start running. If they do, start making noise. If they run that means they are alone. If they don't start running then they are either in their own neighborhood already or they have help around the corner. This means that *you* have to get moving. You don't have to run if it will make you a bigger target but don't be ambling along. If you sense that there are worse dangers than simply losing your wallet, however, get out of there as fast as you can go.

46 | How To: Talk to People

Again, I am an introvert. But I *want* to be an extrovert. This can cause some internal tension at times and a great deal of painfully awkward interactions. But it can also lead to meeting some great people! And that's what it's about. We need human interaction. Some of us are blessed with a great family or friend group, full of caring, supportive, wholesome people. A lot of us are not. As such, we have to go out and relentlessly search for those connections. And if you're like me, it can oftentimes be frustrating and difficult. But fear not! If you continue to try and put yourself out there you *will* find those good people who will treat you the way you deserve to be treated. Here are a couple of tips to get started:

Leave the issues, problems, and dilemmas behind.

Now, that's not to say that these aren't important to talk about. We all need a healthy space to vent and air out our innermost thoughts. Everybody has their problems. But when you are just meeting someone, it is important to try and simply *be*. It takes time for fellow humans to warm up to people enough to be able to lend support. We have to like them first! I practice a technique that I think is called 'The Locker' (Thanks, Chelsea!). I imagine the various feelings and emotions I am experiencing as different versions of myself. Then I imagine a steel gun safe. Upon opening my gun safe I can see the coolest, most expansive man cave anyone has ever seen, complete with a hot tub and pool table. I practice leading the versions of myself experiencing these emotions into the locker/man cave and closing the door. They will be fine in there until I am ready to experience them fully. This usually opens me back up to the experience of *being*, communicating, and thus, being open to hearing what the other person is saying.

Compliments.

Make sure to leave the notion of sexuality or flattery behind here. You are trying to make a lasting, friendship-based connection, not find a partner. Unless you are, of course, and then go ahead. The love of your life is only going to walk through the door for the first time once. But you probably aren't thinking that way every day. So, use compliments wisely and to your advantage. I like to focus on things that I truly admire about the other person. Their posture, their laugh, their style, etc. I also like to comment on things that they have clearly put a lot of time and effort into. This often equates to hair and tattoos, but it can be anything. We are all human, life is hard, and we all crave the relief of hearing that we are doing something 'right.' If you start with a compliment, you are far more likely to start a great conversation.

Put down your phone.

Just think, when you are by yourself at a coffee shop, what do you do after you grab a coffee and then find a seat? I'm going to go ahead and bet that you whip out that smart brick. And then I'm guessing that you spend the next ten minutes browsing all of your social media accounts, checking your email, making to-do lists, and otherwise not focusing on anything around you. And then when you finally do come back to yourself it feels like it's too late. Now it's awkward to look around and start a conversation, right? Too much time has passed! It hasn't but that is definitely how it can feel. The trick is to be present in the moment. Simply sit with the awkwardness and anxiety of being in a new place. Let it wash through you, over you, and out of you. Look around the room, don't be shy, and see if you catch an eye or two. If you do, great! Give them a quick smile. If they smile back, great! That's an invitation. If not, move right along. You are now present in the moment and can easily transition to talking to an actual human being. If not, well, there's always your smart brick.

Eye contact.

This has always been difficult for me due to an intense desire to try to keep my problems to myself. I do not lack confidence, it's just that the eyes are the windows to the soul, and I am deeply afraid that people will look into mine, see nothing but pain, and recoil in fear. But that's just me! We all struggle with our own battles. Whatever it is for you, practice eye contact. It is a very quick way to establish trust and camaraderie. It is also the best way to effectively show someone that you are…

Listening.

We all have room to grow when it comes to listening. Well, hopefully, you don't, but if you're anything like me, you do. I am highly excitable, passionate, and usually anxious enough to try to override it with lots of talking. I care deeply about what the people around me are saying, I just get so excited that I can sometimes bite off the ends of their sentences in my rush to connect and join the conversation. Often, this makes people feel like I didn't hear what they had to say. I'm working on it! And this is what you'll need to do too. We can all be better listeners. I've found that focusing on their face and their words at the same time helps me stay focused on the essence of what they are trying to convey. I also have found that biting back the instant replies that my mind cranks out helps to keep me from taking away from their words. A good rule of thumb is that if what you were thinking of saying is important, you will remember it when it is your turn to speak. If we are simply waiting for our turn to speak then we aren't listening to what the other person is saying. Another trick is to actively listen. For me, this involves actively trying to picture their story like a movie in my mind or to see the words coming out of their mind as words they are writing on a page of paper. Just leave the highlighters on the table! Sometimes all we need as humans is for someone to listen to what we have to say. If you can practice actively listening, without interrupting, you are going to have a much easier time having rewarding conversations.

No judgment.

This isn't just the hardest part of holding a conversation, it might be the hardest thing we ever have to learn in our lifetimes. We are conditioned in a tribalistic, xenophobic, racist society to form our groups and hate what we don't understand. As a kid who grew up in a *very* liberal community and then moved around to every single corner of this country, I can honestly attest to the fact that this includes everyone, regardless of their political leanings. Remember: if you are angry about something someone said it means that you don't understand them. It's that simple. When you are having conversations with people, reserve your judgment, practice empathy, and try your best to remember that we are all human. Also, remember that everyone's opinion is valid, no matter how much you might disagree with it.

47 | How To: Talk to Police

Unfortunately, you are most likely going to have to talk to the police at some point. I have had to do this way too many times and every single time it has happened, I have immediately started categorizing all the things in life that I was going to change to make sure that it never happened again. But hindsight is 20/20 and you are in whatever situation you are in *now*. And, believe it or not, there are a ton of ways to make the situation worse in that particular moment. So, pay attention:

Be respectful.

Every single police officer that has ever lived has been routinely treated like shit far more than the average person. Think what you will of them. They are the only actual buffer between you and the dangerous/nasty elements of our society. This gives them leeway, both legally and culturally. There-fore, if you treat them like shit, you are going to immediately get on their nerves and activate whatever legal recourse they have to make the situation more intense for you. Regardless of how unjust the situation might be, and believe me, sometimes the situation is completely *unjust*, you still have to treat these officers with respect. You don't have to go over the top. You don't have to say 'sir' and 'ma'am' with every other word. Just look them in the eye, tell them before you yank something out of your pocket, and generally do exactly as they say. If an officer is being unreasonable and yelling at you to do something unreasonable, just imagine how much *more* unreasonable they are going to be when you tell them to screw themselves!

Let them do the talking.

Cops aren't legally required to tell you what they are hassling you for immediately. Stay patient, remain respectful, and fight the urge to apologize. Simply remain curious. They are always looking for you to incriminate yourself. If you say as little as possible then you can find out what they are trying to get out of you. Don't give them what they want!

Always ask: "Am I being detained?"

When it is your turn to talk, that is. It's not a rude question. Most cops operate under pretense and assumption. Usually, they don't have enough proof to keep you there. Most times they use the words that you say to cite you! So, simply ask whether they are detaining you. If they are not detaining you, then you are free to leave.

Keep your hands visible.

Cops are twitchy and gun-happy. Don't give them a reason to overreact and make the situation a crime scene. No sudden movements and keep your hands where they can see them. Make sure that your car is in park, your window is either all the way down or cracked, and don't reach for anything until asked to do so. If you are pulled over at night, turn on the light inside your car as well.

Stay public.

Anytime a cop wants to speak to you privately this is a sign that they are trying to get you to reveal sensitive information that is most likely damning to you or someone close to you. Stay public. There is no arena that cops operate in that should be private. They are (ostensibly) Defenders of the Public after all. If you *want* privacy, of course, this is a different matter entirely. But if that is the case, I would be questioning my motives.

Never consent to a search.

The vast majority of the time, police officers do not have the evidence or probable cause to search your car or your person. They may claim that they smell something, but this is not admissible in court. Never, ever consent to a search. We are humans, we forget things, and you never know what may or may not have fallen out of your pockets. Or worse, your friend's pockets! Now, cops can order you out of the car and they can search your person if you have committed a crime, such as failing to yield. That is perfectly legal for them to do, and you should immediately comply! But if they find nothing on your person then they have no legal grounds to search your car and you should deny them the opportunity. If they *do* search your car without permission, then make sure to note that. Anything they find cannot be used against you.

Keep it very, very simple.

It's always tempting to get anxious and do a lot of talking. I have friends that claim that they can always 'talk their way out' and who have also done several stints in jail. Every single one of them later told me it was because they talked *too much* and said things that later incriminated them. If you are in trouble or, more likely, they are trying to shake you down because you 'look like trouble,' just give short, polite answers. If you are in *real* trouble then they will have to appoint you a lawyer and, if that's the case, simply wait until they arrive to do any of the talking.

48 | How To: Tell if Someone Is a Good Person

We all need human interaction and a sense of belonging. The reason I have included this section is because oftentimes in our pursuit of community, we can become desperate, accepting, and attracting people that are not in our best interest. They aren't necessarily 'bad' people but they are not 'good' people for us. Therefore, it becomes imperative to know how to spot 'good' people and how to attract them into your life. Here are some things to look for:

Honesty.

Most people lie. Ok, everybody lies. But some people lie *a lot*. Either they are trying to be something they are not or simply seem like someone they are not. Doesn't matter which one it is, such people are being dishonest, both with themselves and with you. Your goal should be to find people who are authentic and honest and, as a result, are open and forthcoming about their faults. Ideally, these people are willing to work on their faults as well but that might be splitting hairs. Honesty is the greatest indicator of integrity, and integrity is the foundation for being a good person.

Accountability.

Everyone makes mistakes. Some of us make more than others. Doesn't matter in the end. The difference between slags and good people, however, is the ability to take accountability for these mistakes. This is not always as simple as apologizing. Take this example: say you see someone hit another car as they are pulling out of a parking spot. Taking accountability is getting out of your car, checking for damage, and if there is any, waiting for the owner of the other car to return or leaving a note on their window with your contact and insurance information. Not taking accountability is simply driving away and hoping they don't find out it was you. Who would you rather be friends with? If you said the latter, think about this. What happens when that person is allowed into your home, around your friends, family, possessions, pets, and (possibly) your partner? Do you trust them now? Yeah, me neither.

No judgment.

Good friends don't judge each other. The best people don't judge anyone at all really. But let's focus on friends. Your friends are your friends simply for the fact that they are supposed to accept you exactly as you are. If you see potential buddies running around judging people, gossiping, and talking behind people's backs, it's a near guarantee that, given the first opportunity, they will do the same to you. Look for those people who are accepting and accommodating. Don't let them go!

Helping people.

It can be as simple as holding the door open for someone behind them. There are a lot of nasties out there that are only out for themselves. Good luck to them. You aren't looking for friends like that. Trust me, no matter how much fun they might seem like they are having, or how much they include you in said fun, they will always leave you hanging. And when you are living on the razor's edge, most likely out of a backpack, this can be a dangerous proposition. Watch people's actions and carefully note the person who holds the door open for people, the person who lets people into their lane in traffic, and the person who is friendly to people they meet, even when they are in a hurry. These are people who know the value of human connection and who are going to be there for you when you need them.

Courage.

This isn't a hard and fast rule. I have met a lot of very courageous people that were some of the most despicable humans the world has ever known. But there are also those people who have anxiety, shaking like a leaf in front of a Shop-Vac, leading the meeting full of down-and-out former drunks. These are the people who have such a strong sense of purpose and desire to improve that they are willing to do things in direct opposition to their deepest fears. That is true courage, and these are the people you want to be friends with.

Kids and animals.

You can bullshit an adult. You really can. We all choose to see what we want to see and, as we get older, we can oftentimes be conditioned or coerced into only seeing certain things. As adults, we also make measured choices. We let more things slide than perhaps we should. None of this applies to kids and pets. They can feel our energy, sense our intentions, and otherwise simply *tell* what kind of a person they are dealing with. When you are observing people, observe whether kids and pets are drawn to them. If they are, chances are that they are good people at heart and very worth your time to get to know.

They take the time for you.

As I was writing this book, I went through a lot of different things. My life has always been tumultuous but this was *next-level* difficulty. There were a lot of days when I didn't truly know if I was going to survive it. And yet, I found out who my friends were. For years I was drunk, alone, and uncommunicative to the world. I was a hermit wrapped up in the blanket of pain and problems, a lot of which I had either created or helped to create. And yet, when I began to go through what I thought was unsurvivable, my friends began to appear. Relentlessly. I have not gone one day since the events that destroyed me without having an hour-long conversation with someone I was *sure* didn't care for me at all. These are your people. The ones who reach out. Who take the time to focus on you, whether you need it or not. The ones who will drop everything and take you to lunch, or an interview, or pick you up from the airport. If they are willing to take time away from the things they are passionate about to help you out or simply spend time with you then they are the community you want and deserve.

49 | How To: Throw a Punch

Look, the goal of your life should be to be in a place mentally where you can walk away, laughing, from any potential fight. You should *want* to *not fight*. That is the ultimate measure of success. It means to a high degree that you have conquered the majority of your demons, dealt with your traumas and dramas, and have a strong sense of self-worth. Not to mention, that you live a happy and fulfilling life.

But shit doesn't always go down that way.

Sometimes somebody takes a swing at you for absolutely no reason. Sometimes you show up at your mother-in-law's house and your favorite emotionally-stunted brother-in-law with an eighth-grade education gets right in your face about your last fucking *vacation* and keeps dropping r-bombs and f-bombs (no, not the fun kind) and you want to… Yeah OK, I was right to walk away from that one. But the *first* one, where some rando wants to cause you harm for no reason at all, *that* is a really good reason for turning the lights out inside their little acorn hut. And to do that you need to know how you throw a decent punch.

The first thing to drill inside your head is that anyone, and I mean *anyone*, can throw a good punch. It's just like a golf swing. If you can master the form, you can master the punch.

But also consider the infamous words of Ben Parker: "With great power comes great responsibility." Once you know how to hurt someone, the goal should be to never actually do it. Strength is for *protecting* people. We forgot that a long time ago in this country. It's on you to remember it again. The Universe does not pity bullies. It is a universal truth: whenever you think you know everything the world will send you something you don't know. As soon as you think you're tough this world will send you someone way tougher. Do you want to start throwing fists willy-nilly? Get ready to lose.

Another important thing to remember is that in this modern era of anti-bullying, lawsuits, and assault charges, people just don't get their asses kicked that often. This is a key component to understanding the world. You can never truly get the game you're playing until you *lose*. Coming up in the public school system with a crappy home life and an anger problem like I did, it is no surprise that I got into a lot of fights. And because my brother, who resented me for a million different things, was in the grade above me these fights were mostly with older kids. And I mostly lost. And you learn *a lot* when you lose a fight. There is a moment when someone is punching you as hard as they can, right in the side of your head, and you can't even move your arms. All you can do is hope someone pulls 'em off of you. It's brutal and it is inextricably human. Then you have to walk *alllllll* the way home.

That is how you learn how to lose.

Without that knowledge, without those excruciatingly painful lessons of your limits, you can prime yourself to be a rocket headed toward a brick wall. And that brick wall can very easily be death. That might sound like an exaggeration, but I mean this with all sincerity. When grown people fight, adults with years to build muscle and callous and loathing for others, there is a good chance that somebody gets 'accidentally' put on ice. Permanently. It happens all the time. And if you think you're above it, that you'd never do that, then you haven't been in very many fights. You have to *know* what you are capable of before arming yourself, whether it be a shotgun, a Taser, or a really good punch.

Ok, I think my lawyer, therapist, and inner child are all satisfied, so here's how to punch.

The first place that you punch from is your feet.

You need to keep your feet underneath your shoulders. If you can do this, you are already throwing a better punch than you think. The power of your punch comes from your lower body, not your upper. A lot of rookies want to angle their punches *down* and they twist their upper body in an attempt to torque the punch into someone else's face. This is the best recipe for breaking your hand. Rather than this, you want to plant your dominant foot behind you (but under your shoulders) and your nondominant foot ahead of you. There should be a 45-degree angle from your back foot to your front foot, directly towards your target. This is called the 'A-stance' and it is the absolute basic. Do not practice throwing punches yet. You'll probably just learn shitty form. Practice keeping this position and swinging your hips.

Keep your hands up and in front of your face.

You always have to assume that the person that you are fighting, or going to fight, is an experienced fighter. And that they also know how to punch. It only takes one perfectly placed blow to turn the lights out in another person's skull. You don't want to be caught unawares. Keeping your hands up is the best way to be ready to defend your head. It also serves the dual function of keeping your striking fist that much closer to your opponent's face.

Roll your thumb over your fingers.

You want your thumb to be in front of your index finger. If you are punching from your hips and your feet are beneath your shoulders, you have enough power to break your hand. Especially if aren't aiming very well. If you put your thumb *inside* of your hand then I can almost guarantee that you are going to snap one of your fingers, maybe even your knuckle.

Line up your wrist.

The same thing goes for your wrist. It's tempting to angle it a little, especially if there is a difference in height between you and your target. You need to keep your wrist perfectly in line with the rest of your arm so that the entire mechanism is sending the force backwards into your shoulder.

Aim with your middle knuckle.

You want your middle knuckle to be the first contact that you have with their face, wherever that is. Just like when you are playing catch and watching the ball into your hands, you want to watch your fist until it hits the target. Line it up, aim carefully, and make it count.

Slightly bend your knees.

Slightly. Keep your original stance, moving if you have to, but still in the original A-stance. All you are adding is a little bit of bend and bounce to your knees. This keeps you balanced and mobile, so if you have to duck or if you get pushed that you won't just topple over.

Next, these steps all happen at the same time:

Pivot your dominant foot as you turn your knee inward.

Twist your hips so that they are parallel to your target.

Remember, you have been in the A-stance so that your hips are perpendicular to your opponent. When you're done throwing your punch your hips will end up facing them, just as if you were about to grab their waist and start ballroom dancing with them.

Extend your fist (punch).

If your arm turns a little inward that's OK. It's also OK if you lean a little forward. You want to make sure that you don't get out of control either way though. Remember, you are fighting a fully capable human who you have to assume has extensive combat experience and who is immediately going to want to hit you back. You need to be ready for this.

Watch the punch in and follow through.

I learned way too late that the trick to this is to imagine that you are trying to punch a spot two inches behind the head of the person you are punching. A lot of people 'choke' their punches, involuntarily pulling back slightly instead of hammering home the force of their arm and fist. To counteract this, you want to aim with your middle knuckle, watch the punch into its designated location, and aim behind their head so that you get maximum force. Your fist should land with the upper part of your hand facing upward.

Be ready to immediately dodge a counterattack.

Too many people think that punching someone is going to be consequence-free and that they are going to knock someone out with their first punch. Truth be told, you probably aren't. You're probably going to have to land a few good strikes to even get someone to consider backing down. Always remember that the other person is thinking the same thing you are. You still have to *win*. Anticipate their next move and make them pay for it (See: How to Dodge a Punch).

50 | How To: Write a Resume

One important thing to know before you listen to me tell you how to write a resume is that I have never worked a job that made over 80k per year that I wasn't directly offered when I was working another job. I have worked those jobs a handful of times. But I was only 'discovered' by headhunters when I was either tending a bar or running one of my small companies. The resumes I know how to make, therefore, are based on supposed 'entry-level' jobs that for some reason require a great deal of experience and/or education to get. The idea is to spit in the face of a lot of the things I have said in this book to write a bangin' resume that will get you hired. Hey, you've got to eat. All that health and wellness stuff goes right out the door when you've been ramming Top Ramen into your pie hole for three straight nights. And in the world of business, if you ain't hustlin', you ain't tryin'.

So, you're going to want a really good resume. This is pretty funny because all these companies want people with decades of experience yet they don't want to offer them a reasonable amount of money or decent benefits. This means they only attract younger people who are less likely to require those benefits, and who cannot possibly hold the desired amount of experience. What is happening? To put it bluntly, everyone is lying through their teeth.

Now, this can happen in a myriad of different ways. You can embellish your experiences. You can turn a humdrum landscaping job into a 'small business entrepreneurship.' Or a bussing and dishwashing job into a 'back waiter and server's assistant' job. And so on. You can also flat-out lie about jobs you have had. I've seen a ton of this, especially when working at a cool spot in a bad economy. Everyone is just trying to get to the interview stage, where they can turn on the charm and personality. No judgment here. That is exactly how I used to do it. You can also do what everybody else is doing too, which is a mix of both of these. Flub the details, sand the edges, and obfuscate till you're left with an amalgamation of lies and the truth that even you have a hard time distinguishing from. For example, say you worked a job at a bar. Maybe as an ID checker. You can then say that you were a bartender there, a much more lucrative position because you can still adequately describe the place and its management. Then you can give the phone number of one of the cocktail servers there, you know, the one that *really* liked you, and use her as a reference. Bam. Suddenly, you have the experience of a bartender at a place you use to work at.

Now, let's remember that these are flat-out lies. And that your lies *will* catch up to you in the end. It is never OK. Ever. But again, we all have to eat. And this system is set up for people to fail. It wants you to work the shittiest job for the longest amount of time. Every single 'rung' upward on the ladder is harder to get to than the last. Even a college education doesn't equate to diddly these days. You have to ask yourself a hard question: am I willing to lie, and deal with the consequences, to get a head start? For me, back then, the answer was yes. To a degree. I had a lot of experience, but I frequently found myself on the wrong side of a desk or a slamming door. What I didn't have were *references*. So, I lied. I used my friends and family. And it worked exceedingly well. Remember, all these people want is someone who can do the job well, won't steal from them, and will show up every day they are scheduled for a long period. If you can convince someone of that, then you will always get the job. Here are a few more tips on how to write a bangin' resume:

Make it easy to read.

This is one of the few times that style matters just as much as substance. Keep in mind who your audience is. You are one of hundreds of other resumes. So, get on one of the free resume-building sites and make it pretty. Add bold characters to separate the items of your resume that you want to stand out. And make sure that everything is spell-checked and easily legible.

Add pretty pictures.

My favorite resume I ever assembled had an awesome picture of mountains as the header background. It had an awesome font, graphs, and tables, all part of the $19.99 premium package I bought on a resume-building website. It was worth every penny. I used that resume for years. Time and time again I was told that it put me right to the top of the list. That people just hadn't *seen* a resume quite like that. I had also stuffed it with emphatic embellishments and maybe added a phony job or two, but it also had *pretty pictures* which drew the eye and got me noticed.

Don't worry so much about fudging the dates.

We all worry that someone is going to see and judge us for the four-month vacation we took figuring ourselves out down in Mexico in between quitting our last job and applying for this one. But really, don't. You may be desperate for a paycheck, but you don't want to work at a place that is going to negatively view your time off. Also, these places will ask you questions about these dates, so if you fudged them, you are probably going to get those questions 'wrong.' Now you have lied, tried to cover up by lying, and are now caught squarely. The best option is just to be honest about it upfront and then focus on answering the rest of their questions as best you can.

Use multiple kinds of references.

I have seen a lot of resumes. Most of them list only professional references. And that's OK, I guess, but I found that the best references I ever actually talked to *weren't even business related*. I had someone come in and his only reference was his mom. I called her anyway. One of the funniest and best conversations I have ever had, especially because it was right in front of the kid. I hired him on the spot. I have seen people use coaches, pastors, volunteer leaders, teachers, friends, former coworkers, you name it. These are always going to give the best kind of actual reference, from how you work to how you interact with others. Use them all if you've got them. Just make sure to warn them first!

Focus on the skills you learned and developed at each job.

You can't always be the 'ideal candidate' and you certainly won't always have direct experience with the job you are applying for. There are a lot of companies that are narrow-minded and will only hire those exact people. But those aren't places you want to work anyway. When you are listing the jobs you've had on your resume, make sure to detail the *exact skills* that you developed, or could have developed, while you were working there. A lot of people's first job is in fast food. They'll hire anyone with a pulse. Which is great because you can learn a lot of things there. Were you working the window? Great. You were honing your direct customer service skills, attention to detail, and ability to multitask in a fast-paced environment, all in direct adherence to a finely detailed code of health and safety rules. All these apply to any position in that restaurant. Here's another example. Were you working as a cashier somewhere? Great. You were developing your ability to handle large amounts of currency, enact hundreds of correct mathematical calculations per day, provide high-level customer service skills, multi-task in a fast-paced environment, and do it all with a smile. You can do this with literally any position. So, when you are writing down your jobs, don't just write the job titles. Detail what you did, how well you did it, and what skills you developed while you were there.

That's it. Pretty pictures, easy reading, the best references you can muster, and find the best qualities of yourself that you developed doing whatever it was that you were last doing. It's that simple. Don't forget to breathe.

51| How To: Write a Good Cover Letter

It's probably important to note that I do not look at jobs the same way that a lot of people might. I am and always have been picky when I could be. I also have a lot of trauma and complex issues surrounding my past work environments. The corporate ladder and long-term, upward-mobility careers are pretty much out of the question for me. I am never going to last long enough without "showing my ass," as a friend of mine used to say, or getting bored, to be promoted and make the commitment financially worth it in the long run. Therefore, my cover letters are designed to attain niche jobs in hospitality and other exotic fields. Anything different, anything that is fun, anything that is ultimately short-lived. This is how to write those cover letters.

The first step is to get their attention. When I was young and starving to death in 2009 (the absolute worst year to graduate) I would show up to the HR offices of anywhere, and I mean *anywhere*, and talk my way into the actual office. Then I would smile as charmingly as I could and *sliiiiide* my resume on top of the list. It worked. If you're desperate then absolutely do this. Remember, there is nothing a business owner wants more than someone enthusiastic for a low-paying job that they think will show up on time every day and stay working there for a long time. But you're probably trying to find the coolest place to work, for only as long as it stays cool and fun. If you're not this way, become this way, right now. Anyway, these days you're probably just applying online and hoping that someone notices you at these awesome, unique, fun-looking jobs. You need to get their attention. Every job gets 50 responses on the first day of posting. Every cool job? 100s. 1000s. You need to stand out to someone who has already read at least two dozen cover letters. And to do this you need to appeal to what they want in a coworker and an employee.

The easiest way to achieve this is to be unabashedly yourself. We already went over what to do if you're desperate. You are ideally *not* in that situation and are looking for a job that you want in a place that you want to be. As such, you do *not* want to bend over backward to prove that you are the most pliable and 'normal' person who has ever lived. You want the person reading that email or resume to think: "Damn, I can't wait to have a beer with this guy/gal." To do this, you start your cover letter with a subject that is well thought out and an opening three sentences that are heavily injected with your personality. The subject is always the hardest part. You've got to make it look professional, you have to have correct grammar and punctuation, and you have to also attract their attention. I usually just re-write the job title that the position was listed under and then add a few words about it that are different. Use the words 'awesome' or 'enthusiastic'. Just that little touch separates you from 50% of the other emails. Next, start your cover letter with a professional sentence and immediately follow it up with a sentence about your 'awesome' and unique self. Here's an example:

Hello,

My name is Sam, and I am highly interested in the part-time delivery driver position at Marc's Flowers. First of all, I am a full-time writer, so I am looking for a part-time job that gets me out of the house. My dog thinks that I'm part of the furniture around here! Second, I love plants. I constantly get in trouble for bringing too many plants home. They just make me happy. And third, I have a ton of hours of driving experience with Uber, Uber Eats, and Door Dash. Altogether this seems like an ideal position for me, and I would make a fun, positive, hard-working addition to your team.

Bam! This shop owner is *definitely* reading my cover letter. And if there is still a job to be had by the time they read this letter then I am probably already on the shortlist of people to interview. If I'm not? Then they are a bad fit anyway. It's that simple.

The next thing to do, and this is the boring part, is to list your professional qualifications. Most people reading resumes aren't going to read through your resume if you have a crappy cover letter. They just don't care enough.

This is the only place in the 'real world' where you do have to worry about first impressions. Whoever is reading this needs to believe that you can do the job that they need you to do. If you have direct experience with this job, then definitely start with that. Most people do the same job their whole lives. All they understand are people who do the same thing that they do. Tell them what they want to hear! If you don't have experience in that particular job, then try to make whatever experience you have *sound* the same as the job you are applying for. Here's an example of when I applied for a social work position:

> Professionally I have similar experience to this position. I have worked dozens of jobs in the hospitality industry, the tradesperson industry, the business and commercial industry, and have owned several successful small businesses. While I have yet to work in social services, my success in so many different arenas gives me a unique perspective that reflects very well on everyday people like myself. I find myself effortlessly connecting with people of all shapes, sizes, and positions in the 'social hierarchy.' I usually stop and talk longer with the person tearing my ticket for the train than I do with the people sitting next to me on the ride! I know how to work hard, that's a given. I know how to succeed. I know how to push others to reach their potential. I also know how to function well as a member of a group, and how to lead when necessary. These are all traits and values ideally suited to this line of work.

> Life experience is where I am particularly suited for this job. I grew up in a traumatic environment. Young adulthood was no different. I have been shown, repeatedly, the dirty end of the proverbial stick. I have seen my fair share of social workers and therapeutic environments. And I'm writing a great book about it! But I am grateful for my experiences. They have taught me a wide array of things. I am fortunate to have developed a strong survivor mentality and I am proud of how I have always kept empathy and ethics as the driving forces in my life. I think it's this type of experience that led all of my friends and teachers to recommend this position to me. I have always felt like I had some good advice to give, some wisdom to share, and some people who might just need my help.

> I believe I was made to be a strong shoulder, and a soft voice. Everywhere I've gone, and there are a lot of places that I've been, I seem most drawn toward the people like me. Who didn't get a fair shake, or who may have missed the starting gun. I think I am one of those people who others feel safe around. So far, I've transmuted these beliefs into becoming a meditation teacher, writing the aforementioned

book, and to settling in this community. I'd like to continue this pursuit and as such, I'd be the ideal candidate for this position.

Check me out bitches. This is a real cover letter that I sent. And I got the job! Can we all appreciate the lengths your handsome protagonist went to write this book?? Anyone? Oh well (pats own back). Still got it though! And y'all can use my cover letters. Go on, take 'em. If someone tries to get you in trouble you can point straight to these words. Tell 'em Sam said you could.

The relevant point is that I immediately anticipated and addressed their first question then quickly diverted to what I was good at. I bombarded them with other things that I am good at and then appealed to their *ethos* by honestly telling them that I want to do some good in this world. Considering that I was writing to a social services program this was a calculated bet that whoever was reading this was probably similar in that regard. Turned out I was right too. Lastly, always directly say that you will be the best candidate for that position. I don't really know why. Just do it. It works. And then sign off with your name, your phone number, and your email. If they are interested in you, they will immediately call or email you. Bam! New job.

You can do this! Remember to breathe.

52 | How To: Start a Fire

Step 1: Drench the outside of your former house with gasoline.

One side will do, make sure to get as high up on walls as you can without getting on your clothes. Are the lights on? Good! That means they are home.

Step 2: Make a trail into the house…

Just kidding! You are trying to make a fire in the woods out of sticks and logs. Right? Right. Right! Moving on.

So there you are, in the woods, at the mercy of the wilderness. At some point you're going to have to address how to stay warm and, unless you're lugging around a portable generator and space heater, you're going to need a fire. Plus, it's the best part of camping. Here's how to get one going.

Now, everyone wants to roll into whatever turns out to be their camp and then start grabbing these huge logs. It always becomes a competition for who can get the biggest sticks. But what you need is a bunch of *little* sticks. You never know how wet the wood is and you can never really be sure how many matches or how much lighter fluid you're going to need. You want to make sure you get it right the first time. Of course, you can always douse it in gasoline (if you can afford it). But there is no *honor* in that. You are trying to exercise your dominance of nature and fire. You are in command of an *element*. Which makes you, in a certain sense, a Fire God. I mean, unless you want to use gasoline. That's cool too, I guess.

Collect a ton of small sticks.

And I am talking about a lot. At least two bundles the size of your arm or leg. I usually get a wide variety of different sizes, mostly the thinnest and longest ones I can find, but up to as thick as my fingers. Get your minds out of the damn gutter, folks. It'll be dark and cold soon. Anyway, I collect enough so that it's hard to fit both of my hands around the pile. If you have tiny hands, get double.

Collect a bunch of mid-size and a few larger sticks.

I usually have whoever I am camping with do this part. Most people only like to collect these anyway. This gives me time to make my nest of small sticks while they tackle the harder work of dragging everything into camp. Once you get your actual fire going, you'll need a few of these fairly quickly, but just the little ones to start.

Make your 'nest.'

What you're looking to do is create a situation where the fire from your lighter or matches travels upwards and catches on the smallest sticks in your nest. Remember, heat rises. So, if your heat is lighting the smaller sticks, they are then heating the ones above them, and so on. Small, thin sticks will burn regardless of how wet they are, which makes this method almost foolproof regardless of the weather. I start with a couple of fistfuls of small, thin sticks and prop them against a larger stick. It creates a hole that I can fit my lighter under. I then add more sticks on top of this nest so that, when this burns, it will light the ones on top of them.

Pile it on.

As I am holding the lighter underneath the flames are traveling upward into the densest part of the group. At the same time, I am usually adding more little sticks on top of this. The idea is to get as many of them burning at the same time as you can. You'll notice that this is the most difficult part. You are trying to keep as much heat burning at the same time s possible. You're trying to reach a critical mass, where there is enough heat that it will continue to burn without your constant attention.

Make it grow.

Once you have a little bit of heat and flame coming off of your 'nest' you need to immediately start adding slightly bigger sticks on top of them. You are going to keep up this pattern till you are adding your biggest sticks and logs to the pile. But don't forget to add smaller fuel underneath as you go. You are trying to get the heat of your fire to continuously increase. If you expect the larger and larger sticks you are adding to put off the same amount of heat as the original sticks, and as quickly, then your fire is going to die. As such, continue to add smaller sticks underneath the nest as the smaller sticks burn out, and as you continue to add larger sticks on top.

Spread and push.

Get your mind out of the gutter, I said! As your fire begins to grow you are going to want to flesh it out a bit. If there is a side that does not have any flames, add some pieces of wood to this 'hole' and wait for them to catch on their own. You have been focusing on getting the heat of the fire to gradually increase, now you are focusing on creating the biggest pile of embers in the center of your fire pit that you can. These embers burn longer and create more heat. This is what is going to keep you warm and make it much easier to keep your fire going throughout the night. So spread your sticks and logs around the fire pit and push any stragglers in towards the middle.

Gloat and preen.

Don't forget to stand up and flex. It's really important. Brush that dirt off your shoulders. Whip out those tickets to the gun show. Show off that crotch. It's not every day that these mere peasants are in the presence of a true Fire God.

If you don't do that, definitely do not forget to enjoy your fire for a little bit. Life is a series of very small moments. Warming your hands over a fire that you started is one of the more satisfying ones.

53 | How To: Start a Small Business

There are those of us who have a serious problem working for other people. This is nothing to be ashamed of. You'll see commercials for sports stars and celebrities, highlighting how they 'go against the grain' and how they are 'so different from the rest.' They grew up either a foot taller, prettier, or far more naturally gifted than the rest of us. In our society, it is commonly accepted that to be different you have to also be beautiful, rich, or famous. Well, the vast, vast majority of us aren't going to be beautiful, rich, or famous. I would even go so far as to say that the vast majority of us don't *want* to be beautiful, rich, or famous. Well, maybe just not *famous*. It's always better to be crying in a Porsche than it is in a Geo Metro. So here we are, most likely none of those things, and still not wanting to work for low wages for a company that makes exorbitant profits off of our stress and sweat. So, what can we do?

The answer for a lot of people is going to be to start their own business. We are essentially forced to work for ourselves. This type of work comes with a high degree of uncertainty and risk. Small-business is notoriously competitive, income can be highly variable, and you are completely responsible for everything that goes right and wrong. There are no managers to turn to if you get hurt or if there is a pissed-off customer. There are expenses and more expenses. You have to provide tools and materials. Education. Supplies. Insurance. It's all you, all the time.

But you are free.

The word company is widely used but is mostly a misnomer because it implies that you will be working with other people. This could eventually be the case, and hopefully is at some point, but at first, you will be working alone. And that's just fine. It is going to be a lonely road and you are going to have to navigate it by yourself until you are bringing in enough business to justify hiring employees. Now, there are tons of examples on TV and social media showing people who became bakers, crocheters, or social media influencers. Good for them. But that's not what is going to pay the bills for a lot of people. Some of us have different skill sets, different work ethics, different whatever. This article details the steps toward starting a painting business solely because that is the most successful company that I started. It certainly wasn't the only one, but it was something I had a lot of talent in. These steps can be applied anywhere and to any company idea you have. Painting was the best for me because I love to work independently, I had a bunch of tools and handyman experience, and I knew how to grind. If that sounds like you then the sky is the limit, so pay attention to the steps below.

First thing first. Take a big breath and exercise patience.

Starting any company is going to be difficult. If you enter the market thinking that you are going to have overnight success, then you are just going to end up disappointed and stressed out. Everything regarding starting a company is expensive and irritating, from designing your logo to dealing with the government. You're going to need tools, materials, advertising, lead generation, promos, etc. It adds up quickly. Not only are you going to be operating on thin margins but you'll most likely be cutting heavily into your savings as well. Make sure to take time to relax and enjoy yourself. There is no point burning yourself out before you secure your first contract.

Come up with a name.

This could be the hardest or easiest part of the entire process. You've got to first figure out what you're going to call your new venture. Then you need to check and see if the name is available. Make sure to pick a name that people can understand and pronounce. For example, my company was named Chiliad (pronounced \KILL-ee-ad\) because one of its meanings was "a thousand separate things." I am a handyman, writer, driver, photographer, craft-maker, and general jack-of-all-trades, so the meaning of the word worked for me. The problem was, nobody could pronounce it. And I heard later that the simple fact that the name was foreign to some people turned them off of my company. Do I agree with it? Hell no. But that's what they told me. So maybe it's better to pick a name that people can wrap their heads around. And keep track of your ideas. I usually keep a list of four or five of my top ideas at all times.

When you do get your names together the next step is to register it with your city/county/state. Everywhere is different. I started my painting company in Portland, OR. At the time I had to register with the city and the county. They had a website that had a list of registered companies in the state wherein you could see if your desired company name was already taken. Oddly enough, there was already a Chiliad Inc. or something like that. I had to slightly alter what I wanted to call myself. It is what it is. Once you find a name that isn't taken then the fun part begins.

Register with the government.

Prepare yourself for some frustration with this step. You'll most likely be dealing with a handful of career government employees who want nothing more than the freedom to do exactly what you are doing. I am certainly not saying that government workers are bad or rude in any way. But if there was a situation wherein someone could be bitter and difficult to the person they are employed to assist then this would be a textbook version. As such, walk in with patience, offer nothing but kindness and understanding at all times, ask them how their day is, etc. Treat them like the humans they are, and your paperwork will be processed. Treat them badly? Well, then you'll get to see the pinnacle of bureaucratic efficiency.

Every single town and city has different rules and processes for starting your own company so it is hard to tell you exactly what to do. The plus side, however, is that your local government wants nothing more than for you to start a company. Keeping money local makes local politicians look good. So, a simple web search of how to start a company in your state, then an identical search for your county, then, you guessed it, another search for your city, will all yield positive results. The key is to not just take one website's information and hold to it. Oftentimes, your city will want you to pay them to register and file with them but say nothing about contacting the county or the state. As a small business owner, the onus is on you to know. If you're a micro company, it might never matter. No one is going to come after you for the $100 you made at the farmer's market selling honey. But if you want to blow up and make 100k per year then you better have your ducks in a row or eventually you're going to get a serious phone call from someone in your local government and the IRS.

Here's an example. Right now, I am in Asheville, NC. A simple web search brought me to the North Carolina state government web page for starting a business. This site is great. It clearly outlines what business license I am going to need to attain, what taxes I am going to pay, and has a business name-finder tool. Following the registration prompts takes me to a place where I can register a name with the state and the city, both for a fee, and assume a business structure. Business structures can be complicated at first glance, but you are most likely going to want to be a limited liability corporation (LLC). Mistakes happen. We will get into licenses and insurance in a moment. But suffice it to say that it is worth having to spend a few more hours on your taxes each year to insulate yourself from potential lawsuits. Trust me on this. Keep in mind that some sites are great and some are horrible. If you do run into any confusion or if it is unnecessarily difficult to figure out what you need to do, just head down to city hall. They do know the answers and are happy to help, as long as you're not an ass.

Find out what licenses and permits you will need.

This can be a huge turn-off for some because it can be intimidating to have to go and get a permit to prove that you know how to do something. Just keep in mind that it is designed this way to weed out amateurs. It's OK if you *are* an amateur, though. If this step makes you overly nervous, then simply go hire on with a company that operates in your field somewhere. The money from the construction industry is in having your own jobs that you bid on and signed an agreement for. That is why so many contractors hire subcontractors. All the contractor has to do is show up, give a bid, then hire some other people to do the work for them. There is no other practice that pisses me off more. Yet it happens all the time, specifically for this reason. Some people just want the experience of working for someone else so they can branch off on their own. Non-self-employed painters don't make much and the work is very hard. All of this means that you will always find a place that is hiring painters. The same thing goes for any other field you might be in. Spend a few weeks, pick up a few tips and some knowledge, make some quick cash, then circle back to get your licenses and permits.

You really shouldn't be worried though. In my experience, this was the easy part. In Portland, OR, there was a handy tool called the 'handyman designation,' which allowed you to work any job without any permit as long as the cost was under $1000. I may have fudged this a little in the beginning but also most of my early jobs were below that number. As soon as I started scheduling bigger jobs I went and got my contractor's license. I was intimidated at first, but it was much easier than I thought.

While you may not need a license in certain places, you will almost always want or need to have insurance. Sometimes areas price you out of insurance. Either the bond is too high or the rates are astronomical, whatever it is. But this is changing. Now there are large companies that will cover you for small amounts or fewer employees. If your area requires a certain level of insurance, there is usually a workaround with outside companies or by combining insurance companies. Whatever this ends up being in your area just make sure that your health insurance is covered (remember, you are a small business now and can take advantage of business pricing) and that you are at least covered for the amount that you have bid for the job.

Even if you are starting a company that doesn't require a permit, having insurance is always a great idea. If someone slips in front of your booth, or you have a tragic sewing machine accident, or your laser printer sets the workshop on fire, the costs all fall on your shoulders without insurance. Dealing with insurance is a nightmare of twisted people and evil companies but it beats having to sign away your yearly salary for the indefinite future. Just fork it over and enjoy the peace of mind.

Make a website.

I enjoyed this part, but some people hate it. It can be confusing and irritating. I just found a web hosting service, took the name of my company and added the city after it, and made that my web address. Then I used Google to add pictures, reviews from work I had done previously, a quick 'about' page, a contact form, and voilà! I had my web page. Make sure to pay for the security features that protect your info from spam. You're automatically a target for web crawlers and your basic info is automatically listed on the registration. Either pay the money for a service to protect you or go through the steps to change the information on your registration. Currently, I have the number and address of my local District Attorney listed on the registration, you know, just to send the spammers to the place they belong.

Buy equipment.

You are going to need basic equipment. I always brought my multipurpose toolboxes along to every job. You just never know what homeowners are going to throw at you. And while you can always say no, remember that you are already there and if you can add services to the bill and make your client happy at the same time it is a win-win. If you are working in some other field you are still going to need to follow the same principles.

Always try to source your equipment as efficiently as possible. You don't want to buy super cheap versions because they won't hold up. That doesn't mean you need to buy brand-new versions though. Everything you are looking at should be researched and you should have a good idea of what 'good equipment' looks like in your field. Then you can set out to find the best deals you can.

Start at the re-sale stores and re-stores. That isn't to say to buy cheap, crap equipment. Again, do your homework and research what a good product is before you leave. But for things like floor/wall plastic, rollers, drip trays, tray-liners, hand cups, extend-y bars, stain brushes, etc., you can save a ton of money starting here and seeing if anyone has donated some quality gear. Starting a catering company? Check the restaurant supply stores. The point is that there is always a market for used gear that still has life in it. Make it a habit to find where these places are. I spent so much time combing the re-stores that eventually I was approached by a pair of managers and ended up just having them call me whenever they had paint gear come in. I got first dibs on the stuff that came in and they made money achieving their purpose. Win-win. There are other examples of these types of stores: used clothing stores, warehouse supply stores, craft stores, you name it. If you look hard enough you can find a good solution to whatever you're looking for without having to pay for a new version.

When you do have to go to a big-box store make sure that you still shop around. I won't name names but for construction material, there's a red one, an orange one, a blue one… you get the drift. When you're buying in bulk it is well worth your time to figure out who sells what cheaper in your area. For example, you might find that plastic is cheaper at the blue store, while brushes are cheaper at the orange store. If you need a drill, a compressor, or just a wheelbarrow, definitely make sure to look into 'used' places first. But if you have your heart set on 'new,' shop around. Lastly, once you've identified what stores you are going to shop at, quickly get signed up for their loyalty program. Once you hit a certain level of business, you'll want to be saving money everywhere you go repeatedly.

Business cards and swag.

This ended up being my second favorite part. I started by creating a logo. There was a website that offered some basic designs to pick from, then allowed me to slightly customize them. It cost me about $50 and in the end,

I had a logo with my company name that I could put on stuff and things. I immediately did so, getting a bunch of hoodies and t-shirts. Altogether that cost me another $300. It wasn't necessary but I got a ton of attention everywhere I went from my cool logo, which immediately led to handing out my business cards (more on that later), which then led them to my website. It all looked very professional and helped my cause. Altogether I took my logo and put it on some cards, clothes, coffee mugs, and even some stickers. It was a blast and made me feel good. I highly recommend it if you've got the cash to spend. There is no better feeling than waking up in the morning to get ready for a job that you bid on, got accepted for, and are presently pouring some coffee into a mug with your logo on it.

Aside from the swaggy stuff, business cards are easily the most important part of this process. You are going to want a clean, easy-to-read card and you are going to want a lot of them. I went with a white background with my awesome logo on the front. On the back, I simply listed my contact information and website. It was simple, effective, and cheap. People often screw up by thinking that they need a complicated business card with a ton of information on it. Just the opposite. You want a good logo that draws the eye, then a simple business card that won't confuse them. Also, keep them on you at all times. You will frequently find yourself discussing your business in all kinds of places and you are going to want your cards handy to pass out.

Lead generation.

This was the most rewarding and frustrating process of the entire venture. I started by using various sites and apps that I had to pay to send me leads. These are inherently evil, have horrible customer service, and often charge you for 'ghost leads' that aren't real. Several times I have been personally contacted by law offices asking if I wanted to join their class action suits. They were, however, highly effective at getting me some of my first bids. The frustrating part was paying $70 just to talk to someone that I might not even get to give a bid. Then, if I did actually get them a bid, a lot of people were shocked that it wasn't the 1940s anymore and that I was going to charge them more than $100 to paint their entire house! It was stunning. My personal favorite was paying to talk to someone, going over there and having a great conversation, taking an hour to write them up a complicated and nuanced bid, then never hearing from them again. And let's be clear, at this point I had great reviews and was intentionally charging no more than half what my competitors were. So yeah, these lead generation sites are a decent place to start but expect to waste a ton of money in the process.

The number one place that I found customers was at the local paint stores. Now, I am not a salesman. I never have been and I never will be. I am humanly incapable of upselling or overselling and it has dramatically hurt my bottom line in the past. I don't care. I do the right thing, every time. With that said, this method can be easily overdone. Here it is anyway: I would go to paint stores in gear that was splattered with paint. I would usually do this whenever I took a break from whatever job I was already on. This not only gave me a chance to pick up whatever supplies I might need but also just to take a breather. I would then slowly take my time going up and down the aisles. Without fail someone would come in and start talking to one of the reps about this or that, asking for advice on their project. I would then slowly walk up, hand them a business card, and tell them we give free estimates. Then I would walk away. I did this at big-box stores, re-stores, laundromats, and grocery stores. I got used to just keeping my painting gear on as I ran errands. Not everyone called but I got at least one job a month that way.

Another great method I had was just walking around with door hangers. I hated this method because I don't like just walking up to people's houses, but I got at least five big jobs a year doing it. I stuck primarily to neighborhoods that I wanted to work in. Either they were near my house or one of my favorite taco trucks. Whatever it was, I just picked out where I wanted to be and started going door-to-door with my door hangers. These can be easily made and designed on the same website you use for your business cards. Pro-tip: pay your friend's kids or some local college students to hang them for you. If the college kids are old enough, they will most likely work for beer and tacos as well.

I am a loner and like to go my own way but for social people, the best long-term option is probably to join a leads group. These can range from informal bi-yearly meet-ups to expensive, weekly groups. I was a member of two of these, at different times, and we met once a month. It cost me $400 per year. These meetings were a great way to 'network' (man, I hate even saying it) and rub shoulders with good people. It was always a bit much for me but once they got to know my work ethic and craftsmanship, I started to get at least one or two phone calls a week through this organization. Think of it this way. Imagine that you're renovating your kitchen. You've got a flooring person for the floors. You've got an electrician and a plumber. You've even got someone to install the cabinets. If even one of these people tells you that they know a great painter for cheap, well, then you're going to call that person. And if that person is good at what they do and cheap, you are going to hire them. And hire me they did.

The last method that worked for me was using flyers. I printed out a bunch of pull-tab flyers with our logo and pictures of our good work. Then I went to paint stores, re-stores, big-box stores, laundromats, housing developments, huge condominiums, you name it. If there was a large number of people living there with a decent chance of someone moving in or out, my flyer was up in the manager's office. I usually would set aside one day a month to go to some new places and check on old flyers. It was fun, plus, I met some great folks that way.

The overarching point is to be creative. You don't have to pay Google exorbitant prices, practice SEO marketing, sell your soul to various apps and websites, or even put on 'face' that much. I guess it's a little harder this way, but I never once had to try hard to pretend I was a social person. For me, that's what this job was all about. That's not to say I didn't enjoy my clients and occasionally meeting people. I'm just saying you don't have to go crazy with it.

And that's it.

You'll read in a bunch of places that you should hire people at low wages, or worse, hire subcontractors to do your job for less than you bid it for. Frankly, these methods are wrong and everyone knows it. You'll also notice that I do not go into the bidding process or how to actually paint a room. The reason behind this is two-fold. First, this section isn't really about painting. If you are reading this, you probably have enough of an idea of how to do whatever it is you are doing to start your own company doing it. Second, the bidding process is one that I came across organically. Your respective small business will undoubtedly be the same way. It helped to have done the job for a week or two before I set off on my own just to see how one of my mentors bid on projects. You'll discover that on your own. Also, everywhere is different. I would charge a much different price here in Appalachia than I would in Portland. It's just how it is. You can sign up for a service that will help you do this or drink the Kool-Aid of someone who is actively trying to teach you how to rip people off. And that's cool, I guess, but that's not how I operate. I ended up breaking my leg and messing up my back on subsequent hiking trips, so I shut down a year ago. But I still get a call every other week. If that's the type of business you want to run just follow the steps above.

You've got this. Be patient and remember to breathe.

····································

"Don't let anyone who hasn't been in your shoes tell you how to tie your laces."

····································

The Handbook

Oddly enough, the hardest part of writing this giant book was coming up with the title. I always thought that it would be the massive scope of the project, the formatting, or the ridiculous amount of editing you have to do to publish a book that would deter me the most. Nope. The devil was in the title. I mean, how do you name a book that is focused on wellness, travel, survival, alternative lifestyle, and non-fiction stories? There isn't even a category for that. I refuse to admit how many agents and editors passed on this project because it didn't fit into a genre they were interested in. And yet, here we are, with Happy & Homeless.

Still, even with a title it was awkward finding a way to organize everything. It eventually dawned on me to simply organize it the way that I would want to read it. Survival first, then a practical guide, then random topics in an indexed format. That way, if someone is reading it cover to cover they will get a book-like experience or, if they are ADHD like me, they can simply flip to whatever chapter they need at that particular moment. Easy peasy. So here we are at the third and final section, fittingly titled: The Handbook.

The definition of a handbook is "a book giving information such as facts on a particular subject or instructions for operating a machine." Well, there you go. That kind of fits. My first title was 'The Lifelopaedia.' Back in those days stuck smoking pot in the closet with the grandiose idea of changing the world with a book on how to do *everything* this seemed like such a great idea. As I got older I realized how egotistical it was to even entertain the idea of being able to do *everything* well enough to advise on it. So, I moved on to 'The Compass Compendium.' OK, that has a ring to it. The alliteration is great, it has the word compass in it, which smacks of travel, and the word 'compendium' fits and sounds cool. I went with that for a solid year, until a friend of mine informed me that he had no idea what the title meant. And he wasn't the first. It immediately dawned on me that I had done it again. Grandiose ideas and scope had all been consummated in another title that no one would ever bother to figure out. But the show must go on! So, I brainstormed. I meditated. I pounded the thesaurus with my head. And then I simply relaxed, laid back, and asked my higher self to figure it out for me.

And one day I woke up and there it was!

So, here you go. The Handbook portion of this book is simply a (somewhat) random collection of topics and skills that I have regularly experienced in my life. It is by no means complete. I will no doubt be adding and editing this book for the rest of my life. That is exactly why I put '1st Edition' at the beginning. But for now, this is what I have to share. I truly hope that it helps you along in your journey. If it doesn't, keep in mind that I am simply giving the best advice that I possibly can in the hopes that it makes your life easier. Also keep in mind that if any of it makes you angry or upset, I don't care.

Don't forget to breathe.

54 | Acne

There have been very few greater banes on my existence than acne. It may sound vain and trite but for an introverted male with anxiety and depression issues, a criminal lack of basic social skills, and a desperate need to connect with humanity, acne became a fixation. The road is lonely if you're not good at fitting in and ingratiating yourself into situations, which I am decidedly not, so I spent a lot of time alone. Staring at my face. Picking at my face. Hating my face. All of which made my face red and inflamed. Then I didn't want to go outside, so I stayed on the couch, wondering why I was saddled with this pestilence. Wondering why God hated me. Hating myself and ruminating on all the little things I did wrong. I was focused on everything negative. I created an image of myself in my head that was nothing even remotely close to the truth, then enacted an anxious and nervous outlook onto every behavior I had. It was crippling.

I have struggled with acne my entire adult life. Even now, in my mid-30s, it continues to be a problem, albeit much, much less of one. Anyone who tells you to 'just get over it' does not and will not understand, much the same as someone who doesn't understand why anyone would leave the town they are originally from. Acne is a multi-faceted problem whose only solution is wholesale and widespread adaptation. You have to change your *whole life*, just to *figure out* what is causing it. But this is a beautiful thing. Much the same as we must learn how to accept change and difficulty as a positive and as a means of growth, acne directly tells us that there is something dramatically wrong in our body and our mind. That we are 'sick,' either mentally or physically. It allows us to directly affect the course of our lives through the focus on our total health. And in the end, we are the better for it!

Trust me, I tried everything, EVERYTHING, in 'the book.' I have changed my entire life dozens of times. I have cried and screamed and clawed and woosahed, WOOSAH DAMNIT, and on and on into near infinity. Every product. Every pill. Every cream, salve, wash, and ointment. None of it worked. The answer is in my mind and my outlook, i.e. *your* mind and *your* outlook. It is in the food that you put into your body. It is in the food you *don't* put into your body. It is in the mind-gut connection. It is in the physical toxins surrounding you and the toxic people surrounding you. It is in overwashing and over-medicating, while simultaneously under-washing and under-medicating. Yes, I will explain that. It is all about finding your balance and your health. And doing that has way more far-reaching implications for your health and well-being. But for now, we will focus on the steps to improving your acne:

Mindset.

Somewhere along the line, the idea gets in our head that we have to have perfect skin to be whatever it is that we think we have to be. All we see are the outward personas and images of those around us. Makeup, photo editing, method acting, blatant lying, all these are used by everyone around us to create what they hope are positive images in our minds. We rarely see what is real. And most of us know this, at least on a basic level, yet almost none of us can live our lives without letting this affect us. Look at the rates of eating disorders, suicides, mass shootings, homicides, divorce, you name it. All of this is at least indirectly caused by people thinking that they don't measure up to those around them, that they have failed somehow, or, even worse, that they aren't worthy of their own lives.

This is a negative outlook, and we can immediately see from an outside perspective that it is unsustainable. Yet how many times have you or I become entrenched in it? How many times have we browsed social media without realizing how we are comparing ourselves to people who don't exist in the ways that they claim to? How many times have we been ashamed to show our face in public simply because we thought that we would be perceived poorly just because of a few red bumps on our faces?

The main way to get rid of acne is to change the way you look at it. Instead of picking your face and staring at your 'imperfections' close up, take a step back and admire yourself. Smile at yourself. Tell yourself that you love yourself. If this is difficult and awkward, then you have found out where the main problem is. Because if we cannot love ourselves then we are going to harbor all the negative emotions that spawn from that lack. Anger, rage, hatred, anxiety, sadness, grief, shame, guilt, etc. These emotions don't just go away, either. They dig in, build nests and fester. And one of the ways that we see this is on our faces, in painful little red bumps. The first way to combat this is with love. Self-love. Self-compassion. Let yourself feel some positivity. And then go out in the world and do your best to hold your head up, look people right in the eye, and be yourself. Forget what's on your face. Trust me, it doesn't look or appear nearly as bad as you think it does. Once you start to do this more and more often, you will start to see less of them appear. Guaranteed.

Diet.

As Americans, we eat crap. We eat highly processed, injected, rejected, neglected, and under-detected food. I am not a nutritionist by any stretch of the imagination, but I do know that we are composed of the materials that we shove in our mouths. Thus, it is simple reasoning to say that if you eat more toxins then your body is going to have to remove more toxins. While it is a misconception that your skin can remove a substantial amount of toxins from your body, our face is the place where this kind of build-up is going to show up the most. And while sweat and exercise are great means for getting rid of all the crap that accumulates in our bodies, these methods are not guaranteed to remove or prevent acne in any way.

There are advocates of Eastern/Chinese medicine that claim that there are certain areas of your face that evidence certain types of acne. There might be some truth to that. Stress is a primary culprit here. But whether or not this is true is purely conjecture. What is *definitely* true is that your body may not be able to handle your diet. And this inability to process the constituent components of your food is showing up on your face. In my journey, I quickly found that eating dairy brought dozens of pimples, mostly around my mouth area. Yes, that includes butter. Gluten became a big no-no as well. Alcohol too. Bummer! But it was all part of the process. The most annoying thing to do, and the hardest, is to keep a food journal. It took months. But I would carry a little pencil and a small notebook in my back pocket, writing down everything I ate and when. Then, a week later, when my upper lip was a wasteland of red bumps and pustules, I had some idea of what caused it. Seeing a nutritionist to help you with this process is highly recommended if you can stomach the cost.

Over washing.

When you are sitting there at night, face covered in acne creams and other salves, staring at a tiny screen and reading about how to cure your acne, the most common thing you hear is to wash your face two or three times a day. Sometimes they even say to use a medicated wash this many times as well. Now, maybe for some people this works. If it does, stick to it. In my experience, I found that this was overkill. And after a few weeks, this practice actually made my acne worse, which led me to think that maybe that was the plan all along for the company who had sold me the expensive wash. Go this route if you want. Everyone has a different face. I found, rather quickly, that once a day with tea tree oil works best for me. Things come up though! When I work out, get a kiss from my girlfriend/dog, or have to wear a facemask for a while, I just splash my face with some water and pat it down with whatever is handy.

Under washing.

The yin and yang of what works for you can be supremely frustrating. Remember to always *try* to keep your mindset loving and positive about yourself. However, for some people, the issue is not washing enough. I was never one of those people. I've got an oily face in parts and a dry face in others. If I don't wash my face at least once a day I can *feel* the grime and oil. You may be the exact opposite. It all depends on your biology and your face. But if you notice that you've got a ton of acne and you can't remember the last time you washed your face? It might be time to get to a sink. This was more of a problem for me when I was living out of my car and doing a lot of physically intensive jobs. I didn't realize that I would go eight to ten hours with sweat and grime on my face, then head straight to the bar for four hours, then finally hit the shower. Eight hours is a lot of time for stuff to seep into your pores. So, if you aren't washing *enough* that might be the easiest fix you ever made.

Chemicals.

We are human beings. We are not made of metal and we are always much more sensitive to things than we think we are. As such, even though there is a product on the shelves that has FDA approval it still might not be anything close to 'good for your skin'. The most common acne-fighting ingredients are benzoyl peroxide and salicylic acid. These are the active ingredients in the vast majority of acne-reducing products. You may very well be allergic to one or both of them. They certainly aren't natural. Even if you aren't allergic to those, they always come packaged with ten to twenty other ingredients that you would be hard-pressed to pronounce quickly.

As such, remember that your skin is a sensitive organ. Be gentle with it. You could be exposing it to the very chemicals that are *causing* your acne.

Natural acne fighters.

It took me years to finally try some holistic ingredients to fight off my acne. It happened at the same time that I, big reveal here, started to address my mental health and anxiety issues as well. But it was also important to get me away from the chemicals as much as I could. They just weren't helping and who knows what other problems they were causing. The two major things that work for me are tea tree oil and witch hazel.

Tea tree oil was an especially helpful revelation because I quickly found that it was useful for my face and my head. I had always had a ton of acne on my scalp. No matter what I used, it always lingered. Until I found a shampoo with a ton of tea tree oil and not much else. I use it once a day and leave it on my head for a minute. I haven't felt any acne up there for a long, long time. With my face, I have seen more mixed results. I will say this, since I have used tea tree on my face, especially the kinds with as few extra ingredients as possible, any acne that has shown up has faded faster and been way less severe.

Witch Hazel was another breakthrough in my efforts. I had used things called 'toners' before. Toners are meant to give back a lot of what you stripped when you washed your face. This means adding something positive to your skin and pores, wherein the opposite could be dirt and other crap getting in there instead. A lot of these were expensive and hard to remember to use. But then I found witch hazel. It's cheap, it smells weird, and it is the most effective part of my skincare routine. Since I started using it, I have noticed a dramatic decrease in the number of blackheads and pimples that I get, especially on my cheeks and forehead.

There are more holistic/natural ingredients that can help your face. For example, if you have a huge, golf ball-sized zit (this has happened to me) then the best remedy is a paste of turmeric. Just be careful. It is tempting to assume that just because you can physically see the ingredient, and you have eaten it or otherwise used it in the past, it is going to be good for your skin. This isn't necessarily the case. It is always a crap shoot and everybody's skin is different. Make sure to try things slowly, be patient with them over time if you are going to use them, and don't *over*use them. The world has a million different remedies for everything and most of them... don't work. Take your time, breathe, tell yourself you love yourself, remember that your skin and appearance really don't matter, and then keep trying.

Probiotics.

Simply put, the research on the gut microbiome and how that affects your entire body is criminally underfunded and inconclusive. Everything I tell you is strictly from my own experience. But I will say that, without a doubt, when I started eliminating the crap food from my diet and started actively taking probiotics, my acne started disappearing. And the acne I did get was nowhere near as severe. I also noticed a significant change, for the better, in my IBS symptoms, heightened energy, an easier time switching between activities, and a whole lot of other little benefits. You should be taking these, at least once in a while. And if you have tried everything and nothing is having an effect on your acne, this might just be the missing link.

55 | Airplanes

Here we are again, at the dangerous crossroads of ego and humility. This is not a travel blog. There are a million different tips and tricks for how to take advantage of everything on an airplane. Frankly, others have told it better and given better advice. Oh well! Here are some of the things I know about airplanes:

Breathe.

The whole thing is stressful, from leaving the house in the morning to the final descent. Unless you're an alien and love being around all those people, I guess. Then it is invigorating? I can't possibly understand that mindset. For me, it is a necessary evil to achieve my goals in life and it is utterly exhausting. So, the goal is to breathe, over and over, until I can be present and calm enough to effectively regulate my emotions. You've heard it dozens of times already in this book and you will hear it dozens more. Breathe. Take slow, calming breaths and center yourself on the moment. Find things you are grateful for and that you appreciate at the moment. Feel the oxygen coursing in and out of your lungs, then feel the seat underneath you. Take your time, watch your breath, and enjoy the ride.

Bring food.

It is wise to always have food with you every time you are traveling. A couple of small bags of candy can make a huge difference when something stressful goes down. This is especially true with airplanes. While it may be easy to forget amongst the rigors of actually getting to the airport and then going through the boarding process, you are inevitably going to have some downtime before you get on the plane. And then there's the actual plane ride. I cram whatever healthy snacks I can into whatever space I have left in my bag. Dried fruit and protein bars are my favorites. They don't take up a bunch of room and won't expand like crazy when the cabin is pressurized.

Vitamin-C.

Traveling is notorious for spreading disease and airplanes are one of the chief culprits. You are crammed in a little tube with hundreds of other people who just shared a crowded terminal with thousands of others. You are thereby being subjected to the breath of thousands of people. And if one of them was sick? You get the idea. I try to drink orange juice all the time while I am traveling and especially if given the opportunity on the plane.

Don't take off your shoes.

A lot of people sweat through their feet when they are nervous or walk a bunch. That is perfectly normal. What is not perfectly normal is to get into a highly pressurized cabin that recycles air over and over again and let loose the foul concoction that has been brewing in your socks for the past eight hours. It is disgusting. It's like farting in an elevator. You might get away with it, but you always know that it is wrong. Wait until you are off the plane to do so.

BYOB.

This is for my people who aren't sober like me. Just because I can't do it doesn't mean I can't share some wisdom.

Most flights have caught on to people bringing nips/mini-bottles and have imposed severe penalties for doing so, but call me old-fashioned. I always used to bring a bag of nippers with me. You don't want to bring too many. First, they are always the cheapest, nastiest liquor that the company who bottled it can find, repackaged as whatever they are pretending it is. And you don't want gut rot on an airplane. Second, remember that thing about being in a highly pressurized cabin? Yeah, so if you drink a bunch of alcohol it messes with your head and dehydrates you. You are then guaranteed a hangover *before you even step off the plane*. Nobody wants to start a weekend with a hangover. Third, as I mentioned, a lot of airlines make their money off of selling the concessions on the flight, so they have cracked down hard on people bringing their own booze. This is not to mention the increasingly troublesome amount of people acting like animals on airplanes, leading to airline workers wanting nothing to do with drunk or buzzed passengers. So, bring 'em but don't let anybody see them. I used to wait for drink service to roll around, grab a Coke, and relax.

Always give away your window seat to well-behaved kids and nervous flyers.

I don't care if that seat cost you an extra fifteen bucks. I could go on and on about why life is about service to others, what it means to be a good person, and how selfishness only hurts you in the long run. This is just one of those things that you *do*, like opening the elevator door for someone running to catch it. You aren't in their head. You have no idea how much they might be panicking and it helps them to be able to see and have something to focus on. Just do it.

Sleep-gear.

This is redundant but it's worth mentioning. Have your headphones, some kind of blanket, and a sweatshirt you can roll up as a pillow conveniently nearby. If you *can* sleep on a plane then these will greatly help your cause. And if you're an anxious flyer then these are essential.

Audiobooks.

I only learned about these late in life and I feel like I may have wasted some time without them. I guess podcasts are a great thing too, but I can't stand them for some reason. Maybe it's the bold opinions, the crappy editing, or just the silly format... Who cares. If you dig podcasts, have some downloaded before you leave. The same thing goes for audiobooks. For years I was a forlorn window starer. I loved melancholy music and some targeted self-loathing at every opportunity. Traveling alone gives you every opportunity to watch as the world goes by and ruminate on your past mistakes. Yeah, so now I listen to audiobooks a lot. It's a great way to read without having to focus my eyes on anything in particular. I find that hours go by as I am off in Storyland, navigating the cosmos. Way better than simply staring at the back of a chair or watching the same movie I've seen a dozen times.

All airplanes have earplugs and ibuprofen.

No matter how crappy the carrier, they always carry these things for emergencies. If you struggle with crowds as much as I do, these are essentials. And if you forgot to pack some, they are always available. If one steward says no, usually with a tired and sassy tone, just ask the next one that walks past. It oftentimes helps to go to the back when the seatbelt sign is lifted and politely ask for some.

56 | Airports

I had to be careful here not to sound like a travel blog or as someone trying to seem cool because I fly around a lot. You know the type. That's why I've kept this section as simple as possible. There are a million different tips and tricks to how to best navigate airports, so I'll just stick to the ones I know. I'm sure you'll figure out some more on your own.

Sleeping.

If you are planning on sleeping at the airport, you'll need to consider a variety of things. First, you don't want to if you can avoid it. They keep the air cold to help prevent disease and... people sleeping there. On top of that, security is not always OK with it and they make sure that there are no comfortable places to lie down, both to keep everything in camera view and to keep the homeless from setting up shop. The trick is to make it look like you just dozed off for a few minutes. Set up your pack or your bag and lay against an ATM or behind a row of seats. This gives you some degree of privacy while also making it look like you belong there. Also, keep your ticket close by. There is nothing worse than getting rudely awoken by airport staff after you finally get to sleep, only to be angrily asked where your ticket is. Also, take your passport, wallet, and anything else that is flat and valuable, bunch it up, and put it between your waistband or under your shirt *in front*. If you travel with a laptop or just value the bag that you have, make sure to wrap it around your arm or leg twice. I usually loop it around one leg, so that if some dickwad runs up and tries to steal it, they will quickly find that they are stealing me as well, which is a dangerous proposition.

The best places that I've caught some sleep are in empty terminals behind the back rows of seats. Although it *was* pretty unsettling waking up to a bunch of people sitting in them that you didn't see coming. Always travel with ear plugs but it's worth mentioning that these are especially key in this context because of the constant announcements they blast over the loudspeakers. The same thing goes for an extra T-shirt to cover your eyes from the bright lights. Lastly, I know I said earlier to always act like you've been there before. This is one of the rare cases where the opposite is true. If confronted, always pretend like you are super annoyed and that you really don't want to be there; like you absolutely cannot wait to get on your plane and out of there. All airports are different. In some, it's illegal to sleep. In others, it's perfectly fine. Regardless, acting like having to sleep there is the biggest inconvenience in the world will help your cause. They will automatically assume that your plane was delayed and that you got stuck there against your will.

Don't get flagged.

This actually happened to me. I remember flying through Denver on my way home to a funeral. I was a mess. I was anxious, trying to hold back tears, and sober for the first time in days. I was on the phone and kept talking about how nervous I was to fly. It did not help that every security officer within a half-mile was openly staring at me. I tried to talk myself out of it, but they were *really* staring at me. It didn't help that I hadn't bothered to unpack all of my hiking gear from my pack when I had left Bryce Canyon, where I had been working. They had confiscated four knives, a hatchet, a butterfly stove, a large water bottle, and some iodine pills. Looking back, I can see why I might have been on their radar. I can also see why I was promptly searched. Twice. Of course, when they reluctantly let me go, I headed straight for the bar, which probably made me look even better.

This pattern of searching hasn't left me *to this day*. I have been inappropriately and illegally searched in several foreign countries, openly sexually molested in at least six airports throughout the U.S., and generally harassed at every opportunity when traveling via plane. It could have been because of that day in Denver or it could have been any number of other times I acted like a fool in an airport. Whatever it was, it has greatly inconvenienced my travels ever since. Oh well, it is what it is. But it doesn't have to be that way for you. Here are some tidbits of wisdom for you:

● **Don't talk about how nervous you are.**

Flying is stressful and can be downright terrifying at times and it's OK to be scared. There's even a section for that! Just avoid talking about it before or while you are going through security. They are always listening to and observing you from the time that you walk through the front door. A little bird once told me that in TSA training they are instructed to look for people who exhibit visible signs of nervousness. Foremost among these signs is talking about it out loud. So, while you might be shaking like a leaf and dreading your upcoming flight, do your best to keep the fear from coming out of your mouth.

- **Try to avoid nervous gestures.**

Picking your nails, wringing your hands, rubbing your shoulders, and even yawning a bunch can get you singled out. They are looking for anything that can prove their exaggerated budget. OK, maybe that's a little cynical. Maybe they are just good people trying to keep the world safe. Either way, just keep it cool, focus on your breath, and act like the person in front of you.

- **Don't complain.**

Whining and bitching are a normal right of passage of every traveler from time immemorial. And yet, TSA looks at any amount of whining as one of their signs. This means that you have to keep it under wraps as best you can. Having a complaint-based meltdown will definitely get you flagged.

- **Don't pack liquids, chocolates, coffee, herbs, gemstones, or a bunch of cash.**

These things might seem arbitrary to you, but they are some of the things that the scanners are looking for. Chocolate can look like explosives. Drugs are oftentimes packaged in coffee. Herbs look like drugs. Gemstones can be used as a weapon. And a bunch of cash? Might as well have a sign that reads: I am on the run! All these things are immediately picked up by the x-ray, which will slow you down by getting you searched, then will get you flagged.

- **Leave the guns at home.**

Never thought that I'd have to say something that obvious but here we are. If you do all these things above and leave the Glock at home though, you'll probably save yourself from being flagged.

How early you arrive depends on three things: the size of the airport, the amount of traffic, and the weather.

The age-old axiom of 'arrive two hours early' doesn't apply to Kalispell, Montana, where you can throw a tennis ball from either side of the airport.

I have shown up to flights here with fifteen minutes to spare and *still* had to wait. But if you're headed to a large airport with tons of people, head two hours early. If it's raining, it's Friday, and you're in Seattle? Go four hours early. You'll be glad you did.

Bring an empty water bottle.

This is one that I only remember to do half the time. The security checkpoints won't let you carry a water bottle, which is dumb, but they can't say anything about you having an empty bottle for water. In my experience, you are best off with one that is see-through. I have had all kinds of water bottles confiscated for various reasons, usually because they could ostensibly be used as a weapon, but never the clear, formerly full water bottles. Throw one of these into the side pocket of your backpack and then just fill it up as soon as you get through security.

Always bring an extra charger.

I carry two brick USB ports and two cords. I don't know if it's the repetitive stuffing in and out of a bag, the X-ray machines, the constant use, or what, but these cords don't last and break at the worst possible times. You will want an extra, probably sooner than later.

Bathrooms.

If you're on a layover, or if you habitually show up really early (raises hand), then chances are you're probably going to need to use the bathroom at some point. If you're a man, then you know about the horrors of the men's room. A symphony of horrendous noises, smells, and odors. I've never been in a women's room, but I would imagine it to be the same, especially in the airport. Nothing is going to help you if you're in a hurry. But if you get the chance to pick, you can up your chances of not having a trauma-inducing experience by picking well. My trick is to wait/look for the bathrooms near planes that are currently departing or have just departed. This is especially true near the end of the terminals. The traffic is lower and, at the very least, you usually don't have to wait in line.

Bring a sweatshirt.

As I mentioned, airports are kept intentionally colder to keep people moving and to discourage disease from spreading. You're going to want a sweatshirt for the airport and the plane, even if you are heading somewhere tropical. The key is also to wear anything bulky that you have in the actual airport so that you can maximize the amount of space you have in your bag.

Grab a shopping bag.

If you have too much crap or if you are a little over the bag weight limit, ask for a shopping bag from one of the stores accessible in the concourse before security. You can pretend like you just bought something as you were waiting. This is especially helpful for carrying any snacks, food, or water that you are bringing in from outside the airport.

Don't eat anything unless you have to.

It all comes off of the same truck, from one of two major companies that are extremely successful because they adhere to virtually no standards of health or nutrition. Everything that is wrong with food is on its best display at the airport. And if it doesn't agree with you, causing indigestion as all crap food truly does, being up in a plane is going to make that bloating and cramping much worse. If you're about to be on a plane for a long time, forget about it. I'd rather be hungry than miserable.

If you do have to eat, resist the temptation to eat large, complex meals. Stick to the healthiest options available. You may not want to eat healthy when you're traveling or stressed but this is the exact time that you should. You want your body to be on the evenest keel that it possibly can. Not only does this take the stress off of your guts but it gives your body the energy and supplements it needs to recover from the stress that you are putting on it. Stick to the salads, rice bowls, and smoothies if you can.

57 | Alcohol

I am not going to harp on anyone for using alcohol. I used to drink every day, so no judgment here. The only thing I will say here is that your actions do mean something. There was a day when they didn't. You could get away with just about anything, almost anytime. Not anymore. And that doesn't even begin to get into Karma, a higher power, and all that other stuff. That applies to men, women, kangaroos, whatever. While it doesn't define you, and you can overcome mistakes, a great deal of who you are *is* what you *do*. And life is infinitely easier if you don't make those mistakes in the first place. Keep asking yourself questions. Keep being curious. If you feel like drinking, simply ask yourself why. That's it. That simple conversation will pay immense dividends. Might even keep you out of jail.

The second, and last thing, I am going to say about alcohol is this: if you don't think you have a problem with alcohol, then do not drink it for 30 days or more. If this is difficult then you might have a problem with alcohol. It's not a condemnation. You don't need to run off to the nearest AA meeting and dump all of your friends. You just need to realize it's a problem. That's it. That's the start. As a nation we stigmatize mental health and, as a result, we suppress a lot of our crap with alcohol. We work 65-hour weeks, over and over again, then we get wasted on Friday and Saturday, sober up on Sunday, and rewind the tape. We are trapped in an unhealthy system. No one is at fault. That's why all you have to do is see if you can take 30 days off. If you can, no sweat, carry on. If you can't, you might want to do something about it. Maybe you don't. It's a beautiful thing, this world, that you can do most things you want if you put your mind to it. If you *do* want to do something about it, then simply admitting you have a problem is a huge step forward. The next step might be to get a counselor, talk to someone who has more money than you, open up to your friends, or make some changes in your life that improve your mental health. I'd recommend licensed doctors and counselors. They helped me along the way, and they have the degrees and the know-how you probably didn't know you wanted/needed. 30 days. What do you have to lose?

58 | American Football

American Football is the greatest sport on Earth. It is the closest we get to the primal, hunter mentality we are instinctually driven to at our basest level. Nowhere else is there a set of lines wherein the best athletes in the world walk onto the ground and proceed to beat each other nearly to death, all for the entertainment of the masses. It's tough. It's brutal. It's glorious.

That said, for some people sports are boring as hell. I get it. To me, watching baseball is worse than watching paint dry. And I ran a painting company for two years, so I loved watching paint dry. Meant I was either taking a break or was done for the day. Still, sports are an inherent part of our world. Some people say it's because of an instinctual urge to be 'part of the hunt.' Some people claim that we just need to be entertained and find ways to be distracted from our mundane lives. Regardless, they are here to stay. This means that you, whether you enjoy them or not, are going to come face to face with sports situations in your life. Therefore, it is a very useful skill to be able to at least pretend that you enjoy them or just have a few comments to throw around to be part of the scene. Here are some things to say to make it sound like you understand football:

- **"That D Line isn't getting enough penetration."**
- **"They are getting outcoached."**
- **"I miss John Madden."**
- **"What a great tackle!"**
- **"That was pass interference!"**
- **"They need to get more pressure up front."**

- Just sit there, intensely watch the screen, and say "Pick, pick, pick, pick, PICK!"
- You can do the same thing with the phrase: "Get him!"
- "They missed that facemask."
- "What a bad spot."
- "I think that coach is on the way out."
- Wait for a completed pass then: "What a read."

If you've been watching for a few minutes and you are really in over your head stick to these time-tested favorites:

- "What are they DOING???"
- "Where's the flag on THAT?"
- "C'mon, get a stop!"

59 | Basic Travel Phrases

I have no idea where you are going to go. I don't even know where I am going to go. What I have done is gone to a bunch of different countries that speak different languages. And sometimes that meant going to different countries with different languages in the same week. As such, learning the entire language of every country I was going to was really out of the question. Even being able to hold a passable short conversation was way out of my reach. But what you never want to be is one of those tourists that try to demand that people in their own country speak *your* language. Even if you can't speak their language you have to show that you are *trying*. It is not only polite, it is the necessary amount of respect that you show to anyone when you come into *their* country. And more often than not, they do know English, and they are happy to speak it with people that make an effort to respect them. So here are some basic travel phrases to learn for every country that you go into. I always just write them down on a couple of pieces of paper (you will always lose one) while I am on the plane. Just use the questions and then get a translator app on your phone.

- **How much does that cost?**

You'll also need a basic understanding of the number system. If not, just use a piece of paper and a pen.

- **Hello, please, and thank you.**
- **I do not speak _____.**
- **Thank you for your patience.**
- **Where is _____.**

1. The bathroom.
2. The bar.
3. The hostel/hotel.
4. The bus station.
5. Taxi.
6. Grocery store.

- **How are you?**
- **I don't understand.**
- **The bill, please.**

That's it. I always added some extras for how to navigate the bar, how to get to various destinations, and some other pleasantries, but as long as you can haggle how much something costs and get to the main travel hubs when you have to everything else is a bonus. You are just patiently waiting until everything falls in your lap. Relax, try your best to speak the language, and smile. You are traveling and (hopefully) on vacation. You are in no hurry. If you seem like an asshole, they will label you as an asshole and they will either jack the prices up or ignore you entirely.

60 | Being a Good Friend

Being a good friend is a simple concept, yet it can be very difficult in practice. We all see ourselves as great friends. Indeed, why wouldn't people want to hang out with us, cherish us, and see us as the amazing human beings that we are? We all have something awesome to offer the world. And some people see this in us more than others and like some of the same stuff that we do. Which means we should be great chums!

The problem lies in our ego and our motives. Where we all might have things to offer, we also all want things that we can take. Whether you see it in yourself or not, you are always using people for something. Sometimes it is simply being nice to someone so that their bad attitude doesn't get directed toward you. It could also just be that you are going through some difficulties and need to talk. A lot. Or it could be something more problematic, like habitually not paying for gas or food when you hang out with people. We can become so engrossed in our own story that we often fail to see how our motives and our egos are detrimentally affecting the people around us. We can easily become a net negative on our friends' lives or worse, an outright burden. Therefore, because we are social creatures and need solid connections in our lives to remain grounded, it is important to know how to behave like a good friend and avoid these common pitfalls.

Take accountability.

Own your shit. I have had way too many friends where everything was someone else's fault. They never, and I mean never, apologized for anything or saw their part in any situation. After a while it became exhausting to hear them talk about their life because the answer was always the same:

they were the problem. I started by trying to gently nudge them in that direction. When that failed, I began to flat out tell them what I perceived to be their role in their misfortune. Eventually, it turned to apathy and cynicism and then, inevitably, the end of the relationship.

I have also been this way at times. I am certainly not a saint. We see ourselves as the protagonist of our own story and I am no exception. I frequently found myself experiencing bad luck or running into the same problems over and over and I would blame everything from God to the entire city I was in. I would rant and rave to my friends and my lover, lambasting everyone within 500 miles as I judged the whole world guilty for my own crimes and attitude. It was, to put it bluntly, a giant pity party. And no one wanted to be around it. Who could blame them? It was a series of hard lessons gleaned through loss and solitude. So, learn from my mistakes. Look at yourself and your role in whatever is happening around you. Once you can do that you can learn to not repeat that mistake, forgive yourself, move on, and thus be someone that your friends look forward to hearing from.

Set boundaries.

"Oh, there you go again. Sam, quit talking about stupid boundaries!"

…

No.

Because boundaries are really important. They are insanely hard to set at times and take a serious backbone. There are a lot of ways that people behave around you regularly that are not going to jive with your morals, ethics, and values. And that's OK! We are here on this planet to be different and to interact with one another. Your experience is just as valuable as everyone else's, whether that be at work, at your in-law's house, riding the bus, or hanging out with your friends. If you are sitting around a table and one of your friends is discussing politics and you *really* don't want to be talking about politics, then you have every right to say so. And you absolutely should. Because if we don't then we are going to gain resentment. And resentments are like hot coals in the pit of your stomach. They aren't going to hurt anyone else but you. Then, when you are good and burned, you are inevitably going to lash out at the people you love and care about the most. This is going to harm the relationship and, most likely, the person who hurt your feelings in some way is going to have no idea how and what they did. The answer is to set the boundary.

Now, setting these boundaries doesn't give you the license to be a whiny bitch. Simply because you don't like something doesn't mean that everyone else does too. You have to first be accountable, which is why that is the first thing on this list. You have to take a brief moment to ask yourself why something that was said or done affected you in the way that it did and handle that emotion like an adult. Once that is completed, if the behavior was truly out of line then you are absolutely in the right for speaking up and putting a stop to it.

Setting boundaries also needs to be done tactfully. You can't just lord over people and throw your weight around. That just makes you a bully. Way too often in this country, we see arrogance and aggression being mistaken for assertiveness and 'standing up for one's self.' I have a few insanely self-centered friends. They go through phases where they take and take and take. This doesn't mean that they are bad people or that I don't love them. It does, however, mean that I frequently have to assert my boundaries to protect my emotional and financial well-being. My self-centered friends rely on me for work opportunities, rides, and emotional support. They are often stressed out and dealing with a lot. So, when they behave selfishly I first put myself in their shoes. I try to feel how they must feel. Then I look at myself and how I feel, especially how I might feel used and taken advantage of. When I have a clear picture of the reality of the situation, I then address them. I talk in 'I' statements only, telling them how I feel, what I think, and how things need to happen from here on out. I then listen to their response. Most often my boundaries are met with understanding and grace. Sometimes they are not. In that case, well, fuck 'em. They can walk home.

Be open.

It's easy to button up in this world and keep everything deep inside of you. This is especially true with our friends. I know that I want to be funny, entertaining, and generally 'not a burden' to the group when we are hanging out. So, I bottle up my emotions and the heavy things I am currently dealing with and try my best to forget about them. This works until it doesn't. When I try to do this, I frequently find myself getting upset over trivial things or rapidly getting depressed for no apparent reason. This happens because I need to talk about what's going on in my life! And the people I am around typically *want* to hear how these things are going. Now, we don't want to turn our social time into long, drawn-out therapy sessions. That is what therapy is for. We like to hang out with people because it is fun, not work! But it is absolutely OK to be open about what is happening and what is going on in your life. It creates connection, allows your friends to feel part of your experience, and opens you up to insight into your own experience.

Give back.

This is one of the greatest lessons that I have learned from the people in my life. I am a generous person. I always have been and always will be. As soon as I like someone, I want to help them as much as I can. It can be a serious defect just as often as it can be an asset. It has led to a lot of people taking advantage of me as much as they possibly could. Still, it is a good quality to have and to develop. The key to using it to better your friendships is to first take accountability, seeing where you are taking from others, and then to make a concerted effort to give back to the person who you took from. This could be buying someone a meal, paying for the toll or a tank of gas, hugging someone, or offering to do the dishes after they did all the cooking. Whatever it may be, it is key that you identify what someone has done for you. Recognition is the greatest way of giving thanks. Then you can find something you can offer in reciprocity.

Listen.

It is amazing to me how few of the people that I am habitually around ever listen to anyone else but themselves. I have certainly been of this number many, many times as well for sure, but there are folks out there who truly think that their opinions and reality trump everything else. In the *entire world*. It astounds me. Because when you are sitting around a table at a restaurant surrounded by your friends, you are staring at a bunch of people with completely different life experiences, viewpoints, and general outlooks than you. You may have a great story or outlook yourself, yet you are no different or better than anyone else. As such, you can seriously benefit from listening to the words and experiences of your friends. Not to mention, the very act of *being* a good friend hinges on listening to them speak what's on their mind! So, try to listen, hear what they have to say, and don't just be ready to say something else.

Be creative.

It's easy to get stuck in patterns and ruts. We are, after all, creatures of habit. We like the same coffee shops, restaurants, and hole-in-the-wall bars. We have favorite vacation spots and weekend activities. And some of us even like to make the same jokes over and over! But the onus is on you to try to be creative with some of these things. That's not to say that you should sacrifice the key elements of who you are for the sake of the group. It is good to get out of your comfort zone but if you get panic attacks every time you go to a punk show, definitely stop going to punk shows! The idea is to find things that you and your friends might like and then suggest those activities to the group. See a fun pop-up restaurant flyer outside of your apartment? Great! Grab your chums and give it a shot. Is there a new escape room opening downtown? Perfect. Get the gang together. Putting some effort into creative ways to hang out with people can improve the morale of the entire group and lead to some fantastic memories.

Let things go.

People are, well, people. We all have our defects. Some more than others! We tend, as humans, to try to pigeonhole people close to us into our ideals and viewpoints. Simply put, we see them differently than they are. And this creates a set of expectations that only hurts you in the long run. The answer to this is to let things go. When one of your friends is habitually late it is really important to set a boundary regarding that behavior, as your time is valuable, but it is equally important to forgive and forget. When we hold grudges and resentments, we create a wedge in our minds against the people that we love. We create a boundary between our love for them and our expectations for how they should behave. And in the end that only hurts you. So, as one of my mentors likes to say, let that shit go, bro.

Give honest advice.

A lot of us like to sugarcoat things and support people regardless of whether they are right or wrong. This is easier for us because we are simply telling our friends what we think they want to hear. But in reality, we are hurting them, oftentimes severely, in the long run. Because friendships are all built on trust. I trust my friends to tell me when I have spinach in my teeth and ketchup on my shirt. I also have to trust my friends to tell me when I am falling into a trap that I have fallen into before. The responsibility lies on all of our shoulders. To be a good friend you have to be honest and courageous with what you tell your buddies. You have to be strong enough to tell them what you see about what they are telling you. A lot of times this might go exactly opposite to what your friend is saying too. I have almost gotten into several fistfights with some of my more hotheaded friends because I stood up to them and told them that what they were doing was wrong. I have also had that reaction many times as well when I was called out. But that's the thing. You have to be able to trust your friends to tell you when you are making a mistake or getting in your own way. And they have to be able to trust you as well! So, give honest advice and feedback. While it might be more awkward in the moment it will lead to much better friendships in the long run.

Be there to help.

This one is pretty simple. If your friend is going through a crisis or if they desperately need help with something, be there. Head to their house and help them change their flat tire. Bring over some steaks after their latest emotionally unavailable girlfriend broke their heart. Or just sit there and throw tennis balls at them as they try to mow their lawn. Whatever works! If they need you, be there.

Take time.

It's easy to get buried in work, relationships, and temporary obsessions. Personally, every time I start a new sci-fi novel I involuntarily check out for a week or so… whoops! We can get wrapped up in the day-to-day routine of getting everything done and then relaxing that we lose track of our friends along the way. The key is to *make* time in your busy schedule to see them. This can mean showing up for twenty minutes to inhale a burrito, give them a high five, and get a quick rundown on their latest jailbird love affair. Or it can mean doing errands together, as this is the only time that you have available that week. If you carve out the time out of seemingly thin air, then you are effectively demonstrating to your friend that they matter and that you prioritize the friendship. And this is how to strengthen that friendship in the future.

61| Booking Hotels

When I was a lot younger, I bolted from a decent job at Crater Lake National Park because I was scared. There was a beautiful woman there who treated me well and I just couldn't have *that* in my life, so I ran. I headed out thinking I was going to hike and camp my way into… well, I had no idea what I was heading out into, but my nuts felt as big as boulders and my dreams of adventure were as tall as skyscrapers. I figured I could live on a thin roll of foam on the ground for as long as it took to see the entire world. I vividly remember stopping at my brother's place before I headed out. I didn't know when I'd see him again, so I wanted to stop by for the night and reconnect. We had a damn good time and the next morning he handed me some brownies. I had eaten some brownies before and enjoyed them, but I will never forget the wry look on his face when he handed me these. It was a look that said: "I am going to start laughing as soon as you leave and keep laughing till you call me to cuss me out." In my mind, I was bulletproof so I didn't even notice. I hugged him, jumped in the car like it had a shotgun window, and was off on the highway.

I made it to Idaho that day and stopped at a campground called Craters of The Moon. I set up camp, went hiking and exploring, then came back right around nightfall. I was no stranger to camping, so I whipped out the guitar, drank a 12-pack, ate some sandwiches and read my book, and generally hung out till it got cold. Then I got hungry again, so I ate one of two big ol' brownies my brother had handed me. No big deal. Waited an hour, felt a little woozy, and of course, I ate the other one. Then I got really tired, really fast. So, I laid down and passed out. I figured the worst thing that could happen was the Park Ranger would wake my ass up for staying too late the next day.

I was wrong. Turns out the worst thing that could happen in that instance was a lightning/thunder/rainstorm complete with a small flash flood. I woke up to a sound that resembled a football team of people pounding slapsticks on the side of my tent. Every fifteen seconds there was a flash of lightning accompanied by the almost immediate clap of thunder that reverberated through the rocks surrounding me, over and over, endlessly. It took me at least fifteen minutes to even realize I wasn't dreaming and that I was in immediate danger. Then the storm picked up.

I've been in a lot of intense rainstorms in my life and the obvious thing to do is simply to not panic. Typically, it sounds and feels way worse than it is. This was not one of those cases. This was a flash flood in the middle of nowhere punctuated by a lightning storm right over my head. The hair on the back of my head was sticking straight up, which meant a lightning strike had hit close. Real close. Turns out it was the nearest pole to me! But I had not only eaten one of the brownies, I had eaten both. So instead of running to my car and taking off, which would have been an even worse call, I just sat there in my mummy bag and stared wide-eyed at the outside of my tent and… cracked a beer. And then I started seeing things. And hearing things.

At first, I thought that aliens were here, and they wanted my butthole. Man, I was going to get probed *for sure*. Then I wasn't so sure, as I kept seeing small, prong-headed devils dancing in the light conveniently provided by the frequent lightning strikes. It was about this time that the water started to pick up the tent and rapidly push me down the campsite. Ever wonder why they put those big logs on the sides of the concrete pads that you camp on? They aren't just there for looks. They are there to stop your tent from physically moving down into the water drainage canals carving up the middle of the campgrounds. At least, I know that's what mine were for. And in between covering my head to protect against the aliens trying to invade my butthole and stay away from the little demons slapping the sides of my tent, I just started howling in fear. It was primal. I barely knew it was coming out of me. But fuck it if I wasn't going to crack another beer and enjoy my last minutes. You know, in between bouts of complete terror.

When the storm finally let up, centuries later, I immediately jumped out of the tent, grabbed my remaining beers, and sprinted to my jalopy. As soon as I got in I felt better, so of course I broke down in tears. I sat there, wide-eyed and high as a kite, until the sun came up. I then heartily threw all of my soaking gear straight in the car with as little thought or care as possible and started to drive away. Everyone in the entire campground was staring at me. And no, I wasn't just imagining it. As I passed the small park ranger booth, I could see them laughing.

I can see you thinking: "What is the point of that story?"

The point of this story, other than why you shouldn't do drugs kids, is that shit happens and it's usually something you never expected. And when it does all of your most carefully laid plans can mean nothing. I still remember driving through the bright sunshine, exhausted and shaking, chain-smoking and blasting Rage Against the Machine, until I physically couldn't anymore. I was shattered, emotionally and physically, embarrassed, humiliated, and completely alone. I had to take the first hotel I saw. It was a crumbling shanty of a roach motel, disgusting and horrible, and still in Idaho somewhere, which was further humiliating because it was so close to 'home.' But I had no idea how to find a better one, or a cheaper one, or how to plan ahead. I had just assumed that I would camp for cheap no matter what. That was an OK plan until it wasn't. What I have learned over the years is that eventually, you're going to need privacy and a good shower. You're going to need four walls to calm down and recharge. Oftentimes the only place to get that on the road is a hotel.

Therefore, you need to know how to find one and book one, most likely on your phone as you are driving. There are a million tricks and tips here, so I've just laundry-listed them below. Not all these are 'rules,' so they won't always apply. But for the 1000s of hotels I've stayed in, they tend to be the norm.

● **There is a difference between a hotel and a motel.**

A hotel is typically a big building with multiple floors and doors that face an inner hallway. This means there will probably be an elevator, a big lobby, food in the morning, and some kind of security. A motel is a one or two-story building where all the doors face outwards, typically toward the parking lot.

● **Hotels tend to be nicer and safer.**

● **Motels tend to be cheaper.**

● **Motels are far more likely to offer 'weekly rates.'**

These can be a lifesaver if you need to hole up somewhere for a week or two and you're sick of sleeping in a tent or your car. The most common times you'll be looking for one of these is either if your car breaks down, you break down, or you decide to settle down in a city for a while. Whatever it ends up being you'll want to do some research on it first.

● **When you find a hotel/motel with weekly rates, check the parking lot.**

If you can, and it's legal, it's wise to hang around and watch the parking lot for a few hours, especially around rush hour. What you're looking for are children. That sounds weird but if you see kids running around and playing, you're in the right spot. Parents, as a whole, don't want their kids playing in super dangerous areas. If you see kids, you can automatically assume that the staff takes security seriously and that there aren't a lot of dangerous people hanging around. Also, a lot of people that stay in weekly hotels are hard-working people who are in-between apartments and frequent travelers who stay in different places for a few weeks at a time. These are the types of people who you'll see return around six o'clock. Keep your eye out for people in work clothes, uniforms, or just dressed nicely. You'll be able to spot them pretty quickly.

● **If you don't see working people, frequent travelers, or children, you need to be very careful.**

I've had a lot of good and bad experiences and they weren't strictly correlated to how much money I was spending per week. Most of the dangerous 'motel stories' that I was part of, however, happened at cheap weekly motels where I didn't scope out the location before I paid up and checked in. Some other warning signs that you're in the wrong place are:

1. **Plastic/glass screens that prohibit people from reaching across the desk.** These are thicker and more intense than the hanging sneeze screens everybody has nowadays, which are normal and no cause for worry. If there is only a slot to fit your ID under and a heavy security door into the office? Yeah, not the safest place to be.

2. **Places that simply don't let anyone in the lobby.** That means there has been a serious issue, most likely very recently, and the owners are *done* with their clientele. This also indicates that something serious has happened more than once.

3. **Furniture sitting outside of the doors.** This either means that people spend a lot of time outside of their rooms or that there is the presence of bed bugs. If people spend a lot of time outside of their rooms there is a good chance that either the beds are terrible, the AC doesn't

work, or they live there permanently. In my humble experience, none of these are good things.

4. **Broken down cars in the parking lot.** Hoods up, flat tires, cars held together by bungee cords, all of these indicate that these cars don't run and haven't run in a while. This means that the management isn't concerned with regulating the parking lot. This can also mean that some people are staying there that are getting desperate. Again, this does not mean that these are bad people. It is just a situation that you want to avoid if you can.

5. **Broken windows.** A lot of times this isn't the obvious shattered glass and caution tape you see in TV shows. Most often you see where someone taped it together, or where someone had to paint and caulk the outside of the seal. It can also be cardboard taped over parts of the window.

6. **Police drive-throughs.** If the place is dangerous then it is a spot-on guarantee that there have been arrests made there recently. Think what you want about the police. They do their jobs. Part of this job is to drive through places that have a bad reputation. If you are hanging out, scoping out the place and seeing if you want to hang around, and a cop drives into the parking lot slowly, drives through, then leaves, you head right after them.

● **Sign up for every app and rewards service.**

If you are going to get around, you are probably going to *get around*. And you'll quickly find that all the types of hotels and motels that you are familiar with might not be the places that you are going to end up staying. Everywhere is different and everywhere has its way of doing things. I keep a notebook app on my phone that I back up to Google. This has a list of all the different apps and programs that I participate in, along with passwords and logins. Currently, I use about fifteen, and every single one offers some kind of rewards program. I never pay for these services, but I oftentimes reap the rewards.

● **Find out which rewards programs apply to which kinds of hotels.**

And which companies own multiple chains! If you start to look into this, you start to get an idea of what the 'good' companies are, and which ones are horrible. You can also start to pick out good and bad hotels just based on the brand, the company, the location, etc. After a while, it becomes second nature.

- **When looking for hotels a great way to go about this is to pull up the map of where you'd like to go.**

Before this, I always gauge how tired I am vs. how much coffee I've had, how much sleep I've been getting, what I want to do that night, etc. Then I give myself a rough idea of how much longer I want to keep driving. Once I do that, I look at the map and start randomly picking cities and seeing how long it will take to drive there. This will dramatically reduce your options. Then I refine the search to the radius of how far I want to go, pull up the available options, then start to analyze and process reviews and where each hotel is located. Once I have narrowed it down I either drive to the location I picked out and scope out the hotels or just book something and hope for the best.

- **Hotels and motels can be much cheaper by calling them in person or going through one of your hotel apps.**

This is irritating and confusing, I know, but it is just how it works. Some hotels understand that hotel apps take a large percentage off the top for their services. As a result, they will lower their rate to *just under* the amount that it would cost them to rent a room through, say, Expedia. This is why you call. When hotels do this you are going to pay less than you would normally. But not all hotels and motels use shrewd marketing strategies. A lot of front desk people have no idea what they're doing. And that's OK! These are the ones that will straight up tell you to book through the major booking sites. They don't care, you don't care, nobody cares. In that case, take the cheapest rate available on whichever app you have.

- **If you're traveling with a dog, always call and ask about their pet policy.**

Hotels and motels love to charge you extra for your pet because they can, even though they do nothing extra after that pet has left the room. And oftentimes the pet fee listed is incorrect. There is nothing worse than paying a nonrefundable rate for a room that suddenly doubles because the front desk person is afraid of your pit bull.

- **A lot of hotels and motels have bucked the trend of using any kind of web-based service to display their location.**

And this includes Google. For whatever reason they just want to attract people that drive by. There is nothing wrong with this! Screw The Man!

More power to 'em. Not coincidentally these have been some of the best places I have ever stayed. Also, not coincidentally, these have been some of the worst. You're never going to know what you're going to get with these spots. They are typically people who have owned the hotel for a long time. Or they are people that made some money somewhere else and wanted a business to retire with. Again, this can go either way. Sometimes it's cabins in the middle of nowhere that are cheap as dirt and positively wonderful. Sometimes it's poorly maintained roach motels on a country road in the middle of nowhere. It's a crap shoot. You either hit the lottery or you can't get out of there fast enough. Let it ride, baby!

- **AAA deals.**

I try not to advocate for various companies. Mainly because I don't want to get sued by anyone. But AAA is a service that you should have. Also, if you are booking hotels face-to-face (i.e. not through an app) then they almost always have a AAA discount of 5-10%. Which is awesome.

- **Using an app to get a hotel, I have never once correctly listed the number of people that were staying in the hotel.**

For some reason, hotels charge more for more people. Even if they have zero amenities. I worked for a decade in the hospitality industry. I *was* an all-powerful front desk person. I have yet to get a straight, informative answer about why it's alright to charge extra for extra people. Don't talk to me about 'utilities.' Maybe it is simply to avoid having a clown car situation, wherein forty college kids are stuffed into a room together for the night, having too much fun. I don't know because that situation has never arisen, in my experience. Just sayin'.

62 | Burnout

I once worked in a small town in Alaska with 4,000 residents. There was a large ski resort there with a massive hotel. I can't remember the exact number of employees but suffice it to say that the majority of the town either worked for the resort or had a job that was there because the resort was there. Now at this time in my 'waiting tables' phase I was good. Really good. I also hated it, didn't fit in, and was starting to realize that despite all the money I was making, I hated my job, my life, and people in general. This is the last classic stage of 'burnout.'

If you are not familiar with the term, 'burnout' is defined by Merriam-Webster as: "exhaustion of physical or emotional strength or motivation usually as a result of prolonged stress or frustration." At this point, I hated everyone and everything and started drinking way too much. I also started taking my frustration out on the employees around me. I had worked in over fifty restaurants and knew what talent looked like. Most of the people I was working with at that time did not have any. They regularly screwed up and, in my head, cost me money. Which led to more stress, more frustration, and then, more drinking. I was a mess. One day, as I was complaining to the general manager about the new employees she had hired, she asked me a good question:

"Do you know how many people I have had to fire, *multiple times*, in this town? Do you have any idea how hard it is to vet, interview and relocate employees in the middle of the season?"

Good point. It was at this time that it all dawned on me at once. Not only was the talent pool in this tiny, barren little town not enough to satisfy the demands of a huge resort, but even the employees you could import had such a high turnover rate that the importation process had to be *constant*. And these are people who you most often interviewed (back then) over the phone and had never actually *met in person*. It was a crapshoot of humanity showing up at your door, put to work in an environment of people they had never met, hopefully with enough experience to at least tread water, all with a constantly overwhelming workload. Welcome to seasonal work! The salient point is that these companies are investing serious time and energy into maintaining a stable of warm bodies that they can throw at the meat-grinder of assholes showing up at their resort. These assholes need to sleep, eat, drink, and ski, and all those things require a full staff to provide those services. This is where I came in. The problem was, as it always is, that a business that has invested always wants to *maximize* that investment. They want you to show up and start working right away and they want you to keep working until the people stop showing up and they can boot your ass out of town. To these businesses, you are a lemon and they are using you to make lemonade.

You just have to make sure that you don't end up as pulp.

It's important to remember that without seasonal labor these companies would cease to exist. They simply wouldn't have enough bodies to keep the whole thing running. Therefore, to find enough people these companies are forced to advertise and recruit, spending large amounts of money and time in the process. When they do find and secure these employees, they then have to pay HR to get them set up, feed and house them. Only once this is all complete do you actually get to work. Therefore, hospitality companies want you to work. A lot. For most this is just part of the game and what they are looking/hoping for. A good amount of people work their asses off for six months and then 'retire' for six months. Instead of this, I just kept working, season after season, drinking more and more and becoming ever more miserable. I was burnt out. I had worked myself into the ground until I was too miserable and frustrated to dig myself out. I had been pulped. And the real problem is that seasonal work is often the most challenging, mentally and physically grueling work you can find. And once you are committed you are in till the end. Unless, of course, you crash and burn, get run out of town by a pistol-waving old woman (RIP Susie), get fired in 'disgrace,' or generally just burn rubber on the nearest highway. But the entire idea of this book is that you *don't* have to act like I did. And that you never become as miserable and lonely as I became.

Any astute observer would, at this point, illustrate that the entire point of this book is to break you out of the 'norm' and out of the constructs surrounding you that keep you unhappy. So, why wouldn't you just leave a job when you are burnt out? Why work and strive to keep a job in your life that actively makes you suffer? The answer to this is simple: you oftentimes don't have a choice. I cannot count how many times I had to use my very last dime to buy the last ticket to the place I was going to show up and work at. Again, you should always save your first paycheck so that if the job is abusive or just flat-out sucks then you can leave. Not all of us do this, so you might be broke when it becomes apparent that the situation has become untenable. Hence, you have to manage your burnout till you can.

● **Always keep a good rapport with your manager, if possible.**

Hey, I get it. Usually, this is the exact person who is causing most of the stress and grief at your job. But if you can keep it friendly and professional with them. When you start to identify the signs of burnout in your day-to-day, you should immediately go to this person and see if they can give you some extra time off, put you on some shorter shifts, or otherwise work out a solution. If they help you out, maybe that's a better job than you thought! If they tell you that you're on your own, or worse, that you need to 'suck it up,' then you know for sure that it is time to move on when/if you can.

● **Reach out to your people.**

This is where I regularly failed myself through a long and tenuous process. Long story short, I often had no one to call or talk to because of the snowballing effect of my long-term burnout and increasingly reclusive habits. The idea is to not get to that point! So, when you are starting to become frustrated *all the time*, or if it seems like you are dreading coming off of your weekend, or, most importantly, you are starting to develop intense anxiety, then you need to immediately reach out to the people in your life that you trust. The 'venting' process is key to not holding residual anger and distrust. Not to mention that hearing yourself talk can often solidify and clarify the realities of a situation, such as if there is an abusive or neglectful element of your job that you need to get away from. Or you might just find that it was a rough week and you needed to dump it on someone. Whatever it is, pick up the phone and make a call. That phone can feel like it weighs a thousand pounds at times. Imagine the weight that you'd carry if you didn't get it off your chest though!

● **Reach out to a therapist or mental health professional.**

If you are like me and have often found yourself without anyone you connect with or if you just want to use your money to prioritize your mental health, you should reach out to a therapist. Don't let cost deter you. Nothing is more important than your mental health. Even if you don't have insurance most therapists will work out a deal with you, or you can just schedule to see them a handful of times, maybe even just once a month.

You'll be amazed how many small towns have a handful of therapists to choose from. Even though you are paying them the benefits of talking to someone who you can share your experience and emotions with are incalculable. And you might just learn a few things about yourself in the process.

- **Lay back on the drinking.**

First of all, if you are dreading going back to work and your weekends are filled with constant dread for 'your Monday,' then you are already burnt out. It is at this stage, particularly in resort towns, that people start to hit the bars and drink heavily. I know I did. My weekends would consist of some crazy activity on 'my Friday,' like climbing a mountain or heading to some crazy bar in the middle of nowhere. But the next two days would be spent sitting at home, taking care of my laundry and bills, and generally getting my mind ready for another grueling week. And that's if I had two days off in a row. The answer that I never saw at the time was to lay off the drinking. I was spending most of what I made trying to blow off enough steam not to hate my job. That much alcohol was also messing with the hormonal balance in my body, negatively altering my brain chemistry, and creating intense consequences via my organs and digestive tract. In essence, my drinking was holding me back and making everything worse. I'm not saying pull the plug on it entirely. This is never a bad thing, but I get it if you aren't 'all or nothing' like me. Try to take some nights off though. Hydrate. Watch some movies at home. Get your mind and body right while you save up your money. You'll thank yourself when the time comes to leave.

- **Try to enjoy what there is to offer.**

At some point in my hospitality career, I realized that I was working so much, and so burnt out, that I wasn't even enjoying the things that resort life had to offer. I wasn't skiing, hiking, camping, or even checking out the local restaurants. I was drinking heavily, avoiding the friends I had made, isolating myself outside of work, obsessively thinking about money, and generally fiddling away my time without having any fun. You work to live, not the other way around. And if you forget that then you need to reprioritize your life. Force yourself to go to the local attractions, no matter how touristy. Go get dinner, hit up the mini-golf spot, take a tour, and watch a play. Get out of your head and your wallet for a minute. It might spark a desire to continue *having some fun*. God forbid, right?

- **Be ready for the end.**

I am certainly not saying that it is a foregone conclusion that you are going to leave your job. I understand that it may sound pessimistic. I'm working on it. I am also not saying to *be* pessimistic and let your behavior dictate a hasty end to your employment. What I *am* saying is that if you are burned out it can happen suddenly and with great conviction. And it always comes as a surprise, particularly when your work and living situation are intertwined. Suddenly you are out of a job *and* a place to live. And if you live in the middle of nowhere then you certainly aren't going to just walk down the street and get a job at the gas station. Even if you wanted to, they aren't going to hire you. No, now you have to also *switch towns*. And most likely that means hiring on with another company far, far away. If you are starting to hate your job, are struggling to remain positive, and generally find yourself upset and exhausted all the time, mentally prepare yourself to have to move on. The worst-case scenario is that you are correct but prepared.

- **Look forward to the future.**

In my life, I have often fallen prey to the 'devil you know' type of thinking. Even though the situation I had put myself in was toxic and untenable I could at least understand what was going on and why. I often found myself afraid of anything else. This is what caused even more distress and burnout. I would hold on as long as I could, desperately trying to make the situation work for longer. This is a difficult way to live. We fool ourselves into thinking that we are going to fail if we try something new. We cannot see a life where our needs are met and we are fulfilled. Trust me, there is such a life for you. For all of us. So, if you are experiencing burnout, to whatever degree, try and imagine a life where you are moving forward with purpose and success. Picture yourself in this new situation. Allow yourself to feel it, then believe that it is possible. We are trying to live in the present at all times, for sure, but it is also healthy to visualize and imagine a bright future. It is key to living the life of our dreams. So, when you are in a job that you have identified isn't for you, look forward to the future. Think of the positives, the ways that you can improve, the steps you can take to make it happen, and how you can add the purpose and well-being that you are seeking to your life.

63 | Busses

Everyone has either heard about or seen a bunch of Greyhound buses. They are ubiquitous to American travel. They go everywhere and their old, decrepit stations are a fixture in every single American town, large and small. And for good reason. They dominated the 'bus industry' for a long time, and for good reason. It is a low-cost option for getting from point A to point B. But nowadays, Greyhound is not the only carrier that can get you there for cheap. There are a myriad of different low-cost carriers that have jumped on the low-cost bandwagon. It is well worth noting that when you are considering heading from one point to another, look for a cheap bus route that heads that way. You can save a ton of money and have a chance to relax between destinations. There are, however, a lot of potential pitfalls that come with this as well.

Busses are often the lowest cost of travel that you can find. It is no wonder that bus travel dominates travel in less developed parts of the world. I once made my way all over Peru and eventually to Columbia solely off of bus travel and paid pennies for the privilege. I found out later that the borders were extremely dangerous (whoops) but I brought two cases of beer with me and we all had a great time. If they were planning to rob me, I think they forgot. Anyway! Whenever you utilize the lowest cost of anything you are going to deal with what I call the 'lowest common denominator.' Ever been to a Walmart? Yeah, you get the idea. Hostels are like this. Cheap hotels, flights, and 'discount days' are like this. Yes, I know how negative it sounds. I am working on it. But it does have a decided element of truth. If you are dealing with 'lowest common denominator' travel you are going to have the highest chance of being stuck with people who act in the worst possible way, with the worst manners, and the least concern for people around them, AND THAT SLURPING NOISE, GOD HELP ME. Anyway. I am not saying that these people are worse, or that they are bad people in any way. It just has the highest chance of hitting on whatever pet peeves you might have.

You might be wondering about the all-caps words above. I always do my research. And even though I have traveled on buses hundreds, if not thousands of times, I still had to get the raw version again so I could tell you about it. So right now, I am sitting on a bus writing this as I ponder murdering another human. OK, that's way over the top. Break his nose? Wrong again. OK. I am sitting on a bus and I want to scream in another person's face. For a long, long time. This dickwad is loudly talking about basketball while everyone around him sleeps. And, perhaps more damning, he is loudly, and I mean LOUDLY, slurping and sucking on nuts, chips, jerky, whatever this horrible little monster can get his hands on. I adamantly realize that life circumstances that I created and am accountable for put me on this bus in the first place. And I also realize that, again due to these circumstances, I am tired, lonely, off-balance, and extremely irritable. Compounding this is the fact that my stupid headphones just *will not* stay charged, meaning that I can't just drown out the people around me with music or ambient meditation music. I am fully at the mercy of this inconsiderate twenty-something monster.

This could have been easily avoided. And *should* have been avoided because I took every step necessary to avoid this. But shit doesn't always go the way you want it to. And that is why you follow my advice, because your handsome protagonist goes through the legwork for you. So, the next time you end up exhausted and irritable on the bus and you want to murder a human being so bad that you can't even yell at the guy because it'll come off so angry that it'll cause a brawl… you'll have everything you need. Or it won't happen to you in the first place.

● **Never, ever, have a long conversation on the phone.**

This applies to everywhere indoors but sometimes it's just not possible. You're busy, you have to get groceries, and you need to coordinate things before you get home. Does that mean you need to be on speakerphone? Nope. And yes, this section directly pertains to the Don't Be a Crappy Little Monster (i.e. What You Do Effects Everyone Else) section as well. But when you're traveling it is imperative to understand that *everyone else* is just as bored, uncomfortable, irritated, annoyed, or whatever it is that you're feeling. They don't need to hear you talk to your mom for 45 minutes. They don't need to hear your opinions on whether Tom Brady has another year in him. And they certainly don't need to hear you going on and on about wherever it was that you just left from.

- **If you don't have headphones, keep your phone silent.**

I can't believe this needs to be said to other human beings but do not put your phone on speaker and have a chat with someone, play videos of cats, or my personal favorite, bump whatever music it is that you're into at the time. No one else cares and certainly no one else needs to hear it. Which reminds me.

- **Always bring two pairs of headphones.**

Grab a cheap set of earbuds, have two nice sets, or get Air Pods. Do whatever you have to do. One of the most annoying situations, while you're on a bus, is to have a bunch of people who think they can rap, sing, or politically commentate, or any of the other things I am listening to right now. Are they charged yet? Please?

- **Stay positive.**

Alright, enough negativity. Traveling can oftentimes be difficult and annoying. Infuriating even. But you have to take time in these moments to remember all the great places and things that you've been enjoying and all the places and things that you're headed to now. There is always something to look forward to and be grateful for. Even if it's just getting off the bus.

- **Be nice to the driver.**

I have seen way too many people treat the bus driver like crap and I've never understood it. This is the person who is in charge of getting you to your destination safely. Why on Earth would you piss them off? Or worse, treat them like a lesser human being? Not to mention, if you pass out, they are the ones that are going to wake your ass up and make sure you get off in the right town. Trust me, waking up in the wrong town on the wrong day is not only very possible but also very expensive.

- **Bring snacks.**

Oh man, you never know how hungry you're going to be until you're four hours into a nine-hour ride. I always stop by Aldi and grab a bunch of snacks and sandwich-making stuff. While there might be food at the bus station it is going to be dramatically overpriced and most likely bad for you. Also, do you trust the food handling at a place like that when you're traveling long distances? Hard nope.

- **Have a blanket.**

Even if it is just a small, thin one from an airplane, having a blanket can make a huge difference. The air is often kept too cold to try and limit the spread of disease. And frankly, buses can be dirty and decidedly unfriendly environments. So, having a creature comfort like a blanket can trick your brain into thinking that it is comfortable and relaxed which, in turn, can lead to you *feeling* calm and relaxed. It's worth lugging around if you are going to be on a lot of buses.

- **Sit in the middle.**

In the front, you have the driver and the lonely person most likely talking to the driver. There always seems to be at least one Chatty Kathy in the first few rows. Avoid those. You don't want to spend countless hours making pointless small talk with someone you don't vibe with and will never see again. In the back are the bathrooms. And these are typically going to reek to high heaven. Plus, there is no doubt going to be a constant procession of people going in and out of this smelly commode. Thus, the best place away from both of these hazards is square in the middle. If you have to hedge, go toward the front. But don't make eye contact with Kathy.

- **Bring that thing you've been meaning to do.**

On a long bus ride, you are a captive audience of one. You can think that you are going to be satisfied watching movies and reading books for twelve hours all you want. Eventually, you are going to get bored or want to be somewhere else. This is the absolute perfect time to whip out some work that you have been delaying, like that book you need to finish, those pesky taxes, or just some letters to old friends that you've been putting off. Not only does it feel really good to get these things done, but it also has the magical effect of making your next movie or long session of staring out the window seem much more enjoyable.

- **Keep the existential dread at bay.**

Just, keep it at bay. Try not to think about your exes, or your reflection in the mirror, or any of the… just, keep it at bay.

64 | Cell Phones

Cell phones and smartphones have become synonymous with everyday life. Regardless of age or socioeconomic status, nearly everyone has one. And with the rise of the gig economy, they have become an essential asset to a lot of people's survival, myself included. As a result, cell phones have become arguably the single most useful tool for making a living on the road that you can own, and it is important to know how and why to get an affordable phone and what kind of phone plan to get. These plans constantly change, and phone companies rapidly upgrade and alter their operating systems, so this section is short and sweet.

Get a monthly plan.

As soon as I traveled abroad, I became aware of how much they screw us on wireless plans here in the States. Nearly everywhere else in the world, it is cheap and easy to buy a sim card that you can put into almost any phone. Here we are caught by the balls/ovaries by the major cell phone carriers who have traditionally dominated the market. This is rapidly changing because competition in the market is driving the price way down. Still, companies lure you in with a cheap monthly installment plan (it's not actually cheap) for the latest phone (it won't be 'the latest' for long), all the while charging you exorbitant fees for account activation, monthly maintenance, and early termination. Avoid all this by getting a pay-as-you-go, month-to-month plan. Also, buy an unlocked phone so you can take advantage of deals provided later by companies who want you to switch carriers. With an unlocked phone, you can switch services almost pain-free at any time. The ultimate benefit of this is that you can pause your service when you are going to be out of service for long periods, like working in the woods or at a National Park, and keep your number.

Buy unlocked phones.

Phone companies and chat boards will try to scare you off of this by claiming that unlocked phones are less secure, but this is ridiculous. Hackers are going to hack, scammers are going to scam. It's up to you to make smart decisions about what websites you visit, who you give your debit card information to, and who you choose to talk to online. No one can help you if you aren't going to help yourself. So, buy an unlocked phone. The main reason behind this is that you can choose to switch carriers at any time. I do this regularly. I use one of the niche carriers listed below until either the trial period ends or I get a better deal. Then I wait for one of the other companies to offer me a promo to get my business back, they send me another sim card, yada yada. It may seem like a hassle, but I like to save money and an hour of my time is always worth a cheaper phone bill. Even if you don't want to play hot potato with phone companies, you at least have the option to sell the phone when you are done with it if it is unlocked.

Buy cheap phones.

The entire matrix surrounding you is designed to keep you wanting more stuff. Buy, buy, buy. Consume, consume, consume. It keeps the wheels turning and keeps everyone happy, right? Right? Except you really wouldn't be reading this if you were truly content, would you? So maybe, just maybe, you don't need the newest phone that comes out seemingly every ten minutes. The makers of phones are all rapidly losing lawsuits regarding their 'planned obsolescence' tactics, wherein the software of older phones was designed to slow and break down over time. This is becoming a thing of the past. Now phone manufacturers are focusing instead on more and more frills to sell newer and newer phones. You do not need the latest and greatest. Get the model right behind it, or better, get a phone that is two or three models behind. You can still effectively run the apps you need to work, check your email, and make a call. And from a guy who has dropped a lot of phones into rivers, streams, and off of cliff faces, these older models are much easier to replace!

There are better ways to buy used phones than others. Go to a pawn shop only if you're desperate and there are no other options. The same goes for eBay and similar sites. Nothing is worse than getting a phone only to realize that it's been locked because the previous owner didn't pay their bills. Or worse, that it's been reported as stolen. Usually, you aren't getting your money back. Customer service will laugh at you until you hang up. I have had the best luck going into the stores and bribing employees with coffee and donuts. They usually have phones lying around. Also, check the smaller phone repair stores. They always have phones for sale, they are usually cool, and if it breaks you can usually take them in to be fixed for free. The point is, shop around, try and stay away from online unless you're going to buy a new phone, and think for a minute about who might have decent phones that they don't want much for.

Have anti-spyware and anti-virus software.

I know. It's annoying to buy any kind of tech and go through the process of being nickel-and-dimed for everything from the case to cloud storage. But having an asset requires maintenance. And the most basic maintenance that you need is that of security. This is doubly true for an unlocked phone. You don't have the same level of protection that being tied to a major phone carrier affords you. Shell out the $20 per year to have a firewall and virus protection. It'll give you the peace of mind you didn't know you needed till you have it.

Try not to use public WiFi.

Everybody I have ever talked to in cyber security tells me the same thing: avoid public WiFi. Well, you try and travel on a shoestring budget in a foreign place without having a home network to connect to, buddy. Sometimes I am going to have to use the laundromat WiFi to get a job, a place to live, and a plan for the next three weeks before my clothes are dry. And to do that I am going to need WiFi. The trick is to treat it like you would any other public space: dirtier, noisier, and with a much higher chance of having anything bad happen there. And when you're done using it, clean yourself up. In this case, this means running a check for malware.

Always have a case.

It is uncanny how many times I have dropped a phone when I didn't have a case for it. This typically happens the first day I got it too. And because I am prideful, I used that cracked screen for months. Would it have been easy to get it fixed? Yes. Cheap too? Also yes. But there I was, staring at a huge crack and pretending it wasn't there. Anyway, as soon as I get a case around my phone it stays glued to my hand as if drilled on with a lag bolt. Even the cheap ones will save you a lot of trouble. Just make sure to get all of your cases online. The phone stores and big box stores count on you wanting to protect your investment, so they upcharge the hell out of the cases. Online retailers just want to sell as many as possible so you can get the same case that you had your eye on for half the price.

65 | Cheating (on People)

There is never a good reason to cheat on someone else. It just doesn't exist. We convince ourselves that this person was abusive, or they didn't or don't care about us anymore, or that they frequently mistreat us. But in that case, the onus lies on you to leave. Or talk about it. There is no excuse to not have a serious and frank conversation about your relationship. Rather, most people use the person they are with for whatever they are using them for while they run into the arms of someone else. This is betraying your partner and yourself. You are stabbing your subconscious in the eye while you are stabbing them in the back. And there is no person alive who deserves this.

In my life, I have always told my partners to simply *tell me* if the relationship is over. Why not? I am not a puppet master controlling every aspect of their lives and their day. Even if I wanted to I could never control whether or not they wanted to stay with me. And people have definitely made it known before that they wanted nothing to do with me at a moment's notice. And I have certainly done the same. But some of these women went behind my back about it. And that is what hurts someone the most and makes it hard to trust future partners. That is what creates the scars that lead to complexes, trauma, and trust issues down the road. All because two people couldn't have a short and uncomfortable conversation.

I remember a relationship I had when I was in my early 20s. I had taken off and landed at Mt. Rainier. It was glorious. My life was a party and I was finally free. So, what did I do? I fell in love with the absolute worst match for me that could exist. She even had the gall to claim that the feeling was mutual. She yanked me around for an entire season and when it was done, somehow agreed to keep a long-distance relationship going. My goodness, how silly that was! I *believed* that this woman was being good to me while she was partying her ass off in college, thousands of miles away. I took this horseshit for six months until we finally got another job together in Yosemite National Park. It was an instant nightmare. The woman I had waited for had turned into the most flirty and promiscuous woman I had ever met. She claimed that she wasn't sleeping with everyone she met. And I believed it! But I was still too spineless to have an upfront conversation about it. Instead, I would drink to excess and rant and rave out in the woods, all while she was in someone else's company. I angrily pushed my way out of that job and landed us a gig at another park. It was going to be better, she'll see! Nothing got better. She immediately fell in love with a guy there. It was plain to see. And then I got the call. My uncle had died and my mother was suicidal. I had to get home. Fast.

I immediately hightailed it to the nearest airport, six hours away. I was at the funeral two days later. Consoling my mother and my brother took all of my time and energy. I had no mental space to think about what was going on back 'home.' I dared to think that my girlfriend and I could do a lot better when I got back. That our troubles had been my fault, not the complete lack of respect that she was showing me.

When I finally got back, five days after I had first taken off, I was shocked when I saw them standing close together. I had loved and trusted this woman so deeply that I couldn't fathom that she didn't feel the same. The boy walked away and she started to as well. I was calling out to her but a friend of mine quickly walked down the hill and put his hand on my chest. He whispered in my ear: "Don't do anything stupid." I will never forget those words. He probably saved my life because all I could feel was a primal rage, a wellspring of hatred and self-loathing that could have leveled a mountain if let loose.

The pieces were told to me in starts and stops over the next few days. I barely remember speaking to her and her new boyfriend. I barely remember punching the kid in the face or walking, humiliated and zombie-like, through the crowds of snickering coworkers for what felt like years. I had spent all of my money on getting back 'home' the first time, so I had to work and stay in that hellscape for another three weeks until my next paycheck. I must have smoked a pack of cigarettes per hour. Everything that I had believed had been shattered, crumpled, and pissed on. I had been a hopeless romantic up to that point. That died, then and there, on the Paunsaugunt Plateau. She even had the nerve to tell me that while she was getting screwed by this guy, she had started yelling *my* name. What do you even make of *that?*

As I see it, none of that crap needed to happen. That woman could have told me the first week that we knew each other that she didn't want to have a relationship. I could have had valuable experience learning about myself and how to fill my internal chasm, rather than trying to fill it with someone else. She could have run off with anyone she wanted at any time.

Ultimately it shattered my persona, my mental state, and my faith in humanity for months. I take full responsibility for the poor choices that I made next, but that event was the catalyst for a lot of pain and suffering that could have easily been avoided by one simple conversation. Cheating is never acceptable. Ever. If you want to bone someone else just *tell your partner first.* Then you're free! You can be free anytime you want. Anytime! But what will chain you, tethering your soul to guilt and shame, is betraying someone else. Going behind their back. Being too much of a coward to simply tell them that it's over. It's that simple.

66| Couch Surfing

As I mentioned in an earlier section of this book, couch surfing is a grey area in the realm of a conscious, healthy lifestyle. It can be exactly what you need to get ahead just as often as it can hold you back. For this reason, this chapter did not exist in the early drafts of this book. But over time I realized that, because it was such a part of my early story, the lessons I learned might be able to help a great many of you. As such, here we are.

Couch surfing is a delicate situation to be in. Typically, this means that something has gone wrong or that you are in a difficult situation. It's important at this juncture to clarify the difference between couch surfing and simply staying with someone. Couch surfing is not staying on your friend's couch for the weekend. A lot of your friends will cherish and appreciate having you stay with them for a few days while you are on vacation. Any effect you might have on their lifestyle is mitigated by the fact that you are only staying for a short amount of time and that it is inherently a novelty. Couch surfing is when you are either traveling or living somewhere and need a place to sleep for at least a few weeks. When I was in this situation, I was either between places, had abruptly been kicked out of somewhere else, or I had burned all of my bridges in another town and needed to establish myself somewhere new that did not have any other options I could afford. It was always based on need, rather than simply for fun. And because of this, I had to establish a firm set of rules for myself to maintain my good standing with my host and thereby solidify my survival. These personal rules not only kept my relationships with my hosts sound and healthy, but they also kept me sane during these periods of upheaval.

Give back.

For the vast majority of times that I have been couch surfing I had just become unemployed. While I was obviously fixated on getting another job as quickly as possible, I nevertheless had some free time on my hands. I always used this time to do things around the house that I was staying in. I would deep clean their kitchen, living room, blinds, etc. I would do things that they might not typically have time to do, like gardening or power washing the driveway. This creates value for you in the eyes of your host and is an opportunity for you to show that you appreciate the free ride that you are being given. As someone who has frequently hosted couch surfers as well, there was always a tracker in my mind of who was willing to do something around my living space. Even if it is as simple as ordering pizza for the house or having the dishes done when I got home, I greatly appreciated my guests taking the time and effort.

Fit into their lifestyle.

A lot of times when you are staying with someone you will be sleeping in a high-traffic area such as the couch in the living room. This means that you can easily cramp their style if you are not aligning with their schedule. There is nothing worse than having someone staying with you that becomes an immediate nuisance through their self-serving behavior. If your host is going to bed at 8 pm then you shouldn't be far behind them. Because that means that they are going to be up early in the morning and want the use of their entire house. They cannot do that if there is someone loudly snoring on their couch. The same goes if they are night owls. A lot of people I stayed with loved to watch movies or play video games on their living room TV until the wee hours of the morning. This either meant that I was adjusting to staying up late and hanging out or that I was falling asleep, sitting up, with a ton of noise in the room. Either way, you certainly do not want to impede upon what people want to do in their own homes. There is no quicker way to overstay your welcome than to show your host that they cannot live their own lives the way that they want to.

You'll notice in this section that I focused completely on couch surfing with people you already know. Just know that this was intentional.

Bring something.

Never show up with your arms swinging. Always, and I mean always, have some token or gesture of appreciation when you show up at someone's door. This could mean a banana or a pretty rock that you just found. This doesn't have the same meaning as a bouquet but it isn't *nothing*. There is a subconscious shift that occurs when you see someone show up empty-handed. You suddenly, without thinking about it, see them as a dependent. This is not a good thing to be as an adult. I would always call ahead and see if they needed anything. Usually, people would say no out of their sense of self-reliance or simple politeness. I would slightly press the matter and ask if they were running low on milk, cheese, soda, etc. You don't want to be pushy, but you do what to find something useful to them if you can. Avoid beer and alcohol unless you are in a party house. This sends an immature message, namely that you are willing to spend your sparse funds on alcohol when you are ostensibly using their place as a leg up. Toilet paper and paper towels are bulky but send a great message. The same goes for a bag of fruits and vegetables. Whatever it is, put some time and effort into what you are bringing and then present it when you arrive with a heartfelt thank you for their hospitality.

Pay for what you use.

This is pretty simple. If you are staying in someone's house and you go to the fridge and eat all of their yogurt, then you need to head down to the store as soon as you get a chance and replace it. The same goes for toilet paper, things you break during your stay, and gas for their car if they are shuttling you all over town. This prevents your host from seeing you as a parasite. It is also immensely beneficial to your general outlook and self-esteem as well. When you are in this situation you are inherently struggling with self-sufficiency. By paying for the things you use you are telling your subconscious mind that you can still take care of yourself. It can have long-lasting and beneficial effects on your self-esteem.

Let them know you are coming.

This is another concept that is very simple but oftentimes gets neglected. It can be difficult when you are bouncing from town to town and having fun to set to a specific schedule. But this is exactly what you need to do. People want to be able to expect company and to know when to have their space available for guests. If you are postponing, even worse, showing up a few days early, you are putting your host on the spot. This can give them fits of anxiety and other issues. You have no idea what is going on in the head of whoever it is you are trying to crash with. You need to be as predictable and stable as possible for their sake. I always tried to give as much notice as possible. This didn't always work out the way I wanted it to. Traveling is difficult and time-consuming. Flights get derailed, trains are delayed, and busses break down. Shit happens. Simply remain in contact with your host and do your best to give them appropriate time to prepare for your arrival and you will be fine.

Be very clear about how long you need to stay.

And then stick to that plan, no matter what. People can be very hospitable at times, particularly when they care about you. That does not mean that they wouldn't prefer to have the space that they have worked hard for exactly the way that they want it. Most of us work way better with adversity when we know when it is going to end. This isn't to say that you are 'adversity' when staying on someone's couch. It is simply a gray area where a lot of negative things can arise quickly. And you, as the guest, have to assume that sooner rather than later your host is going to want the full use of their house back. As such, figure out either beforehand or within the first day how long you are going to need in their space. If you quickly find that you are going to need *more* time than you originally said, then do not ask them to stay longer. This will immediately make you look like a dependent to them and the tension will start building. Instead, find another couch to stay on. Rinse and repeat. Your goal should be to find a place of your own as quickly as possible, but this can be overwhelmingly difficult for some. I get it. Just make sure that you don't burn any bridges when you don't have anywhere to go. Set a time limit for how long you will be staying, try to get off their couch before the end of that time limit, and if you need more time find a similar situation elsewhere.

67 | Dealing With People You Leave Behind

You never really think about how most of the people around you will be affected by your absence. We do, in a sense, try to imagine it for some. Like if someone we care about is all alone in a new place, or if someone is forced into a situation of solitude by various life events. What we don't think about is how the people around us live their lives, either with us in it or without. We can't. We are too busy living our own lives; too busy being ourselves. Some would say it is impossible to ever truly experience someone else's life, even for a moment, as we are so inherently ourselves. Still, we all know that our absence or presence affects those around us. As such, it is reasonable to wonder how that is going to be.

The answer is, resoundingly, that they are going to react poorly. Your parents, family, and close friends won't blink an eye. Okay, maybe they will. But they'll get over it and get used to it. Leaving for considerable periods has been the best barometer in my life for determining just who in my life is worth keeping around and who isn't. Most people are going to shun you immediately. These folks don't live a flexible life. They have an arc, a trajectory, that is filled with goals and aspirations that effectively dictate how they are going to progress through their work, family, and social lives. There is nothing wrong with this kind of life or this kind of person. You are most likely *not* this way, so it may seem a bit foreign looking at those who want a slow and steady life. However, for those of us who are not willing to accept a nine-to-five job, have the work ethic necessary to continue moving around, have little interest in maintaining a single career, and don't want kids, this type of life is a jail sentence.

These two realities are directly opposing. A vast amount of people are not going to stop and try to consider your way of life as equally valuable and fulfilling. They are going to judge you as lesser, particularly your lack of possessions, and find ways to exclude you from their social sphere as often as they can. It is how they maintain their own set of priorities and principles. They are not afforded the luxury of reconsideration. Once you have children and a mortgage you are locked in for life. Unless you want to spend the rest of your life regretting it, as a lot of people do. But that is up for a higher level of judgment than either I or anyone else is capable of.

This is not to say that everyone in the world are assholes and that they just don't understand and never will. You will meet a lot, and I mean *a lot*, of unhealed, judgmental people who will put you down and insult you for no better reason than they feel like they can. Also, they undoubtedly have a *ton* of unresolved issues from their life and their childhood that they take out on everyone around them. That's just most people in this country. We are not a happy country of healthy and well-adjusted people. We are the lazy, psychologically broken members of a dying empire. Even with this constantly in mind, these people will tax you to the absolute limit on a daily basis. Amplify this by the fact that people treat outsiders *much* worse than they do people that they know they are going to see again and the propensity of people to act selfishly while on vacation (people you will be surrounded by) and you have a recipe for a worst-case scenario that you have to be prepared for.

By now, you know you are going to leave. Probably over and over again. And people are most often going to react badly to this. Whether it is co-workers, people you have been living with, friends, or family, you are going to immediately see who can handle the fact that you will not be present anymore and who cannot. The best way to get yourself ready is to know how to handle leaving. There are two ways to do this:

Just leave.

The first method is to just take off in the middle of the night or first thing in the morning, without any warning or advance notice. Your first thought might be: "Damn, I can't do that. They'd never want to see me again!" And to a degree that sentiment is spot on. A lot of people have abandonment issues (raises hand). So, if you just leave them like that, they might hate you for it. If you choose this option, you need to *make sure* that it is a place you do not want to return to. At least, not for a long time. This can be an act of mercy at times. Relationships that aren't working out but where there is a lot of love and affection. Abusive friendships. Toxic work environments. You name it. Sometimes, a carefully worded and heartfelt note, along with your absence, can be the easiest way to make a transition. You just have to actually *go* at that point. There isn't any turning back.

One time I remember particularly well was when a girlfriend and I were working in New Zealand in a very small town. Very small. We started working at the local market/restaurant. To say that this was the only show in town would be an understatement. It was literally the only business in town. There wasn't even a town. But it was spectacularly beautiful. Virgin, untouched beaches, an amazing lighthouse, deep-sea fishing… absolutely glorious. The problem was the woman we worked for. She was, let's say, a tad bit of a feminist. No problem, I thought. I can work with this as I have often in my life. Until I spied my girlfriend staring at our boss one day as she was talking.

I had never seen her with an 'I am going to commit murder' look in her eye before, so I had no idea what was going on. I had been tuning all of them out, as I am wont to do when I am the only male in a group of females. When I reentered this plane from my perfectly good daydream of the aforementioned beach and my girlfriend in a very skimpy bikini, I was immediately confronted with a tirade against men. Oh wait, it wasn't a tirade against *men*, it was a tirade against one man. Me. And evidently, it had been going on for quite some time because my girlfriend's face was going beet red. It also became evident that my lack of participation in this tirade was making it much, much more emphatic. I can't remember her exact words. What I can remember is that it was a speech designed to cut my balls off, feed them to me, and then withhold my check until I could pay her for the privilege. Remember what I said about unhealed people? Yeah, that didn't sit well with anybody.

Now, you're probably thinking that I should have just taken off, no problemo. The problem with that we had been there about three weeks at that point. We had gotten to know the shop owners, their beautiful children, and members of the staff and town. I had gone fishing with the male equivalent of the Betty Frieden wannabe who had so frequently cussed me out, and had developed a pretty strong bond in the face of all that hostility. Long story short, we had somehow become part of the family, despite how most of the town simply referred to us as 'the Backpackers.'

After that last virtuosic display of misandrist opinions and a thoroughly enjoyable display of how to correctly wash dishes, I had had enough. My girlfriend wished she had a shotgun. It was extremely clear to us that we had to leave. It was my opinion that the best option would be to just leave a note, profusely apologize, and never look back. We were poorly paid travelers who were getting treated like crap. We owed them nothing. My girlfriend, however, thought differently and convinced me to go to their door and tell them that we were leaving the next day. The husband was there and accepted our resignation fairly and gracefully. At least we thought before the door slammed loudly in our faces. We were then inundated with text messages from Betty all night long. The last one came through at 4 AM I had already booked us out of there, so when 5 AM came around we were ready, willing, and able to get the hell out of there. I handed my girlfriend a cup of coffee and gave her a very tired smile.

"Ok, OK!" She said, "You were RIGHT. You don't need to rub it in." It was pretty funny by this point. We got our bags together, hoisted them on our backs, and spat the ugliest-looking thing we could muster in the middle of the floor. And then we got in the taxi and never looked back. This was in the middle of the week, meaning that we hadn't received a paycheck yet and were due for one. It never came.

Give notice.

The second way to leave a place is to give plenty of notice, tell everyone your plans, help them find a replacement (if it is a work situation), and otherwise make an effort to see people and participate in the community before you leave. This seems, at first, to be a much better way of doing things. Perfect in theory, right? Except that you are headed somewhere else. Most likely you are excited about the change. Everyone can see this in you. And a lot of these people aren't going to react well to seeing that because they have lived their own lives in their own experience, and they invariably have a lot of things that they haven't dealt with. It is extremely common for people to feel *stuck*. As if they wasted their 'best years' working for goals that they realized they didn't want in the end. They may have spent their entire lives in that place, rarely taking the vacations or trips that they've always wanted to go on. And instead of delving deep into their minds and dealing with their long-held issues and problems, they are going to place all that baggage on *you*. It is easier for them that way.

When we look at it objectively this second way is the better ethical, moral, and emotional way of doing things. Especially when it comes to family and friends. I would highly recommend doing it this way most of the time. But there are situations where it doesn't benefit you to do this. The main one is in a work situation. I cannot count how many times I have been screwed over just for putting in my two-week notice. What is mind-blowing about this is that giving notice is the best thing for both parties! You give them time to find a replacement and don't force others to have to cover the work you were originally scheduled for. It rarely works out this way in the real world. The best example I have of this was when I was working a job near Bigfork, Montana.

I was one of the two bartenders working there. It was a very busy bar and the management was just too damn cheap to hire another one. They had hired another one because they had deemed me *persona non grata*, despite how I had worked 50-60 hours per week for them since I started. So, it was already going downhill. But this was right at the end anyway, so it didn't affect me all that much. I did meet my ex-wife there. She walked in the door and we immediately fell in love. This was a problem because the owner's son claimed he was in love with her as well. He never really said, that but it was painfully obvious to everyone. The timing of which perfectly coincided with them hiring my replacement. Doesn't take Sherlock Holmes to figure that one out.

My ex-wife had known these people for a long time. She knew who and what they were. I was blinded. I had been so lonely for so long that I thought they wanted me to be part of the family. Hoo-ey, was I wrong! So, as we started to become an item the tension started to rise. Not coincidentally, she started to convince me that I didn't need that place or those people. As a matter of fact, I didn't need to even be a *bartender* anymore (See: Burn Out). Also, not coincidentally, I had already bought a ticket to go off to Europe. One way. It was no surprise then when the owner's husband came down one morning and attempted to get me to 'work harder.' He told me I had been 'slacking.' I was dumbfounded. I had just worked the Fourth of July at a bar directly on the lake, *by myself*. I had made over $1500 in tips. In one day. And if you average about $1-3 in tips per drink? You can imagine how utterly exhausting that would be. No barback, no servers, just a full bar of people for *fourteen hours*. Now this spineless asshole was telling me to 'work harder.' That was it. I could take the cold shoulders, the childish demonstrations of ignorance, and the continued disrespect. But this was too much. I sat on my patio with my ex-wife all night long. We decided that the best thing to do was to just pack up my stuff and leave. Right then. Of course, we were drunk, and driving wasn't an option so... I didn't.

Instead, I put in my two-week notice the next morning. For some reason, I still respected them enough to give them that. Big mistake. At least they had the grace to pretend that they were sad about it. For me, it was liberating. I texted the other bartender, who I adored, and asked him if he'd come in early for me. I had never asked for a single thing since I'd been there. Just the opposite. I had always picked up the extra slack. He begrudgingly obliged. I called my ex-wife and we headed out on the town. We celebrated, telling everyone about my newfound freedom. It was glorious. I never knew how deeply I'd been chained. We were so happy and enthusiastic; it was no surprise that I was oblivious to the trap that had been laid.

I had rented a beautiful beach house right next to the lake. Unfortunately, that meant it was right next to the bar I worked at. And in the parking lot of the bar lived the cook who, of course, was an 'ex'-convict. We had stopped for a six-pack on the way home and were happily buzzing back from my car when the cook stepped in my way and took a beer out of my six-pack. I didn't like that and I told him so. That's the last moment I remember clearly. The only thing I remember was coming to, drenched in my own blood from head to toe. I remember tackling him and trying to punch him. But my fist kept swinging six inches away from where I was aiming. I don't remember who pulled me off of him. He immediately jumped in his car and spit gravel in all directions as he left.

I didn't know that the guy had tried to kill me until about four days later. If I had, I probably would have pressed charges. I thought that I had just been head-butted. That I had lost a fight. That made me (somehow) weak and embarrassed. What had *really* happened was that this cook had taken a beer and when I had voiced my disapproval, he had clobbered me in the head with the bottom of the full bottle. Four times. I don't know if it's possible to have multiple concussions simultaneously, but if it is, I did. For some reason, I refused to go to the hospital. I don't know what I was thinking. Probably nothing. Instead, I took a needle and thread and laced up my gaping head wounds, cleaned at least a half-liter of blood off of my body in the shower, and waited. For some reason, the bar owner's son barged into my house. I screamed at him to get out and when he didn't, I punched him right in the face. That's all I remember.

The next day I was fired via text message. Let me repeat that, the next day, the owners *fired me*. Via text message. I met with the husband a day after that for my last check. He seemed sad. All I told him was that they were lucky they weren't all in jail. I don't know why I didn't call the cops. It was very, very clear that the woman who owned the place had put a hit out on me. And that someone had actively tried to end my life. There was something in me that pitied them. That sad, sad hole that they lived in was consuming them. I was just chaff falling off from the rapidly increasing amount of bullet holes. I decided it was best to just head out, hit the road, and never look back.

There are a lot of lessons I took from that bar. The first was that there are times and places where it is best to *just leave*. Without a word, no note, no warning. And that will always be up to you to decide. A lot of times you will be in a healthy, solid environment. In that case, tell them all about your plans and help them out until you go. But a lot of times you'll be in the exact opposite situations. Job, housing, and community openings frequently exist because someone couldn't take it and left. And when you are in those situations make sure to ignore the money for a moment and take a good, long look at the people around you. It is so easy to take respite in various things at the expense of other things. If you are lonely, it can be very tempting to stay in a crappy situation simply because you enjoy most of the company. But what I learned from that bar is that there is no remedy worth the side-effect of losing your self-esteem, your physical well-being, or your long-term hopes and dreams.

Whichever way you choose to leave a place, make sure that you stick to the plan you choose. A lot of jobs will try to fire you as soon as you put in your two-week notice. It's a bizarre occurrence. But keep working hard, keep doing your job, and just know that you were right to leave. A lot of friends will put a lot of effort into seeing you before you head off somewhere. Keep them close. Make sure that you spend time with them. Then keep in contact after you leave. A lot of friends will just disappear. It is the unfortunate side effect of leaving that you will be forced to find who was a real friend and who wasn't. The same thing goes for family. Especially family. Siblings, cousins, parents, etc. It will all come to a head eventually. You are inadvertently forcing a reaction. To create the best kinds of reactions you need to make a plan that you think will best suit your situation. And when you make that plan, you have to stick to it. Let your gut dictate your plan, let your head navigate that plan, and let your heart say goodbye. It'll make things easier and more efficient. And who knows, it might just save your life.

68 | Dealing With Toxic/Abusive People

We are constantly faced with toxic, abusive people. Life is hard! It is easy to let the difficulties and hurts that we encounter in this world skew our outlook toward the negative; to see people as lesser or as our enemies. And it is very easy to convince oneself that we are the only one who thinks that way. As such, we encounter a lot of unnecessary spite and negativity in our interactions with others. Now, we can stoop to their level and become petty and negative ourselves. All of us do it and none of us are above it. But we can also choose to address our issues, challenge ourselves to respond rather than react, and ultimately do our best to make the world a better place. Effectively and intelligently dealing with toxic and abusive people also has the added benefit of being one of the main ways to achieve prolonged happiness and satisfaction in this world. So, there's that too.

We all hear these hippies preaching about 'love' and 'acceptance.' Bleeding hearts who haven't had to deal with a gun to their head or a lifetime of getting kicked around, right? Right? Well, maybe not. Because the main way to achieve the frame of mind necessary to enact love and acceptance is to have experienced the exact opposite. We need to see, hear, feel, and touch the evil that humans are capable of to understand why it is so important to see your fellow humans as, well, *fellow humans*. Is it any wonder why so many soldiers come back from war and become adamant anti-war advocates? Or how most of the counselors in drug treatment have had a problem with drugs in the past? Or even how when you get to know someone you are routinely surprised or engaged by how many things they have been through/overcome? Because we have all been through a great many things. Life is hard! At the end of the day, the ultimate goal is to *be* loving, to spread *peace*, and to generally treat people the way we want to be treated. The primary means of doing so is realizing that every human around you, even that Karen who skipped the long line you were waiting in to ask for special treatment, has been through their fair share of horrible things and, despite their grievous trespasses, deserves to be treated with kindness. Not to mention, treating these dickbags with kindness *completely removes* their impact on you.

Which means the hippies are onto something.

So how do we do this? How do we take the high road when Captain Purple Hair and her ridiculous-looking vehicle are trying to run you onto the highway shoulder? How can we possibly stand there and *not react* when these godforsaken shit birds are calling us names and disparaging our honor? The answer is impossibly simple. And I mean that literally. It is simple, yet seemingly impossible. And that is:

Don't react.

I can hear you now. "Shut up, Sam. No one is Jesus." But it's true. The ultimate way to get someone to freak out is simply to not respond, or worse, laugh in their face. Why is this? Because people use you to get the reaction that they want so that they can find an outlet for feelings/thoughts/emotions that they cannot handle. Their emotions and reactions occur because, somewhere along the line, they were treated poorly. Now they are recreating a similar situation to assuage their bevy of emotions that have been simmering in their brain for who knows how long. And by reacting to them you are then *participating* in the re-creation of their trauma. You are now part of it. *But you don't have to be.*

'Kill them' with assertiveness.

I have been told countless times in my life to 'kill them with kindness.' Frankly, this is a load of bullshit. Simply accepting the abuse that these nasty people throw at you isn't healthy for you or them. You were not put onto this Earth to be a doormat. You were put here to step into your power, your truth, and your being. You are a miracle of mathematics and humanity. So, despite how terrifying it might be at times, you need to assertively tell them that their behavior is inappropriate. That they are out of line and that they are wrong. This is not reacting, this is responding. You are addressing the situation, standing up for yourself, and also, in a way, trying to help them grow as a person. Win-win. Never hesitate.

Don't hold on.

As someone who has been with several abusive, narcissistic people, I can tell you: it's easy to hold on. You want them to change. You see flashes of brilliance. You believe in their potential. Sometimes there are even long stretches where they are a decent partner. But in the end, and there will definitely be an end, they will never change. It will always be your fault. They will always revert to the belief that they are infallible, and they will create a reality in which they are the victim. They will most likely either betray you, cheat you, rob you, slander you, or a mix of all that. And that is *after* all the manipulations! Just let it go and do it quickly. The longer you hold on to them the more they are going to eventually take you for.

Boundaries.

This goes right along with being assertive but deserves its own section because of how important the practice is. And it is a *practice*. It's hard to do, even harder to do well, and oftentimes seems impossible in situations like work or family. So, we *practice*. Always try. Never get complacent with people abusing you, talking down to you, or otherwise treating you like you are lesser. This isn't to say you should be over-sensitive. If you are hyper-emotional and highly sensitive, you are probably prone to over-reactions. And we are trying to *respond*, remember? Yet there is nothing wrong with asking someone to clarify what they just said. Or making sure that they add a please and thank you. Or simply walking away. That's my personal favorite. Fuck you very much, you can try talking to me when you've taken that ridiculous ego and shoved it up your ass. Boundaries. Set them, set them again, and then set them permanently. The harder people resist these the more you know that you need to remove them from your life.

Write down how you feel about them.

This especially helps when you are close to the person. I recently went through a breakup. It was horrible, gut-wrenching, and humiliating in a lot of ways. And for a while, I was right back in the guilt/shame cycle that she had wanted me to live in (hint: it's how they manipulate you). But after talking with dozens of people, from therapists and friends to shamans and mentors, I began to realize that my relationship wasn't nearly as one-sided as it seemed. As I wrote a list of my experiences several words began to pop up a lot: narcissist, compulsive lying, cheating, abuse. I had endured a lot. My reactions to this? Not great. But was there some room for self-love and self-acceptance in there? Absolutely. And by writing it down it became easier to process how complicated and mixed-up my emotions had become. I could see her clearly. I could see myself clearly. I could see why it had to end. And I could break the cycle of manipulation and control because despite my intense emotions, there it was. Right there on the paper. How could I argue with the facts behind my pain? How could I avoid the truth when it was staring me right in the face? I couldn't. Write it down. Then write it down again. It is the easiest and clearest way to get to the truth. And like they say, the truth will set you free.

Don't get family involved.

I had to learn this the hard way. Relationships and breakups can be messy. There are always things left unsaid, questions left unanswered, things you want to do, and of course, the horrible, mind-twisting back and forth of 'fuck them' and 'good God send them back to me right now.' It is so tempting to use family as a mediating in-between. The problem with this is that families, regardless of what 'side' they're on, are intensely invested in the subject. They have strong opinions and strong feelings. And for good reason! You really wouldn't want them around if they didn't! But this is exactly why you have to avoid this type of situation. You want to progress and get through this, not make matters worse. And there is no more surefire way to make a breakup worse than to involve family members from either side.

69 | Death

What a weighty chapter title, eh?

Death is inevitable. None of us like to think about it and it is awkward to discuss. It is easy to put out of mind, especially when there is so much going on in life. It is why we sometimes feel a slight aversion to looking at the old and feeble. It is why we tend to overlook the news stories of hundreds dying in a train crash or war. We do not want to look at the absolute fact that our lives are going to end someday and that we have zero control over when and where that happens. Because death is going to happen to all of us.

Living the lifestyle that I have lived for so long has taught me just how precious life is. In an alternative lifestyle, you see and experience a lot of things that bring you close to the edge of life and death. I have had my fair share of near-death experiences. I have had to make literal leaps of faith across mountains and rooftops, have survived multiple attempts on my life, and have been in enough tuk-tuks to have had a few close calls. These immediately show you what is important. You find yourself thinking of things that you wish you could do at that moment. You want to call people simply to tell them that you love them. That you forgive them. You have strange sensory memories like the smell of a smoldering campfire in light rain. And you have a hyper-awareness of life, with every single one of your senses on full magnification, and each passing second becomes a solitary snapshot of the grand experience of life. It makes the rest of your bullshit come into stark perspective.

Even if you don't have any of these experiences you still begin to come to a gradual awareness that life is fleeting. You see multiple environments, rather than the same ones over and over. You see elderly people with not a lot of time left just as often as you see little ones who haven't even started. You see the broad spectrum of humanity pushing, pulsing, cavorting, and contorting. You innately develop a clearer view of what your purpose should be and why you are here. And once that becomes illuminated you realize that it isn't going to be forever.

So… death.

It could come at any time. You could be t-boned by a drunk driver outside of your kid's school at seven in the morning. You could have an aneurysm at 6:30 PM as the game comes on. Or you could die in your sleep for no apparent reason at all. You really never know. We all see the Hollywood take on the matter, with long, drawn-out scenes depicting final words and epic sacrifices. In reality, death happens alone. We come into this world alone and we die alone. Whether or not you believe this is immaterial. You still have to prepare for it and understand it or it is going to lead to horrible difficulties both in your life and in your last moments.

All you can hope for in death is to have no regrets, that you can see it coming, and that you are at peace when it happens. That's it. Having no regrets means that you went out and achieved your goals and became the person you want to be. You made amends for your mistakes, particularly with yourself, and generally tried to be the best person you could be. Seeing it coming is simple. While we all might hope for a quick death, ideally you are going to want one that you can see from a ways away. It might be scarier and more uncomfortable but this way you'll have a chance to confront that fear and live out the remainder of your life in a way that brings resolution as you pass. This means telling your loved ones how you feel about them, cherishing your last moments, and otherwise tying up loose ends. And this brings me to the third point: peace. That is the sauce on the enchilada. We can live an awesome life and achieve great things but if we are not filled with some semblance of peace and serenity in our last days then we have done it wrong. This is the penultimate goal after being a good person for the entirety of life. And as such, it is all we can hope for when we die. It is the endeavor toward achieving these three aspects of your death that you should focus on rather than the question of what comes next.

Eventually, you're going to find out. It is, without a doubt, the most important thing to be prepared for.

70 | Depression

This is another aspect of mental health that belongs in the beginning, but this is a guidebook, not a wellness manifesto. Still, depression is a stark reality of any kind of nomadic existence. I'm tempted to say that no one who is truly happy would ever voluntarily leave their hometown and their family but that doesn't come close to doing it justice. Some of us just need to see it for ourselves. Some of us are introverts, outcasts, outlaws, loners, or all the above. Some of us have an instinctual yearning to keep going over the next mountaintop. In principle, there is nothing wrong with this. In reality, there are several problems with this, foremost among them being that humans need contact with other members of the species to be content. It is a basic human need. And the road can be hard, lonely, abusive, and… depressing.

I will never forget sitting at a beach-front bar in Ft. Meyers, Florida, during Spring Break. I had no interest in being on Spring Break. I had no interest at all other than trying to make some friends. I was working on a small island two boat rides and an hour's drive away. There were seven other employees on the island, none of whom liked me that much. You could even say that they *really* didn't like me. I cared about that stuff back then. Anyway, everyone on Gilligan's Island took turns getting four days off every two weeks. It was my turn, so I went to the nearest place where I had an 'in' at a cheap hotel. My lucky day, it was Party fucking Central, with kids my age streaming in to get wild all day and night, screaming and hollering and playing beach volleyball. As much as I wanted to pretend, I had no business being among those types of people. I just wanted to get drunk, maybe watch some football, and smoke some cigars on the patio as the sun set. I had been isolated for so long that I was having trouble controlling my anxiety. It showed. I think some people took pity on me because every so often someone would come over and talk to me. I guess it helped a bit. Then this older man came up and slapped his hands on the bar.

He reeked of gin and had that hard leathery skin a lifetime spent at the beach must give you. His head was bald, popping with varicose veins and dark cancer-y-looking freckles. He slapped me on the back. "Good luck!" he loudly proclaimed, clanking his fist on my beer bottle. "You're going to need it!" He said this way, way more ominously than I thought was appropriate. It was so random, so cruel, so jarringly mean. People are nasty, backbiting, horrendously self-centered parasites at times. I have had people treat me in horrible ways. But this was just such a low blow at a time that I absolutely couldn't handle it. I was such a weak puppy, furtively wagging my tail and trying to attract some other puppies to play in the sandbox. And this guy, maybe unwittingly, poured a bottle of cigarettes and beer all over my face. Metaphorically speaking of course.

I didn't show it immediately but soon I had left the beach, gone and got two 12-packs and a few cigars, and headed to my room. It was still early in the afternoon. I think I made it another hour or two before I broke down in tears. I couldn't stop till the sun started to set. I was silent. Learned to cry that way early on. Nobody wants to be around a grown man, a grown anything, chest-wracking, snot-spewing, ugly crying. I could hear the people on the beach laughing and screaming. The other balconies were full of people having the times of their lives. I remember bribing a room service guy to grab me two more twelve-packs the next day. I was too ashamed to show my face again.

Now, it's easy to look back at that younger version of myself and identify the obvious issues. Hey, maybe you shouldn't drink so much, eh? Why don't you try some therapy, some self-compassion, and maybe some activities you actually enjoy? Maybe stay out of Florida? But these things are only clear in hindsight. And no matter how positive and hearty you think you are, you can and will break down on the road. It is only a matter of time. It is a fact of life that when faced with monumental difficulties your brain is going to find a release valve and depression is the path of least resistance for all that tension. Having a plan for how to deal with it when it comes up is essential.

Get a therapist.

You'll see me say this a lot, in this section and throughout the book. I'm pretty sure it's legally required. Even if it isn't, it's still absolutely true. I have been to 20+ therapists in my life, most times for just a handful of sessions, in places all over the world. It helps. Life is hard and thinking about it all is harder. These people are paid to help you figure it all out. If you think you can't afford it, you're wrong. And if you think you don't need it, you do. And anybody who is telling you *not* to go to therapy *definitely* needs to go to therapy too. The online, text-based versions are crap. Don't waste your time and become disillusioned. You need an in-person (or telehealth), real person, who takes real time to help you with your very real issues. If only just to hear yourself talking about your problems out loud.

Take the time to deal with it.

Travelers are usually taken advantage of. Whether through low-paying jobs with little to no benefits or just through price gouging and manipulation, the vast majority of people are xenophobic when given a chance. Jobs will offer you housing, free meals, maybe even an activity or two, then try to work you to the fucking *bone*. No matter what it costs you financially or in 'the eyes of your employer,' take the time to address the fact that you are bottoming out and need some time to recharge. Every single time I either ended up in jail, getting kicked out of a place, fired, or just plain abused, it was because I was depressed and wasn't dealing with it at all. The only thing I have ever regretted about those times is that I didn't just put myself first and hole up in a hotel for a few days. Or, God forbid, take a few days off!

Write something.

I get that everybody doesn't love to write things down. You can stick to the 200-character rule if you want, doesn't matter. The key element is to get what you are thinking out of your mind and onto a piece of paper or on a screen in front of you. If I am writing some pretty sad, depressing, or messed up stuff, I like to put it onto paper because then I can burn it later. Letters to people who have hurt me, letters to people I've lost, political rants, really all kinds of rants, and anything else that just needs to be purged, all this needed to be expressed physically through my writing. And burning the writing is a great way to go about getting it off your mind for good. Whatever it is you choose to do with it just make sure you take it out of your head and put it in front of you. This helps you process it and stops the cycle of overthinking.

Get outside.

When I am sad, I isolate myself. You probably do too. Currently, I have been in the hotel room I have sequestered myself in for six days straight. My car broke down in a tiny little town where I can't even catch an Uber. I could still get around if I really wanted to, but I haven't so I am starting to get cabin fever, feeling constantly like I am missing a train and that my veins are pulsing. That I am missing out on life. It doesn't help that somewhere my wife (now ex-wife) is out hiking with her new boyfriend that she doesn't think I know about, that my company is almost defunct, and that my life is slowly spiraling into the pits of Hell as I type… Anyway. The answer is to just put aside all the worries and concerns you might have and get out of the environment you are in. This hotel is dark and depressing. So, I need to get around some trees, maybe find a ridgeline with a view. Hikes are the best. If that's not possible then just a walk around the parking lot. Fuck it if it looks weird. You have to prioritize yourself. And even just a few moments of something different can kickstart a new mental state.

Keep pushing forward.

Make yourself progress. Read articles about your psychology. Read a sci-fi book. Try and do something that opens your mind and creates a situation where you are bettering yourself. This could be as simple as posting something positive on social media. Or this could be working on a side hustle that makes a few extra dollars a month. It doesn't matter what the monetary, professional, or personal gain might be. Psychologically you are progressing at a time when you most likely feel like you are backsliding and this halting of imaginary momentum is essential to getting you back into a place mentally where you can progress out of feeling so down.

Exercise.

Get those steps in. Sometimes I just pace back and forth, talking to myself and God and going over whatever is important to me at the moment. Ideally, you can go for a run or hit the treadmill. But sometimes we don't want to be seen and that's OK too. You're aiming to get your heart rate up and, again, get out of your headspace. If that means jumping jacks and pushups in your studio apartment, then that's what it is. If you are moving and your heart is beating, then you are doing it right. Prioritize this, especially if you are experiencing a lot of negative self-talk.

Give yourself some slack.

Most often we find ourselves depressed when we are ragging on ourselves. Beating ourselves up. Not giving ourselves the benefit of the doubt. Usually, I don't even realize I am doing it till I am writing my thoughts down or talking to someone else. Then I see that I am negatively painting myself in a certain light and that if I practice a little bit of self-compassion, I can let some things go and be more positive. This positivity is the first, second, and last step towards busting out of the funk.

And don't forget to breathe.

71| Education

I've got some whip-smart friends. One of them is a jack-of-all-trades, with an innate ability to pick up various abilities and apply them almost instantly to whatever it is that he is doing. It is wild how this guy can learn so quickly and adapt to situations and yet… he can't read. What? I thought that to be successful and abundant in this world you *had* to go to college and get a degree. At the very least I had to get an associate's degree. And yet, here is this guy, absolutely killing it, making way more money than I am, generally successful in just about everything, happy and abundant, and this guy can't even *read*. Meanwhile, I have multiple bachelor's degrees, graduated when I was 20 years old, am ridiculously good at trivia, have been everywhere, can manage complex situations, arguments, and equations… and I almost drank myself to death and ended up broke, broken, and miserable. I had no idea how to live life. Or enjoy life! Thriving? Embracing trust, love, and acceptance? What are those? I am worthy of making… money? Naw. I can speed read though, that's important, right? Right?

The point is that everything you know about education is bullshit.

The reason this is a separate section is that, for a variety of different reasons, our society has de-prioritized real education. We bicker and bullshit over what textbooks to allow while the truth is that our kids aren't learning anything practical or effective. Our public education system is a joke, our community college system is on life support, and our university system is fundamentally and effectively worse than our health care system. Please explain to me how universities and hospitals that are expected to make giant profit margins are going to be effective at doing the basic functions that define them. I'll wait.

I grew up in the public school system of this country. I remember being forced to recite the Pledge of Allegiance between 1st and 2nd periods. We were forced to love and adore a failing empire. And we wonder why so many people don't understand what is happening here. I also remember being told, over and over, that anything less than a 70% average would lower the funding for our school. This was because 'standardized testing' and 'rubric benchmarks' became a political rallying cry. The 'No Child Left Behind' policy was implemented way before it was actually implemented, thereby leaving entire generations of children to be taught according to a standardized test that every child in the nation had to take at the end of the year. The information on this test was dubiously true in the brightest of opinions. This means that for entire years of children's lives, their most formative, they are fed bullshit, taught to write formulaically (boringly), forced to learn math by rote, and otherwise shown that learning is boring, oftentimes painful, and altogether not worth the time. There is nothing else on this planet that is less true than that sentiment. And yet, most people hate to learn.

What can we take from this? Riot? Armed revolt? Vote for people who prioritize education? Lop off some fucking heads and bathe in the blood of the oligarchy? Sorry. My bad, went a little too far there. Or is it? Yes, it is. I mean... yes, it is. Anyway. What can we do? You don't need to go to an online college that doesn't teach you anything just to prove to yourself that you have a degree. You don't need to go to college at all. You don't need an AA degree. You don't need to head off to every certification course and expensive retreat or whatever you think you have to do. The answer is way simpler: read some books. Go take some classes. Or just take *a* class. The entire notion of adding monetary value to pieces of paper is nonsense. I have had a degree for a long, long time. Not once, and I truly mean not *once*, has anyone asked to see my diploma. It is just a piece of paper in my office.

From very, very early on as a child it was drilled in my head that I was going to go to college. I was pressured and pushed in every way possible to get good grades at all costs. I wrecked my nervous system in middle school (absolutely no point) and high school (even less of a point). I took all the tests, applied to all the 'big' schools, and even got accepted to two of them. For only $46,000 a year after my generous grants and scholarships kicked in! Yeah. Turns out, I ended up taking the free ticket to a state school because of my GPA and my writing. My mother and I sat at a table and discussed the whole thing. It only took one minute. We looked at each other, looked at the cost, and the decision was already made. Do you know what kind of a noose that kind of debt puts around your neck? For *life*? For jobs you *might not even get*? Yeah, I took the free ride.

Turns out that was the best decision I ever made. See, I had been *told* that I was going to go to college my entire life. I had never even considered whether or not I *wanted* to go, whether I *should* go, or whether or not I would be *happy* going. And as it happened, I was miserable. From bad roommates to an inability to handle large groups of people, and then the workload of classes, all of it combined to lead me to drink and smoke pot at levels that were extremely unhealthy.

I quickly realized that I had been duped. I thought that the only way to live your life was to get into college, succeed in every way, and then enter the 'real world' with a degree and an instant skill set that would allow me to get *the* job and thus, afford *the* lifestyle that I never wanted in the first place. And there I was, in a state school with standardized classes, a drinking problem, and friends who I didn't care for but felt that I needed to have. It all resulted in me *flying* through. I started taking double the class load. I isolated. Oh yeah, I also held down two jobs to pay for rent and even more classes at the community college. I set myself so firmly toward a goal that it consumed me, without ever thinking about what I was working *toward*. I had regular panic attacks. I cried more often than a human should ever cry, and for what? A degree I never ended up needing to do what I wanted to do.

When I graduated it was a pretty big day for my mom. Whoopee! The abusive narcissist could now tell her friends that her son was a *college graduate*. I remember walking across the stage and getting handed my piece of paper and then hugging her, who against all the rules was standing right by the stage, then immediately taking off my gown and hat and walking away. I didn't even stay for the commencement speech or any of the parties. We just went to lunch. I remember the only thing that went through my head, the entire time, was: "Thank God that is over."

Because education has nothing to do with a standardized test, a degree, or a fancy hat that you can throw in the air. It has nothing to do with your parents' approval or societal pressure. Education is solely about learning more about yourself and the world around you. And the age-old paradigm of how to make this happen is to get someone who is presumably an expert on the subject to stand in front of you, give a boring ass lecture, have you take notes, then take quizzes, study, take tests, and maybe write some research papers along the way. And this isn't necessarily *bad*. But we are starting to see that it isn't the only way. All these professors publish their findings publicly. There are an amazing array of classes, even from the highly esteemed Ivy League schools, for *free*. Online! Education has become so widely available that *not* educating yourself in some manner has become almost impossible. Because it's not all about Biology or Economics. It can be about how to read people. How to remodel a bathroom. How to travel. Who cares what it is! If you love doing it then you should be learning more about it. It is almost a crime not *to*, as there are so many ways that you can either monetize your interests, or simply follow your interests, that we are beholden to ourselves to look into it. We should always be educating ourselves. Whether it is on how to grow better tomatoes or how to bake the perfect macaroon. You are your own professor, and this world is your university. Never let anyone convince you that you should have a degree.

Of course, there are elements of education that you can focus on if you are looking to diversify your skillset, advance a particularly demanding career, or just dominate the service industry like Ben Affleck in *The Tender Bar*. I am extremely grateful for my opportunity to get a degree solely because of the ways that the material taught me to think and decipher information. I am just as grateful for the classes I randomly took for free online, the technical skills I learned from courses at the local community college, and some awesome certifications I got along the way. I've added these subsections for you because I think they are the most important. And if you are looking for direction, you can start here.

Always be educating yourself.

As I mentioned previously, the onus is on you to educate yourself. People dump their kids in college because they want them to somehow pop out with a brainiac mentality and a well-developed sense of manners and etiquette. These kids just turn into people who *really* know how to party with fancy hats and slick pieces of paper. Whether you have a degree or not doesn't matter. Life is about learning as much as you can. You have to educate yourself. And this can be simply doing the crossword every morning. Or reading a mystery novel before bed. I like to add potential learning moments throughout the day. An app for teaching me languages. Meditation. Reading. New music. Really anything. Tons of people love podcasts. I think they're horrendously obnoxious personally, but my friends swear by them. Whatever it is for you, if you are learning something new, every day, you are doing it right.

Critical thinking.

If you start to get into meditation, which could be the only real education you end up needing, you will be bombarded with people telling you to 'be curious.' What that stems from is a gentle way of getting people to start analyzing their lives and the lives of those around them. To get thinking about how your brain ticks, what is going on, how to apply rational thought to everyday interactions, etc. This is how you learn to adapt and master whatever situation you are in. This doesn't mean dominance in these situations, but rather confidence. Both in the sense that you are doing the right thing and doing it the right way. And this comes from critical thinking.

For example, look at the political situation in America. There are two sides. Two. This is, unequivocally, the stupidest way to run a democracy of 330 million people that I could imagine. Let me let you in on a little secret: both of the parties are crap. Absolute, unadulterated, horseshit. And it's because, to survive, both parties have to cater to as many people as possible. They have to cast a broad message. Yet 330 million people have a *lot* of different viewpoints. And to have only two parties speaking for all those viewpoints? Idiotic. No wonder everyone is at each other's throats. And if you *really* want to get into the critical thinking of this, you can watch some of the videos of the KGB defectors from the 80s. You know, the other side of the Cold War? Those guys? They openly describe how they have intentionally spread misinformation and propaganda throughout the U.S. to *directly* create division in the political sphere and thus, create a divided society. Just like the one we have now! Oh my God! That's crazy! It's almost like we lost! Wait, did we lose? Yes. We did. And yet everyone is locked into their unsubstantiated viewpoint, waving flags and putting up passive-aggressive political signs in their yards. Most people honestly think that the enemy is their neighbor, just because they have a different opinion and vote for a different person.

Critical thinking isn't just important for politics either. It is crucial in your family, your work environment, and your community. Everyone needs a diplomat. Someone who can solve arguments and disputes. And every diplomat shares the quality of being able to use critical thinking to examine each side of a debate, then come up with a reasonable solution. Be the diplomat. Don't be the person lobbing Molotov cocktails or standing with body armor and an AR-15 next to an old statue. Be the person trying to calm everyone down. Be the voice of reason, logic, and compassion. We all *know* this is the best way to be. So why aren't we like this? When you answer that question for yourself, you'll have figured out why this is so important to your education.

Follow the money.

Almost everything in this world relies on money. Even churches need income. It should be no surprise to hear then that behind everything you see there is most likely a monetary reason that you are seeing it. This is a basic concept so I will not go into extreme detail. Just remember to apply critical thinking to everything. Political events, community happenings, relationships, anything really. And then apply this principle: follow the money. Who wants the money? How are they going to get it? Who is benefitting from this? How can they afford to give money back to me? Where are they making their profit? Does that mean I am getting swindled in the long run? Follow. The. Money.

Find real information.

I wish I could just list places to find information and talk about them but there are two problems with that. First, these things change all the time. People sell out. Supposedly reputable places to get unbiased information become biased, in a hurry. Opinions become advertisements; advertisements become opinions. Everything is malleable and constantly changing. Second, I don't want to get sued. It's just a hassle. Anyway, the issue here is that to appropriately navigate through the world, you are going to need at least some information. And you do want to operate with *correct* information. So, what is reputable?

The premise of 'following the money' is probably the best way to easily go about finding good information. The more money that is behind something the more likely there is going to be opinions, advertisements, and 'spin' applied to it. If a news company is owned by a major conglomerate or has major conglomerates as their sponsors, you are being fed a heaping load of crap as supposed 'facts' and 'news.' These 'news sources' are only out to serve the interests of capitalism. There are, however, large sites that operate off of very little money that are solely devoted to providing worlds of information, for free. Even better, people who post to these giant troves of information are required to submit references and resources for where they got the information. This way you can follow the trail of where it all came from. This is just one example of how to use critical thinking to start finding better information. It is not an exact science. Sometimes, when I need breaking news, I sign on to the blue website, doom scroll for a moment, then immediately sign on to the red website, and proceed to doom scroll for another minute. The entire time I am aware that both of these sources are crap. But somewhere between them is the truth. At least a kernel or two of it. Just follow the money, pay attention, and try to figure out where the lies are. If in doubt, look for sources and references. And if there are none…? Well, what do you think?

Books.

Read them! Even ones that are pulp trash. God help me, but I love pulp-trash Sci-Fi. Whatever it is though, read something. Have your brain working, your vocabulary increasing, and your imagination broadening. Books are *always* better than movies because they can encompass so much more than you can process with just an image. And you won't even notice how much you are learning while you are doing it. Grab a book and read it.

Higher education.

Now, I didn't say that all college/university is a horrible idea. The point that I would like to make about college is that for most people it is a racket designed to suck you in with the promise of success and then hamstring your finances for life. They never promise that you'll get a job though. Curious. And getting an 18-year-old to sign themselves up for a lifetime of crushing debt? That's evil. And when you add in the fact that universities are for-profit institutions? Also, evil. Therefore, to have college work for you, you'll need to have a really good idea of what you are walking into and why you are spending the money.

You need to go into college with a mission and a vision. And that's not what everybody goes for. Ever met an 18-year-old going to college? Ever asked them what their intended major was? Psychology. It was psychology. Let me stop you right there because it's boring. Most people never even take a second class. Kill that dream with fire right now. How many people do you know who became shrinks? Yeah. I always advocate for people to go out in the real world after high school. Take a year off and see how your life goes. Get a crappy job and a rattrap apartment. Or a good job and a good apartment. Both will do the same thing. See what it's like paying bills and having roommates that you depend on for their share of the utilities. You might just find that you are happy as can be without going to college. Or, it'll make you *beg* to go to college. And that's the right attitude if you are going to commit to that. Because college is *hard*. If you are going to learn something you should have a really good plan to do it, as well as an intense drive to learn it. Be pragmatic. Be smart. And have a good idea of what you are trying to do, along with how you are going to pay it all back.

Some of the happiest people I know didn't even bother with the college crapshoot. They went to a trade school to be a veterinary technician, a carpenter, or a lineman. They now make more money than most of the people I know. Just a thought. If no one has told you this yet, I will tell you. You do not have to do the same thing for your entire life. You do not have to decide your entire life when you aren't ready. And frankly, most people are *never* ready. There is nothing wrong with doing something you find interesting. Want to be a construction worker? Awesome. It's really fun until your back starts to hurt years down the road. Want to work with animals? Great, be a veterinary technician. Want to work on cars? Sweet, be a mechanic. All these are much shorter commitment times and will give you valuable skills for your entire life. And if you hate them a few years later? No problem. Try another one. Or go to college! You always have options. Never forget that.

If you *are* planning on going to college here are the actual classes and subjects that will help you the most. Some of them are boring as hell but I have added them because they have saved and made me a ton of money over the years.

- **Accounting (follow the money)**
- **Finance (follow the business' money)**
- **Photo-editing**
- **Math (i.e how to finance a house/car)**
- **Psychology (it is nice to know how people tick)**
- **History (history repeats itself)**
- **Political science (Study Realist Theory and you will understand the entire world)**
- **TEFL (Get a certification to teach English abroad)**

72 | Finding Your Passion

A misconception in this world is that you have to do what you love for a living. This is just way too complex of an idea to pigeonhole into how you put food in your mouth. I struggled with this concept for years, constantly bouncing from job to job, working four or five side hustles at a time, transferring cities, starting new ventures and companies, and making new friends and connections. I always came back to the same point: not liking it all that much. Sure, I liked the grind. The hard work. I loved the thrill of turning a profit from nothing. And getting a comma in your bank account balance is a panacea to most of life's problems. But it wasn't fulfilling and the same old problems that had nagged me since my adolescence would rear their head again and BAM, I was back on the road, looking for the next ticket to transcendence.

I am glazing over a lot, but the point remains the same. The world constantly tells us to do what we love and to chase our dreams and our passions. To flourish as dandelions in the cement of the concrete jungle we all must live in. These are great concepts and ideas to start with but without the additional components that make them feasible they are nothing more than inspirational posters that mean nothing. We have to add personal context, subtext, and subjective meaning to every action we perform. We have to find those mediums of social interaction that appeal to our particular needs from society. We have to find the qualities within us that we want to develop. We have to define which of our behaviors leads to the most joy and fulfillment.

Those sentences are all pomp and circumstance when viewed in a vacuum; an inspirational poster in a noisy dentist's office. Our mission in life is to make our passion and joy for life so intrinsically part of our existence that they overcome nearly everything else that we know. That is true success. That is real power. That is heaven. It also happens to be the most difficult thing to achieve, with an impossibly complicated route filled with an infinite number of roadblocks and obstacles. We overcome this by systematically approaching the entirety of our own experience.

You can start any way you like. The Universe *will* guide you if you pay attention. But you can save yourself some serious time if you focus on what and who you love while trying to be the best person you can be. Again, reminiscent of an inspirational poster, but try to dig into the meaning behind a systematic approach to your well-being.

It can be overwhelming at first. Maybe forever. I am overwhelmed daily by the number of things I try to mentally undertake. But they are all things that I love, that I cherish, that I am present for and that, ultimately, bring me joy. I am a work in progress, as I will always be, but I find much more happiness than I used to. I am no longer reliant on drugs, alcohol, cigarettes, or other things to find peace and joy. I find it easy to be in my own body, two feet on the ground, present in my environment. Perhaps, most importantly, I find it much easier to shrug off when things go 'wrong.' All these things can be attributed to a commitment to living a life I love to live. And it is hard. Finding the drive and motivation to push yourself toward joy every day can be exhausting. Not to mention stressful. Exchanging the daily grind with the security of a regular, standardized paycheck for one where paydays and payoffs can be either sparse or irregular can breed a mentality of scarcity in your mind.

But it's worth it.

Here are some keys to finding your passion(s) in this world. Keep in mind that there will never be *one* thing that completely transforms your world. Not children. Not a partner. Not a job. No one thing is going to fulfill all of your innermost wants and desires. You are going to have to identify *all* of your passions. And some of these aren't going to have names or descriptions. They may be feelings, basic activities, or even strange talents. Whatever they are to you, *you* have to find out what they are, why they make you happy, and how to best incorporate them into your life.

Pay attention.

We most often attribute our daily lives to common parameters. If you went to work on a Monday and you didn't get fired, you might say to yourself that it was a good day. But pay attention to the *exact* things that made you happy. Did you make some money? Great. *Why* does that make you happy? Are you providing for your family, so that you come home feeling success-ful? Do you feel more secure? Can you now buy a bunch of new shoes? Pay attention to the exact moment that you felt better than any other moment and examine what about it was fulfilling. That small realization is the first step. Knowing why you do what you do. Knowing what about your day is making you keep doing it. And then, knowing what part of it you can focus on to create more of those moments.

What you are doing in your free time?

Our weekends and our time off are key to understanding what our pas-sions are. What you are doing when you feel like you have taken care of the routine tasks to stay alive and don't feel pressured to be doing anything else is key to understanding what you *want* from your existence. Do you 'veg out,' binge-watching shows and eating snacks? Do you seek out adventure on the trail or the river? Do you climb walls? Or do you head to the bar to drink and be merry with friends? All these can be indicators of the small, minute satisfactions that drive you.

Most passions are small.

We are commonly fooled into thinking that 'our passion' has to be singu-lar. Very few people are going to have one overarching passion. If you do, more power to you. But that isn't all (or even most) people. And this is how we get stuck. We spend our whole lives searching for that *one thing*, but some of us just like to relax, get naked with our partners, watch a movie, walk our dog, take a drive, maybe even all of them in one day if you're lucky. And these small passions come along with a myriad of different thoughts and feelings, all of them contributing to your overall experience of this world. Find them. Cherish them. Make them happen more often! I keep a list of all the small passions that I have. They do change regularly. But I focus on the ones I have now. As I write, some of those currently are: feeling close to my girlfriend, being a good Dad to my dog, bringing in income to house and feed myself, fixing things, and, naturally, writing. These might be the same for you or something completely different. Be prepared. Your list is going to be *long*. Keep that in mind and take the steps forward to make them more frequent.

Strengths and weaknesses.

This is where a lot of people get tripped up. We all know that one person who is amazing at drawing, yet won't do it professionally. This baffles us. Why not make a living off of it? The answer to this is twofold. A lot of us convince ourselves that because we aren't the 'best' at something we could never spend all of our time doing it. We would surely starve. Also, there is a fear that if we do it all the time it would lose some of its magic. These are real fears that should be listened to. Not all of your passions need to be monetized. Some things in this world need to be just for fun! Which goes to say, fuck everyone else. If you like to draw, draw. Even if you 'suck at it.' Who cares? You *love* to do it. So, love to do it. Don't overcomplicate it.

That leads me to point number two. We are often told to either work on our weaknesses to balance ourselves or to focus on our strengths to be better at what we do. Neither of these tactics are effective. Because we are perfectly imperfect people. We may want to work on our weaknesses and improve some of those things one week and then focus on our strengths and embody those another week. We do not have to make a concrete decision based on one reading of the tea leaves. We do not have to take a personality quiz and then say: "OK, that's me. It will always be me. And I am going to base my life, career, and personal time on this little quiz." Hell no. Remember, you are perfectly imperfect. You are going to change, warp, and adapt to your surroundings. You do not ever have to decide on what is going to make you happy or that you are passionate about for longer than the time it takes for you to make that decision. It can happen fast and it can happen slowly. Don't stress or worry about these things. Just pay attention to what your strengths and weaknesses are in that particular moment and then go with it. Especially if you *want* to monetize something, or if you just want to *do* something.

Ask your inner child.

This is what I had to learn. I grew up fast and early, way before I should have had to. There are billions of people just like me in this regard. Maybe you. Regardless of what your childhood looked like though, it is crucial to talk to our 'little selves.' Ask what the younger version of you would like to do. How you might please the child that is always there with you. Want to head to the dollar store and buy those bubble-blowing kits? Hell yeah. Want to make a water slide on the lawn? You know it. Want to quit this lame-ass job and take that job opportunity in the Virgin Islands? Already buying tickets. Ask that kid. Most often it's the best thing you ever did.

Get ready to be awkward.

A lot of the things that are going to call to you are going to seem out of reach and scary. Joining a meet-up group or a new soccer team is going to be intimidating. The first page of a book is going to seem like the first step up a giant mountain. And quitting your job to set out blindly into the unknown? Holy shit, it's terrifying! And lonely! But when you look back on your life you are not going to remember that fear. You are going to re-member that you took the chance and went out on a limb, risking countless hours and dollars and that somehow, 'win' or 'lose,' that journey was what ended up making you happy. Get ready for some awkward interactions and hours spent waiting, staring at the wall. Those are the hours that you *really* start finding out what you need and want to be happy in this world. The risk is negligible. The reward is *everything*.

73 | Forgiveness

Simply put, forgiveness is the key. Things are going to happen to you in your life. Bad things. Maybe they already have. Doesn't matter. No one is going to get out of this thing without being subjected to some terrible events. We are creatures of light and dark. And wherever there is bright light there are dark, dark shadows. Which means that you are going to be forced to choose. Most of us choose to remain in pain, becoming bitter, jaded, cynical, or just mean. It is the principal reason that there are so many assholes in this world. We don't *deal with* the events that happened to us. How they made us feel, how they scared us, how they created walls and blockages in our minds. Instead, we build over the scarred tissue. We adapt and contort our lives to avoid pain. And in doing so we become mentally and physically malformed, contorted to the point of becoming unrecognizable. The answer is and always has been forgiveness.

A lot of terrible, horrible things have happened to me. When I was fifteen my father pointed a loaded gun at me in front of a friend. As if the first fourteen years of abuse weren't enough. I have had three separate and deliberate attempts on my life since then. I have nine confirmed concussions. In my early 20s my best friends growing up decided to all ghost me at the same time. I have been cheated on, betrayed, abandoned, humiliated, emasculated, ridiculed, robbed, stabbed, burned, punched, kicked, spit on, and how many more things do I need to write? It has been a hard road. Really hard. I like to say that I have always played the video game of my life on Extreme difficulty. Except that it wasn't a video game. We don't respawn when we die.

All these things that occurred in my life have added up. I am fortunate to have developed, within myself, the drive and tenacity to change at an early age. This is why, now in my mid-30s, when I became aware of the fact that I again needed to change, it has been less of a monumental undertaking.

I have always resolutely tried to turn the other cheek. To open myself up and remain gentle and kind to the world. It hasn't always worked. It seems downright impossible at times. This is why, when I became aware of how negative, cynical, jaded, and defensive I was, I had to come to terms with it. I was miserable! Life had turned from the mystic to the myopic. I had had so many things *actually* happen that it wasn't just anxiety anymore. My paranoia had manifested in *actual* events. It wasn't just a mental construct. My walls were *necessary*. I had pushed the world away and built my walls high. The problem is that no one can live that way for long. Neither the people inside the walls nor the ones who want to get in. And the only way to start to deconstruct those walls is to learn how to let some of this stuff go. To learn how to forgive.

Now I could go on and on about anger and the constituent emotions that stem from trauma. But I am not a shrink and who cares anyway. The important part to take away from this is that your anger and your emotions *only hurt you*. The person that robbed or belittled you is not going to suffer because of your feelings. They don't spend any time thinking about what they did. They have moved on to the next victim and you are stuck behind. The absolute only thing that you can control about interacting with these people is how you respond and how you feel about it.

The hardest part of all this to understand is that your emotions are completely under your control. I get it. They are overwhelming. I still have anxiety and panic attacks. I am oftentimes a walking example of how my emotions are not under control. But under all those layers of adaptation and contortion, you are the one making the decisions. You are the one behind the wheel. Counseling and therapy are incredibly useful because it helps you to understand this fact. When you can peel back the layers of your onion and find out what makes you tick the way you do, you regain the *feeling* of control. You never really lost it. You just made the machinery of your engine too complicated to fully grasp. When you can break down your reaction and turn it into a response then you are no longer on the hood of the car swerving on the freeway. You are behind the wheel. And when you can regain control of these powerful emotions you are then able to start to let them go.

Isn't that just a bitch? Everyone keeps telling you, over and over, to let it go. Fuck them, right? What do they know? They have no idea how… scared you are. Wait, what? Scared? Not me! I'm angry! I am powerful! I am too tough to be scared! I am… scared that it will happen again. Which is why I am angry. Avoidant. Cynical and jaded. Reserved. I am too scared to let the pain go because it has become so much of who I am. The coping strategies that I employ to deal with my traumas have come to be the very measurements that I *define myself by*. My passions, joys, and humor all come from these same adaptations. And now you are telling me that I am *scared*? And that most of the constituent parts of me are all, at least partially, based on *fear*? On top of that, you are telling me to just *let it go*? And on top of *that*, I am supposed to just *forgive* these people? *And myself*??

Well, fuck.

But that's exactly it. We start our lives innocent and free. When we are introduced to pain we adapt. We spend the rest of our lives trying to either avoid pain or channel it into various things. Most of the time we don't even know we are doing it. And then one day you are unhappy, and you don't know why. Of course, everything is much more complex and complicated than this. But the answer is not. Forgiveness. Such a simple word, yet the hardest thing in life to achieve. Because when we can truly forgive others, we release ourselves from whatever it is that happened. We will never be able to go back in time and change things. What has happened, has happened. But what we can do is release ourselves from it. The exact permanence of history is the exact reason that the present and future are so malleable. We are here because of what has happened and, with that knowledge, we can then make the conscious decision to *let it go*. We can *decide* to forgive, not be angry, not be afraid, to turn the other cheek, and *move on*. Oftentimes we are afraid to do this.

In the past, I have been addicted to the pain. It is terrifying to release it because then who would I be? What am I but the amalgamation of all of my actions and memories? And therein lies the answer: I am who I am right now. And by choosing to forgive and let it go, I am consciously taking control of the present and thus, the rest of my life. I am forgiving the past to allow for a future. This is the key to freedom.

74 | Getting Arrested

We all make mistakes. One of the main goals in life is to make sure that you don't repeat them. But hey, sometimes we repeat them anyway. And sometimes we make long, decidedly ignorant *series* of mistakes. Decisions piled on decisions, all of which, in hindsight, are dumb as well. Don't act like you're better than me, Karen. All humans do this to varying degrees. Some of us just like to push this to the extreme. And we are the ones who have to know what to do when you get arrested.

Don't say anything.

Anything you say can and will be used against you. A police officer has to see you commit a crime to arrest you. Like, you know, peeing on the door of a local fraternity. Or steaming up the windows of your pickup truck at the drive-in theater. Just examples. Don't get mad or upset. Remember your rights. Police officers most often give you a ticket or a charge because of *what you say*, not because they saw you do something. If you stay silent, they will most often have to let you go. Make sure to 'invoke your rights.' You have to tell them that you are going to be silent. Otherwise, they can use your silence against you, like saying that you can't talk because you are intoxicated, or something silly like that.

Do ask: "Am I being detained?"

This is the one exception to the above rule. Because if the answer is 'no,' you can legally walk or drive away.

Be polite.

We all know a lot of police officers are monsters. That doesn't mean that there aren't great police officers. That doesn't mean that *most* of them are evil. So always be polite. It will frustrate them more than anything because they are used to pushing and intimidating people into doing what they want them to do. You can stay silent and not be rude. If they see you as disrespectful it is almost a guarantee that they will find a reason to put you in jail.

Do not resist.

I have never had a serious charge. My short stays in jail have all been for relatively victimless crimes, aside from my liver of course. But even then, I have been rudely thrown to the ground, had my head slammed against a car, and otherwise been treated like shit for no apparent reason. As I said, some police officers are monsters. Don't give them a reason to step on your neck. If you resist you are going to waken their inner need to control the situation. This is going to legally allow them to use more force than necessary. And you don't want to end up on the wrong side of a 'resisting arrest' citation, or a body bag.

Don't believe a word they tell you.

Police will always lie. It's just how they do their job. Their reports will be lies, their promises will be lies, and everything that comes out of their mouth is going to be lies. They are used to dealing with hardened criminals who are really, really good at being hardened criminals. The system just isn't set up to eliminate crime. This means these frustrated officers are used to having to use whatever means necessary to do their jobs. It isn't an excuse. But know the reality. They are typically full of shit.

If you do get put in 'the tank', be nice to the person at the window.

I have, unfortunately, spent a few nights in the drunk tank. You do want to avoid this. But if you can't, be nice. These folks are used to dealing with screaming drunks, assholes, and people at the end of their rope. So, if you're *friendly* then they will take care of you. You might just end up with some sandwiches and coffee.

Smile for your mugshot.

You are probably enjoying the worst day of your life at that point. And it may seem like a very far cry to try and visualize a bright and positive future at that moment. But try you must. Make sure to smile so when you look back on your life, you'll get a laugh out of it.

75 | Getting a Lawyer

The only thing that my father told me that ever stuck with me is this: "As soon as you step into a court, you've already lost." Think about it. Regardless of which side you're on you are overwhelmingly likely to be in a courtroom for a crappy reason. Unfortunately, as I type this, I have to take a con-man pseudo-contractor to small claims court to recover my entire savings that was supposed to be spent on a new bathroom. It is a complete injustice, and I am owed thousands of dollars. It is still nerve-wracking and heartbreaking to even be going through the process. And yet, sometimes you just have to do it. Hopefully, you won't. If you do, here are the basics.

Look for legal aid programs.

A lot of states have 'modest means' or 'affordable legal advice' programs wherein you can go through their service and get a lawyer for super cheap. These programs range from good to barely usable. But if you fall under a specific category or have been wrong in the 'right' way, you might be able to find someone who will take on your case 'pro bono' (for free).

Public defenders.

If you are in big trouble, get a lawyer. If you can't afford a lawyer, then there are always public defenders. Some of these are terrible. Some are great though! It is the luck of the draw. But they are always, always better than doing it yourself. If you need a lawyer this is the first and last resort.

Lawyer referral services.

Lawyers are a notoriously 'bad' breed. Not all of them, certainly, but there is a reason for their reputation. This means that if you need a lawyer and can't get a public defender or free legal aid then you are going to have to find a lawyer that isn't a scumbag. And you are going to have to find one that will take your case, with experience in whatever specialty you find yourself in trouble with. On top of this, this lawyer has to see a monetary benefit to them in your case. All this makes simply calling up lawyers an intensely difficult and time-consuming endeavor. In comes the lawyer referral services. These will match you with lawyers in your respective area and slim down the choices. It's still a crapshoot from there but it will narrow it down.

Get ready to pay a retainer.

This is a set amount (usually large) that you pay upfront, wherein a lawyer can then charge their fees to that account. This is why you need to have some amount of trust in your lawyer, as you will not directly see what and why they are charging this account. Lawyers ain't cheap. You're going to need to hand them a bunch of money immediately and probably more later. It's a system rigged toward the rich, so get ready to be gouged.

76| Hangovers

From years of working in bars, I learned a lot of lessons. Some were bad, some were worse. Some were good though! My time as a bartender showed me some of the best and worst of humanity. I was spit on, punched in the face, hit with beer bottles, betrayed, berated, belittled, cussed at, and one guy even tried to stab me. But I also personally arranged two couples that are still married, kept a lot of people from getting roofied, gave countless free therapy sessions, and generally saw the gregarious, fun-loving, and compassionate side of humanity too.

And I got drunk. All the time.

This was fun while it was fun. I don't drink anymore and for good reason. I think I'd be dead! But at the time it was completely normal to drink an insane amount of alcohol per week. This was compounded by the fact that I worked a lot of hours as well. In a bar. And if you have ever gotten drunk before you know that you can't just tell your body "Hey! Time to not be drunk now!" Nope. You've got to let it run its course. And if you are scheduled to work at 11 AM but you were up drinking till 5 AM... then those two realities are going to butt against each other. As a result, it became imperative to figure out how to either 'fix' a hangover or delay it to a better time. Here's my advice. It is based on copious amounts of personal experience and a bunch of pseudoscience. But you can trust me. I was a bartender.

If you feel like you're going to throw up, just get it over with.

Get up, chug two or three glasses of water, head to the bathroom, and let it rip. If you are hungover enough to throw up it's going to happen eventually. We always hold onto the brief and illusory hope that if we can just lie on our side in *this exact position* then maybe we can fall back asleep and wake up and this will all be *over*. But that is a fallacy and it isn't going to happen. If you're going to puke, just make it happen and then the healing can begin.

This is also a point where I should mention that if you are facing this situation frequently then your body is trying to send you a message. I'm not your father or your therapist. But it might be time to slow it down a little. If it's New Year's Day and you just had the time of your life? Just *survive* baby.

The second critical thing is to remember what *not to do*.

One of the conventional methods for dealing with a hangover is to pound coffee and this is absolutely wrong. Do not drink coffee, do not smoke cigarettes, do not take ibuprofen. Do not introduce anything that is a foreign substance into your body that it is going to have to process and remove. If you are a smoker this is a prime example. You are most likely partially hungover *because* of the cigarettes. Your body just can't remove toxins that fast and it is going to focus on the alcohol first. Coffee is another huge no-no because it effectively stops the absorption of water into your body for a designated amount of time after you take the last sip. This can be hard because we are all addicted to caffeine to various degrees. But your body is very dehydrated and needs water to recover. Adding coffee is just going to delay the process by at least an hour. Lastly, ibuprofen is another no-no. It can upset your stomach, cause extra strain on your liver, and generally gunk up the works. If you've got a raging migraine just wait till you eat to take pain pills.

Take a shower.

Even if you don't like showers, this is a game-changer when you need to flush your body. My trick was to roll right out of bed, hop in the shower, make it as hot as possible for as long as I could stand, keep my towel on after I got out, and do it again thirty minutes later. Your skin is the largest organ in your body and it is also one of the vessels for removing the crap you put in it the night before. As such, if you can open your pores and get your skin working then you are rapidly speeding up the process. While I found that a single shower did the trick it also left me smelling like hard alcohol for the rest of the day until I could take another shower and wash it off. That's where the second shower comes in. You can either repeat going as long as possible at the highest temperature you can stand, or just a quick couple of minutes to rinse off the tequila pumping out of your pores. I usually come back to this step after eating.

Get some food.

I strongly advocate for eating *before* you go to bed. Not only is this going to slow your body's absorption of alcohol and thus reduce the impact over time but it is also going to give your body the vitamins and nutrients to combat the oppressive amount of alcohol overwhelming your system. There is also strong evidence that eating during a night of drinking can slow the absorption of alcohol enough to give your liver adequate time to process the alcohol in your system as it comes in, allowing you to potentially avoid a hangover entirely.

But chances are, you didn't do that, and you are most likely wondering what you can do *now*. People usually gravitate toward breakfast food because it is greasy. It isn't a bad tactic. For a bad hangover, I used to start with just a single piece of toast though. It came back up easily if I needed it to. Eating said piece of toast seems to have a calming effect on the stomach that then allows you to down more water. Then more food, then more water. Repeat, repeat, and repeat again. When you can 'stomach' the idea of a full meal, breakfast food can be great *if* you don't have a sensitive digestive system. Personally, greasy food helps me the most and I strongly believe that there is an unstudied connection between the fact that most cholesterol is produced in the liver and that we humans tend to crave greasy foods (high cholesterol) when our liver is struggling. There is no science behind this but trust me, I was a bartender. I don't care what *is* scientifically proven, adding salt and potassium to your body actively helps your cause, which also lends credence to the 'breakfast food theory.' Salt and potassium hold onto water, thereby decreasing dehydration, which is your main enemy at this stage. If you can't 'stomach' the idea of a full meal, stick to pretzels (salty) and bananas (potassium). I used to whip up a smoothie with bananas and whatever I had in the fridge, then down that and eat a salty egg (cholesterol). And drink more water!

Deal with your headache.

If you've ever had a really bad hangover, then you know what 'the cycle' is. You try to down water but that makes you puke. You try to take pain pills so that you can get some food down so that you can drink water but *that* makes you puke. You're stuck running back and forth from the bathroom just to dry heave. It's horrible.

The steps above are simply to get you out of 'the cycle.' Once you have some water going into your system, and hopefully some food in your stomach, you can then start dealing with the accompanying headache and stomach ache. It might seem a little masochistic at the time, but it does need to be done in this order if you want to make it as short as possible. Just remember, no one made you take that eighth shot of tequila. It was just a really good idea at the time, damnit! But you're here and ideally out of the worst of it so now you can start dealing with the side issues. Keep drinking water. Anything to keep the toxins and alcohol flowing *out* of your body. Also, now you can add coffee, ibuprofen, and tea (peppermint or ginger) to the mix. If you're like me then you drink coffee every day and probably need to deal with a caffeine headache by now. This will give you a little boost that you should use to do something active. I'm not saying to hop on the treadmill and run ten miles. Take it easy on your body. You're basically running a car without any oil in it. Baby yourself. But drinking some coffee and engaging your lymphatic, muscular, nervous, and circulatory system forces your body to produce endorphins that are going to make you feel better. I always recommend a little activity over the pain pills, as you will most likely see the same results, but if the migraine is crushing you then start with a low dose and move yourself up. Remember: baby yourself.

Vitamins.

Nobody is going to eat a salad when they are hungover. Maybe a smoothie, when you're done with that stack of waffles, of course. Still, the quality of the food in your fridge or cooler probably isn't the best so you're going to need to supplement. You want zinc, vitamin D, and a vitamin B complex. Ideally, you already have these and can just pop a few, after you eat some food. Did you hear me? After the food! Trust me, taking zinc on an empty stomach will destroy your world. And if you have to acquire the cheap versions at your local drugstore, this will still help your cause, just not nearly as efficiently.

Hair of the dog.

I didn't put this first because I remember the days when I was so consistently hungover that it became routine. Frankly, I was lonely, miserable, and directionless. Not to say that you are these things. That was just me and the direction/actions I chose. I wrote this book in the hopes that you wouldn't have to go through the things that I did. So yeah, this part could be at the front of this section. It certainly throws a Band-Aid on the problem. Your body is in withdrawal. For some reason, a night of heavy drinking turns your body into an alcohol machine. FEEEDDD MEEEE. So, while what you actually need is water, vitamins, nutrients, and minerals, what you can do is add more alcohol and 'punt,' essentially delaying the hangover until later in the day. I used to call this 'tucking and rolling' because yeah, I was in a freefall toward sobriety, and yeah, hitting the ground was going to hurt, and if I could bend my knees just right as I hit the ground *maybe* I could roll out and lessen the impact…

Yeah.

Anyway, if you are going to go this route keep in mind that the same stuff that got you there probably isn't going to fly. You probably can't stomach the same tequila or cheap beer that you were pounding just six hours earlier. A good friend of mine used to swear by sugary drinks that she would never *actually* drink in her right mind. But during a hangover? Sweet ambrosia. A bloody mary might be an option simply because it *does* have some vitamins in it as well. Some people really like mimosas but frankly, my body just can't handle wine or champagne, so this always made things worse. Whatever it is, stick to small amounts, keep drinking water, don't mix alcohol and pain meds, and if you feel the need or desire to take a nap then do so. Worst thing you can do? Tuck and roll yourself into a full-fledged bender. You'll come out of it broke, disillusioned, and the pain the next day will be astronomical. Trust me. I was a bartender.

77 | Hitchhiking

I almost left this section out because of how precarious this subject is. In a lot of places hitchhiking is straight-up illegal. There's also the issue that if your favorite traveler tells you how to do this and you end up getting in the car with a serial killer who makes you into sausage, then your parents would try to sue me instead of processing the fact that the world isn't fair. So, I'll put it this way:

Never, ever hitchhike. It is extremely dangerous, and you just never know who you are getting into the car with. This is me, Sam, explicitly telling you to never do it.

But for those who are going to do it anyway, here are some (hypothetical) tips for how to be as safe as possible.

Always go for the truck bed.

I have hitched many a ride. These came in all kinds of different vehicles, from 18-wheelers to Astro vans. Easily my favorite rides were always in the back of pickup trucks. Safety concerns aside, I was getting a free ride where I didn't need to make awkward small talk, there were fewer unpleasant smells, and the danger of getting stabbed was almost nothing. The weather was often a concern but frankly, something is charming about getting rained on in the back of a pickup as you roll down the highway. I love to lie down and watch the sky go by.

Don't get discouraged.

Nobody is going to pick you up if you cop an attitude and start looking sullen. When I was much younger and pursued these kinds of rides, I would often get irritated when people wouldn't pick me up. Now I know how silly that is but at the time it seemed perfectly reasonable. I mean, there I was, a super good person who just wanted to get to the next town and had no way to do so, and nobody was picking me up. So *unfair!* Still makes me chuckle. But the people driving by could have a million different reasons not to pick you up. They could be late, have kids in the car, or maybe the car is chock full of groceries. Who knows, maybe they just don't like people! It is easy to assume that everyone is a traveler like you as well and that they understand the difficulty of getting to some places without a vehicle. This couldn't be farther from the truth. Keep in mind that most people stay where they are for the majority of their lives. If they don't know you from somewhere then they certainly aren't going to trust you enough to let you in their car. The trick is to maintain a positive attitude regardless of the weather, your financial situation, or how long you have been walking along the highway. Don't smile like a psychopath at every car that passes. That will invite the wrong kind of attention. Simply stand up straight, put out your thumb, and maintain your positive attitude. Visualize a friendly couple on their way to the movie theater pulling over and hollering at you to hop in the back of their truck. Stay patient and positive and a ride will come. If for some reason it doesn't, then:

Keep walking.

The easiest way to get frustrated is to remain in the same spot all day. Sometimes when you are pursuing this very difficult mode of traveling you are going to end up walking long distances. It is what it is. If you remain in the same place all day this can have a crushing effect on your morale. So, keep walking. When you hear potential rides coming up behind you, turn around to face them and show them that you are a good person who needs a lift. Positivity, positivity, positivity. If they don't stop, simply turn around and keep walking. Believe me, the people in the cars will be watching you the entire time. This is important because oftentimes people will stop and pick you up if they see you still walking some time later when they have returned from the errand or wherever they were going. People aren't always good. A ton of people are horrible. But that doesn't mean that there aren't billions of great people out there. And these are the folks who are going to pull over for you.

Watch for the turn-around.

By far, the most common occurrence for getting a ride is having someone turn around a few miles up the road and come back to offer me a ride. We are all human beings who experience fears, doubts, and uncertainty.

But the people who are going to pick you up are those that can process these emotions and then still decide that you are worth taking a chance on. Sometimes this takes a few minutes. As such, they are not going to slam on the brakes in the middle of the highway just to pull over right next to you. Rather, they are going to wait until there's a safe place to pull over, wait for traffic to clear, turn around, then head back your way. Trust me, these are the folks you want to be riding with. Good-hearted, conscientious, and safe. This is also why you have to always remain positive. Because if you are kicking rocks and lamenting your bad luck, you might just miss the person who decided to come back for you!

Be ready to talk.

The very first thing anyone is going to do is ask you where you are heading. This is really to give them a chance to size you up before they unlock the doors. It is human and perfectly natural. Be friendly, open, and honest. If you are headed to somewhere far away, then chances are your ride will only be going part of the way. Make sure that you can negotiate a good place to be dropped off before you get in the car.

If you aren't in a truck bed, then you are most likely also going to have to talk for an extended period. Extroverts I have traveled with have loved this part. As someone on the other end of the spectrum, this has been the most exhausting part of traveling. Regardless of your personality, you are going to have to talk a lot. Everyone is going to want to diminish any nervous feelings they have about you by finding out who you are and what you stand for. And that goes both ways. My trick was simply to be as open and honest as I could. I never explicitly told people what my travel plans were. I intentionally left a lot of details vague, as I didn't want to fall into any kind of trap. But I was extremely open about where I was coming from, where I had been, and the things I was hoping to see. In a pinch, simply ask the person what the best parts of their hometown are. People are more than happy to talk about their lives, their homes, and their families. This is the best way to find out about lesser-known swimming holes and things like that. It is also a great way to pass the time!

Stay away from highway entrances and exits.

If there are any restrictions on hitchhiking in your area, then make sure to follow all the rules of the law. With that said, if you are not heeding any of the direct advice I have given you, then make sure to avoid highway entrances and exits. There are two reasons for this. First, there is oftentimes no place for someone to safely pull over. This is by design. Highways are intended for people to get places faster. As such, you are expected to speed up quickly when you are merging on and slow down rapidly when you are merging off. It is simply not safe to pull over for someone at either of these times. Second, because there is an inherent safety risk in these places, police officers will not hesitate to order you to move along. They are simply doing their job and keeping everyone safe. It is in these instances that you are most likely to get cited for this as well. So, pick other spots to try and get a ride.

Gas stations.

Speaking of other spots, these are the best places to try to find someone going in your direction. While there are plenty of different spots where you can get a ride, large gas stations with tons of traffic are easily your best bet. It can help to have a sign, but I have always preferred to simply put out my thumb. I always took a moment to analyze where most people were coming into the gas station and made sure to post up there. This gave people the chance to look me over as they pulled in and then think about whether they wanted to give me a ride. If that didn't work after an hour or two, I would simply grab some snacks and then start talking to people who were taking a break in the parking lot. I looked for those with vans, trucks, out-of-state license plates, or surfboards on top of their vehicles. These were the folks that I got along with best. Once I could get to know them a little bit, they were usually happy to shuttle me a few hours down the road.

Offer gas money.

Nothing in life is free. If you are hitchhiking and trying to hoard your pennies, then you are most likely doing it wrong. Even if all you have is three or four dollars, make sure to try and offer some gas money to whoever is willing to give you a ride. Nine times out of ten these folks will decline with a smile. And if they don't, they probably are in just as tough of a spot as you are. So, help them out! This is especially key if you find a ride that is willing to take you a long distance. If you don't have any cash on you, ask them to drop you off near an ATM so that you can compensate them for taking you so far.

Pay attention to how you look.

I am not going to go into the difference between male and female hitch-hikers here. You know what those are. The point is that you need to make yourself appear, to the best of your ability, as someone that you would willingly pick up. Trim your beard, wash your face, clean your clothes off to the best of your ability, and otherwise try to present yourself as the cleanest and tidiest person that you can. If you look too appealing or too unappealing you are inevitably going to attract the wrong kind of attention.

78 | Hostels

After you get older and you've been to a few places you start to find and talk to other people about where you've been, what you've seen, what you did, on and on, blah, blah, blah. This kind of talk always bores me to tears, particularly how much people want to brag about all the places they've been in this never-ending circle-jerk of geography. It's annoying. Also, places change so fast these days that telling someone to go somewhere really has no significance. The restaurants you loved have probably sold out. The bands you saw are either broken up or have also sold out. It is the world we live in and it is beautiful. Anyway, talking to people throughout the U.S., I have noticed that a startling number of people are not familiar with hostels and how they function.

Simply put, you cannot travel around or land in new places for pennies on the dollar unless you utilize hostels, cars you can sleep in, or weekly hotels, in that order. You have to have a way to head into a new place and set up shop long enough to make enough money to move on. Or, if you're not a partying alcoholic like I was in my 20s, you need to budget your money and spend it wisely. The main way to do both of those things is to spend as little money as possible on sleeping and eating as you can. Hostels are the number one way to make this happen.

Hostels function by having a ton of beds in the same room. These rooms are loud, dirty, and occasionally very weird. They are, however, dirt cheap. Like, less than the price of a hamburger cheap. And hostels also understand their clientele. I should know, I was the general manager of one for a long eight months. They know that you are traveling on a shoestring budget. And they also know that you want to do things and have a good time. So, they offer all kinds of things to either keep you staying there or operate in conjunction with other businesses that pay the hostel to send you to them. For instance, in big cities, the hostels downtown often offer free 'pub crawls,' where a paid employee of the hostel will take you to each bar, show you around the town as you walk, and generally translate between as many people as they can. There's always something, whether it be drink specials on Tuesdays if the place has a bar, free tours around the area, or discounts at sightseeing locations nearby. Combine this with the extremely low cost of living there and this makes for the ideal home base, or lily pad, to establish yourself and find out where you are going next.

One thing that a lot of people don't know is that hostels most often function with volunteers and low-pay employees. This is rapidly changing in a lot of places as laws have been passed to prevent places from overworking their staff, but the principle is the same. Hostels always need cleaners and because their business operates under slim margins, they need to get their cleaners to work for very little. The workaround is to 'hire' people who can work off their stay for a set number of hours cleaning per week. I ran a 198-bed hostel with two large buildings, four kitchens, rooms of all shapes and sizes, and even camping spots. I kept a designated room for 'staff,' which contained eight beds. These beds were theirs for as long as they wanted to keep working there and most of them stayed long-term. They had to work six days a week for three hours, typically between 1 AM and 2 PM, when we had to flip all the beds and get them ready for check-in. The only times this changed was when I needed someone to do something random, like paint a door or mow the lawn.

Hostels also have a constant need for receptionists and front-desk workers. It's a hard job. You are dealing with people who expect the hostel to live up to insanely lofty expectations, which is impossible, and people who have been traveling the hardest way possible, meaning that they are tired, hungry, and exhausted. None of those people are easy to get along with. As such, there is a very, very high turnover rate for front-desk workers. But, if you can hack it, you can easily work off the weekly rate for your bed and then make a chunk of change on top of it. When you're living with minimal bills and costs of living this can easily add up quickly.

Hostels also commonly offer low-cost meals and food ingredients. If the hostel you are staying at offers free breakfast and/or dinner *always* volunteer to do dishes or help out in any way you can. Not only is this just the right thing to do, it will buy you serious points with the staff and with the cooks. The first time I ever went to South America I started from Big Sky, Montana. I took a bus, had a long layover somewhere, hopped on another bus to Seattle, took a train for two hours to the airport, had another layover, then a flight to Boston (for some reason), yet another layover, then a flight to somewhere in Florida, I could barely remember my name at this point, then a five-hour flight to Lima through heavy turbulence. At no point during this thirty-hour slugfest did I catch more than two hours of consecutive shut-eye.

It is no surprise that I immediately fucked up royally by leaving my only debit card in the ATM right behind the Customs gate of Jorge Chavez International. When I finally gave up trying to convince the security guards to let me get back in to check the ATM, it was an hour-long taxi ride to Miraflores, where my hostel was. Luckily there was a shop next door, so I grabbed two beers and headed to the reception desk. I was a mess. I looked like a wreck, and I must have sounded like a wreck, 'cause the girl at the desk immediately put down her phone and gave me an encouraging frown. I told her what had happened and that I had pulled out enough cash for a few days, then after she had shown me around, she led me to their little dining hall. It was full of people and they were serving spaghetti. Awesome. I must have eaten more than everyone else there combined but I didn't care. It was warm, it was food, and it was free. Immediately afterward, I started clearing everyone's plates and helping the cook with the dishes. After about an hour of this, I heard a 'tsking' and some clucking, and the cook and the front desk lady were both smiling and waving me up the stairs. I hit the rack and fell asleep till late the next day.

I stayed in that hostel for two weeks, subverting my initial plan of traveling all around Lima and staying everywhere in the massive city. I couldn't walk by the cook without her waving me into the kitchen and handing me a bowl of something delicious. I guess I was pretty skinny back then. I helped her cook a few times, I helped her clean up every time, and any time I had the chance I would grab a broom and sweep up the hallway. What I didn't know at the time was that there were a bunch of people doing the same thing, except they were getting *paid*. Still, they let me stay with no money until my new debit card arrived, fed me a steady stream of beer and posole, and got me hooked into every free tour and pub crawl they could find. I loved that place and I will never forget it.

These places are essentially communal living spaces designed for like-minded travelers to hang out, eat and sleep. If you are looking for a community of people just like you then make sure to hit as many hostels as you can. Some are legendary, some are god-awful. All of them require a positive mindset and a willingness to interact with other travelers. If you can keep your chin up and do your best to keep from being cranky, then these are the absolute best places to land when you just need a place to hang out. Here are some tips and tricks for living comfortably:

Ask about weekly rates.

First book the place for three nights to see if you dig it and can handle it long-term. If you can't, move on to the next one. A lot of times hostels only allow a certain percentage of their rooms to be booked via the major hosteling sites. I know I always kept four or five beds in reserve for people who came in on foot. This is important because if you can't find a website that can book you in for a few weeks then a quick chat with the front desk might give you what you're looking for. And for cheaper.

Always have your door stopper.

Not for your room, that would immediately piss everyone off. For the *bathroom*, if there are private bathrooms (a lot of them are going to be shared). Remember, these are high-use facilities that aren't always in the best repair. Nothing is worse than having some dickwad barge in on you at the worst possible time just because the door doesn't lock very well. And when humans are embarrassed, they will immediately blame you for it, which is equally frustrating.

Bring your own sheets and towel.

Hostels never charge for sheets, but they do clean them as fast and with as little soap as possible. Not to mention that if you aren't used to cheap soap, you're going to be itchy as all hell. You're always better off with your own. They also usually provide towels but a lot of them charge for this so it's best to have your own.

Take the bottom bunk.

It's easier to get into, you don't have to climb stairs every time you have to pee at night, and it's easier to hang your sheet from (see below). Most hostels have sturdy, well-built bunks designed to last for fifty years. Some, however, have rickety, creaky metal bunks that sway and sag. You may feel safer on the top bunk but believe me, trying to sleep through the creaking and swaying can be difficult.

The other reason to bring your own sheets is to provide your bunk some privacy.

My favorite trick is to hang my extra sheet across the 'entrance' to your bunk so that you can hang out, sleep, and change without having to leave the room. It also has the added bonus of shielding your eyes from older naked people (they are always older and do not care about burning your eyes).

Earplugs.

People snore, people talk, people are people. Hostels bring you face-to-face with the best and worst people that travel. Make sure that you're prepared if someone tied one on and is now chainsawing their way through a bad dream or if someone thinks they can quietly get frisky without waking anyone up (don't do this, it's amazingly selfish). I always bring a bunch and if I hear someone loudly sighing or tossing and turning, I turn on the flashlight of my phone so they can see me and quietly walk over to offer them some. It's a human thing to do and a great way to make a friend.

Always wear sandals.

Everyone in the hospitality industry does their best. People who clean do try, very hard I might add, to keep the places they are working at as clean and tidy as possible. It is just not possible to keep these areas clean all the time. From bathrooms to hallways there is so much traffic and human interaction that you have to accept that this public domain is not going to be as clean as your home may be. A lot of people just can't accept this and that's too bad. But in a hostel, you have to or you're going to have a nervous breakdown.

This is where sandals come in. You need to wear these, or socks, at all times. You can get anything from warts to worms walking around with bare feet anywhere, and in such a high-traffic area you dramatically increase your chances of exactly this happening. This is especially true in the bathroom. You don't want to pick up a wart on your foot. They hurt a little but most importantly to get them removed you have to go to a dermatologist or doctor once a month for two to five months. And for roughly $100 a pop if you don't have insurance that works in the area. This can add up! Sandals, on the other hand, cost $5 and fit easily in any bag you might be traveling with.

Take advantage of work opportunities.

Around a hostel, there are always jobs and work to be done. This doesn't mean you need to pester the front desk person multiple times a day or constantly carry around a stack of resumes. The way to go about this is to be observant. Check the bulletin board. Strike up a conversation with the front desk or the cleaners and casually mention that you like the place and could use some extra cash. There are always things to do around a hostel and any manager worth half a grain of salt is going to at least trade a bed for some yardwork. In my experience, there are a lot of smart companies, mostly moving companies, that posted flyers or routinely called the hostel looking for cheap, temporary labor. If the people working there know you are looking, they will happily hook you up. I did this regularly and my cleaners and employees were always super stoked to make an extra hundred bucks or so.

Cook your food.

I have watched too many people ruin their budget and their trip by getting wrapped up in eating out twice a day for their entire stay. It will drain your finances really fast. Every time I ever stayed somewhere like this for even a few weeks I would always source some cheap Tupperware or Saran Wrap and bowls, then make 'large' meals that I would munch on for a few days. That doesn't mean that you aren't picking up a gyro or four as you pass by, but it does mean that the majority of your nutritional intake is taken care of for cheap. A lot of people like to cook communal meals this way, but I don't eat dairy or gluten so this immediately became a non-starter for me. Another great way to save a bunch of money though.

Be welcoming, compassionate, and friendly.

You aren't traveling to be a snob. And you certainly aren't traveling to prove that you are better than anyone else. So often I have seen wonderful places to meet like-minded people turn into high-school-esque dramafests, simply because people didn't take the time to get to know one another. If you're American you are going to quickly, and I mean *quickly*, find out that most people from other countries *automatically don't like you*. Who can blame them? When you start to see other Americans in the wild, walking around like they're better than everyone else, insisting that everyone speak English in *their* home country, and generally making asses of themselves, there will be a little tickle of embarrassment in your chest. And this isn't limited to

Americans. I have seen this in a large number of people, mostly from other Industrialized/Commercialized democracies, and it leads to people being ostracized, belittled, and judged. All the things that we all left our 'homes' to get away from. Don't be one of these people. Doesn't matter if they are local, don't speak your language, are dismissive, are young or old, or just got there and look stressed, whatever it is, everyone deserves grace and respect. And if you are the one being friendly to all these people? If you are the one demonstrating that you are someone worth knowing and caring for? You are bucking the trend. You are holding up a torch for those around you for how to be. Not to mention, being a good and decent human being is the only way to go about it.

79 | Hotels

There's a section later on detailing how to actually pick a hotel but there are also some things you should know if you plan on spending a lot of time in one. Most people are in hotels infrequently, only when they have some business or when they take a quick trip. But regardless of whether you spend a lot of time in hotels, or any other forms of rental spaces, then here are some general tips and tricks for getting by.

Always tip your cleaners.

Their job sucks and they get paid nothing. They are cleaning up after your mess, including your body hair and all the trash you didn't throw out. Forget the barista, if you are ever going to tip a human being then tip your hotel cleaners.

Be nice to the front desk.

It is rarely their fault for anything that goes wrong. Sometimes it is but not often. Even then, guess who is the only one who can fix it? Yup. The front desk person. And if you're super friendly they have the power to waive pet fees, resort fees, etc. I've even had my entire charge magically disappear before. These folks deal with the most difficult kinds of travelers regularly. Make sure not to be one of them.

Take a quick check for bedbugs.

These insects are not smart. They aren't digging away and scurrying from view like cockroaches. They hang out in plain view or poorly concealed underneath the sheets. Take a peek and see if you can spot them before they get a chance to get in your bags, or worse, into your skin.

The tap water is always crap.

Do not drink it if you can avoid it. Older hotels can have lead pipes, which is really bad. Newer hotels can have lead just as easily (which is somehow even worse). If they don't have that these hotels most often have poorly maintained and never cleaned water tanks. On top of this, a lot of hotels 'soften' their water, where they remove all the minerals to make the showers and sinks easier to clean. This isn't inherently bad until you think about the maintenance process for this as well. Are there cracks in the ceiling? A crappy paint job? Are the rugs nasty and stained? If they are, then how well do you think they are cleaning and maintaining the things that you *don't* see? Don't drink from the tap.

Clean off the remote.

Even without considering any viruses, TV remotes are never cleaned, and everyone is touching them. You just never know who was in the room before you. That remote could have been in a dog's mouth, a child's mouth, or between the butt-cheeks of the last overweight, middle-aged man who was sitting in bed watching murder porn. Wipe 'em down before you use them.

Always lock the door, deadbolt and all.

It doesn't happen that often, but it happens. The all-powerful front desk person can accidentally give someone else a key to your room. I've been handed one of these. Walked right into a room where an old guy was sitting on his bed, buck naked, dick in hand. Phew. I used to let my dog into rooms first but that habit stopped that day. Lock your door. You don't want to have any unwelcome visitors.

Put up your 'Do Not Disturb' sign.

This should go without saying but I'll explain it anyway. Unless you're with a large group of people who are going to be going in and out of one another's rooms frequently or if your family are in adjoining rooms, you aren't typically in a hotel for social calls. Without fail, whenever I am in a hotel and forget to put my sign up, I am taking a shower when the housekeeper lets themself in to clean my room. Considering I have PTSD and a pitbull, this creates a myriad of different problems. Make sure to keep your belongings safe and tucked away too, but the first line of defense against anything unwanted is that little plastic dongle hanging from the doorknob.

Have earplugs.

This is addressed at other spots, but it is equally important here as anywhere else. Earplugs can make the difference between a good and bad vacation.

Nowhere is this more prevalent than when the 'next-door neighbors' start having a knock-out-drag-out fight at two in the morning, or when someone is having *too* good of a time.

Don't leave your door open and don't blindly open your door.

My favorite example of this was at a cheap, rattrap hotel in Stockton, CA. Now, there is nothing wrong with Cadillacs. Nothing at all. But when you see one, decked out and upgraded to the max, with rims that have diamonds and gold paint on them, sitting outside of a *dive hotel*, you can guess the profession of the person who owns it. And if they are there, odds are that their 'employees' are there too.

I checked into one of these dives with a couple of rookie travelers that were hitching a ride with me. I had just cracked a beer and started to settle in when there was a knock at the door. I had a feeling what this was. I did not unbolt the chain and I stepped to the wall-side of the door. This is so I was not in the way of the door if someone tried to kick it in. I barely cracked the door open and immediately started saying 'no thank you,' over and over. A woman who had no business trying to sell her highly neglected body was standing there looking bored. "You called for some company?" she asked, putting a hand on the door. I immediately shut it, yelled that I was calling the cops, then called the front desk.

I let him have it. Someone was trying to force their way into my room to offer me services I didn't want for an employer that would no doubt threaten and coerce me regardless of what I did. I truly hate even the notion of being a Narc, but they forced my hand. The hotel manager was there within seconds, telling me that this had happened before. I saw the Caddy pull out a few minutes after that. The cops were there two hours later, right on time. The message here is to always lock the door, check who is outside before you open it, or just don't answer it at all.

Do a thorough room check before you leave.

Ruffle the sheets. Look around the sides of the bed. Check the shower, the bathroom, and the wall for chargers. I get all of my stuff in the car, including my dog and girlfriend, then head back into the room, take a big breath, and lazily scope out things I might have missed. I always find a dog toy or a book that had fallen into some crack or crevice. Just make sure to take a few minutes to check. Whatever you leave behind is gone, so make sure not to leave it!

80 | Housesitting

There isn't going to be a lot to this section simply because there isn't much to say. Most people can figure out how to open a door and not take advantage of people when being paid to do exactly that. The point here is to detail that this is an option that you might not have been aware of till now.

Simply put, housesitting is where someone pays you to watch over their house while they are gone. Most homeowners want to be sure that their possessions are going to be secure while they are away. And if they have dogs and plants, they are going to want to make sure that they are well taken care of and alive when they return. You are functioning in the same ways that the homeowner would if they were present.

The only potential pitfall to getting into this type of arrangement is finding the opportunity. For this, you'll want to go through one of the certified websites designed for this exact purpose. You can use Craigslist, but I wouldn't recommend it. With the amount of scams present on that platform these days you are just inviting someone to steal your personal information and get you into a precarious situation. As such, this advice is catered specifically toward utilizing these sites.

Have experience.

Don't worry, you have the experience. The point of that statement is to get you thinking about how to prove that to another human being. You'll need to be prepared to answer their inevitable interview questions about whether you have taken care of animals, lived in a house, traveled, and otherwise been responsible in your life. So, start to think through your mental resume of doing just that. Even if you didn't grow up in a home or haven't rented one before, think about how you have maintained an apartment or something similar in the past. Anything that details how you can take care of four walls, a fish tank, and a dog.

Create your resume.

Once you sign up and pay for whatever platform you'd like to use for your housesitting leads, you'll need to create a profile. Think of this as a mix between your social media and work profiles. You'll want a picture that makes you look friendly, you'll want to detail your qualifications, and then explain how you fund your travels. Everyone wants to see anyone who is going to be in their home for even a short time as reputable, employed, and otherwise trustworthy. I am going to assume that you are all these things so do a quick personal inventory and list these qualities of yourself on your profile.

Research the location.

When you do find a place that looks appealing to you, research the place before you respond. You need to see if you are going to like the place, if there are things that you want to do there, and if it is going to be a good fit for you. When you are initially reaching out to the homeowner who has posted the ad you are going to want to add these pieces of information. Homeowners can smell desperation from a mile away. If you are frantically looking for a place to stay this is not going to be the best option for you or anyone else. You want to have a good reason for wanting to be in that particular part of the world. Are there great hikes nearby? Great, you can take the homeowner's dogs hiking with you. Have you always wanted to live in Italy? Awesome, tell them that. Then they will be comfortable trusting *their* travel plans to you actually showing up. Know what you are talking about before you even reach out.

Don't be a robot.

Be yourself. The homeowner is going to grill you over all kinds of details of your life. You'll have already passed a background check by now so there is a basic level of trust between you, but now you are going to have to discuss the details and prove that you are the reputable person that you say that you are. The best way to do this is to be yourself. Answer in your own quirky way. Tell them about your passions, why you want to travel, why you are leaving wherever you are at that moment. Tell them about your family, your partner, whatever it is that means something to you. This creates a connection where you can also hear about their life and see if that is an environment that you want to be in. By resolutely being yourself, you can also save yourself some trouble down the road because if they aren't a fan of your personality then you probably weren't meant to live in that house anyway.

81 | Make Time to See Things Worth Seeing

When I started writing this book, I had a huge whiteboard that I put up in my office. Really it was a piece of white exterior board that I had picked up from the Orange Hardware Store and screwed to my wall, but it worked just fine as a whiteboard. It covered the entire wall, and I could stand there all night long and write down all the ideas that popped into my head. With a book this immense and (hopefully) all-encompassing it was crucial just to have that space to empty my mind on. During one particular late-night session, I started listing places I have been that had ties to stories that might be worth telling in this book. I'm sure you've noticed some of them by now. As I was listing these locations, I realized that there were a *ton* of them that were in cities and locations that I had only traveled *through*. I couldn't tell you a single thing about the actual city because all I had seen were the bus stations, some high-rise buildings downtown, a short stretch of road from a taxi, and then the airport. I hadn't seen or experienced much there.

Now I am not saying that traveling through a place isn't a good way to experience it. And I certainly feel grateful for being able to have been there in the first place. But most often we travel because we want to see and experience cool stuff. We travel to *enjoy it*. So, this section is short, sweet, and simple: make sure to take time out of the rigors of travel and do something that will make you *remember* the place you traveled to. Find out what the best restaurant is and get yourself there. See an art museum or a zoo. Look for a weird art installation. Or even just the best bar in town. Just make sure that you intentionally looked for something in that place that makes you happy. You just might get some good stories out of it.

82 | Picking Hostels/ Hotels

Most times when you are picking hotels you are going to be on the highway, driving along and starting to plan where you are going to stop for the night. Either that or you are headed into a city where there are no campgrounds or other cheap places to stay and you're sick of Walmart parking lots. Even if you've been to the city before it's almost impossible to remember everything about it, so you're staring at a map and trying to read reviews and figure out what the best, or most tolerable, cheap hostel/ hotel is in that area.

It used to be that you had to drive up to a hotel to check it out. That way you quickly saw what its condition was, what neighborhood it was in, and if there was a good bar nearby. Nowadays you are probably going to book the hotel before you show up, so you probably aren't going to see its condition, neighborhood, etc. before you get there. You need to be able to determine some basic, sight unseen, from a basic map of blue and yellow lines on your phone. Here's what to look for:

Watch out for clovers.

These are multiple highway off-ramps that branch off from where two highways meet. Engineering-wise they are brilliant. Regardless of what direction you are going, you can get off the highway in that location. The problem with these is they generate a ton of traffic and road noise, making the land less valuable. Who swoops in to buy it up? Hotels and motels. They then advertise that they are 'conveniently located.' These aren't necessarily bad hotels. But if you are looking for cheap then most likely they aren't going to have good insulation, meaning that you are probably not going to sleep that well. Additionally, clovers are at the intersection of two highways, so getting around on foot is probably more difficult than it is anywhere else. If you're sick of driving, don't have a car, or want to take your dog for a long walk, these hotels will be anything but convenient.

Look at other businesses.

You always want to look at what is around a hotel. This is not a hard and fast rule and there are exceptions. In my experience, you want to look for bad chain restaurants, pawn shops, closed-down stores, loan sharks, major discount superstores, adult stores, strip clubs, laundromats, and unfortunately, thrift stores. None of these types of stores are inherently bad in a vacuum. And they may be the exact places that you need and want to go to. They are not the places that you want to live around. It is a fact of life. Remember, as a traveler with a car most likely packed full of stuff, you are a target. You are already at risk. You want to minimize this risk by trying to insulate yourself as much as you can. Being in high-traffic areas is only going to increase the risk that someone might smash in your windows and cherry-pick your gear. But wait, Sam, I don't have any money or anything of value! Doesn't matter. They don't know that. If the place is surrounded by a bunch of disreputable businesses, chances are there is a lot of crime going on as well. Avoid it if you can.

Look at what else is around.

This is the hard part. Typically, you're looking at a list of hotels that show doctored pictures and you are trying to get the cheapest one you can with reviews that don't mention 'roaches' or 'bedbugs.' What you need to do is take that location, switch over to maps, punch in the address, and take a quick dive into the location. The Streetview function is great for this if you have it. You're looking primarily in a two or three-block radius. Nowhere is perfect. But some red flags are warehouses and shopping complexes nearby, chances are they are abandoned, garbage dumps, manufacturing of any kind, wrecking yards, factories, truck stops, pretty much anything that might have large and loud machinery. A lot of these places operate primarily at night too, which can be supremely irritating if you were looking to have a decent night of sleep before you hit the road again. Lastly, a lot of times it's a red flag if the hotel isn't around *anything*. This *can* be a good thing, and oftentimes is, but it can also mean that you are surrounded by abandoned buildings and properties, which hold the highest chances of housing someone who needs your stuff more than you do.

Urban areas.

Anytime you are going to get anywhere near a city center you are going to pay for the privilege. You rapidly enter a far more complex area than the last small town you passed and this likely drives up prices and taxes dramatically. That's why if you find a cheap hotel in an urban center you need to be very, very wary. These places are naturally a hotbed for various types of criminal activity. They are also going to attract people who are running out of options. Again, that does not mean that these people are bad or that they deserve scorn or ridicule. The reality is that this world is a cold, hard place. And if you push people hard enough, they are going to have to make really tough decisions. Cheap hotels in the middle of an urban center are going to attract *a lot* of these people, which adds to the odds that something bad is going to happen. Even if a hotel in an urban center isn't cheap, that does not mean that you are going to get what you pay for in the quality of the hotel itself. You are paying for the privilege of being near more things and also for the hotel's costs of doing business in a much more expensive area. This can easily lead to cutthroat maintenance like painting over mold, an absolute lack of security, crappy customer service, or exorbitant rates for a dive hotel.

You may be asking why any of this matters. So, in the famous words of Heath Ledger's Joker: "Why so serious!?" Well, the truth is that the hotel industry isn't known for being a shining beacon of health and quality. I have stayed in some incandescent pearls of hospitality, class, and maintenance. Some hotels can demonstrate the absolute height of humanity at its finest. Typically, however, if you are operating on a shoestring budget you are going to come face-to-face with business owners who know that they are operating on a predatory basis. They know that you aren't going to be as picky because you want the lowest-cost option. They also know that if you don't like it *you are going to leave anyway.* They aren't interested in your repeat business and don't care about your reviews because they are the cheapest in town. There will always be a subsection of people that will choose that hotel simply because it is the cheapest. With that in mind, here is what to look for in a good hotel:

● **Always look for air-conditioning, parking, and Wi-Fi.** You'd think these are standard, but they are not. After days, weeks, or months on the road without Wi-Fi, you are going to need it to communicate, plan your next moves, resupply if you have to, and generally do research on what's ahead. Air-conditioning is obvious. If it's super-hot out and you're paying for a place to get out of it for a minute, then it damn well better have some AC. If it doesn't, it should have a fan or three, so make sure to ask. Some hotels have the nerve to charge you for parking. But there is a common rule that most people don't know. If they don't advertise that they charge for something, then you do not have to pay it. And they are legally obligated to agree with you. It is extortion to charge a non-refundable fee for a hotel bought online, sight unseen, and then add charges that weren't agreed to upfront.

- **Look for recent reviews.** Hotels and motels change hands frequently. Everybody thinks they can do it better than the last owner. Some of them actually can and put their money where their mouth is. If you see reviews that are older mentioning how run-down the property is and how they 'saw bugs,' then you see a bunch of newer reviews mentioning how polished and clean the place is, then chances are that someone new bought the place and sunk a bunch of money into it. Most buildings can be fixed and renovated. Bugs can be killed with great efficiency. And sometimes the hotels with older bad reviews and newer good reviews actually can be the best places to go because you know that someone recently came and dealt with the problem.

- **Read the negative reviews first.** This isn't a pessimistic thing! You need to know what the problems are first because there are non-negotiables. If there is a recent review mentioning bed bugs *and* roaches? Deal-breaker. If there are *old* reviews mentioning these things, then maybe they have been solved in the past few years. But if there are recent negative reviews about crime, thefts, and break-ins, well that means that the property owner is either unable or unwilling to do anything about it.

- **Then read the positive things.** Every business is going to have its fair share of people that were happy about the place. If it doesn't then it will fail quickly. If a ton of people got a good night of sleep and were happy with the overall experience, then the chances are that you will as well and that they aren't all fake (they could be fake). One caveat to this is that most people are pissed about 'the breakfast' that these places advertise and offer. I have never understood this. Is anyone expecting a hotel breakfast to be *good*? If you are, where are you from? What planet? I have seen thousands, and I do mean *thousands*, of reviews that are incredibly pissed about how a hotel's breakfast was either canceled due to COVID, shitty, or my personal favorite, *sub-par*. It's yogurt cups, mass-produced oatmeal, microwaved eggs, and pancakes. Come on! It's crap! Why are you splitting hairs? Anyway.

- **Look for 'fish-eye' lens shots.** This includes any distorted photos at all. They're fairly easy to spot. If your mind sees a picture that is distorted you will get this funny little tickle on the sides of your eyes. Your brain might jump in with comments and judgment but your eyes can't be fooled. Follow your eye-guts, because usually if there are distorted photos then a property is trying to make its rooms look like something they are not. This is very rarely going to benefit you.

OK, storytime. I was in Bozeman, MT, with a girlfriend and I was feeling the itch to hit the road. I was miserable and I hated it there so naturally my negativity was attracting all the parallel negativity held by all the negative monsters that live in that horrible, negative little town. OK, I'm just kidding, Bozeman is a great place with *some* great people. OK, lots of awesome people and it is a great, if cold, place to live. I just had a rough time mentally when I was there, so I desperately had to get out. In hindsight, I went about this the absolute wrong way.

Why was it so bad? Well, the day we were leaving my girlfriend was having minor surgery on her foot. In my defense, the doctor had assured me that it was going to be extremely minor and that she would recover within a few days. Before I had scheduled this and made this happen (she was very stubborn and had been limping for months) we had paid the money to get out of our lease. I had worked my ass off driving Uber, pulling moving gigs, and getting my brain melted by pothead pseudo-scientist teenagers, to make enough money to comfortably get us somewhere else. The morning of the procedure we showed up with my old F-150 loaded up and ready to rock. That's just how we rolled, always ready to take off. We walked in as if this surgery was going to be nothing.

I knew it wasn't 'nothing' after the first hour had passed. I had been assured that this would be a fifteen-minute, in-and-out type of deal. If you can't tell by now, I also deal with a good amount of anxiety. So, by the time the clock turned over the first time I was four cups of coffee deep, had asked all three of the receptionists to check on the procedure at least three times apiece, and was intensely pacing back and forth in front of the door where they continuously assured me they would come and get me shortly.

It was exactly one hour and forty-three minutes from when they'd walked her through the doors that I heard the nurse on the other side of the door quietly tell someone to come and get me. She didn't even make it through the first door before I barged in and started walking toward where the recovery area was. I had had a procedure here a month earlier, so they remembered me and how spectacularly amusing I am after anesthesia. That's probably why they let my behavior on this visit slide.

Within seconds I saw how pale my girlfriend was and knew I had fucked up. I barely remember the doctor telling me that they had had to cut a lot deeper than they originally thought. The recovery was going to take months rather than days, I was going to have to change an intense bandage twice a day, and I was going to have to get her to a place where she could be in bed for at least a month.

Well, fuck.

Now, my girlfriend was a tough little lady. Ride or die, bitches. She was also really high for the next seven days so I shouldn't have listened to a single word she said. But she said it was no problem and I loaded her into the car. It felt amazing to get out of that town, even with a completely loopy navigator who could barely talk, sang horribly and loudly, and drooled every five or ten minutes. I think we made it a few hours down the road before I started to hear a low whine coming from her throat. I'm not completely sure she knew she was making it. At this point, I still hadn't had to change the bandage, so I didn't know how bad it was (it was really bad). But I knew she was in pain. When we were checking out from surgery she had declined the pain pills, but I had laughed in her face and had them double the prescription. That might be the only thing I did right. I pulled over, ran around the side, and barely caught her as she tried to slide out of the cab. I made her take two, lifted her back in, and tried to make her comfortable. Just imagine someone with their lower leg completely wrapped, splayed across a massive bench seat, alternately sagging into their chest and groggily humming along to AC/DC. Yeah. She should have been in bed. At home.

Eventually, I caught her wincing at every bump in the road despite the pain pills and I decided to pull over. This is where the 'hotel' part comes in. I was panicking. I can handle my injuries. I've walked off a broken leg, multiple concussions, not to mention some large and nasty cuts in the wilderness. Now, dealing with someone else's injury? Someone who I cared deeply about? New territory. I was making poor decisions based on snap reasoning, none of which made any sense. And that is what led us to stay at the good ol' Vegas Hotel in Billings, MT.

I didn't do any of the things I described above. I didn't read the reviews or check the location. I didn't think about it at all. I just saw this cheap, crumby, flea-ridden, cesspool of humanity and booked it. Pulling up in the parking lot it may have dawned on me how much of a mistake this was because *a guy was getting mugged in front of the door*. So, we sat there, my girlfriend moaning in pain, watching this guy pull a knife on another human, then run off with a cheap phone, some small bills, and a pack of cigarettes. I even laughed. And then I walked in the door.

I mentioned the mugging when checking in and the flea-ridden woman behind the desk just mumbled something about it 'being taken care of.' I helped myself to their wheelchair, which was very considerate of them, and went back for my girlfriend. She was drooling again so I lifted her out of the seat and put her in the chair. Bless her heart, she immediately woke up, laughed, and yelled out: "You wannnnnna gaaaamble?" Which was hilarious because we already had, already were, and sure, why not. So, we did. I got a cheap drink, grabbed her a hot dog, she wanted a hot dog for some reason, and within minutes we won $400. It wasn't all bad, I guess.

But then we headed to our room. Only took a minute before I spotted the first cockroach of the evening. It was OK with me, though. She was lying down with her foot elevated, just like the doctor told me, swathed in ice up to her hips, and heavily, heavily sedated. Even nodding in and out of consciousness, mumbling like fucking Charlie Sheen, she still managed to rag on me for picking the shittiest hotel in Montana. Yeah, remember when we talked about things to watch out for that may be in the neighborhood? Anywhere that they allow gambling is definitely a place to avoid staying in or next to. But I had her safe, comfortable, and healing and that was all that mattered. I put on a movie and tried to calm myself down.

It was around 11:30 at night. I was wired, anxiety making my hands shake, migraine splitting my skull, watching her sleep as if I could *make* her heal faster with pure, undiluted concern. I had just spotted my fourth cockroach skittering by on the far wall. An apocalypse movie was playing on the TV. Out of nowhere, someone began screaming with great conviction in the hallway. I had double-locked our door and put my door stopper underneath, which is probably what stopped it from getting rocked off of its hinges when the door and the entire wall buckled as something slammed into it, with even more shouting. Then I hear the very, very distinct sound of a pistol round being chambered. I didn't think. I pushed my recently-operated-on girlfriend as hard as I could off the side of the bed, rudely waking her up and causing her untold amounts of pain. She was in the middle of her first "WHAT THE FUCK, SAM" when my body crashed on top of her. I immediately went to one knee and yanked on the far side of the mattress until I could pull up and get the whole mattress standing vertically on top of the box spring. Another cockroach scrabbled its way across the now-exposed box spring surface. The door was banging, hammering, and the shouting noises had devolved back into screams back and forth. We had no idea what was going on. I could see a large blood stain seeping through my girlfriend's bandages.

Turns out that there had been a junkie who had gotten high and left his door open, exposing his drugs and needles. Also turns out that this wasn't the first time he had done this. The front desk person saw the open door, saw the junkie, saw the drugs, and naturally called the police. When they started pulling him up and putting cuffs on him, he freaked out, at which point he was thrown against our door and a gun was put to his head. We didn't know this at the time. I figured that somebody else had gotten mugged and hoped it was 'being handled.' I got my girlfriend cozy again, swapped out the outside bandages, and changed out the ice bags. I fell asleep right before the sun came up.

I went to the front desk the next morning because there was no way in hell I was leaving that room before 9 AM, cockroaches and all. I was exhausted, stressed, disheveled, and pissed off. I had also gone out to the truck by now, which had a few scratches around the door handles meaning someone had tried to break in. Evidently, they were too lazy or too weak to undo the ratchet straps holding in a bunch of valuable tools. But what do I know? I was positively floating on a whimsical cloud of vitriol when I made my way back through the Hell Gates. There was a new woman behind the counter. I didn't dance around it and demanded my money back. She rudely refused. Over and over. I remember her face, craggy and angular, with the dark bags under her eyes that spoke loudly of insomnia, all atop cracked rosebud lips smothered in cheap purple lipstick. I remember exactly what she said. I think about it every time I am considering a cheap hotel.

"I mean, didn't y'all win some money?!"

83 | Health Insurance

Health insurance is one of the most controversial, lightning-rod topics in American culture and politics. Oh wait, it's not? Wow. Alright then. Well, by now you know that I think that the American health care system is the epitome of the failures of unchecked capitalism, i.e., the 'tragedy of the commons.' Hospitals and healthcare facilities are not required to post the costs of their procedures. They don't have to tell you what it COSTS for goodness' sake. This is because they charge whatever they can get away with in an intricate dance of chicken with insurance companies. And who has one of the most powerful and expensive lobbies in Washington? Yup, you guessed it, hospitals and major insurance companies. In any given year it is a guarantee that the American Hospital Association, the American Medical Association, Pharmaceutical Research & Manufacturers in America, and every major insurance company you can name (Regence, Premera, Keiser, etc.) are among the top 50 in annual spending for lobbying in Washington, D.C.[32] They subtly and overtly dictate policy nationwide, thereby maintaining a status quo that allows our healthcare providers to arbitrarily fix rates and charge us unreasonable prices for low-quality services. This is not peak capitalism, rather it is the opposite. This is what happens when wealth is consolidated at the top, allowed to privately (and artificially) fix prices, then fund legal processes to maintain the existing system.

So how does this affect your life? As we saw earlier, maintaining your health is extremely important. It can also be very costly. This is where in-

---

32   "Leading Lobbying Spenders in the United States in 2022." Statista, 5 Apr. 2023, www.statista.com/statistics/257344/top-lobbying-spenders-in-the-us/. Accessed 12 Apr. 2023.

surance comes into play. If you have good enough insurance, you won't be paying much, if anything, for occasional services. If you don't have good insurance? Better start praying harder. I cannot count how many times I have been seriously injured and simply tried to tough it out for a few weeks because I didn't think I could afford it. I walked on a broken leg for two days just because I was worried about how much it would cost if it was broken, even when I *did* have insurance. Again, these companies charge whatever they want. And if you piss them off they will find a way to charge you double. The system is fucked. The only thing you can do to stay out of bankruptcy is to try and navigate it the best that you can. Here are some tips I have found along the way:

The Marketplace.

Say what you will about universal healthcare. Keep in mind that I don't give two shits what you think. A government should exist for two reasons: 1. To keep its citizens healthy. 2. To keep its citizens safe. And that is it. If a government is *not* doing that, then you have serious problems. The U.S. government has never truly done this for its citizens since F.D.R. was in office, and even that was iffy. Passing a healthcare bill is the only thing that the U.S. government has done in my *entire lifetime* that I fully agreed with. And currently, it is the only reason that millions of Americans have healthcare. If you aren't signed up for this, do so immediately. At the very least you can get a 'catastrophic' plan that will pay for something really bad happening. It won't pay for anything else, but you are covered if you end up in the hospital for a few weeks.

PPOs vs. HMOs.

This is one of those subsections that details another thing you should have been taught in high school. It is a crucial element of a crucial component of surviving the capitalist jungle that we live in. Insurance is complicated and is designed to confuse so much that you don't use it. As such, understanding how to get what you need is crucial. Here are the basics:

● **HMOs**

1. Everything is in a certain network, i.e., that particular hospital group.

2. Anything outside of this network is barely covered, if at all. If that hospital group has shitty doctors and specialists, then you are stuck with them.

3. Most often you have to have a PCP, or primary care physician. This is just a doctor that you have to see if you want to get anything done or see any other doctors.

4. This means that if you think you need an x-ray on your broken hand you have to go to your PCP first, who then can request that an x-ray be done.

5. This can be annoying and difficult, as you have to jump through a bunch of hoops just to see someone you already know that you need to see, like a psychiatrist or a gastroenterologist.

● **PPOs**

1. You'll still need a PCP because you'll need referrals for *some* things. Also, you need a doctor that you see regularly (or once a year) to stay as healthy as possible.

2. Oftentimes you can simply look up specialists 'in network' and make appointments, without having to talk to your PCP first. I have a PPO and recently was able to schedule a psychiatrist and a naturopath this way. But I wasn't able to schedule an MRI for my brain (too many concussions) without a referral.

3. This type of plan will cover a lot of the cost of 'out of network' providers. It is still better to stay 'in network,' but it's not as much of a financial cliff as an HMO.

4. These plans tend to cost more because they aren't as evil.

When you are looking for healthcare plans, these are your two options. It'll help you tremendously to look at your area and then figure out what plans are associated with which hospitals, and thereby what is available to you. For years I had insurance in Oregon but was rarely ever actually in the state. So, I picked a plan with a hospital right by the airport. Every year I would fly in, see my mother, hang out with my friends, head over for my annual visit, then hop right back on the plane. It worked for me at the time. Just make sure that whatever you pick (or that you can afford) has services in your area. These companies just want your money so watch out for their pitches. They are usually bullshit.

Another thing to understand is that insurance plans come with 'deductibles.' These are just a set amount that these plans want you to pay before they actually pay for anything. The higher the deductible the more you have to pay before any of your benefits kick in. This can be a serious pain in the ass because you're already paying a monthly premium. And then, God forbid, something goes wrong, and you have to pay *more* before you can get your leg fixed? Yay, Capitalism! But it's how it works. And for a lower deductible, you are going to pay more per month, unless you are low-income and/or on the Marketplace.

The last thing to know is that insurance is usually going to try and screw you over. They know a million different ways to make things *so difficult* that you won't want to fight it. They will deny things that they clearly should be paying for, drag their feet and needlessly make you wait for weeks or months, change your 'representatives' multiple times, pass you off to other employees endlessly, and on, and on, and on. Dealing with insurance is a nightmare. But keep in mind that there *are* things you can do about it. Always stay nice to these people. That's the main trick. If they start to dislike you, they are going to make the process even harder. And while you are being nice to them, continue to assert that you are right. You might have to go through a few appeals or file a ton of paperwork, but eventually, you'll get your money. Just be prepared to stand up for yourself against this skewed system.

84 | Heartbreak

There is no substitute for family. It doesn't exist. Yet there are so many of us who try to find it, create it, forge it. There are even more of us that desperately try to hang on to the shreds of 'family' that we thought we had; vague memories of fragments and pieces that we imagined were what we needed. If you are reading this then you probably know what I am talking about. We are a tribal species. Bound to the base, to the spine, of the fundamental truths of our territorial existences. We believe that we know more than anyone who came before us. We are the penultimate expressions of our familial line. We know *better*. The problem is that we don't. We are steeped in the problems of our past, our parents' past, and the past of our ancestors. We are the confluence of a great many rivers. Of emotion, of debt, of will, of solace and solitude. We are the remainder of a fuck-ton of division.

All this is an expression of the loneliness we all face. However, I would wager that most of us travelers face more of it. It's something I've seen thousands of times. Everyone has a story but let's face it, travelers have *better* stories. And better stories usually start with heartbreak. The movies and the books glaze over it, showing only the cliff notes of trauma and suffering. They only want a montage. But some of us lived through years of discrepancy. Some of us went through decades of loneliness, of shame, of feeling like we were aliens in a world of humans. Some of us go through that today. But we can't be aliens. We are all human. And we crave the same things: Belonging. Acceptance. Trust. Love.

Some of us even venture so far as to say: I can attain this through a partner. I know I have. I have scoured the Earth for a partner. And for the women who have looked into my soul and seen something worth holding onto, I can only thank you, despite how it ended. The fact is, we see only at the *end* of a relationship that they could never save us. They could never be what we missed, what we never had. They could never have filled that 'unfillable' hole inside of us. There are very few things that can heal such a tear. Being dependent, or codependent, on another person is never the answer. The only thing you can fill that hole with is the wholeness created by *you* loving *yourself*.

Now this doesn't mean you should turn into an asshole and treat everyone like crap. And frankly, you see this equally in all genders. When you watch anything produced in Hollywood over the past ten years you will see a different story, but the truth is it is a 'war' between both sides. And both sides are losing. We are two sides of a whole, yet we are turned against one another. We are twisted and jaded and confronted with uncomfortable truths. First and foremost, among these truths is that we are not complete without another. Yet we cannot accept such completeness without first accepting ourselves. We have to find the peace and understanding that lies within our souls to fully give ourselves to a potential partner. We have to figure out who we *are* before we can think of completing ourselves with someone else. Think of it this way: how can you possibly find the right puzzle pieces to attach to, if you don't even know what your own puzzle pieces *look like*?

We are going to go through our fair share of relationships. But heartbreak is a different beast. It hits us all the same, yet feels so irrevocably unique. You pinned your hopes, your dreams, and your passions, all on the same person. And now they are *gone*. Ideally, there are as few as possible of these relationships in your lifetime. You do only want a few. It decomplicates things at the end. And in the end, only the end is what matters. Make sure you hear that because that is what is going to get you through. You were looking for a partner that was going to cover up all the ills and ailments of your past. You were looking for the puzzle piece that fits into yours. Then maybe you could have taken that dual puzzle piece and plugged it into another world of puzzle pieces… but now it's gone. And you are left alone. One piece, drifting in a world of… what?

And here is where we circle back and summarize. You have deficiencies. Everyone does, yet all of us are the same in thinking: "Nah, it won't happen to me." Except that it does. It happened to our ancestors and our parents. Now it is happening to us. We are all flawed and people are going to leave us. We all think that if we can just find those perfect puzzle pieces then everything will be OK from that point forward. Except that it's not and it won't. Putting aside all the personal growth and general spiritual work that every person needs to do to be a healthy adult, then we *still* need to work well together. And because you are here, because you are reading, it means that *it didn't*. So, what comes next?

Well, what do you have? You have one piece to the puzzle. You have *you*. And that is how you are going to get out of 'the hole.' By focusing on *you*. It is too common in failing and dying relationships to shower each other with scorn, contempt, and insults. You start to believe that the other person's hatred of you for not fulfilling your role in their life is true! Don't get me wrong. The words of a dying and failing relationship can be the best catalyst for finding the best and truest version of yourself. Some of the criticisms that come out of a breakup can be the best criticisms someone can receive. Listen to those and take them to heart. But do not, under any circumstances, believe in the scorn and vitriol. This relationship may be dying or dead, but you certainly are not. And you only grow a plant by watering it. You only raise an animal by feeding it. And you are only going to bring yourself out of 'the hole' by nurturing yourself, educating yourself, and generally treating yourself the way you deserve to be treated. That's not only how to develop yourself to your highest potential, it is how to get over heartbreak for good.

85 | Insomnia

As anyone who has gone through a period of high stress or tension can attest, not being able to sleep for long periods can dramatically affect your quality of life. In recent history, the world has only sped up; adapting, evolving, and becoming more demanding. And more stressful! We are affixed to screens, for better or worse. We stray ever further from our instinctual roots of foraging along the forest floor, subsisting on hunted game and berries. We wear custom-tailored clothes and communicate mostly on keyboards. All this has led to our natural and instinctual rhythms having changed. I won't begin to claim that I know the first thing about why or how this works. What I do know is that I consistently battle anxiety and PTSD, which regularly leads to sleepless nights. Here are some tips for how to handle them:

Embrace it.

Don't fight it. Don't get frustrated and angry, or worse, even more stressed because of the day you have planned coming up. There is nothing you can do that will help the situation besides relaxing and taking it as it is. I have time limits for myself. If I am in a high-anxiety mindset, I give myself twenty minutes before I get up to walk around my house while taking long, big breaths. I regularly just get up to stretch out my bad back and meditate in my living room. It takes you out of the mindset you are in before you're caught in a cycle that will most likely last all night. If I am angrily tossing and turning in half sleep, I give it an hour before I do the exact thing. A lot of time just changing your body position, stretching, and taking yourself physically out of the place you were inhabiting can 'reboot' your brain, allowing you to create a relaxing and soothing mental environment for you to fall asleep.

If, however, you are in the dreaded 'stasis zone,' where you are wide awake, alert, and find it hard just to keep your eyes closed, it becomes even more key to embrace your situation and try to find the positives. If you're in this place, then you are most likely going to be awake for a while. I used to get pissed about this. I was exhausted from my day, physically and mentally, had to work again the next day, and I couldn't just *sleep*. It kept me up even longer, eventually turning to angry ruminating about this and that. When I embraced it though, thinking, "Well maybe now I am forced to read that book I've been wanting to" or, "Hey, the TV is open, I'm going to play video games,", everything changed. It became an event, rather than a burden. It became just another thing. Of course, I was incredibly tired the next day. It was not sustainable, and I had to figure out what was causing it in my own life and take the necessary steps to remedy it. But it made the effects lesser. I wasn't up for an entire night. I was able to scavenge three or four hours of snoozing. Believe me, from someone who has involuntarily spent days awake, it is better than none.

Have a plan.

Know what you're going to do beforehand when you can't sleep so when you start to get frustrated you know what you need to do. As I type this, I hate my girlfriend and dog. I don't really hate my girlfriend and dog but right now, somehow, I hate them with a strong, powerful passion. My girlfriend is sick, meaning that she is loudly tossing and turning, making smacking noises with her mouth, calling out in her sleep every twenty to thirty minutes, and *shooting* out of sleep to loudly trumpet blast out of her nose at least twice an hour. This is torture on my dog, as he just wants to protect and nurture us, so he is antsy and nervous, meaning that every time my girlfriend moves, he moves. And every time he moves, she moves again. I have already stood outside for an hour since midnight. Usually, I would just leave the room and go sleep on the couch, but we are staying in a one-room cabin at the moment. Where there is no escape. No escape at all.

I know that every time the insomnia kicks in for me, I have to get up and write something. That's it for me. It takes me out of whatever mindset I had been in, drains the frustration, and makes me super, uber tired. I know that as a last resort, I can always whip out the laptop and type until I am drowsy enough to pass out. Your plan may be much more elaborate, or much less so, but this is mine. Either it works well and I get right back to sleep, or I get a ton of work done. Win-win? Maybe. Making the best out of a difficult situation? Definitely.

Find support.

A friend of mine has insomnia and it has taken a toll on her over the years. She finally found a solution that works for her but when she was in the middle of it there were a lot of sleepless nights for her. One day she referenced her 'late night buddy' and I immediately paused. "You're going to want to explain that." Turns out, she had polled her friends and found out that not only did two of them have insomnia, but that they were both in a later time zone than she was, meaning she could talk to them about it *earlier*. This blew my mind. I always thought that insomnia was the eminent domain of the lonely. A reclusive right-of-passage for the stoic nightcrawlers who inhabited the dark. Turns out it was an extremely inclusive club that anyone could be part of. Occasionally I would wake up to her giggling, typing away on her phone. She wasn't sleeping, but at least she was enjoying her time.

The point is to find some kind of support. Someone or something to talk to about what's going on in your head. For me, I have some gratitude boards and meditation apps that I like to participate in. For my friend, it was talking to friends and sharing memes. Tomato, tomato. Whatever you do, try and have some kind of support set up for the times that you can't sleep. Not only will it help you eventually get to sleep but it will encourage fewer nights like that from happening.

Move around.

I have to fight this one all the time, but it is key. I get it, you're in bed, you're tired, it's late, and you don't want to deal with absolutely anything else today. But you have to *get up*. You have to shake out your limbs, take a walk around your place, and even go outside. Sometimes walking my dog has been the best cure for insomnia, especially when it's cold. He's standing there, wondering whether to lift his leg on this particular bush, and meanwhile, it's fifteen degrees outside and I just got hit with an icy blast of wet wind, right up into my butt crack. And then finally, he pees. He poops. And then we are rushing back inside, I'm taking off my coat… and then I am not thinking about my dickhead neighbors. Or family. Or the monster client I have to deal with the next day. Instead, I am thinking of my warm bed, with my cold dog (who will warm up) and then everything seems a whole lot more manageable. So, get up. Walk around. Shake your limbs, chomp on an ice cube, and maybe even water your plants. It might just help you take your mind off of it long enough to put you to sleep.

86 | Investing

Most of us are never going to be rich. Capitalism was established with a set of rules that benefit those with resources and impede those without. If you have a ton of money in this system, then you get to set the rules and rig the system so that you can make more money and stay in power. It is how humans have always functioned as is especially prevalent at this time in history. Unless we evolve much more efficient brains, then this is how things are going to be. Most of us are going to fall into the lower tax brackets, middle class at best. A ton of us are never going to even break the cycle of living paycheck to paycheck. Or hand to mouth. But that doesn't mean you have to *be* most of us.

First of all, throw away the thoughts of the mansion and the expensive spouse. Focus on quality of life. Focus on the health of your body and your happiness. These are the things that will save you the most money along the line and allow you more funds to play with. You can always make small investments that pay great dividends down the road. It is a focus on your future that leads to wealth. You are not going to win the lottery. If you do, call me. I'll be the first one to admit I was wrong to say that. But I am not wrong. You aren't. They advertise those stories of the lucky people who do win to keep people thinking that they can actually win it. They can't. What you *can do* is turn some of your money into *more money*. If you can make the right series of decisions, then you can eventually have enough to eventually coast by on. The idea is to use your money effectively to reduce your workload and increase your quality of life as much as you can, as fast as you can.

The Capitalist system is designed to get you to participate in 'entry-level' jobs, i.e., a job that 'anyone else' could do. This is supposed to convince you that you are only worth the minimum wage allowable. Do you see the mindset that inevitably puts you in? That you are easily replaceable, only worth starvation wages, and that you 'need' supervision to do a menial task. Not only this, but you also somehow deserve to make less than all the people you are 'serving' in your job. No wonder so many people get credit cards! And no wonder so many people do not believe that they can *ever* invest, not to mention ever save enough to be comfortable when and *if* they retire.

To become 'wealthy' you have to invest in yourself first. You have to establish in your head that you are worth more than the minimum wage. Not to say that entry-level positions aren't a necessity for most. Everyone has to eat. And if you have anyone depending on you at all, you have to bring home that bacon. But you owe it to yourself to not get stuck there permanently, or even for a long period. When you convince yourself that you are more than just a cog in a simple machine, then you immediately realize that you are capable of achieving your goals, aspirations, and dreams. You are worth putting time, maintenance, and money into. It is not that much of a stretch to realize that once you condition your mind to believe that you are a unique miracle of mathematics and spirituality you can become more than you think that they think that you are.

Once you can break yourself from that negative chain of thinking that our current society brainwashes you into then you can then focus on how to best utilize your money. Investing your time in the practices detailed at the beginning of this book, combined with meditation and mindfulness, can and will lead to better mental and physical health. This is the most important thing to invest in. But the world does revolve around money. The bottom line is that we do need some degree of currency to make our lives comfortable and worth living. To best achieve a balanced and healthy income stream throughout our lives we have to focus on investing in three major categories: long-term investing, short-term investing, and quality-of-life investing.

Long-term investing.

This is the common form of investing that most people know and dread learning about. It is the playground of the wealthy and frankly, it's a minefield for casual investors. This system is designed to lure you in and take your money to exact profits for middlemen and traders aligned throughout the system. Everyone has heard and seen the stories of people who played with fire, investing everything they had in stocks and bonds and losing it all. It truly is a house of cards managed behind a curtain. We will never see the inner machinations. When this system collapsed in 2008, ruining the lives of countless people, this did not hurt this industry *at all*. The executives in charge got *bonuses*, all while their companies were getting bailed out with money taken from the same taxpayers that were robbed by the system. When engaging in this system, never forget who you are dealing with.

This is not to say that this 'market' cannot profit you in the long run. In particular, everyone needs to have an IRA. While the returns on an IRA just barely outpace inflation, they are tax-free, meaning that any amount that you put into an IRA you can write off on your taxes. That money stays in there till you retire, making a set percentage, and thereby can vastly change your fortunes when you are older. Do yourself a giant favor and start an IRA when you are young. Put twenty bucks in per month, every month, for 20 years. When you are old enough to even start considering what you're going to want to do when you're old, you will feel like it is attainable. If you listen to one thing I say in this book, this might be it. Slowly accumulating wealth via an IRA is the safest and lowest impact way to set yourself up well in the future.

I would write about CDs, money market accounts, savings accounts, treasury notes, and bonds, but as of the writing of this book, the rates on all these are dramatically lower than inflation. These are bad bets. With inflation the way it is these 'investments' will lose you money. Quickly. But they are worth looking into if this situation ever changes. The way I grew up, these were all useful tools to 'make your money work for you,' or to be making money off your money while you are waiting to spend your money. The odds of that happening again? Currently low.

Another old concept, and for good reason, are precious metals. Mainly gold and silver. I am a huge proponent of this because: A. I think it's cool to own shiny things and B, every time the world goes to shit, everyone wants gold. If the world collapses, we are going to need some kind of currency. Not to mention, gold is the most effective conductor of electricity that is available. As we use more and more of this finite resource it is going to become more valuable. I certainly feel more secure with gold than I do with my meager stock portfolio. Correction, than I *did* with my meager stock portfolio, which I sold at the first whiff of a recession. I do not want to lose all of my hard-earned money just because somebody can't keep from invading someone else. I like gold because it's shiny, in any environment or situation it is going to be worth something, and I can keep it locked away in a safe somewhere. Just food for thought.

Perhaps the oldest concept of them all is to buy land. Most people don't know that land can be affordable if you're down to get a smaller piece that is in the middle of nowhere. Frankly, that is what appeals to me most. But if you are willing to save up for a while and do the work of getting it surveyed and soil tested, not to mention paying property tax every year, you have a section of the Earth that you own, permanently, that you can do almost anything you want with. Most importantly, you own a piece of land that you can park on for as long as you want. And, as one of my favorite quotes goes:

"Buy land. They aren't making any more of the stuff." – Will Rogers.

There is a lot of talk about cryptocurrency going on and this can be appealing to a lot of people. Currently, I make money off of various passive income streams like my online meditations, some How-To videos I made, etc. It is very easy and rewarding to immediately turn this passive income into any number of fun and new types of cryptocurrencies. There are two convincing sides to this argument. Yes, the blockchain-based, online currency might be the 'wave of the future.' But currently, it is open to all kinds of attacks from a wide array of different sources. The very things that make it appealing to us are the same things that make it appealing to people who can and will steal all of your stuff. It is incredibly easy to get into the cryptocurrency game as you can buy very small amounts at a time. Just remember that nothing is guaranteed in this game. And appearances can be deceiving. A completely online currency whose value is determined by incredibly complex factors is volatile and a ripe opportunity for larger investors to manipulate. Be careful and only play with money you can afford to lose.

Altogether, just remember that you can put your money into different avenues that can ultimately make you a steady income. Imagine if you put 5-10% of your income aside for a year, put a down payment on a piece of land, built a bathroom and ten campsites on it, then rented them out on Airbnb. There are a lot of steps involved in that and a lot of things can go wrong but this is one idea. And this idea could bring in a considerable amount of income if you were to pick a smart location, use your assets wisely, and ultimately create a successful enterprise. The point is to get you thinking about how to invest in yourself. You are not defined by your wage, your tax bracket, your car, or anything else. You are infinitely more than all those things. And you deserve to invest in yourself, currently and in the future. By saving as much money as you can and putting it into the right places, namely the places listed above, you can greatly increase your chances of making your life much easier and reducing the amount that you are going to need to work to make enough money to make, and keep, yourself happy. That's what it's all about.

87 | Mental Health

You'll be noticing at this point that I talk a lot about mental health. Why is that? Are you padding these pages, Sam?? Nope. I keep referencing it because it is so important. Everyone on this Earth has to prioritize their mental health, *especially* in this country. We are run as a business that wants to squeeze, squeeze, *squeeze* us until we are nothing but a pulped mess and someone is drinking a lemonade made of our constituent parts. That is an incredibly important reality for everyone. But 'everyone' doesn't mean *everyone*. All of us are different. That's just how it is. Some of us are *mentally* different too. Some of us, they got into early. Messed with the way we perceive the world. Some of us have been in survival mode since we were infants. Some of us have had too many scrapes with the other side. Some of us have 'the shine.' Some of us are trying to keep our heads above water every single second of every single day and these pills *don't fucking work, Bill.* This isn't an elite group, this isn't a club that you want to be a part of, and it certainly isn't a distinguishing factor. This is a section for those of us that this world broke into a million pieces, over and over, and who have relentlessly tried to adapt and put the pieces together. It's for those who have struggled just to stand in a crowd and who have always felt like aliens.

And anyone who just needs a fucking hand.

The first thing most people who work in mental health will tell you is that they know a great place to 'check you in,' you know, 'if you need it.' Then they have you go over your symptoms, your thought processes, your child-hood, your experiences. These aren't caring and compassionate therapists. These are mental scalpelists trying to quickly diagnose you and then pump your brain full of chemicals to keep you tottering along in the pulp line. OK, that was pretty negative. They are trying to help you in the only way they know how and they think that the only way to improve a chemical imbalance in your brain is with other, man-made chemicals. It is perfectly rational, it is perfectly sane, and these are good people who try their best. It is also almost completely ineffective in the long run.

Normally I would keep what I think about this issue to myself because it makes me too vulnerable but I think that mental health issues are a particularly prevalent problem in the 'traveling community.' It makes sense. If you struggle to maintain a basic level of communication, achieve lasting or fulfilling relationships, generally ostracize yourself from jobs, friends, and family, or otherwise act in a way that could be embarrassing, then it is perfectly natural to want to take off and leave somewhere. I have done it dozens of times. I left college, countless jobs, towns, counties, states, and even countries. All because of my mental health and the fact that I couldn't keep a reign of my emotions, my demeanor, and my mouth. Everyone experiences mental health issues in their own ways. I certainly have mine. But living an alternative lifestyle can be overly stressful and trigger you in a myriad of different ways, far and above the norms of a 'regular' life. As such, it is important to detail some steps to mitigate these issues.

It is important to explicitly state that I am not advocating to get off of any medications you may be taking. I am simply stating that trying to address all of your issues by taking pills is like trying to pound in a roof's worth of nails with a raw turkey. It just isn't going to work. Additionally, I have no medical license of any kind, nor am I planning on getting one. You can and always will need to seek professional help alongside these recommendations.

Meditate.

Have you heard it enough yet? It is the pursuit of finding oneself that leads to inner peace and calm. We are hardwired to spend our lives distracting ourselves from and numbing our sources of pain. And that's putting it bluntly. We are inundated with messages of 'how to be happy.' But happiness isn't sustainable and fulfilling. It just isn't. Happiness is inherently *designed* to be fleeting. So, chasing it is going to lead to… unhappiness. Rather, we should be seeking peace, calm, and self-reflection. This is achievable almost exclusively through meditation. A lot of us can achieve an indirect form of meditation through means that we aren't even aware of. Ever broken into a rhythm while working out? Ever lost track of time singing in the car? Ever lost track of a few hours with your lover in bed? These are all flow states and thus, primitive meditation. Imagine if you were able to recreate those moments of flow and tranquility without needing to physically exert yourself or go out of your way. Because you can. It is all, and I mean *all*, in your mind. Meditation has the most direct effect on your mental health that you can achieve. It's the single most important factor in regaining control over your thoughts and emotions. And it takes years, decades, to 'master.' So, start now and do it as much as you can.

Exercise.

Even if it only means breaking out of your routine once a day for five minutes just to walk up and down the stairwell one time, do it. Whatever it is for you, just do it, then do it again when you can, then do it more when you're up to it. Exercise is the key component to jump-starting everything. Whether you're in a rut or need some inspiration, taking a fifteen-minute jog is going to expel the excess negative energy you might have hanging around. It is going to give you an intense feeling of accomplishment and achievement. If the world seems against you and the obstacles just *keep coming*, then you need to energetically and physically drag your mind out of the ditch. Start by moving, then keep moving.

Call people.

Everything these days is online. We are barraged by the dinging of our phones, whether it's an email, text message, notification, or chat board. It's isolating when nothing is authentic or if you're just trapped in your head. I've learned to call people just to hear their voices. My mind does tricky things to me when I am texting. I hear people's voices through the lens of my fears, trauma, insecurities, and past life experience. Even those people who are truly well-intentioned come off as cruel and uncaring. And it's not a far stretch of the imagination to think that we are all like this to a certain degree. That's what makes phone calls so important. We can hear the inflections and tone of the other person talking. We can hear them laughing out loud! It's a different experience entirely. For me, this is enough to get me away from the often negative thoughts that I am having and to help me move into a constructive and positive headspace. If the phone feels like it weighs a thousand pounds, make sure to lift it until someone answers.

Do something every day that makes you uncomfortable.

This might be the hardest for some because of all the rules and boundaries we set for ourselves. We are trying to avoid embarrassment, pain, anxiety, terror, abject depression, etc. We have created a system of yeses and noes in our heads that puts us into a hamster wheel, which in turn compounds the things that made us miserable in the first place. The best and easiest way to create situations in which you can feel like you are learning, growing, and evolving is to push outwards on your boundaries. Try something and try hard to succeed, then pat yourself on the back whether it went well or not.

Always, always, always give yourself some credit.

We are conditioned to be hard on ourselves. To a degree, this can lead to success. If you are lazy, you run a much lower chance of succeeding. This does not mean that you have to regularly and continuously push yourself past your limits. Sometimes 'not enough' is perfectly enough. Sometimes 'average' is plenty. And oftentimes we achieved way more than we thought we did, especially when we are being hard on ourselves. Some days you are going to hit every one of your goals and on top of that, the beautiful woman at the counter who just sold you dog treats is going to hand you her number with a wink. Some days it's enough to just get up and take a shower. Be your own greatest supporter, whether that means celebrating or commiserating. You deserve credit for simply being you and doing the best that you could in any given circumstances.

Try the medications.

Again, medications by themselves aren't inherently bad. They *become* bad when you learn to rely on them. When you use them as a crutch to base everything else in your life off of. Especially when you use them to justify poor decisions and behaviors. Remember that medications are designed to give you the distance and objectivity necessary to fix your problems *on your own*. They are a Band-Aid, not a life sentence. I have had resounding success with these at various times in my life. They stopped working for me but that might not be the case for you. If you are having a really hard time getting your mind out of the negative twists and turns then turning to a medication for a while might be exactly what you need.

Find a mental health professional that you like.

My last experience with a psychiatrist went poorly. He kept prescribing me things that gave me rashes, heart palpitations, and twitches on the side of my head. I have PTSD and I was also experiencing a time of intense stress and anxiety. I am not trying to die though. I switched to another provider and instantly knew I had made the right choice. I actually belly-laughed during a psychiatric appointment! Good stuff. The point is: don't stop until you find someone you like and trust. Someone who has your best interests in mind. They are out there, so don't take no for an answer.

Set boundaries.

The absolute most effective way to get someone else who is taking advantage of you, abusing you, or otherwise lobbing their toxicity at you, to freak out is to simply utter the word 'boundaries.' It is a lighctning rod. Because there is no hiding or escaping from them. They are the light in the darkness. And enacting them? Extremely effective. You need to sleep, so turn on the 'Do Not Disturb' button on your phone. Whoever freaks out that you aren't texting them back probably needs *even more* boundaries. Are your parents abusive assbags? Tell them you aren't going to tolerate their negative put-downs and general attitude. And then when they start yelling? Hang up on them. Boundaries. You will not only quickly find out who in your life is real, but you will also rediscover your self-worth and just how iron-clad your spine is. Plus, it's satisfying seeing these people who routinely treat you like crap start to piss themselves.

Trust.

This is a hard one to write. I am probably the biggest and least successful version of "Those That Cannot Do, Teach" right now. I have let my trust issues eat me alive for almost my entire existence. I have pushed hundreds of potentially good friends away because of perceived slights. I have self-sabotaged myself in some way every single day for the past twenty years. And for the past five years or so, I have even been *conscious of doing it.* I have to tell myself daily that the people I care about actually care about me too and there is no reason that they would want to betray me. I even worry about whether my dog loves me! What the fuck, eh!?

What we forget about trust is that it says everything about us and nothing about them. If we trust our partner and then they go out and stab us in the back, that is on them. They are the monster, not you. You have done nothing but put faith in your decision-making and ability to judge character. If you are wrong? Oh well, you can learn from it. It is going to hurt. But everything hurts. Brushing your teeth too hard hurts. What doesn't hurt is having a resounding and unbreakable faith in yourself and the goodness of the universe. Finding a connection to the Spiritual World helps in this but if you don't have that you can still find the same effect in a connection to the good and wholesome parts of yourself. Start by trusting yourself. Then move on to other people. And God, if you're so inclined. This is the hardest part and arguably the most essential. You don't have to take your hands off the wheel. You should but that's just one man's opinion. You just have to trust yourself enough to know that you are driving to the place you need to be and with the people you should be with. I believe in me. You believe in yourself. It's that simple.

Micro-goals.

Lots of us set these huge, lofty goals all the time. And those are great. Have them. When you achieve them, it is the best feeling in the world. But we can't achieve them every day. And a lot of the time we get lost because we don't see the end of the tunnel. The walls close in. The ice cream stops tasting so good. And how do we break out of the monotony without small joys like ice cream? Set small goals. Hourly goals, daily goals, weekly goals. I used to count how many people I could get to smile every day. I didn't have any friends back then, so this was hard. I remember one day I was at the bar and got to talking and I told a joke really loudly. Everyone laughed and it was glorious. I still remember my total: thirty-three. I got thirty-three people to smile that day. I can't tell you the address of the first house I ever bought but I can tell you that one day in the spring of 2015, I made thirty-three people smile in one day. Micro-goals!

Listen to music you loved as a teenager.

I don't know why this always cracks me up. Back in the day, I went through every phase. Emo. Hardcore. Metal. Thrasher. Country. Emo again. Indie. You name it. I loved 'em all. And now when I'm down I'll put on some Everclear and start laughing my ass off. Or rockin' out. Depends on the breakdown. Try it, it just might save your day.

Talk to yourself.

I talk to myself all the time. Best conversations I ever get. My dog is also a fantastic listener. And the more I talk to myself the more I realize how awesome I am. Even when I 'don't deserve' to be awesome. Know the feeling? Yeah. Talk to yourself. Tell yourself that you love yourself in the mirror. Tell yourself how much you like your new shirt. Tell yourself anything positive. Because we are all inclined to look at ourselves negatively. And that negative self-talk finds a permanent home in our subconscious mind.

Next thing you know, the negativity is permeating out into the present. So how do you stop it? Tell yourself differently. As often as you can.

Probiotics.

I have no research or studies to stand on here. What I do know is that my guts were tremendously messed up for a long period. And when they were, the inflammation throughout my body was extremely high. When I started taking probiotics my guts were so messed up that it made me an insomniac for two weeks. I never slept. The shock was so intense in my guts that I was wired, anxious, and stressed to the absolute max. But this is exactly why you should take them. Balancing out your intestinal tract is the best way to reduce your anxiety. Plus, it is just plain good for you to have a highly effective gut lining. If you have ever taken antibiotics this is doubly so. After four months of taking probiotics, my body started to show clear signs of recovery. I had more energy, the constant pain in my abdomen was gone, I was way less cranky all the time, and my anxiety reduced *significantly*. This was so evident that I can now trace a lot of my anxiety directly back to what I ate, either that day or the day previously. Your guts are constantly trying to tell you things. If you listen and give them what they need, your entire body will benefit.

88 | Places to Take a Shower

Hey, to each their own. Some people hate showers and can go forever without them. Makes some sense. There's a school of thought that says using soaps on your skin can remove 'healthy' bacteria right along with 'unhealthy' bacteria. I think that showers are God's gift to us to keep us healthy, sound, and sane. They are a blissful reprieve from the world where we get a free mild massage and get to sing loudly while we reimagine conversations and previous interactions in a much more positive light. I take as many as I can. Whichever side of the fence that you're on, doesn't matter. When you're on the road you're going to get dirty. You're going to be sweaty, you're going to regularly slop coffee and ketchup on your favorite shirt, and after long enough even your soul is going to feel grimy. Eventually, you're going to *need* to take a shower. And if you aren't trying to stay in a hotel then you're going to have to get creative with where that is going to happen. Here's a list of places that I have frequently used:

Gym membership.

I currently have a membership with a large chain gym. It's purple. It is chock full of way too many annoying people and the music is awful. But it is clean, has great showers, and only costs ten dollars per month. And they exist *everywhere*. This means that no matter where I go in the country, I can always go to one of these gyms and get a shower or use the bathroom. Not to mention, you know, actually going to the gym is good too.

Gym day-passes.

Don't want to pay for a membership? That's OK. All gyms offer a day pass. Might cost you ten bucks but it sure can beat having to pay for a hotel. Make sure to bring all of your stuff in to shower in a closed bag though. Occasionally some of the staff can get weird about people walking in with flip-flops and a bag of toiletries. Doesn't make any sense when you look at it sideways, but it is what it is. Walk in like you're going to work out, then just take a shower and leave.

Truck stops.

Truckers need to get clean too. These can be hit or miss but the rule of thumb is that the bigger the company the better the showers. The cost fluctuates wildly and they usually do a time-based, 'appointment' schedule, where they will call your name when your shower is ready. These can be absolutely foul, but they can also be very nice. If you're on the highway these are always the best choice. Just make sure to avoid the end of the day when they are super slammed.

Hostels.

Hostels know their clientele. I should know, I ran one. They usually offer some kind of 'day pass' where they will let you charge your phone, get a shower, and generally just recharge. If they don't, bribe them. They usually do though. Or you can just pony up the extra $20 and stay for the night.

Community centers.

The odds of getting a shower at these are 50/50. They either have a shower or they don't. Oftentimes they do and will offer showers for around five bucks. This is clearly to dissuade the homeless from using them. The ones like this that I have found tend to be pretty nice and well worth the money.

Yoga studios.

Yoga is a great way to relax from the road. As a bonus, they oftentimes have a shower on the premises. If you're nice they will usually let you use it. If not, bribe them.

Campgrounds.

These are easy. All you have to do is get by any kind of kiosk at the front and then find out where the bathrooms are. Don't lie. It's tempting, but don't. If you have to, buy the day pass. Or just level with them. Usually, when I've driven all the way out to a campground I want to be camping there anyway. Sometimes you can meet resistance (some of these attendants are way too overzealous). But more often than not you can just drive in and grab a quick shower for free.

Churches.

This is hit or miss, surprisingly. A lot of churches just aren't open most of the week. And you can encounter a *lot* of hostility at times. But occasionally you can get some needed help and reprieve. It's also always nice to have the whole church practically to yourself for an hour or two, especially if you're the praying type.

Community Colleges.

This is often a long shot, so I usually call first. But there is usually a gym at most large community colleges, and they will sometimes let you just take a shower there for free. Act like you belong and like you've been there before. Who are they to argue? If that doesn't fly and there is a super-serious Karen overseeing everything, see if they offer day passes.

89 | Relationships

My experience/advice on relationships can be summed up in three ideas:

Treat those assholes the way you want to be treated.

If you can't do that, get help. If *they* don't, can't, or won't do that, leave. It's that simple.

Watch their parents.

Traits and behaviors are learned early, yet they often take a lifetime to fully manifest. There are exceptions to every rule, but you can get a very good idea of the person you are dating by looking at how their parents act. If, for instance, you notice that her mother is a monstrous, narcissistic psychopath, then there is a high likelihood that the woman you are involved with has some of those traits as well. And if *his* mother is a self-centered, neurotic, alcoholic? Well yeah. There's a *slight* chance he might be too. If you can take the rose-colored glasses off of your eyes for a moment and take a hard look at their parents you can oftentimes save yourself a great deal of headache and heartache down the road.

Never cheat.

I don't understand polyamory or open relationships and I never will. To each their own, love is love, fuck who you want, none of my business. It is my opinion that the only way to carry through life is to attempt to find a partner and a soulmate. I cannot do that by being intimate with multiple people at the same time. In my view, cheating on any partner is cheating on yourself. You are betraying the (supposed) most important person in your life and thus sabotaging your highest goals and desires. Whether you want to own a home, get rich, jerk off in space, have a family, whatever it is, if you follow it far enough down the road of thinking, you eventually get to the point where you are going to want a partner. If you train yourself to think that betraying any human being is an OK practice, you are training yourself to betray your hopes, desires, and dreams. Somewhere along the line, a whole hell of a lot of people convinced themselves that having no moral compass or adherence to their higher path was worth sacrificing for momentary pleasures. I don't look at it this way, especially if there is someone I care about involved. A lot of people don't look at it the way I do though. And we wonder why so many people are so damn apathetic!

If you feel the need to go after someone else just be honest with yourself and what you want. That is always OK. It is always acceptable to have a frank conversation with someone, even if you are afraid that they aren't going to take it well. The way you feel and the things that you think are always valid. And you can always tell your partner these things. If you can't, refer to number one. If that is the case, you shouldn't be in that relationship in the first place. And if you cheat at that point, you are either saying to yourself that you're not strong enough to be brave and honest, or you are just cheating on your hopes and dreams.

Good luck and don't forget to breathe.

90 | Sleep

Your sleep should be a high priority in your life, even if you've convinced yourself that you don't need it. I remember being twenty years old and invincible. I graduated college in three years while working at *least* twenty-five hours per week, taking double the course load from my university and online classes from the local community college for cheaper 'general ed' credits. *And* I would get up early to get coffee before my first class. Classes would be stacked one after another in the morning so I could clock into either the bookstore on campus or whatever restaurant I was bussing for at the time. Around 3 o'clock I would be back at class until after dark. Right after that would be the gym for an hour, then the library to crank out as much homework as I could until I couldn't see straight. At which point I would grab a burrito and head home to study. Around 3 or 4 in the morning, I would finally pass out, only to wake up the next morning and do it again.

I had my first nervous breakdown outside of one of the Halls on campus. I had stayed up all night finishing a monster of a project, something akin to eighty or one hundred pages. It was a math class that taught us how home mortgages work, car loans, credit cards, etc. Pretty much everything that you needed to know about selling your future away to raise a family. Halfway through the project, I realized that the entire exercise had no poignancy for me. I knew I wasn't going to live that life. Why the hell was I doing this astronomical amount of work? For what? For who? I didn't know. So, at 7 AM I walked from my house to campus, dropped off the ridiculously thick folio into the mail slot, walked to the small park nearby, hit the dirt with my knees, and started to cry. Even at this early hour and in this relatively remote corner of campus there were still people buzzing by in my periphery. None of them stopped. I don't remember walking home, skipping work that day, or anything for the next week. I ended up getting a B+ on the project.

My next nervous breakdown was six months later. I had transferred my lease to my brother, packed up my meager amount of things, and jumped in a buddy's car. I set up shop at my mom's house back in Portland and was taking my last collegiate course online at Portland State. I was already working two jobs and interning at a city-wide advocacy group. For some reason, I couldn't let myself relax. I felt like if I wasn't pushing myself to the absolute maximum then I wasn't working hard enough. There was a constant impending sense of doom and chaos that followed me everywhere. I drank at least twelve cups of coffee per day, smoked a half-pack of cigarettes, and then drank beer nonstop when I went home. At no time did I ever average more than four hours of sleep per night. So, as I walked across Broadway one morning, it was no surprise that I just simply *broke down*. I was a van on the highway, engine smoking, busted tires flapping, rapidly flying off toward the shoulder. I don't even remember sitting but the next thing I knew, there I was, down on my knees and crying again, this time in the middle of the street. Luckily someone did care this time. I felt a hand on my shoulder and a friendly voice in my ear.

"Hey, buddy. Let me buy you a cup of coffee, eh?"

Sometimes it's going to be alright, you know?

Now, I should have taken this instance as a watershed moment and turned my life around right then and there. But I was young and didn't pay enough attention to the signs glaring right in front of my face. I was bulletproof, right? I kept doing exactly what I was doing for another month. I remembered what that kind stranger had told me over coffee. He had gently gone over what happens when you push your body too hard. Doesn't matter if you're wearing a suit or a toga. If you try to wring out your body, you're going to end up in the wash. Smart guy. Unfortunately, the coffee was too good. I was back at work that day. But the important things in life have a way of coming full circle, regardless of whether you want them to or not.

As you might have guessed, things started to fall apart. I had been going full-tilt for two years now. I was fired from one of my cooking jobs because I kept messing up the orders. I was a damn good line cook. I didn't mess up anything. *They* were wrong. Assholes! Then one morning I slept through my alarm. Huge surprise. I was late for my job as a package handler. They let it slide the first time. The second time, two weeks later, they were not so nice. I was let go immediately and with a check that had been printed before I got there. Damn. Last, I freaked out at my internship. I can't say why. I was working on a grant and all of the words started to melt together. The phone was incessantly ringing. And the other intern just kept babbling on and on and on. I just remember getting to the bottom of the elevator and then walking all the way home.

I started drinking when I got there. It was 10 AM. I finished everything in the house by noon, then passed out. When I woke up, I jumped out of bed, thinking I was late for work. It was 7 AM the next day. I saw the sun shining through the window in a carefully orchestrated display of hope, generosity, and gratitude. I wasn't spiritual then. I had no idea the confluence of magic and miracle that I was witnessing. All I knew was that I had finally, *finally*, gotten some sleep. And it felt amazing.

It wasn't till much later in life that I saw all these events with clarity. I had become depressed and anxious to an exceedingly unhealthy degree. I had pushed everyone I loved away and had buried myself in work. I was voracious. Then I stopped sleeping. My brain was 'maxed and taxed,' leading to a complete dependence on caffeine to stay operating and awake, and then alcohol and drugs to get it to turn off. My stress was impossibly high. Also, when I stopped sleeping my brain and body never had the time to recover. I was a car that I just constantly kept putting an ounce of gasoline into at a time, forever on the edge of running out of gas, always on the verge of breaking down for good. I was lucky that events conspired to pull me out of this before I legitimately had a heart attack.

See, we are not indestructible. That is why all humans sleep. It is regenerative. It is soothing. It is essential. And when we neglect it we effectively stop the promotion of positive trends in our body and relegate the body's purposes solely to removing toxins, thereby keeping us in survival mode just long enough to chaperone us to our next breakdown. We need to sleep. Moreso, we need to *prioritize* our sleep. No matter how young you might be or how 'capable' you might think your body is, there is always a price to be paid. It could be in a little bit of brain fog and it could be on the molecular level in one of your organs. It could be a complete cascade of failures throughout your entire nervous system (raises hand). Doesn't matter. All of your healthy decisions start with a good night's sleep. So here is how to avoid the mistakes of your favorite travel writer and how to make sleep a priority in your life:

Try not to lie in bed unless you are sleeping.

This was the hardest part for me to master. I am in my mid-30s and still struggle with this. Because now, my bed is awesomely comfortable. Side note: when you finally do 'settle down' and buy a nice mattress, you will never want to leave it. But leave it you must. I remember living in trailers, double-wides, studios, renting rooms with awkward roommates (and staying away from them), and otherwise having every excuse in the world to use my bed as a base of operations. My bed was often the only thing that fit inside whatever room I was staying in. You might be looking at the same thing right now! Yet, you still have to make a serious effort to stay out of it until you are ready to sleep. You have to make your brain associate your bed with sleep and only sleep. No matter what you have to do, this is the absolute key ingredient to allowing you to fall asleep easier.

Stay off your phone before bed.

This is the second hardest thing to do. I love to check the news and my crypto, play some trivia, and otherwise just dink around on my phone before bed. The problem is that I sleep like crap most nights. Thanks, trauma! But these sleep problems are greatly exacerbated by being on my phone before I try to lie down. It's either the stress of the news, the wild amount of information and sensory data a phone provides, or just the fact that I am using my brain when I should be slowly shutting it down. Whatever it is, you will notice a decided difference in how fast you go to sleep and how well you sleep if you can stay off your phone before you lay down. I had to start with five minutes before I closed my eyes. Then I increased that to ten, then to fifteen, then to thirty, and so on.

Turn off the blue lights on your phone.

To be honest, I don't fully understand the science behind this. My ex-wife was adamant about me doing it so I do it. Funny what we hold onto, isn't it? There *is* a ton of research behind blue lights and how they ostensibly limit melatonin production[33]. Considering that melatonin is one of the major chemicals that lead to good sleep and productive sleep habits, you don't

---

33   Silvani, Marcia I., et al. "The Influence of Blue Light on Sleep, Performance and Wellbeing in Young Adults: A Systematic Review." The National Library of Medicine, 16 Aug. 2022, www.ncbi.nlm.nih.gov/pmc/articles/PMC9424753/. Accessed 18 Mar. 2023.

want this limited. I have noticed a decided uptick in the quality of my sleep since I have permanently limited the blue light on my phone.

Don't toss and turn.

I used to think that if I was in bed, I was already doing the best I could do to get some sleep. But all I was doing was stressing myself out more and staying in a low-level, low-quality sleep that didn't help me much. When I am tossing and turning, I always start to mildly freak myself out, thinking: "I only have *this* many hours to get some sleep, I am going to be so tired tomorrow…!" I'm sure we have all been there, especially when we have to get up extra early. The trick is to nip it in the bud. You want to get up and move when this happens. Stretch. Walk around your space. I sometimes even go outside for a minute or two. Let my skin cool off and my senses relax. I breathe deeply and bring myself out of whatever mental circle/ cycle I had gotten caught in. And then I head back, lay down, and try to sleep again. And usually, it works! If it doesn't, I go back to the instructions for insomnia.

No caffeine after 2 PM.

We are all way more sensitive to drugs and chemicals than we think we are. It is just a fact of life that we do not think things affect us as much as they do. Or that we hope they don't. So even if you are on your fifth cup of coffee and are experiencing diminishing returns on your coffee-to-energy ratio, the idea is to stop drinking coffee and focus on getting rehydrated. Because the following cups of coffee or tea aren't going to rev you up as much as you'd like and then they are going to actively affect your sleep quality *later*, which will, in turn, make you more tired the next day. So cut off the coffee around 2 PM. I have heard that noon is actually a better time, but c'mon. Who is going to get all of their stuff done before noon? These dumb nerds aren't going to run *my* life, damnit! Also, what if I want a burger for lunch? This is America. And maybe after that gut bomb I am still regretting, I might want a last gasp of coffee. So yeah, 2 PM, hard cut off, then hydrate as best you can.

Take a nap.

Really, take an *early* nap. I have read multiple times that 'sleep specialists' recommend to not take a nap, ever, if you are going to sleep well at night. And frankly, these people need to be fired. Most of us can't sleep because of our anxiety, which kicks into high gear around bedtime. Whether it is intense, long-term anxiety, or just a smattering of sudden, short-term worries, these anxieties start spinning and keep us up. Maybe sleep specialists are recommending not to take naps without having considered this notion. But what is the best way to calm yourself down and reduce anxiety? Take a nap. If you can, of course. The trick is to do it as *early* as you can. It's not always a possibility with work and social life. If you were up late not sleeping and you have the ability the next day, skip the coffee, get out of bed, and do your thing for a bit, then head back and try to catch fifteen minutes or so. It will help to regulate your anxiety and the stress hormones from the day/night previous. And this reduction will help you sleep later that night. Just make sure not to nap close to bedtime or you'll be up all night.

Work out midday.

This just works for me, so I included it. I have always stressed, in my mental health struggles, to exercise as much as I could. And I found over time that working out in the afternoon was when I had the best sleep. It tires my muscles and makes me feel accomplished so that when bedtime rolls around I can take a shower to ease my aching muscles and joints and use that relaxation as a springboard to hop into bed. Call it momentum building. Or maybe slowing? Either way, it works. And for me, all it takes is twenty to thirty minutes on a treadmill. Ideally, I am doing more but this is a great start and it helps my sleep immensely.

Have some OTC sleeping pills on hand.

I will probably always have trouble sleeping. There are a lot of people like me and a lot of people who aren't. It is what it is. But regardless of whether you have trouble or not, always have a backup plan. I rarely ever take these things. I have no idea what their ingredients are or how they affect people long term. What I do know is that, in a pinch, they can goad you to sleep. I keep them on hand for those rare occasions when I *have* to get some sleep and am having serious trouble.

91| Sleeping in Public Spaces

To be honest, I didn't want to add this section. Both because I didn't want to admit that I knew these things and because I would hope that all the other elements of this book would lead to you never having to use this information. But then I remembered that I don't give a single fuck about what anyone thinks of me. I also remembered that stuff happens. All the time. And if it happened to me, it will happen to you. So, you might need to know this.

I think I am legally obligated to tell you that this is illegal. Sleeping anywhere in a public space is trespassing and most likely vagrancy. This is amazing because if you are traveling or homeless, or both, you do remain human and thus have the same needs as other humans, which include sleep. But I digress. I am not telling you specifically to do something illegal. You should never do anything illegal, no matter how much sense it might make.

Another thing you need to know is that sleeping in public is dangerous. People are going to try to steal your stuff and mess with you in any way that they can. And on the range of possible outcomes that isn't the worst thing that can happen to you. You need to be aware that when you try to sleep in a public area you are putting down your guard in an area where danger might be actively looking for you. Always keep your hands looped through your bags, always have some kind of deterrent, and always be ready to either run or fight if you have to. It is a dangerous world out there and, unfortunately, you might have to sleep out in it a time or two. With that said, here's a bunch of tips to make it easier.

Warm clothes.

We live a lot of our lives indoors. A lot of people even live *most* of their lives indoors. And even if there is no air conditioning or heat in a building, the temperature is still much better (usually) than it is outdoors. So, when we are suddenly forced to sleep outdoors, potentially without even a blanket, then we are rudely woken up to just how cold outside can be. No matter how warm it is during the day you are going to want layers, from thermals to t-shirts to sweatshirts and back down. Maybe even a big, thick jacket. And definitely another layer on your lower half. Two pairs of socks won't hurt either.

Try to stay awake.

It is going to be really, really hard to fall asleep the first time you have to do this. Frankly, it never got any easier for me. This is why I started carrying a tent and stopped hanging out in cities so much in the first place. But that isn't always possible. When you have found a spot that you think is going to cut the mustard, you've layered up, and now you're trying to catch some sleep, try your hardest to stay awake. Don't whip yourself into a neurotic, anxious frenzy. Just try hard to stay awake. You'll be asleep in twenty minutes.

Protect your valuables.

Hide your ID and phone in your pants. Do not play on your phone for hours. It'll make you a target and kill your battery. Don't wear a watch if it is visible. Put any jewelry in your socks. Loop your arms or legs through your pack. If you are not advertising that you have anything to steal, then you are making it much less likely that you'll have a 'buyer' come and peruse your store.

Cardboard.

Just a small piece can make a huge difference. Because the vast majority of us wear shoes most of the time, we completely forget just how *cold* the ground is. It is not warm, fuzzy, or cozy. And when you are sleeping on it, all that coldness (and not fuzziness) tries to leach the warmth from your body. Especially if it is damp. Laying a piece or two of cardboard underneath yourself creates a thin but highly effective layer between you and the ground. It is a massive difference.

Find awkward, weird, hard-to-get-to spots.

The harder the better. Most homeless are either in a shelter, have a tucked away spot that they aren't telling anyone else about, or don't care anymore so they sleep wherever. If you can find a spot that has a little bit of greenery that requires a little climb, or maybe just a short walk, skip, and jump, go for it. Hiding in plain sight is always the best because you want to be near people if someone tries to mess with you, but you don't want anyone to find you first. There are a million little spots like this so train your eyes to see them. This also applies to pull-offs on backroads and other state and national parks. If you have a small tent, you can easily pull in past dark, set up in a few minutes, then get up early and be on your way with no one the wiser.

Rooftops.

Now, everything that is built is owned by someone. Whether it is privately or publicly owned, there is a property line for every building you see. So no matter what rooftop you sleep on, you are trespassing. And trespassing is illegal. So, yet again, I am going to explicitly tell you not to do this under any circumstance. Angry property owners can get twitchy and defensive at a moment's notice. Always best to avoid any such confrontation.

Were you listening to my stern advice never to do this? No? Ok, well, if you are in the city and need a place to lay your head, rooftops could (hypothetically) work for you if the weather isn't bad. They are inherently isolated and the difficulty of actually getting to one dramatically decreases the chances of running into someone else. The things to watch for are fire escapes (which can be lowered), staircases, outdoor elevators, and even indoor staircases and elevators. You'll want to avoid abandoned buildings. They are crawling with people who will put your neck hair on edge. I would always rather be sternly told to leave and have to hit the ground running in the morning than wake up to some kind of other hostility. Or worse.

Busses.

If you're not flat broke and busted, pony up a few dollars for a day-long bus ticket. You are inherently safer because of the presence of the bus driver and a lot of buses have cameras on them. Plus, most people don't get on a bus to start trouble. There is always the risk that the driver will kick you off but that's OK, that's why you buy the day pass. You can just get on the next bus going in a different direction and try again. If you need a nap and aren't comfortable where you are, this is a great solution.

Libraries.

You have to play this right because they are so used to having homeless people come in and cause trouble. As such, they have a hair trigger for kicking people out. It's why the computers have a time limit on them. But if you pick up a heavy book, find an isolated corner, and don't look completely disheveled, you can usually catch a great nap. If you are young enough to look the part and also don't look/smell like garbage, you can also pull off university libraries as well. These usually have tons of places for kids to study, so whip out your phone and headphones, grab a textbook off the shelf, and pass out. If anyone asks just say that you just pulled an all-nighter!

Laundromats.

These are hard to pull off because so many homeless people use the bathrooms to shoot up. A lot of these places also have people who work there to stop people from sleeping. But I added this because it *is* possible. I always took the opportunity to wash my clothes and take a nap in between cycles. I would wash the clothes in my bag as I took a short nap. Then I would go to the bathroom and switch to the clothes I had just washed. After that, I would wash the clothes I had been wearing and take another nap. Voila! Nothing they could do about it and at the end of the day I looked and felt much cleaner.

Well-lit areas.

If you are forced to sleep in a very public space like a doorway or a public park *do not* go to the darkest spots and try to hide. This is a recipe for getting killed. Stay in the light. You are already in a very dangerous situation. You do not want to make it worse by inviting the darkest and evilest people to the party. Getting a ticket or ending up in jail is always better than getting hurt and ending up in a hospital. You aren't going to sleep very well in these areas anyway. Do the best you can, stay visible, and try to hide in plain sight.

Hostels.

I am creative and adaptive. There is always a creative solution to every problem, *especially* if it doesn't seem like there is. One of these is with hostels. They are inherently more traveler friendly than hotels, which might seem counterintuitive, but it is not. Hostels tend to deal with people who are on a lower budget, and they are always looking for people who are willing to clean. I have been flat broke a handful of times and in a cold place, like Denver. It is pretty embarrassing to walk into these places and tell them that you have no money, but it is always worth a shot. I have told the hostel front desk person before that I am happy to clean, cook, paint, mend, whatever they need. I just needed a place for that night out of the cold. They always understood. One time I had to pull a mattress out and sleep in the common room but it was free and it was 12 degrees outside. Way better than freezing to death.

Shelters.

I have mentioned these before, so you probably know my feelings about these. I like to think that these places exist to help those people who are in intensely unfortunate circumstances. I have always been a traveler, moving throughout the world on my own volition. It just seems like taking advantage of the system to me to use these types of programs when I willingly put myself in the situation that I was in. But they are there, they are warm, and they are usually staffed with caring people. If you have no other option, then look one of these up and go there. Just remember to stay wary and keep your stuff close.

Sunglasses.

These are your best friend if you are sleeping somewhere during the day. Parks, fields, squares, malls, etc. If you are wearing shades then you can back cup against a tree or a wall and catch a nap, oftentimes without even appearing to be asleep.

24/7 restaurants.

These are tricky and take a lot of luck to make work. Usually, I just used these as a warm place to be for as long as I could on cold nights when I was traveling from town to town. A lot of the time busses will arrive late at night and then they will close the waiting room till morning. If your next bus, train, or plane isn't till morning then you have some hours to kill. And if you have a couple of bucks, you can afford some coffee. Whenever I pulled this move, I would always be very upfront and honest with the waiter working the graveyard shift. I would always tell them that I was hard up and just needed a warm place to hang out till I could get on with my life. Every single time they were understanding. Maybe a little bit gruff about it but understanding nonetheless. One time I tried to give the waitress my last five dollars for a cup of coffee and a tip. She laughed in my face, poured me coffee all night long, and kept bringing me little 'mess up' food from the kitchen.

Sometimes it's just going to be alright, you know?

Avoid wealthy neighborhoods.

Whether you are sleeping in your car, looking for a spot to stow your van, or trying to find a place outside to sleep, always avoid the wealthy neighborhoods. These people have too much time on their hands and a lot of fear. They are terrified of anyone and everyone. Of course, they don't want to admit this, so they act pompous, but they are really just scared. And because they are scared they will not hesitate to call the police on a moment's notice. Also, they are more observant and tons of them take early morning walks. So, if you are sleeping and they see you, you'll get woken up much, much earlier than you would elsewhere.

92 | Supplements

Our diets are usually crap. It should come as no surprise to any of us. We eat crap. Drive-through fast food? Crap. Assembly-line sandwiches? Absolute garbage. That bangin' Chinese food shack with tattered awnings that look unsafe to walk under but holy crap their General Tso is amazing? Yup, that is not helping you at all. And why not? I thought this was America!?! Usually, there isn't much choice. Either there are no healthy or decent options available, or we just worked our asses off for ten hours and want tacos. But over time the fact that we aren't always eating salads when we should be is going to take a heavy toll on your overall wellbeing. Diets like these are most likely deficient in something. Or a lot of things. And if our bodies are deficient in vital materials then they aren't going to function efficiently. And in come the health problems. Anxiety. Constipation. Other 'gut issues.' Fatigue. Trouble sleeping. You name it, these problems are starting and ending with your diet. And the adage will forever ring true: "You are what you eat."

The good news is that we live in a time in which the constituent parts of our diet have been dissected and analyzed. We now know exactly how many calories our food has, what vitamins and minerals are in it, as well as how much sugar and salt hang around in there too. We can look at a box and tell exactly how good or bad something is for us before we even buy it. And if this information isn't immediately present, then you can hop on the nearest internet-enabled device and get a really good idea. Now, none of us want to live our whole lives counting calories and trying to be a paper-thin 'influencer.' You want to enjoy it. So, you can skip a lot of those details. The important part is that you try to pay attention to the food entering your body and then figure out what *isn't*. When you can get some kind of idea about this then you can figure out how to effectively supplement.

The first thing to remember is that this process is going to take a lot of time. There is no easy solution and there is no simplified way of figuring this out. I wrote earlier about getting your blood tested. This is a great place to start. You can immediately find out if you have an issue with iron, vitamin D, cholesterol, or a myriad of other things. But the rest is going to be purely by feel and by paying attention to your body. For years I would feel like crap after eating. Didn't matter what it was. My guts would distend, I would get supremely tired, and I generally just felt *slow* all the time. Then I cut out dairy. Took a full six months to get it home, as it's in everything, and I felt better! But not entirely. So, I cut out gluten. Bam! I felt *way* better, almost immediately. I had spent thousands of dollars on doctors and treatments. None of it helped even remotely. Then by removing these ingredients I suddenly felt like a human again. I was free to start examining the things I was eating and how they affected me. I am not saying that you have to cut these exact things out. These are just the steps I took to start figuring out what my body did and didn't need. It took years. But when I could finally put my body in a place that wasn't constantly in shock, I could start the process.

I quickly found out that I was missing some things. I lived in Portland, Oregon, at the time, and it is incredibly common in the Pacific Northwest to be deficient in vitamin D. When I started taking this daily, I immediately noticed a positive shift in my mood, more energy, and generally less sad thoughts. Considering this was during quarantine, that's saying something. This sent me down the rabbit hole. I started looking more and more into how supplements can change your life. I realized how personal of a journey this was. I could read self-help and supposed 'health' articles all day. None of their data (if there was any) was going to be helpful or relevant to me. The only way that I could figure this out was by making educated guesses and by feel.

I bought some absolute trash vitamins at first thinking that I was helping myself. For instance, have you ever eaten gummy vitamins? Yeah. Those aren't helping you. They are making it worse. The citric acid messes up your teeth (might as well just eat candy and enjoy it), the 'sugar' gives you cancer, and the companies themselves cannot even guarantee that there is any actual nutritional value to them. That's right. Dig deep into their websites and there will always be a little message that details how the 'vitamins' they are offering may not *actually contain the very vitamins they are being sold for.* And then I realized: what the hell are these vitamins made from? Even if they exist in the little pills I am holding, *where did they come from?* I did a ton of digging and usually couldn't even come up with that answer. This is a huge red flag! What I did find was that the crappy supplements I was taking were made of synthetic nutrients that were stuffed with toxic additives. More crap. I ended up throwing them all away.

As a quick side note, a lot of people are going to try to sell you on a bunch of different stuff. Anyone who does that is a con artist or it is a scam. Multi-vitamins are worthless. Vitamin packs are trash. Most vitamins sold in stores aren't even what they say they are. They are just trying to get you to buy a placebo pill to make yourself feel better for all those trips to the taco truck. Even if they do contain the supplements that they claim they do, the form that these are provided in is probably not effective and the quality is probably extremely low. In short: you are wasting your money buying vitamins and other supplements at big box stores, through celebrity 'wellness' programs, and grocery stores.

So how the hell can you get some decent supplements? It's easy. You are going to have to go online and spend more money than you thought you would. And that's OK. Keep in mind, supplements *do not* have to be taken every day to be effective. And you don't have to take these for really long periods. Just the opposite. You should take these for long enough to make a difference (a month or two) then take a break for the same period. This gives you the maximum benefit of the supplement, provides your body with what it is missing, and helps you to avoid side effects, if there are any, as much as possible. Of course, there are exceptions. I still take vitamin D every day because I'm pale and I don't get enough sunshine. This practice will help you control costs and maximize the benefits for your body. You want to look for companies that care about what they are putting into the supplements. I try hard not to list actual companies because I don't want to be affiliated or tied to for-profit enterprises that might shift what they are doing and make me the asshole. But these companies do exist. One of them has product bottles that are mostly white with blue lettering. That's what I buy. But look for companies that offer supplements that contain:

- **High grades.** Pharmaceutical is the best.

- **Bioavailable ingredients.** The supplements have to get absorbed by your body to do anything. These ingredients do this better than others.

- **Third-party tested.** Meaning someone independent checked to make sure the company wasn't full of shit. Most of these are absolute lies though, so you have to dig to find reputable accreditations.

- **Distribution.** Do not buy your supplements off of Amazon or other cheap, warehouse stores. Most vitamins and supplements need to be kept within a temperature range to stay effective. In the big box distribution centers this does not happen. You want companies that are cognizant of this. If they mention that they ship probiotics with an ice pack, then you have a winner.

- **Sourcing.** You want to know where the supplements were derived from. If this isn't listed, or the information isn't available, then you might not want to take it.

One last note. As I mentioned before, finding the right supplements to take is a long, long process. Don't buy a ton of them and take them all at once. This is just going to overload your system and potentially cause some issues. If you have a serious condition and need some help, spend the money on a naturopath or holistic doctor. Otherwise, take one supplement at a time and pay attention to your body. I started with calcium. I paid attention to my food and noticed that none of it contained *any* calcium. So, when I started taking it regularly, I noticed some positive changes. Now, I take some once a week. It took years to figure all that out. So be patient, get help if you are unsure about anything, and commit to a long-term approach to your overall health and well-being.

93 | Thrift Stores

Despite how cheaply you can get everything online these days there is still a great amount of money and time that can be saved by going to thrift stores. These are everywhere. And that means that there is a wide range of outcomes that are possible whenever you head into them. Some thrift stores aren't actually 'thrift stores' at all. These are the stores that get everything donated to them for free and then try and sell them for almost what they would cost new. A lot of these places will also encourage haggling, which no one wants to do. Avoid these. It's like voluntarily going to the used car dealership of old furniture and used clothes. Real thrift stores are usually small, non-profit outfits that exist on slim margins and high volume. There is always a charity that benefits from it and volunteers that work there. When you find one of these spots remember where it is. If you scan all the thrift stores in a particular area and keep track of the good ones, you can usually find what you're looking for and typically save a ton of money in the long run. Here are some tips to get you started:

Check-in weekly.

There are no set 'delivery dates' for most of these. They just get stuff when they get stuff. And good jeans for five dollars are going to sell quickly. Eventually, you get to know the place so well that you can scan the place in just a few minutes.

Be ahead of the season.

I can't count how many different places I have been in around the holidays. Wherever you are, you still want a tree and some decorations. But what's the point in spending any money on it? The trick is to be on top of it. Thrift stores will put out Christmas decorations right after Thanksgiving. You can roll in, take your pick of whatever they've got, and be done for ten bucks. And this is for every holiday. If you're really smart, and you've got the space to keep some stuff around, you'll check in after the holiday is over and get the things that others have donated at the end of the season.

Know your measurements.

If you're looking for furniture, know what is going to fit in your space. If you are looking for clothes, know what your sizes are. There aren't always rooms to try things on and you don't want to haul a bookcase home that won't fit in the door.

Stay away from fancy areas.

The thrift stores in these neighborhoods have higher rents, which means that they are going to charge a lot more for their products. Yes, you can get designer name brands here, but you're going to pay almost what it costs to get the same things on Amazon. It's never worth it. Stick to the working class and run-down neighborhoods.

Small towns.

Small-town thrift stores are always better. They have better stuff and it is usually much cheaper. Plus, there are always a few things that are weird and funny, which is really what we're all in this for anyway.

Avoid weekends.

Everybody and their mother are going to be there on a Saturday. It's annoying. Go at the beginning or in the middle of the week. You won't feel pressured, and you won't have to constantly wait for really slow people to make really slow decisions about cheap, used junk. OK, that was negative. Just avoid the weekends.

Look for certain things.

There are better things than others to buy at a thrift store. A lot of these are things that we will often need but that other stores make you pay a premium for. By picking these up ahead of time and used you can save yourself a ton of money. These include:

- Jeans
- Furniture

- Picture frames
- Dishes
- Flower pots
- Bags
- Luggage/Duffel Bags
- Clothing hangers
- Books
- Art supplies
- Holiday stuff (+wrapping paper)
- Sporting goods (always be looking to upgrade your gear)

94 | Trading Skills and Services

Everybody is good at something. Some people have been doing it their whole lives; some people are just born with an innate ability. Whatever it is, we are usually paying a considerable amount for all the rigamarole that it requires to get that skillset to the market. Take, for instance, a mechanic. Let's assume that they own their shop. This mechanic is probably paying a lease for the space used for their equipment, marketing, advertising, payroll, accounting, utilities, etc. You get the picture. It's expensive. The same concept applies to just about any trade, skill, or service, too. We all have to spend money to make money.

Except that sometimes we don't.

Running a painting company, I was constantly amazed by how many people would offer me various services (get your mind out of the gutter) in exchange for a simple paint job. Blew my mind. Something so simple and easy to me was a monumental undertaking to some. I was able to trade painting services for photography, mechanic work, carpentry, book-editing services, spiritual counseling, hairdressers, and even massages. Win-win! And a lot of people are just as excited to trade as you are. Bartering is in our blood. We have not always functioned with a fiat currency. Bringing a trade-based system back is something a lot of people will jump at the chance to do.

Now, there is no run-down of how to achieve this. There is a Barter section on Craigslist which can be useful if you randomly come across the right person. Frankly, using this I was typically just inundated with ads and spam. I had more luck with social media and trading apps, where there are

S.C. SANBORN

entire communities of people who were looking for the same thing. If you pursue these avenues, you will be amazed by how much value you can get. Ten massages for painting a single room? Yes, please! Simply analyze what you are good at and what skills you can offer. Then look into bartering and trading groups in whatever arena you currently participate in.

95 | Trains

I was staying in Miami Beach when I came to the startling conclusion that I just didn't belong there (imagine that), and I had my eye on an old pickup truck up in West Palm Beach. So, there I was, sitting in the lobby of one of the worst hostels I have ever stayed in, researching how I was going to get the hell out of there. And then it hit me. A big town like Miami *has* to have a train service. Lo and behold, it had its *own* train service. Jackpot. Two hours later I was headed to the station.

Any traveler who has never taken the train needs to do so immediately. Personally, I hate airplanes and will spend weeks getting somewhere just to avoid them. Some people like it quick and dirty and I get that. But for those of us who like to stay on the ground, this is an avenue you'll want to explore. First of all, it's dirt cheap. I spent $25 getting out of Miami. Then when the old truck turned out to be a junker, I spent $50 on a train from there to Jacksonville. Ridiculous. Gas in that old rust bucket would have been twice that. Second, there is a service car where you can sit and have a drink or five. I mean, they're really expensive and the selection is terrible, but you're just rolling along, bouncing side-to-side, and *ridin'* those *rails*. It's a damn good time.

What isn't great is that it takes forever. This is where most people get turned off about it. You're stuck in an open seat with people coming and going and you never know what you're going to get. Most of the time you get normal, hard-working folks with their families that don't have the money to either fly or drive. It's usually a good mix. Sometimes you get dickwads. But that's everywhere, right? And with the torrential influx of intensely angry people currently assaulting the airline industry, this is a great respite.

It's also dirty. Let's just get that out of the way. The bathrooms are gross and being surrounded by that many people in a closed environment for ten hours lays a thin sheen across you. These cars and tracks are old. They're government owned and, frankly, have seen better days. Still, though, there's a charm to the dirty. It's like an old car that is way past 250k but you love it so much that you're just going to run it into the ground, damn the consequences.

Just because it is so cheap is the best reason to give it a try. If you are on the corridor that they operate on it can save you serious money, even if you're just using it to get to another city with cheaper airfare. There's a reason a lot of their stations are located close to airports. So, when you do try them out, here are a few tips to get you started:

Always be calm and respectful to the attendants.

They work long hours and *do not* put up with any shit. They will take care of you if you show them respect though. And keep in mind, they're the ones that make sure you get off when you're supposed to. If you doze off, it's a really good thing if they have your back.

Bring water.

Lots of it. I have yet to figure out why this is, but I always get off feeling intensely dehydrated, grimy, and tired. I usually take the train for very long periods (14+ hours) so take this with a grain of salt. During this time, I am usually trying to work, drink, and generally pass the time as best I can. Rarely does it occur to me to pound water and take care of my body. Which means I regularly pay the price later. Don't fall into this trap. Drink a bunch of water, even if you're having a good time, and stay away from the tap provided by the train. Do you trust the filters on that thing? Yeah, neither do I.

There's usually an empty car somewhere.

Keep track of where you see people coming and going. If there aren't a ton of people heading in one direction, then there's a good chance that there's an empty car that way. These are great if you're on a long haul and need a break from people. Or if you have any trouble sleeping in the chairs. I've been rudely woken up a few times but most times they don't say anything about it.

Always get out when you have the chance.

You may be worried about your stuff but don't be. Everyone is thinking the same thing. And you will seriously regret it in two hours when your legs are cramping because you haven't moved in two hours. If you are too worried about somebody tampering with your stuff then make sure to stand up and stretch in the aisles. I usually set a timer on my phone for every 30 minutes and do this even while the train is moving. Make sure to take every opportunity presented to you to move or you are going to be miserable halfway through the trip.

BYOF.

Train operators will say not to bring food and other goodies, so definitely bring your own food and other goodies. If you're looking to party, make sure to bring the party favors. Or just a sandwich or five. Head to Aldi or somewhere that sells food at a reasonable rate and grab some snacks as well. It is worth the cost of a rideshare and is immediately compensated when you see how much food costs at the station and on the train.

Bring books and things that don't require service.

All trains claim that they offer reliable Wi-Fi. None of them do. Ditto for cell service. Cell towers are arrayed to maximize the use of people traversing their everyday lives. Railways are placed and located in areas that very specifically aren't around these areas. As such, you are going to experience a lot of outages. I have always used train rides as an opportunity and excuse to get a lot of work done. But you have to anticipate and expect not always being able to do this. A good book/movie will keep you sane when the lights are off, you can't sleep, and there's no cell service.

Have a cover.

This can be either a blanket, a towel, an extra sweatshirt, or whatever. Small blankets work best for me because I can roll them up and keep them outside of my backpack. In a pinch, I use it as a rain cover. Regardless of what works for you, have something that you can throw over your lap. Just like with planes and buses, trains keep the temperature low to discourage the spread of disease. This means that, while the temperature might not seem low when you arrive, after a few hours you might be feeling nipply. Just a thin veneer of fabric is usually enough to cozy you up enough to either doze off or be able to relax.

96 | Van Rentals

I've already gone into van life, so this is just a section for how to go about renting a van. It's pretty simple if you think about it. What do you need? A place to sleep that you can also drive around to everywhere you want to be. And in a lot of countries, this is how they have set up a considerable part of their tourism industry and their public spaces. Looking at you Australia and New Zealand. But you can rent these anywhere in the world. Not to mention, van life is a blast, and living out of a van next to the beach is a type of freedom that most people dream about. And, if you do it correctly, it can be cheap too! But that is only if you get yourself the *right* van.

How do I know this? Because I have, routinely, picked the wrong fucking van. I had just finished a long year of working in New Zealand and I was finally back on the road traveling. My girlfriend and I decided to head to Australia, but we didn't have much of a budget. So, when we showed up in the country, we had to figure out a cheap way of traveling down the coast. We knew that there were a ton of companies who rented vans out, so I immediately found a cheap hostel and started looking at our options. It didn't take long to narrow them down. Some vans are *really* expensive to rent. These are those walk-in Sprinter vans that you see on Instagram posts and travel magazines. Not only are these vans way more than you need but they can also be more than the cost of renting a car and then just staying at decent hotels along the way. For us, those were definitely out of the question. I laid out three options for her (I always gave her three options to pick from because I am awesome) and she immediately picked the one that said 'Hippie' on the outside of the van. I can't make this stuff up. I could see immediately that these were the shittiest, dirtiest vans being advertised anywhere in the country. And they were dirt cheap. Like, one night at a hotel *per week* cheap. We jumped on it. Well, *she* jumped on it. I still had my reservations.

Turns out I was right. The advertisement claimed that their vans were automatic. They were not. I am a very good driver and know how to use a manual like the back of my hand. That does not mean that I *want* to drive a manual. Especially on a casual backpacking trip. In a fucking *van*. So, when the salesman finally made time for us in his busy schedule and took us out to inspect the van, I immediately pointed this out to him. He claimed that that was the only van they had 'ready to go.' We were surrounded by vans. All of them read 'Hippie.' All of them were dirty, crappy-looking vans. I am 100% sure they had an automatic we could have used. But whatever. I was hungover. Tired. Hungry. And I had been in the country for days and still hadn't seen the beach. Plus, my girlfriend was already in a bikini and gave me that pleading, *c'mon* look that she did so well. *Damnit.* I went along with it, signed the papers, and waited till the guy walked away.

And then I remembered that these savages all drive on the left side of the road. This meant that I was not only driving a stick shift van on the wrong side of the road in a foreign country, but I was going to have to do all this with my *left fucking hand*. And when I pointed this out to my girlfriend, she took the cider she was chugging out of her mouth just long enough to laugh and tell me, without breaking eye contact:

"Well, you *are* the expert remember? I ain't touching that thing."

This was going to be a blast.

And that was that. We were at the nearest beach within minutes, throwing sand at each other and playing in the surf. Until we saw the signs detailing how there are crocodiles in the surf that will eat you, at which point we sprinted back to the van. But an hour later, at another beach with no deathly 'crocodile in the surf' signs (real thing), we were having a blast. And aside from gaining a few wrinkles dodging wallabies and losing some hair learning how those psychotic Aussies like to drive, I quickly adapted and a week went by in relative bliss and harmony. Until our van started to fall apart.

The first thing we noticed was that the bed frame was starting to cave in toward the middle and lean back toward the rear of the vehicle. I thought that I was just putting on a few pounds and that I kept parking on an incline until my cohort said the same thing. I examined the actual components of the thing and there it was, a huge crack in both the rail that held one side of the springs and the board that constituted the bed. "OK," we said, "No worries. Nothing is perfect." And we carried on our merry way. Until the next day when the brakes started to make a little whining sound. And come to think of it, the seat I was in kept slowly sliding forward and

I couldn't slide it *back*. I am a tall man. This was a problem. Still, not worth ruining the vacation over. We parked for a few days and just enjoyed the beach. And then we got to Brisbane and the whole thing blew up in our face. I had just navigated my first round of psychopaths, dodging traffic going over endless hills using my left hand and somehow remembering not to turn right *automatically*, when suddenly I switched into third and the entire van slammed forward a few feet. I could smell burning rubber and I was having trouble getting the damn thing to stop moving. The stick wasn't responding either. Normally I would have just pulled over, but we were in the middle of the bustling city, with psychotic asphalt demons on every side, all of whom were now visibly staring at my smoking Hippie van.

She was laughing while trying not to because of my rapidly impending nervous breakdown. Smartly, she quickly jumped onto our 'free campsite and parking' app and found us a spot that we could pull in a few blocks away. Shuddering, stopping, starting, billowing black smoke, with me generally screaming at everything and everyone around us, we made our way through the twisting city blocks. I don't remember much because I was trying really hard to not kill anyone. It was like breaking in a wild, bucking, aluminum colt. Named Mitsubishi, of course. I do remember turning onto the street we were supposed to go to and being faced with hundreds of people. Didn't matter. This van needed to stop and we didn't have a choice. Some dickhead had tried to block off a parking spot with cones so we just ran them over and parked. I turned off the van and let the smoke clear. I didn't bother trying to turn it back on again. She handed me a beer and a cigarette, and I jumped out, hands still shaking like a percussion gun. Not fifty feet away was a Greek Festival. At least that van knew a good time to quit.

And the gyros weren't bad either.

So yeah, even though there might be good food at the end of the road, you're going to need to know what to look for in a van rental. Make it a point to go over what you are renting and be *annoying* with what you see wrong with it. These vans are routinely beat up like a bad UFC fighter and these companies know it. They do want to charge you for all the bumps and scratches that other people put on these junkers. And if you break something they are going to try to charge you double what it costs to replace it. The cheaper the rental the thinner the margin that these companies are operating under. They are trying to make their money back off of *you*. Keep this in mind:

Buy the insurance.

Always buy insurance for any rental you might have. Otherwise, your entire trip is going to have a little cloud hanging over it. That 'what if' question will be in the back of your mind. Buying the insurance doesn't necessarily absolve you from all ills but it will absolve you from *everyone else's*. And this is essential. You are renting this van to have a good time. Possibly even to go on the trip of a lifetime. Trying to save a few bucks shouldn't prohibit you from doing so. You don't want to be constantly worrying about some asshat nicking your doors or a rock flying off on the highway and chipping the window. Buy the insurance and then forget about it.

Read the contracts and agreements.

As I mentioned, a lot of these companies are operating on razor-thin margins. The salespeople are given bonuses and commissions based on how many vans they sell and how much money they can bring back from their customers. Every time I have taken the time to read the contracts, I have found something in there that wasn't advertised, or that was directly advertised *against*, and brought it to their attention. At which point they acted like they didn't know what I was talking about, walked away, and came back with another contract that didn't contain that crap. I get it. You're going to be tired, weary, and decidedly *not at the beach*. But take your time with this part. Get the right van and make sure the contract is agreeable. If and when something goes wrong, you will be glad you did.

Check the outside of the vehicle.

Start with the tires. You don't have to go crazy with this. Just be ready to tell them 'no' if they are trying to get you to take a vehicle with four completely bald rubber donuts. This will be your first pass around. Prepare yourself to circle the car four or five times. It'll look weird but you'll have plenty of opportunity to give yourself the time to think about what you are looking at. Next, check for scratches, nicks, and dents. Log them all. Make sure that the salesman is also marking them down. I always take pictures of these, even the ones on the roof. If and when they try to come at you for these later, you have proof that these were there before you took off. On your third pass look for things that might have fallen off previously, i.e., the bumper and the headlights. You'll also want to check that these work. Getting a ticket on vacation for someone else's mess-up is never a fun deal. And then just take a leisurely stroll around the vehicle to make sure you didn't miss anything. Never hesitate to be as annoying as possible at this stage.

Check the inside of the vehicle.

First thing first, check the seatbelts. They don't always work, especially in the older vans. Also, try all the knobs, levers, buttons, etc. Occasionally these will simply fall off and if they do, you need to let the salesperson know. These are the highest chances of you getting an unsuspected bill after you bring the van back. Make sure to also look for tears and rips in the seats, the overhead liner, the doors, and the 'trunk' area. Make sure that all the knobs on the dash do what they are supposed to do, especially the radio and the blinkers. Last, check the floor for stains.

Look at the engine.

You don't have to know anything about what you're doing. You don't even have to pretend. The person 'selling' you the van probably won't either. You just have to look for anything that is *visibly* messed up. Because those are the same things that will come back to haunt you.

Take it around the block.

I have rented so many vehicles where they just assume that you're OK with grabbing the keys and that's it. Blows my mind. I always insist on taking it around the block once. How else am I going to be able to check the brakes? They will make you sign the paperwork first. You don't want them in the cab with you anyway. Don't hesitate to take that thing right back if you have a bad gut feeling or if you have trouble getting it to stop or turn.

97| Waiting Tables

There truly is no better way to work and travel than to wait tables, bartend, or otherwise work in a restaurant. Eating food is an inherent part of the human experience and every restaurant needs warm bodies to work there. These jobs usually come with cheap housing and various incentives to keep you there for the duration of 'the season,' at which point they kick you out into the wild. While at no point do they care about your mental well-being, offer benefits of any kind, nor will they take care of you if anything goes wrong, there is a ton of money to be made if you know how to work it and stay positive. Which is easy, because these people know how to *party*. It is no surprise that most of my best and worst stories come from this line of work.

Know this, I spent too much time working in restaurants. I got jaded and antagonistic. It was a major life event the day that I finally decided to give it up for good. Crazy stuff. I wouldn't recommend spending your life doing this. Still, if you're going to join the club and be a waiter, here's how to be really, really good at it:

The Basics.

The first part is getting a job. The easiest way to do this is to just find a place you want to be. There will be a restaurant there and they will forever and always be hiring dishwashers, cooks, and bussers. All these are dirty, crappy jobs. If you have the choice, take the front-of-house job. That's the only way to watch what the 'servers' are doing. I always detested that word. They are waiting on you, not serving you. Only people who are truly bereft of anything good in their lives think they need someone to *serve* them. Get a grip. Anyway, be a host or a busser or whatever you need to do. Everyone needs to start from the bottom. The trick is to not *stay there*.

A good busser, host, and dishwasher are worth their weight in platinum in a restaurant. Everyone, and I mean *everyone*, who is on staff is hoping that you will keep doing that job well for your entire life. Oh sure, they will say that they truly care about you. Some will 'tip you out' better than others. I certainly did. But I also knew, the entire time, that I was making *a lot* more money than they were. Start from the bottom but never, ever get satisfied.

It should take you four to five weeks to get 'promoted' to being a waiter. Anything more than that and they are blatantly lying to you, and you should find somewhere else to work. At this point, you will understand how a restaurant works and you can just fake it on the next job. Just rewrite your resume to say that you were a server, find a buddy or a server at that restaurant who thought you were cool, put *them* down as your reference, and BAM, on to the next job. I mean, ideally, you stay at the same place, right? But every restaurant is virtually the same. The only difference is how much money there is to be made and at what position. Make sure you're in the right position.

There is a caveat. Waiting tables is a bit of selling your soul if you're going to be good at it. I know I did. The happiest people I knew were always the bussers. They made about 10% of what I made but without any of the stress of actually dealing with people. They just pretended they didn't hear what they were being asked or didn't speak English. Legends. So, there's always that. Frankly, I was never really around long enough to see if any of it was worth it in the end, but they were a lot happier and calmer than I was at the time.

But we are going to assume that you want to make money. And we are also going to assume that you have 'worked your way up,' really it is *down* but tomato, tomato (isn't it amazing that you just read that word two different ways without being asked to), or just lied on your resume. Which you should absolutely do. Skip the line and save yourself time. Who said that though? Not me. Anyway, back to making tons of money. Waiting tables is absolutely, 100% about confidence. The golden adage that you should live your life by while doing this job is: "Either dazzle them with brilliance or baffle them with bullshit." I never once, not once, memorized a menu. What I *did do* was bribe the cooks on the very first day. And I continued bribing these hardworking, sweat-drenched assholes until the day I quit with racks of beer and money. Because they would always fix my messes, 'spec. prep.' the orders that I put in incorrectly, and generally take care of their favorite waiter. Take care of your cooks and they will take care of you.

Anyway, I never once memorized a menu. Why waste all that time when I was most likely going to quit or get fired within the month? Man, I had *issues*. Anyway, the trick is to perfect the ability to respond to questions confidently. People are idiots in restaurants. They are perfectly capable of making their dinner at home, or a sandwich, but they typically come to the restaurant for one of three reasons: to impress someone, take a break from regular life, or take out their shitty lives on their waiter. Nine times out of ten the latter is the one asking all the questions. "But is it glazed in pure baby duckling fat? I only eat *baby* duckling fat. I mean, fresh out of the egg. And what was the *name* of this particular duckling? I hate the name *CHAD*." They actually say this crap, looking at their spouse, who is presumably named Chad.

You get the picture though. These people are assholes who are hungry. And they prance around, putting on a big show for the entire restaurant, asking stupid questions, and otherwise making your job way harder than it needs to be. I always just cut to the chase, gave the best answers I could, clipped their sentences (talked just as they were finishing) to establish that I was in a hurry, and generally tried to make their 'orders' as simple as I could. Cooks hate high-maintenance customers and you want your cooks to adore you. If you do this with confidence, ignoring any awkward pauses or moments, and generally just moving on from one thing to the next, you will mitigate the impact of the douchebags in your section and maximize your income. All it takes is unyielding, unwavering confidence. Save the tears till everyone is out the door.

Multi-task.

To wait tables well you are going to have to hone and develop your ability to do multiple things at once. A lot of people fail at this because they think that they can do several things at the same time. You cannot. We were born with two arms, two legs, and one brain. The best that you can do is to make your trips taken between where the food is made and the people eating it more efficient as a means of saving yourself as much time as possible. To someone sitting down at a table, time is going to move much more slowly than you, meaning that an actual five minutes in real time is going to feel like fifteen to them, and it is going to feel like thirty seconds to you. This efficiency might just shave off a whopping 'ten minutes' to your hungry assholes.

The engine behind all this is a rapidly changing and adapting structure of what needs to be done. There are always, always things to do. And this isn't the 'side work' that all restaurant workers despise for good reason. Their wages are slavery wages. If they aren't making tips then they are getting paid only a few dollars per hour because side work doesn't get tipped. Anyway. A great waiter I knew once told me to keep a list of ten things that you have to accomplish in your head at all times. Constantly keep moving to get that list completed. Not surprisingly, this list gets constantly adapted and updated. It is really hard at first because we all want to mosey and chat and generally meander through, so staying direct and focused for a long period can be difficult. But after some practice, you learn to rarely forget anything that people have requested of you, adapt easily to changes, and take care of dozens of people *at the same time*. The perk of this is that while you *physically* work harder, you don't have to strain yourself as much mentally. Your tables can see that you are flying from task to task, pausing only to smile and drop one-liners and ask how they are doing, rather than trying to actively engage in conversation. This was my *Zen*, my happy place, when I waited tables. A bustling restaurant where I stayed constantly busy, but not so busy that I was overwhelmed. Just at the cusp, riding the wave.

You don't have to master this overnight. You are going to make mistakes and you are going to drop things. Hungry assholes are going to behave like hungry assholes. So, when working to reach your multi-tasking potential just keep in mind to keep moving forward and keep achieving things on your list. Hit tables three, four, and seven on one pass with some water. Even if they don't want any you have demonstrated that you are thinking of them amongst your business. Then get to tables three and eight with refills, on the way back drop off a condiment caddy to table five. Table six just got sat? Walk by them while you are doing this, say hello, and tell them you'll be right with them. Are you getting the picture? All ten of your tables see that you are constantly in motion and that you haven't forgotten about a single one of them. You have, no doubt, forgotten about a ton of them, repeatedly, during this time. But your constantly changing and adapting list, combined with your effort and drive to keep accomplishing goals, is what is pushing the cart ever further along the track.

Understanding your customers.

Everything about making money waiting tables starts with a basic understanding of the average diet for most people. It is no coincidence that there are a ton of people who act up in restaurants and other hospitality-based businesses. This is where they want to come so that they don't have to work to prepare any food. They were already hungry before they even got in their car. A lot, if not most, people wake up and immediately start consuming highly processed, sugary, nutrient-deficient food. Their blood sugar raises dramatically after eating this crap and their body immediately starts to strain to process all these ingredients. This process is highly taxing on the body. It should come as no surprise that the first thing any dietician or gastroenterologist will tell you to fix any of your ailments is to start eating more vegetables and less processed foods. Furthermore, a lot of people will feel more groggy and tired around early afternoon and will reach for more coffee or more sugary drinks/snacks. This perpetuates a cycle where they place intense strain on their body and cause dramatic fluctuations in their glucose levels. This is somewhat of a roller coaster in the sense that we cause 'fires' just to put them out. You can't walk into anyone's house in the morning and force them to eat a healthier breakfast. In this country, you'd get shot. So, when these hungry assholes show up you are just an unwilling participant in their glucose/emotional rollercoaster.

Now here these people are, hungry, most likely hypoglycemic, tired, and stressed, and they might not know it yet themselves. They might even have to wait for a table for thirty minutes or so, then another five minutes for you, their waiter, to have time to stop by their table. Remember, they live in a time vortex. To them, they have now been waiting three hours. When you *finally* show up (shut the fuck up, Karen) they are then going to have to wait again just to get drinks, then again for their food, then again for you to bring them a check. Altogether this is an absolute nightmare for this hungry asshole who has willingly subjected their body to a ridiculous amount of stress, refuses to simply make themselves a sandwich, then refuses to have one iota of self-awareness and grace for a bunch of underpaid and overworked hospitality workers.

Sound familiar?

The real trick here is to understand them better than they understand themselves. What they need is sugar for their mini-sugar hangover, crayons to entertain their sugar-addicted children, and the respect that their parents refused to show them as children sublimated into a *need* to have someone *serve* them. Oh wait, can't do that, but you can (temporarily) fix the sugar and crayons part. The first step is to get them something to drink, even if they don't want anything. A lot of times if I would see someone acting up while they were waiting in line. I would just swoop by and hand them a glass of orange juice, 'on the house.' Some people might have been pissed about this but I never took the time to notice. I was busy, I made a judgment call, and I helped someone out before they even knew that they needed it. Just do your best to get them some kind of sugar or coffee or *something* that is going to take the edge off. You'll be amazed how many 'hours' people are willing to wait if their bodily needs are taken care of.

The second thing to pay attention to is that people are in the public sphere. A lot of people fear death, pain, mutilation, and other horrible things. But what do people fear the most? Humiliation and embarrassment. This is why you'll see people freaking out the most about not getting their food when everyone else has gotten theirs. They see themselves as slighted, forgotten, mistreated and all their childhood trauma is now spilling out into your section. Usually, this is because someone dropped a plate or a ticket got lost. But, usually by absolutely no fault of your own, now this person is standing up and yelling at everyone. It is a basic, primal urge to try and reassert dominance and subvert their intense fears of being embarrassed. And this isn't just when they don't get their food. People on dates, couples trying not to fight, loudmouths, business people, young people trying to find out who they are, you name it, a lot of people are participating in the public sphere in an attempt to remedy something they are lacking in their lives. And you are front and center to the whole show. You are the only moving part that it is 'socially acceptable' to treat poorly, or with disrespect, or to complain to if they are hungry.

Next, depending on the type of restaurant you are in, people are either used to being pampered or used to being treated like dirt. Being able to size people up based on this distinction is what is going to make you the most money. If someone is used to being pampered, then they automatically have an overblown sense of self-worth and are most likely chock full of crap up to their eyeballs. These are the people who go to restaurants to treat people like crap, ordering them around and generally acting like they are better than everyone else. You will run into a lot more of these people if you work at a nicer restaurant. Even though most restaurants use the *exact same ingredients* yet charge very, very different prices, people like to assign their self-worth to how much they are paying. These people are the reason I don't do this job anymore. But you *can* make your biggest tips off of them because that is how they try and prove that they are better than you, as they can afford to leave bigger tips. You'll see a lot of waiters bend over backward to fawn over these people. It is what perpetuates the cycle of their behavior. They quickly learn that they can lord over entire restaurants and they will be treated better for doing this. I was no different and I made a ton of money doing it. It wasn't till much later that I realized that if I simply treated them like *anyone else*, I started making even more money. Why? Because everyone else in the restaurant *isn't* like that.

Most people are good, wholesome, 'normal' folks who just want to have a decent meal and need to fix their blood sugar. These are people that are either used to being treated like crap or have been treated that way a lot in the past. All these people are sitting next to each other in adjoining tables. Everyone hears and sees each other. If they see you treating pampered people the same way that you are treating them, you will win them over. People are going to tip what they are going to tip. By maintaining your sense of self-worth, purpose, and general demeanor, and by working your ass off, you are going to maximize your chances of making *the whole room* happy. That is not only the key to maintaining your sanity but also to maintaining your self-esteem alongside it.

I get it. This all sounds pretty negative and cynical. To a degree, it is. In travel, hospitality, and the so-called 'service industry,' you routinely see the worst in humanity. And not only for all the reasons outlined above. Frankly, I knew I was done bartending when a blackout-drunk neighbor of mine came into the bar I was working in, walked right up to me, and promptly spit in my face. This was actually impressive because I am tall and she was very short. There was no provocation for this. We had no romantic involvement, I had done absolutely nothing to her, and I hadn't even spoken to her in a week or so. And the next day? She was right back in the bar. Didn't even remember. To make matters worse, at that moment I had about seven off-duty police officers sitting at the bar hanging out. All of them started to stand and I immediately put up my hand. No need to get a local arrested who's not even going to remember why. Fucking Montana. But as soon as that happened, I felt a seismic shift in my chest. I had faced almost everything you could face behind the bar. I had even been spat *at* before. It was having a random person come out of the universe and directly spit on my face *for absolutely no reason* that finally made me face the fact that the entire industry was predicated on allowing people to take out their problems and place their burdens on someone else, if only just for the five seconds it takes to storm in and spit on their face.

This isn't being cynical, this is reality. And you have to be able to make that distinction. You have to be able to understand who these people are and why they are that way if you are going to do this for a considerable period. If you can't do that then you shouldn't do any of these jobs. There *are* a lot of great people in the world. In this industry, however, you don't always see them. And being able to confront that reality is essential to not only doing your job but to making a ton of money doing it.

Work hard.

Always remember, there is nothing that will get people to convince themselves not to tip you than to appear lazy or uninterested. And this isn't just limited to tips. If you're getting paid to do something, then whoever is paying you is going to be irritated if you aren't at least trying. People work hard for their money. They don't mind spending it, and they certainly don't mind tipping you, but they *do mind* handing over their money to someone who they perceive as working less hard than they do. It's annoying to be ignored; to want a beer and not be able to just go and get one yourself. It's also really annoying to have someone play on their phone when they are supposed to be doing their job. This doesn't mean that you are a robot and that you need to give 100% of your heart, soul, and attention to these hungry assholes. But keep in mind that if people see you being lazy or tapping on your phone while they are in their sugar-hangover-induced time vortex then they are going to decide that you are lazy and do not deserve their extra money.

Look them in the eye and tell them you messed up.

This is the hardest part for some people and it really shouldn't be. I learned to do this all the time. Doesn't matter if I dropped a plate or their toast came out burnt. I was always doing my best to get as many of the things done as they requested of me. When something went wrong, I immediately went straight to them and told them what happened. I never profusely apologized or made it seem like a bigger deal than it was. Hungry assholes tend to be dramatic. But I did look them right in the eye and admit my mistake. More often than not they immediately respected me more and were completely understanding, particularly if it was really busy. Of course, some people are going to freak out and be dicks about it. Comes with the territory. But if your *modus operandi* is to admit your mistakes and own them then you are going to sleep easier and your workday is going to go a lot smoother as well.

Make it right.

When I was first learning how to do this job, I would routinely mess things up, blame everyone else, then try to take the company for whatever I could get away with to make up for my mistakes. For example, waiters are routinely in charge of making their own desserts. This means that they rarely have any accountability with any of the other staff for having to report or admit that they even sold one. The same thing goes for drinks. Pretty much anything that isn't cooked or alcoholic. This means that I would always just offer people a free piece of cake to make up for the fact that I had been on my phone and I had completely forgotten to ring up their order for the (actual) thirty minutes that they had been waiting. Or give them their sodas for free. Whatever it was.

I *was* on the right track; I was just doing it wrong. This is where owning your mistakes, having a good rapport with your manager, and having best buddies cooking your food come into play. Being able to just look someone in the eye and tell them you messed up is the key element to being able to make money. You are not a hustler trying to make a couple of bucks regardless of the consequences. You are here to enjoy your life, make some friends, participate in your community, and generally find a path to happiness along the way. Treating the people you work with as pawns in your pyramid scheme of bullshit is not going to get you anywhere. And anyone who has ever worked in the hospitality industry long enough can spot people like that after one shift. So don't be that way! I learned this the hard way after I was shown the door a dozen different times.

Ultimately the lesson was this: communicate, use your team, and generally 'make it right' for your customers. Forgot to punch in an order? Run into the kitchen and ask the chef to hurry it through. They will do their best because they most likely want you to succeed. They respect you because you didn't try to sweep it under the rug and blame it on someone else. Did you drop a tray of martinis on a nine-year-old girl in her favorite fancy blue dress (true story)? Yeah, go grab your manager and tell 'em. They will probably want to pay for that meal. And if you *do* have anything in your power to make it right with your tables then definitely do so. Just don't steal anything!

There is always a creative solution.

Remember, you don't work in an office where you need to adhere to a strict code of etiquette. You don't have to write business emails, wear a suit, or deal with micromanaging. You are free to do almost whatever you want. And if you aren't, switch jobs, cause that place sucks. This entails that you are given a license to be yourself and pursue creative solutions to routine problems. I used to keep some of the crayons and pieces of paper in the back near my cash register. Before my shifts on Fridays and the weekends, I would preemptively draw a few smiley faces with rainbows and people dancing, or crying, whatever I felt like at the time. When I screwed something up, and inevitably I would screw something up, and the time came to drop their check I would slip this little crayon drawing in there. Then I'd show up, crack some half-hearted joke about how I draw these before my shift and walk away. Nine times out of ten they took the drawing with them. They were funny! And this is just one example. The beauty of the service industry is that no two interactions are ever truly the same. They always have some kind of wiggle room. And this wiggle room is the area in which you can make a ton of money if you put your mind to it.

Bluffing.

You're going to end up bullshitting a lot of people. It's inevitable. You answer the same damn questions over and over again. You tell the same adages and stories. You make the same jokes. Generally, you also go a little crazy in the process. And that's OK as long as you keep the blatant lies to a minimum and never actually start lying to yourself. Always give yourself some slack. It's a tough job and you're doing the best that you can. There are also a lot of things that go down in a restaurant that you just can't tell your tables. They wouldn't understand even if they understood. If the huge vat they make soups in accidentally gets tipped over and for some reason the drain was plugged, then the entire kitchen is going to be flooded with tomato bisque (true story). You aren't going to throw one of your cooks under the bus because they are your best friends, so you're going to have to look someone in the eye and tell them that the soup 'sold out' hours ago. Even with the adjoining table annoyingly slurping right next to them.

The trick to this is looking someone dead in the eye, not wavering or hesitating at all. Confidence is everything in this business. If you say something confidently they *will* believe you, regardless of other evidence that may be surrounding them. If they come back at you with disbelief just shrug, repeat what you said, and if they're still pissed, just walk away. They are going to tip you or they aren't. You are the voice and personality of a large machine that spews out food. As such, you are solely responsible for relaying information to a bunch of hungry assholes who think that the entire thing is *simple*. Have confidence, believe in yourself, and always see yourself as the 'front line' of an army of your friends.

Check-ins.

This is simultaneously the easiest and hardest thing to master in all of the hospitality industry. There is no way to really tell if your tables want you to continue to check in with them repeatedly or if they want you to leave them alone. Everyone is different, everyone has a separate way of communicating, and everyone expects this person whom they've never met to immediately understand their verbal and nonverbal communication style. But checking in with every one of your tables is one of the most crucial elements to making money. You have to show them that you care and that you are doing the best that you can. Also, trying to get them to buy more things is only going to help your bottom line.

Approaching tables.

This is where confidence comes back into play. You are busy, you have a lot to do and little time to do it in, and you have to walk up to a group of people you've never met and start talking. It can wear you out quickly, even if you are extremely extroverted. The key, again, is confidence. You have to simply walk up and start talking. This is especially true if it is a large group of people. Making them all pay attention long enough for you to effectively do your job is like herding cats down a garden hose. So just walk up, start talking, and if they don't respect you, then walk away and keep working. They will eventually respect you because they are hungry.

Dealing with douchebags.

The world is full of douchebags and degenerates. And they all share one thing in common: bringing to bear the things in their lives that they can't or won't deal with on people who don't deserve it. We have all heard that these people must be really unhappy or that they must have an unhealthy home life. While that is probably true, we will never really know for sure. What we do know is that everyone has issues and that most people don't deal with them in healthy ways. On a positive note, that may be changing. There has been a ton of talk about an 'awakening' during the side effects spawned by a global pandemic. Mental health and well-being are at the forefront of the global consciousness more than ever before. The fact remains. Most people are stunted and distorted by the crap that has happened to them in their lives. As a worker who often deals with the public at large, you are not only going to come face to face with these issues and they are going to come disguised as people who believe that they can tell you what to do. And for better or worse, your income depends on it. So, dealing with these types of douchebags, not to be confused with just your run-of-the-mill hungry assholes, is going to be imperative to your success.

The number one thing to remember about dealing with douchebags is *not to engage*. If you participate in their need for conflict and drama you will only bring negativity into your world. This is much easier said than done. It is hard to look someone in the eye while they are treating you like crap or trying to bully you and simply not react. But that is exactly what you must do. The biggest mistake people make is to bend over backward for these people. Either in fear of losing their job or by simply not wanting to deal with any potential negativity, they simply acquiesce to the douchebag. You've heard it a million times. "Yes sir, of course, sir, I am so sorry sir." It's heartbreaking to see. And the cost of this type of back-bending is immeasurable. By doing so you have brought home this douchebag's bullying as part of your psyche. Not only did you actively engage, but you also actively *enabled* this douchebag. You participated in the enactment of their inability to deal with their problems and thereby taught them that *it is OK to act like that*. You cannot be afraid. I am not saying to start an argument or talk to them the way that they talk to you. And I am not saying to not do your job, which is to hand them food. All you have to do is *not engage*. Just stare at them. Smile at their rudeness. This very act will usually get people to calm down. Or get them to ramp up, which is even better because then you can just walk away. If your employer ever had a problem with you doing this, quit immediately. They are most likely douchebags themselves. If you can't do that, keep working with the knowledge that you didn't sell out any part of your soul for a paycheck.

If you must speak to them in this instance, point to the facts as if you would a small child. I perfected my 'Dad' voice early on. When someone crossed the line, even slightly, I would ask them simple questions about their experience. How long they had been there. How their day was. If they 'needed' anything *in my power* I could get them. My tone and the direction of my questions would gently yet assertively remind them that I was human, that they were out of line, and that they were making fools of themselves. Also, that I am not a fucking magician that could pull a three-course meal out of my asshole. Believe it or not, this usually ended up with a fat tip. It is an art, however. If you inject any disdain or shade into your tone you are playing with fire. An angry douchebag playing dress up in a room full of other people who are pretending not to watch them is a recipe for drama. But if you keep it stern, adult-like, and stick to the facts, you can thoroughly embarrass a douchebag in front of the entire room. And it is priceless.

One-liners.

I've heard some really good jokes and one-liners in my travels. They are an extremely useful tool in any job that you work, and this is particularly true in a business where you see so many people at one time. If you are hoping I will list these then I am truly sorry to disappoint you. These are personal things. You have to figure out what's funny to you and then use this to the best of your abilities. If it's not funny to you then chances are you're going to either offend someone (oh no!) or you're going to piss someone off. That, my friends, is how to hurt your bottom line. But keep track of things that genuinely made your tables or customers laugh. Then use it whenever you are uncomfortable or are in a hurry. I used to write them down at the end of the shift over a cocktail. Eventually, it got to the point where I barely had to think anymore when it was busy. I could just pull from a bottomless well of tacky one-liners to keep my tables happy and laughing as I made stacks of dough. Find your own. See what works for you. Then make it part of your 'act.'

Random Advice

- Just show up. 99.9% of life is lived and learned by showing up.

- Don't set life goals anywhere near other people.

- Try to buy gas at night or in the morning. Gasoline expands in the heat, so the colder it is when you're filling your tank, the less you'll end up buying.

- Enthusiasm is the most effective cover for inexperience.

- Put all of the important things you are going to need the next day in or on top of your shoes.

- Bring gum to uncomfortable situations. It calms you down and makes you look more confident.

- If someone hands you a banana, answer it like a telephone.

- Let people pass you if they want to drive faster than you. They will get pulled over before you do.

- Always spin the laundry machine when you are done. There is bound to be a sock or two clinging to the top of the machine.

- TSA will sometimes try to rattle your cage. Just smile, give a little laugh, and walk away.

- Airfare websites track you with cookies. Always delete your cookies before buying airplane tickets, as the prices go up if you've visited the site multiple times. The same thing goes for hotels, car parts, etc.

- If you have to call 911, immediately tell them where you are.

- Let people vent before you give them advice.

- Having a friend with a boat is way, way better than owning a boat.

- Hotel TVs usually have USB ports. You know, if you lose your charging box. Again.

- Highway signs tell you which side the exit will be on by which side the exit number is on the sign below it.

- If you clogged the toilet and are too embarrassed or don't have a plunger, put a cup of hot water and a handful of salt in the toilet, wait five minutes, and try to flush it again.

- I've said this a few times already, but it's important. Always carry a doorstopper. They are the cheapest and most effective way to protect you in any room you are in, especially the bathroom.

- If your car breaks down on the side of the road and you have to leave to get something, like gas or parts, leave a plastic bag hanging out the side of the window closest to the street. This will let the police know you aren't planning to abandon the vehicle.

- Restaurants in the U.S. are legally required to give anyone free tap water at any time, even if they aren't a paying customer.

- If anyone is ever offering a job that is 'perfect for a student,' then they are trying to get you to do a job for half of what it's worth, they are not going to pay you for your gas or time traveling to their location, and it is guaranteed to be labor-intensive work.

- If someone is emotional and you don't know what to do, offer them some water.

- Don't turn your socks right side in when you're folding them. You will always have more energy and willingness to do this in the morning when you put them on and thus, you won't even notice doing it.

- Burned a pan? Don't spend hours scrubbing with a sponge or steel wool. Soak it for an hour then grab a bamboo spatula. A little elbow grease and it'll come right off without scratching your pans to hell.

- Never go to the second bar.

- Put things back (when you do find them) where you first looked for them.

- Las Vegas is a filthy and depressing place if you aren't going to spend a ton of money there.

- If you have to mail a check to anyone, fold up a piece of paper and put the check in the middle. This will prevent anyone who is trying to read through the envelope from seeing there is a check inside and potentially stealing it.

- Everyone is shy. Some are better at hiding it.

- Relationships are never a waste of time. They teach you what you want, what you don't want, and everything you could possibly want to know about yourself.

- Look hard for '3-star' reviews. You'll get the most realistic take on whatever it is you're thinking of buying.

- Unless you really want to be in New York City, do not drive in New York City.

- Don't analyze your life or make decisions past 10 PM.

- If you put a glass of water in the microwave with a pizza it'll keep it from getting hard (in places) and spongey (in the other places).

- Never lie to your doctor.

- When you are 99% done with a large project, like a book, you are only 50% done.

- Go to a pumpkin patch and pick out a pumpkin at least once a year.

- Don't put your hands where you wouldn't put your crotch.

- In a pinch, you can make sausages in a coffee pot.

- Keep an old gift card with $10 or so on it and use it for free trials, shady $1 deals, and the deposit on dive motels.

- Use telemarketers as live auditions for your acting career and impressions.

- If you have to clean up puke, pour coffee on it and leave it for a minute before you get down to it.

- Never get attached to furniture.

- Eat oranges while hiking to keep your muscles from getting sore.

- Always drink a glass of water in the morning before your first cup of coffee.

- Pineapple juice is a better cough suppressant than over-the-counter medicines.

- Walk quickly and intently, with your gaze fixated on the horizon, and the crowd will move around you.

- Empty (and cleaned) chap-stick containers are great money-holders.

- When you are having a bad day, force yourself to smile as big as you can. Probably looks crazy as hell but it helps a lot.

- If someone is acting suspiciously behind your car, take four right turns in a row. If they are still behind you then they are definitely following you.

- Go online and have your mail forwarded the day before you move somewhere else, even if your 'new address' is your Grandma's house while you're backpacking South America.

- Spray flying insects with water. They'll immediately drop and you can pick them up and toss them outside.

- When traveling, always go to the furthest, craziest place on your list first. When you head back to the more 'mundane' places, you'll appreciate them more.

- Embrace nuance. It is art, magic, and the spice of life.

- Read a biography before you ever consider trying to get famous.

- In a pinch, you can use potato chips as a fire starter.

- Coca-Cola can clean just about anything if you leave the object soaking in it overnight.

- Don't drink Coca-Cola.

- Pool noodles are surprisingly handy for a lot of things.

- Always carry some TP when traveling.

- If you get married, sign a pre-nuptial agreement.

Afterword

It's pretty amazing how things come around.

I never thought that this book would ever be finished. I figured it would be a permanent pet project, like a half-built '67 Mustang in the garage. There are an infinite amount of subjects that could have fit into this book. And I have so much left to learn and experience. Just from the time that I finished the first draft to the time I had edited the third, I had gotten divorced, moved states and switched careers multiple times, been homeless, and otherwise experienced more upheaval than a lot of people will experience in their entire lifetime. And going through all of this at a later stage of life forced me to learn new things and adapt in creative ways. Maybe this is how it will always be.

After six rounds of revision, I finally had the courage to send this out to some beta readers. I had this niggling doubt that I should have wrapped it all up with, gasp, an afterword section. But I talked myself out of it. This book stands as it stands. It is what it is. Until I revise, edit, and publish the second version, that is. Several of my beta readers noted that this afterword section would be a great touch. Well, damn it, I was *going to…*

Anyway. Here we are. This book is designed to be repetitive, by the way. I highly doubt that most people are going to read this cover to cover. As such, it is intentionally organized in such a fashion as to provide the most salient and important information at particular places that will be most utilized. Where does a savvy person put their 'yard sale' sign? Outside their house, nestled at the back of the cul-de-sac? Or at the busy intersection a half mile away, with signs that lead you in the right direction? Doesn't take a marketing degree to know how to sell that used recliner.

There are also things that are going to constantly change and be updated. As such, this is just the 1st Edition. I will always be learning and recommend the same. I cannot count how many people I see on a daily basis who act as if they know everything; as if they have it all figured out. I do not see joy or peace in their eyes. Rather, I see pain, boredom, and self-loathing. I refuse to be like that anymore. So, I will be constantly tweaking and updating the edges of these pages. But it is about damn time to put this out into the world!. I hope you have enjoyed it.

I can pretend that it was an absolute joy and pleasure to write but the truth is that it was oppressive and back-breaking. I love to write. I loathe editing. And I had to edit it this entirely by myself. I simply couldn't afford any more help than the bare minimum. As such, there are probably still a bunch of typos and grammar rules that I have broken. Oh well. I feel like I just shepherded a very, very difficult step-child into their college dorm. Now, I get to head back to my car and take a long set of deep, relieved breaths. Let the leaves fall where they may.

The entire point of all of this was to help others. If this book helps just one person it was all worth the effort. If you didn't enjoy it, keep in mind: I do not give a single fuck what you think. It's not about you or me. It is about trying to help the next person who needs a hand. Regardless, I'll be taking a long break, hopefully on a quiet beach somewhere, minding my own business and healing from this exhaustive process. But when I get around to it, I'll be right back with an updated version, complete with who knows what kind of shiny upgrades and pearls of wisdom. And, most likely, a separate book of stories. We'll see.

Till then!

Acknowledgements

There are so many people to thank when it comes down to it. I have been infinitely blessed with the grace and care of some very special humans. I would like to acknowledge the debt I owe to those who have stood by me and given me counsel over the past two years: Arya, Zach, Chris, AJ, Polly, Cindy, Tom, Kasandra, Ken, Gabe, and so many more.

To my mentors, Mike, Brian, Benji, and Jimbo. I will carry your lessons and spirit throughout this world with confidence and a head held high. The high road *is* worth taking. Rest in peace, my friends.

To the thousands of people that I have met along the way that I have not included by name, just know that I listened to your wisdom and it is woven into the fabric of this book.

To Isabella Losskarn, who drew the illustrations for this book. Check her out, she is insanely talented: www.losskarn.art

And last, to Rambo. You are the best friend a man could ask for.

About The Author

Sam is an author, meditation instructor, and avid musician. He currently lives near the beach with his wild beast, Rambo. You can visit him online at www.scsanborn.com or find him on Instagram (@s.c.sanborn).

Did you like the book?

Great!

Leave a review on Amazon.

It helps me out a lot.

And if you stole this book?

Write two.

Made in United States
North Haven, CT
18 December 2023